Praise for *The Mediatrician's Guide*

"When my wife and I were trying to navigate the digital world of devices and social media alongside our three teenage daughters, all roads led to the wonderful Dr. Michael Rich. Drawing on his experiences as a pediatrician and former film-maker, he has the rare ability to offer seasoned and sensible guardrails as we all enter this brave new world together. This book is a must-have and will soon become your best friend, full of daily tips and long-lasting wisdom."

—Sanjay Gupta, MD
Associate professor of neurosurgery, Emory University;
chief medical correspondent, CNN; #1 *New York Times*
and *Wall Street Journal* bestselling author

"Dr Rich offers all of us 'caring but confused' adults—parents, caregivers, edu-cators, and media makers alike—a positive and proactive way to think about the value of today's digital media in our kids' lives. . . . For over fifty years, we have deeply valued research like this and the role it plays in ensuring the media we make helps children grow smarter, stronger, and kinder."

—Steve Youngwood
CEO, Sesame Workshop, and dear friend of Big Bird

"An instant classic, a book where people who fret and worry about what screens are doing to us, especially our children, can find the guidance that truth alone can provide, as well as the authoritative responses they seek. . . . Truly an excep-tional piece of work, a genuine gift to all."

—Edward Hallowell, MD
Psychiatrist; author, *Driven to Distraction*

"Finally! A caring, wise, and joyful guide to the possibilities and the perils of our increasingly more digital existence. As a producer and performer on screens large and small, I am deeply aware of their power to reflect our authentic selves and direct our relationships with others. Just as *Free to Be. . . You and Me* reminded us of our shared humanity, in this book, you will meet young people and their parents as they work with the Mediatrician to optimize their health and development in a constantly evolving world. Dr. Rich's compassion, imagination, and warm humor serve as a compass for us all as we teach and learn from the next generation."

—Marlo Thomas
Activist, actor, and author

"Raising a child in an age of constant screens requires thoughtfulness navigating not only our own digital use but also our children's. We didn't know how to find a balance within it. Dr. Rich has taken his experiences and given us a road map to find that balance!"

—**Hank Azaria**

Father, actor, and more than thirty characters on *The Simpsons*

"This is the essential guide we've been waiting for! . . . This timely, extraordinarily well-written, and thoroughly researched book is the indispensable guide to learn how to stand by your child as they learn to navigate their world. . . . Trust Dr. Rich's guidance here. I do—he is my go-to expert in the digital landscape."

—**Kenneth Ginsburg, MD, MS Ed**

Founding director, Center for Parent and Teen Communication; professor of pediatrics, University of Pennsylvania

"Michael Rich is the Dr. Spock of the digital age. In his practice and in this book, Dr. Rich helps parents help their children—from young tots to late teens— navigate the ever-changing world of connected technology. He does it with compassion and understanding and deep respect for both parents and young people."

—**Larry Magid**

Technology journalist; CEO and cofounder, ConnectSafely

"On the must-read list for all product developers and policy writers working in big tech. It provides evidence-based insights that media companies can leverage to mitigate and prevent potential harms against youth. The book also highlights media opportunities for entertainment and education—critical for anyone invested in understanding how to nurture the well-being of young people growing up in a media world."

—**Tracy Elizabeth, EdD**

Head of family safety and developmental health at TikTok

"A practical and heartfelt path forward for navigating the media landscape. Through the voice of a parent, owning his own successes and failures, the Mediatrician provides explanations and practical approaches. . . . This book can help parents and children reconnect IRL while simultaneously teaching us all how to harness the good in our digital world."

—**Stacy Drury, MD, PhD**

Psychiatrist-in-chief, Boston Children's Hospital; chair of psychiatry, Harvard Medical School

"Parents, educators, and, yes, even teenagers will all benefit from Dr. Rich's thoughtful, timely, and entertaining overview of what it means to grow up immersed in a world of digital ubiquity. His work . . . demonstrates empathy, deep understanding, and strong prescriptions for what ails us all."

—John Battelle
Cofounder of *Wired*; bestselling author; professor
of practice, Northeastern University

"As parents and grandparents, and as citizens of the world, we have a critical role to play as children learn about healthy media use. The most important message that Dr. Rich gives is to always be present for your child. This book can reinforce the most important work we do, nurturing and guiding the next generation."

—T. Berry Brazelton, MD
Author, *Touchpoints*; professor of pediatrics
emeritus, Harvard Medical School

"A brilliant, insightful, and scientific guide that we all need to stay sane and human in today's screen-filled world."

—Tiffany Shlain
Emmy-nominated filmmaker; national bestselling
author of *24/6: The Power of Unplugging One
Day a Week*; founder, Webby Awards

"Through his honest and down-to-earth approach, Dr. Rich takes away the fear and guilt, empowering parents and caregivers with the knowledge to navigate the digital world with their children. He offers guidance backed by research, not sensationalized news headlines, and genuinely provides a sense of relief for parents of digital natives—truly a comfort to read!"

—Tami Bhaumik
Vice president, civility and partnerships, Roblox

"A joyful road map to healthy child development, a clarion call to me and my many tech educator colleagues to listen deeply to the young people we serve, empower them with media literacy skills, and follow them into the future of digital citizenship."

—Richard Culatta
CEO, International Society for
Technology in Education (ISTE)

"Required reading for parents, educators, pediatricians, and technologists. More than a simple prescription for limiting screen time, it's a call to action for collaboration. Dr. Rich has created a framework, based on academic research and firsthand experience as a pediatrician and parent, for all grown-ups to work with their kids or students to create a plan for healthy use of technology and media."

—Catherine Teitelbaum
Head of family trust, Amazon Kids

"The right book at the right time. . . . Thoughtful rather than reactive, nuanced rather than naive, strength-based rather than fear-focused, and empowering rather than overwhelming. . . . I am grateful for this remarkable guide, my new go-to reference."

—Doug Bolton, PhD
Psychologist; educator; former K-12 principal

"Dr. Rich has launched a critically needed new movement that every creator and tech innovator must consider: how to design for evidence-based, human-centered digital wellness. His wise guidance and practical tips for caregivers define a new, more sensible digital diet that attacks the current epidemic of loneliness among our kids, with a caring community at the center. His prescription is one that every responsible decision-maker should consider, starting right now!"

—Michael H. Levine, PhD
Senior vice president, Noggin/Paramount

The Mediatrician's Guide

A Joyful Approach to Raising
Healthy, Smart, Kind Kids in
a Screen-Saturated World

Michael Rich, MD, MPH

with Teresa Barker

HARPER HORIZON

The book, and my life, are dedicated to Lydia, who saved my life
and shared it in raising healthy, smart, kind children
and
to the children, adolescents, and parents for whom I have cared
and from whom I have learned so much.

The cover of this book is a collective piece of art created by hundreds of children, adolescents, and their families who offered their selfies to be curated by the author and art director Belinda Bass into a photomosaic of a beautiful child looking up at us all for guidance, encouragement, and comfort. It serves as a visual metaphor for the subject of this book.

Contents

Introduction

Nicki, age fourteen, and her mother came into my office and took seats just a few feet apart, but the tension was crackling like an invisible high-voltage fence between them. Nicki's mother was the first to break the charged silence. She glared in exasperation at her daughter.

"I feel like I don't know you!"

Nicki slouched, staring down at the smartphone in her hands. "Uh-huh."

Only the top of Nicki's head was visible as her thumbs continued to glide rapidly over the face of her smartphone.

Her mother stared at her in silence, body stiffening with frustration. "We waited . . . ," she glanced down at the screen of her own phone, *"seven weeks* for this appointment. You *wanted* this appointment! And now you can't even look up from your damn phone!" She turned to me. "Doctor, I feel like I have lost her!" She looked at me plaintively. Nicki continued to text.

"When did you first feel you lost her?" I asked.

The COVID-19 pandemic's disruption of Nicki's school routines and social life had been the turning point. "She was on her phone all day and all night, even during online class times. And she didn't do her homework. She got moody. Angry if you ever asked her to stop with the texting. Or even to just pay attention. Never came to dinner. She stayed up way after her dad and I went to sleep. Then she would sleep into the afternoon if I let her. And she was—*is*—never without that phone anymore."

"When did she get her smartphone?"

"When everyone else did—in fifth grade."

"Fourth!" Nicki interrupted, without looking up. I took advantage of the opening in the conversation.

"How can I help *you*, Nicki?"

Nicki broke her gaze from the phone and glanced up at me.

"I don't need help," she said, nodding toward her mother. "*She* does."

Nicki's point couldn't have been truer. Help *is* needed, not only for her mother in this moment but, for most parents, from the time a newborn arrives and as they grow up. Eating, sleeping, playing, learning, loving—time reliably ushers in development along all those fronts. The challenge of the digital age is that screens have become not just ubiquitous features in our landscape but, rather, the immersive environment itself. While we parents may see a virtual world and "the real world," children are born into and live in a single world in which they move seamlessly between the physical and the digital and back again.

For generations, parents' questions and concerns were about children's sleeping, eating, socialization, learning, and growing. *What's normal? Should I be worried? How do I help them grow into the best versions of themselves?* Today those questions and concerns remain the same for parents of children of every age and developmental stage, from newborn to toddler, school age, adolescence, and into young adulthood—but they are transformed by the digital ecosystem in which our children are growing up. Discussions of health and wellness with pediatricians like me, with teachers, and with other parents invariably include questions about children's exposure to and eventual use of digital media. *What are the effects of all this on my child, and how can I protect them from harm?*

What About Screen Time?

We all, adults and children alike, spend more of our waking hours on screens than engaged in any other activity. "Screen time" has become immeasurable. We are surrounded by screens on walls and gas pumps, in elevators and our pockets, on our wrists, and soon on many of our heads. We constantly slide between the digital and the physical. We text, chat, socialize, learn, play, photograph, create, shop, watch, and make videos—all on devices we carry 24/7. We share our photos, our ideas, our opinions. Online we share our upsets, dreams, and even secrets that we haven't shared privately with family or friends. There was a time when *IRL* meant "in real life," interactions in the physical world as opposed to the so-called virtual world. *Face time* meant meeting in person. Those distinctions seem quaint today because our digital interactions are as real as our physical ones—and FaceTime is an app. Video chats, Zoom meetings, remote classrooms, and social media have changed how we live and behave. This reality wasn't created by COVID-19, but the pandemic lockdown moved it from the margins to the center of our families. As interactive screens became the sole tool for everything from school and work to groceries and dating, we could no longer deny that we live our real lives in a virtual world in which we laugh together, cry together, sing together, and are terrified together—even when we are alone.

Since the turn of the millennium, with the expansion of ever-faster broadband internet and mobile devices, children's screen times have grown steadily year after year.

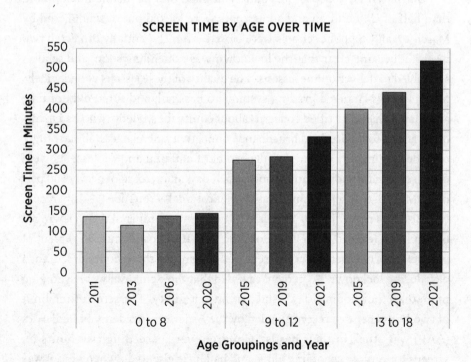

SCREEN TIME BY AGE OVER TIME

Victoria Rideout and Michael B. Robb, *The Common Sense Census: Media Use By Kids Age Zero to Eight, 2020* (San Francisco, CA: Common Sense Media, 2020); Victoria Rideout et al., *Common Sense Census: Media Use By Tweens and Teens, 2021* (San Francisco, CA: Common Sense, 2022).

If it seems as if children and adolescents are spending a lot of their time engaging with screens, it's because most are. A quick flashback shows that trend was well established years before the pandemic. In 2015, nearly all (97 percent) infants to four-year-olds used smartphones or tablets; 90 percent of them started before their first birthday.[1] Between birth and their second birthday, infants and toddlers spend a daily average of forty-nine minutes using screen media; two-to-four-year-olds are using for two and a half hours; five-to-eight-year-olds, three hours and five minutes; eight-to-twelve-year-olds, five hours and thirty-three minutes; and thirteen-to-eighteen-year-olds, eight hours and thirty-nine minutes.[2] Nearly one-third (29 percent) of the time children are on screens, they are multitasking with two or more screens.[3] In 2018, nine out of ten adolescents ages thirteen to seventeen accessed the internet through mobile devices every day; 46 percent reported being online "almost constantly."[4]

On March 15, 2020, as the country lurched into pandemic mode, more than half of US children and adolescents were locked out of school, and by March 25, all US public schools were closed. After the initially projected two weeks, it became clear that the lockdown was not ending soon, and schools scrambled to deliver online lessons. The quality of these lessons varied widely. Many schools changed grading systems to pass-fail, and some did not take attendance due to justified concerns about equity for students who had inadequate access to devices and broadband connectivity. Screen use, already high, exploded.[5] Virtually overnight, 48 percent of children and adolescents were using screens for more than six hours each day, an increase of nearly 500 percent.[6] Most of that screen time was not educational—YouTube (78.21 percent), Netflix (49.64 percent), and TikTok (33.41 percent) dominated their viewing—but children learned from it.[7] Before the COVID-19 pandemic, 60 percent of parents reported that their children used screens for three hours or less each day; during lockdown, 70 percent revealed that their children were averaging more than four hours a day.[8] And parents felt guilty. The screen time limit of two hours per day recommended by the American Academy of Pediatrics (AAP) was stuck in their heads.[9] Children were exceeding two hours on screens for remote schooling alone and had little else to do when school was over—so they stayed online. Their recreational screen time increased by 17 percent.[10] Family conflicts over screen use increased by 49 percent.[11]

The lockdown continued into that summer and fall, when most students returned to remote schooling, delivered in a more organized way. But new issues arose. Many students remained "underconnected," competing for limited bandwidth with parents who were working from home, losing connection and losing interest, using devices like smartphones that were wholly inadequate for learning. Even students with good connectivity and devices had developed habits of "screen grazing," with multiple windows open to text conversations, videos, social media, or shopping. Using multiple media and switching to what grabbed their attention, children were cumulatively exposed to screen content for even more time. Teachers and children became pioneers in the hybrid educational world, using digital devices and applications as tools for learning, researching, communicating, and creating. Parents were increasingly torn between wanting their children to be adept with twenty-first-century tools and concern about what the children were doing with them.

The use of educational technology that dramatically increased with remote learning offered the opportunity to rethink screen use. The AAP's daily limits of one to two hours of "quality educational screen time" were recommended in a time when broadcast television was the primary screen in children's lives. Even then, parents felt unable to determine what was quality and what was educational, let alone effectively enforce a limit. Today, with screens everywhere that we move fluidly in and out of, screen time is impossible even to measure. Let go of the illusion that you can enforce screen time limits or even measure screen time in today's media environment. More importantly, let go of the guilt that you can't restrict your kids' time on screens. That energy is better spent on helping your child learn to use screens in healthy and productive ways—and learning to replace daily screen time limits with daily non-screen minimums. Unless you put your children in a sensory deprivation tank or join a tech-free community completely off the grid, they are exposed to and interact with a media-saturated environment. Most of their personal interactions and communication rely on technology as the interface. Deleting media is undesirable not only because we would be denying them the positive use of the most powerful and effective tools yet for learning, communicating, and connecting with the larger world but because we would not be providing them with the skills to recognize and avoid the negative media influences we fear.

Regardless of the warnings and dogma we hear, there is no simple answer to the complex challenge of parenting digital natives, even for parents who are themselves digital natives. The lightning-speed evolution of media and technology outstrips the pace of human evolution, and even those who grew up worrying their parents about video games and "surfing the web" are grappling with their own children's entry into the digital environment.

So we will not be perfect parents, no matter how hard we try. But we can aim to do our best—and keep perfecting it. As a pediatrician, I can assure you that children are remarkably resilient. They will survive—and thrive—despite, and often *because of*, our shortcomings as parents.

To raise a child well (and to raise a well child) in the digital age, we are orchestrating three moving targets, which we'll track in the chapters ahead:

- the arc of human development, from infant to child to adolescent to adult;
- the constant evolution of the digital environment that stimulates and challenges development; and
- the ongoing transformation in human behavior as we all use these powerful digital devices.

There are several theories about why humans have risen to the top of an animal kingdom that includes bigger, stronger, faster, more predatory, and better-protected organisms. Perhaps it is our larger (but not the largest) brain, our opposable thumbs (which all higher primates have, and some have opposable big toes too), or our ability to walk upright, freeing our hands to use tools (yeah, some higher primates do that too). But a dominant theory is that our greatest strength is our drive to be social, our need and our ability to communicate and connect with each other.[12] Other animals will hunt together or defend the herd against predators, but these herd behaviors are driven by individual survival instincts and are easily defeated by one animal breaking from the herd. Humans build relationships and trust by communicating. From stories told around a fire to sharing images on social media, we have used media to communicate our commonalities, ideas, hopes, and dreams. We have shared laughter and fears. We have built connections that are bigger than us, with family, friends, communities, nations, and religions. Our need to be social and our communication capabilities have allowed humans to rise above our individual desires, needs, and fears to bond with each other, work together, even sacrifice ourselves for a greater good.

Today children are born into a single ecosystem in which they move back and forth between the physical and digital environments. As digital natives, they are early adopters and innovators, finding uses for technologies that their inventors never envisioned. With the rise of hybrid school and remote learning programs, children have learned to use digital devices, applications, and platforms not as toys but as power tools. Regardless of how well they learn, however, many children experience the same physically exhausting, brain-deadening screen burnout that adults often feel working remotely.

Children's comfort and skill in the digital space is just the current iteration of our human need to connect and communicate, to form bonds. Presented with the touch screen of a tablet or smartphone, even very young children naturally form a nimble, flexible, and naïve interface between their minds, eyes, pointing fingers, and these intelligent devices. Human nature being what it is, children can discover the new, create the beautiful, and just as easily go to very dark places. They do not yet have the brain development or life experience to recognize or fear threats, let alone know how to avoid them. But they have us. No matter how rebellious, withdrawn, or sullen your child or adolescent may be, you are still the most powerful influence in their life. Your child, at every age, needs your guidance, offered with as much respect and as little "judginess" as you can muster. Your ability to remain in the moment as they experiment and sort through questions and choices, to listen to your child deeply, and to speak to them authoritatively with respect and compassion will help them find their way and own their decisions. In my clinical practice and as a parent seeking to make sense out of sometimes confusing information, I've found the best approach is to embrace the contradictions and move forward with my eyes and mind open. Absolutes are not the answer. When we shift from fearful and embattled to informed and deliberate with our expectations, we can see the promise and perils of media use and implement reliable strategies to use these power tools wisely.

It has always been the case that each new generation grows up in a different world than their parents did. That is not new. When today's parents were kids, things changed more slowly. Their parents worried about risks in the physical world, including car crashes, cannabis and designer drugs, and teen pregnancy, and communities were more stable—the village that raised the child was nearby, known, and largely cohesive. But now, due in large part to digital technology, the village is global, and change is occurring exponentially. Our world has become increasingly destabilized in ways that can feel alarming. We have seen digital media used as tools for individual gain at the expense of society or weaponized to spread disinformation. To be concerned about our children's vulnerability and to want to protect them is an instinct as old as time in a shifting landscape that feels increasingly dangerous. To protect them mindfully is our challenge. To support their success is our opportunity. Ultimately, the goals of parenting remain the same. We want to raise our children to be healthy, smart, kind—and happy. What we must do is translate our parental instincts and human experience into the brave new world that our children inhabit.

Unlike earlier parent generations whose traditional skills helped prepare children for adult life, today's parents face a different challenge. Our children are adept, learning digital tools more quickly than we do. Smartphones with killer apps, social media, and virtual and augmented reality are in children's hands before we have sorted out the latest, greatest device or application, much less developed a strategy for managing it. But if we acknowledge and respect our children's knowledge, asking them to teach us the technology and share their media experiences, we may have the opportunity to learn key features, identify areas of concern, and share our wisdom and experience that will help them make choices that let them enjoy media and use them wisely.

The Making of a Mediatrician

Like many parents, I simultaneously love and worry about media, for my children and for myself. I know the research showing potential harms from watching television, but that doesn't mean I'd tell you to throw it out the window. From childhood, I have learned much of what I know about the world, the people who live in it, and how I should behave from films, television, music, and, more recently, online interactive media.

Not only have I been a lifelong screen media consumer, but I make media as well. For twelve years, before I decided to become a doctor, I was a filmmaker and writer in the motion picture industry. I had the honor and privilege of working as assistant director to the Japanese master of the cinema, Akira Kurosawa. He made *Seven Samurai*, a sword-wielding action picture that is possibly the greatest anti-violence movie ever made; *Rashomon*, a film that reveals and has come to be synonymous with the many facets of truth in human experience; and my personal favorite, *Ikiru*, which follows the last six months of a dying man as he discovers, for the first time, how to live.

What attracted me to media also attracted me to medicine—a highly technical skill set that allowed me to get close to humans and grapple with the human condition. For me, film combined an intimate exploration of what it means to be human with a unique power to grab people's attention and change their hearts and minds. Media's power to transform lives made me want to make films. It was the same desire to make a positive difference in people's lives that led me to become a doctor. I have come full circle, recognizing the power of screen media to change people, especially young people, who are its heaviest and most impressionable users, and to harness that change to promote their well-being.

We Learn as We Go: Parenthood as a Personal Longitudinal Research Study

Two of my children were born before I became a pediatrician; two were born after. I gave each of them the best I could based on what I knew and believed at the time. Seeing media as a remarkable opportunity to expand their worlds, I provided the first two with music from birth and with educational screen media as soon as they could sit up. They watched videos to learn foreign languages and played with reading and math edutainment software on the computer. With my third and fourth children, I incorporated what I had learned from child health science and clinical experience, limiting and focusing their media exposure to what they needed when their developing brains could process it.

With my original self-assured opinions about screen media, I had not considered the fact that a child's brain is very different from mine—that it's still developing as it receives and responds to audiovisual input and life experiences. One of the great strengths of the human brain is that everything it perceives can change its course of development. As an adult I have had many lived experiences to which I can compare what I see and hear to my entertainment. For a child, who is learning about the world and how to behave in it, entertainment is often their first exposure to various aspects of human experience. If children learn to use a spoon by watching others, trying it out for themselves, and then making it their own, what do they do with what they see on a screen? As a pediatrician, I became concerned that there might be health-related outcomes due to media exposure, so in my patient assessments I incorporated questions about screen media use among other environmental health influences. When I surmised that media exposure might have influenced a child's condition, I recommended modifications in media use, and often the child's health improved. I observed my patients and continued to learn from research. The more I learned, the more I used, and the better my patients did.

As a parent, I have had successes and I have made mistakes. Most importantly, I have learned a lot from my children, as I have from my patients. I have found that one can parent well in the digital age, raising happy, healthy children who are able to use media in positive ways—and to turn their screens off when they are displacing more valuable experiences. I am fortunate to have the unique combination of media knowledge and medical expertise, as well as resilient kids and a partner in parenting who has tolerated my trial and error. I wrote this book to share what I have learned, providing scientific evidence and tried-and-true parenting strategies to replace unease about media effects with knowledge, skills, and confidence to raise wonderful children in a media-saturated environment.

For the Caring but Confused

When I started exploring questions at the intersection of media and children's health, I cared deeply about the issues, but I was just as deeply confused. The news carried stories of how TV watching makes kids fat or playing video games teaches them to kill. But most kids use screen media, often a lot of it, and they are not all obese killers. For every well-intentioned warning from child advocates, there is an artist creating educational games or a tech leader who scoffs at the notion that screen media can negatively affect its users. It is for parents like me, the caring but confused, that I offer this guide to make sense out of the tsunami of information and opinions coming at you. Parenting is hard work—and it is a job with no time off. Each decision, from the food we buy to the schools we choose, and each permission we give, from riding a bike to going to the mall, requires a rapid risk-benefit analysis. Here you'll find the best information for making those decisions in an informed manner that allows you to stay true to what you believe and what you want for your children.

I am sharing with you what I have seen, heard, and learned from more than thirty years as a practicing pediatrician with a special emphasis on adolescents and twelve years as a filmmaker and screenwriter. I bring my clinical experience with keeping kids healthy in primary care and with caring for children and adolescents struggling with problematic interactive media use (PIMU), which includes out-of-control gaming, social media use, pornography use, and/or online information-bingeing. After caring for children and adolescents struggling with media-related health issues for nearly twenty years, I founded the Clinic for Interactive Media and Internet Disorders (CIMAID) (pronounced SIM-AID) at Boston Children's Hospital in 2017, where my team and I have treated hundreds of young people. By passing on to you what I have learned there and at the Digital Wellness Lab, also at Boston Children's Hospital, I hope to build for you a solid foundation of evidence-based understanding of what happens between a growing child and the ever-evolving digital ecosystem. Because the digital environment and how we behave in it are constantly changing, our inquiry at the Digital Wellness Lab will always be a work in progress, from our regular pulse surveys of what is going on for kids, to our longitudinal Global Growing Up Digital (GUD) research with Sesame Workshop, to our youth-directed exploration of their lived experiences in their seamless physical-digital worlds. Our research and clinical care goals will always be moving targets. And our parenting strategies will be the same.

My roles as a parent and pediatrician trump my role as researcher, so *The Mediatrician's Guide* is organized around what every parent desires: to raise a well-adjusted, productive, happy child who has a healthy relationship with media and with others. This discussion naturally includes parental hopes and fears—potential for a child's successes and concerns for their risks—but with the focus on active and preventive health strategies that build a strong foundation for enjoyable, reasonable, and responsible media use in the context of their children's full lives.

This is, after all, an extraordinary era and opportunity for us all. As parents, we should not be fearful, but we should be mindful. We should protect our children from harm but also lean into opportunities to leverage the positives. When screen media use presents health concerns—for any of us, at any age—let's build on evidence and draw on clinical experience to develop fresh approaches that nurture mastery of healthier, more mindful media use.

The Mediatrician's Guide covers the subjects that parents care most about by replacing opinions with an accessible understanding of the science that shows how children's media use can affect their physical, mental, and social health. Building on this evidence, it provides clinically tested, practical strategies for parents, teachers, and others who work with children and adolescents to prevent, recognize, and intervene early on media-related health and developmental problems.

In **Part 1: What?**, each chapter addresses a distinct area of child and adolescent health and development, beginning with a clear understanding of a child's needs, then examining how media exposure can affect that aspect of a child's health and well-being in positive and negative ways. I share what we know, and I examine the ways in which we use media and how that use might influence health and developmental outcomes. I share ways in which the science can inform our parenting risk-benefit analyses, guide our choices, and help us develop strategies for *using* media mindfully, rather than simply avoiding them, to improve our children's present and future. Finally, within each chapter, I write you a prescription, a **Media Rx**, that outlines what **You Can** do to enjoy media, use them well, and be well.

In **Part 2: So What?**, I delve into some specific health problems related to media use, primarily around the *content* to which children are exposed, that worry parents most: anxiety and depression; distorted body image and disordered eating, from anorexia to obesity; aggression and violence; alcohol and other substance use; and a new condition of the digital age, PIMU. On the flip side, I also share positive stories of how young people have leveraged the same media to address problems from climate change to homophobia to bullying in their own schools. Using cases of real children, adolescents, and families (without their real names and with details disguised to protect their privacy), I share the process through which patients and their parents come to terms with media-related problems affecting kids' health and development and how we identify treatment strategies and implement them together, helping children and adolescents recover and self-regulate their media use with the support of parents who are better equipped to be effective guides moving forward.

In **Part 3: Now What?**, we turn our lens away from media content to focus on how the *context* in which children and adolescents use media—when, where, and with whom—influences their health and development. We'll see how the context for a young person's media use affects outcomes of physical (obesity, sleep), mental (anxiety, depression), cognitive (STEAM, creativity), and social (relationships, academics) health as powerfully as the media content they consume. I examine the difference between screen time limits and limiting screen time and why one strategy doesn't work but the other does. While the media content available to children and youth can only be changed gradually through market and legislative forces, the context in which media are used can be changed immediately by the young people and families who use them. Empowered by digital literacy skills, young people can be mindful of how media are affecting them and purposeful in using media in ways that help them be healthier, smarter, and more empathetic and in avoiding media that detract from or actively work against their healthy development.

Finally, **Part 4: Ages and Stages: A Digital Wellness Primer** offers specific, evidence-based strategies and tips organized by children's developmental stages. Since the digital ecosystem in which children and adolescents are living is constantly evolving, the primer offers fundamentals that can be built upon with current information available from the Family Digital Wellness Guide online at https://digitalwellnesslab.org/parents/family-digital-wellness-guide. To keep your skills, confidence, and enjoyment in this parenting and family adventure up-to-date, Digital Wellness Lab resources, which range from helpful checklists to planning and discussion tools for sharing with your school or community, will help you translate ideas into action.

You have all you need to successfully raise your children to be the best they can be. "Yes, You Can!" highlights that you are not reinventing parenting; you are translating your parenting instincts and even what you learned (and what you vowed *never* to learn) from your parents into the physical-digital ecosystem in which you are raising and teaching your children.

You can adapt these parenting tips for practical "best fits" between your family's lifestyle and what is optimal for the health of your children at every age. The primer offers fun alternative activities so screens are no longer the default when your child is bored or restless or when you just need a break. It offers ways in which you can work with childcare providers, teachers, guidance counselors, pediatricians, and school or community groups to get the best for your children.

Don't simply accept what I say as the best or only way. Remember, you know your child better than anyone on earth, and you will be the closest and best judge of how they are affected by the media they use and how they use them. You will make the best choices when you combine information and strategies in this book with your intimate knowledge of your child. There is no absolute Right Answer. There is only the best answer at the time and—if it doesn't work—the resilience to recover and redirect to the next best answer. Remember, living and raising children in a rapidly changing digital ecosystem is, and always will be, a work in progress. This is not a definitive bible of how to parent in our physical-digital environment. It is an invitation to join with me in building on this foundational knowledge and use your own curiosity, observation skills, and nurturing instincts to be a part of the global village that it now takes to raise a child.

This process is dynamic. The media landscape evolves constantly, and as parents and world citizens, we must evolve with it. It's my hope that the principles and perspectives I share will help you parent your children well now with smartphones and tablets and in the near future with immersive, 3D virtual/augmented reality (VR/AR) and generative artificial intelligence (AI). This is just the beginning of our process of mastering the media matrix and using our knowledge to raise healthy, smart, and caring kids in a brave new digital world. Media are here to stay—and they *should* stay as a means of connecting, communicating, and expressing our humanity. I hope that this book helps you and the children for whom you care to enjoy media and use them wisely.

Part 1

What?

Chapter 1

Raising Children Well in a World of Screens

Model, Mentor, Monitor

We look at our kids, and we wonder, we hope, and we worry. They are growing up in a dramatically different and more rapidly changing world than we did. Half of what they face, from climate change to political tribalism to the potential for nuclear war, is what we are handing them. The other half, from sharing memes to talking to each other with their thumbs to speaking a language we don't always understand (WTF?), is uniquely their own. It seems that they pay more attention to their phones than to us. What kind of adults will our children be, growing up exposed to instant and constant bad news, competitive and snarky social media, sexting and cyberbullying, first-person shooter video games, and livestreaming videos of real-life violence? What kind of parents do they need us to be? We imagine the adults we hope they'll be—healthy, smart, empathetic, accomplished, happy—then wonder and worry again. We know we don't have experience, but can we learn how to nurture, protect, and raise them well in this digital ecosystem?

Yes, we can! *Because* you are asking these questions, you *have* the instincts, passion, and compassion to parent your children well in the digital age. All you need now is to understand *with them* the physical-digital ecosystem in which they are growing up and to use the parenting skills and life experience you have to guide them well in their brave new world.

We see the tragic events involving children and adolescents in which digital media play a prominent role. Dire warnings from headlines, teachers, and child advocates—we hear them and we fear them. Yet we, too, are drawn to the latest bright, shiny tech device. And we are loath to be the only parent who denies it to their child. So we give them that video game, that smartphone, that social media app—then we are annoyed by their behavior, and we feel guilty. How do we reconcile how much we love, use, and want to share media with the risks they may present to our children's well-being? And what about us and our own media use?

From the beginning of time, it has been up to parents to safeguard and nurture our children, teach them how to survive and thrive in the world as it is—and to imagine and have the skills to create a better world of their own. Media have long been a part of parenting, from singing songs to newborns to reading board books to an infant to teaching school-age children to read and write. It is important to recognize that while we and our children are using screens for work, education, entertainment, connection, and communication, we have placed screen media at the top of a hierarchy of danger. In 1938, E. B. White, author of *Charlotte's Web* and *Stuart Little,* wrote in a prescient essay for *Harper's Magazine,*

> I believe television is going to be the test of the modern world, and that in this new opportunity to see beyond the range of our vision we shall discover either a new and unbearable disturbance of the general peace or a saving radiance in the sky. We shall stand or fall by television—of that I am quite sure.[1]

Today screens are not an either/or. They are *both* a saving radiance, having transformed our education system and kept us in touch with loved ones during the COVID-19 lockdown, *and* an unbearable disturbance of the general peace as we all, adults and children alike, spend the majority of our waking hours paying attention to one or more screens rather than to each other. We are caught in the tension between what we want for ourselves and our children and what we actually do. And whatever choices we make (or don't make), we feel guilty either for denying our children something they want or succumbing to social pressure and allowing (or benignly neglecting) them to wander the digital ecosystem alone.

Well-intended recommendations to reject or severely restrict screen media are impossible for most parents. And that is OK. Because banning screens, even making them suspect, is actually counterproductive. It misses the point. Screens are here to stay, and what our children really need is to learn to use them thoughtfully and effectively—and to turn them off when they are displacing healthier, more human experiences.

Nicki, whose story opened the introduction, experienced her mother's efforts to curb her smartphone use not as an attempt to care for her but as extreme, controlling, even scary—threatening to cut her off from her world of friends—the world of an adolescent. As Nicki pointed out that day in my office, looking up from her phone with exasperation, "All she wants to do is take my phone away! She doesn't get it—all my friends are there!" Nicki's mother thought she was pitted against the phone, but in truth, she was up against a defining drive of our humanity: we are social animals, and, simply put, media have become our mechanism for expressing our humanity in mostly exciting and creative ways. Whether a book or a movie or a song, media draw us together. We laugh, we cry, and we talk. Media engage us, and our kids, in the most primal and human way. Media are inherently social.

Our fearful approaches and rigid rules generate conflict and guilt but little change. They are no way to equip our children with the skills and savvy to navigate the digital ecosystem and use this powerful technology responsibly. In the now increasingly rare event when a parent proudly announces to me that they have no screens at home, I tell them to go get one. When I was providing health care for a local university in the 1990s, we noticed that there was a subset of freshmen who spent much of their time in the dorm common rooms, even missing classes to watch soap opera marathons and sitcom reruns. Investigating further, we found that many of them had grown up in households without televisions. Like the students who lose control with alcohol, drugs, or sex once they reach the relative freedom of college, they binged on television, seeking a sensation they had not known as children. Deprived of the television experience, they had not learned to manage their screen use, balancing it with their other obligations and activities. The best strategy for protecting your child from potential harm is to teach them not just to survive but to thrive in the screen media environment: to cultivate their awareness, develop their critical thinking, awaken their creativity, and nurture their empathy, providing them with the skills to harness the positive affordances and to recognize and avoid the negative influences of the screens that surround us all.

We are all in this together, living and parenting in the digital environment. We can learn from and support each other as parents, but more importantly, we and our children are in this experience together. In that shared space, parents have tremendous potential to bring insight and purpose to the mix—and to learn from our children.

Parent is more importantly a verb than a noun. Parents parent differently and parent each child differently. Parenting is a journey, an ongoing work in progress that is never done. You know your child better than anyone, and you will parent them better than anyone else could because of that deep knowledge. You will not be the perfect parent; none of us is. As a pediatrician who has cared for thousands of young people from birth to adulthood (and even some of their children), I can assure you that children are remarkably resilient and forgiving. So rather than wasting energy on indecision, guilt, or perfectionism, let's bring a growing body of science together with the time-tested art of parenting and the reality that you know your child as a unique individual better than anyone on earth. While parents' values may differ (even between parenting partners), most agree on one thing: they want what is best for their children. The nuances of that may look different from family to family, but the testing ground is the same: the world around us, as it is.

New mothers text while breastfeeding. Dads check emails at breakfast, while pushing the stroller, or at the playground with their kids. Infants play with tablets to the amusement of friends and the pride of parents. Grandparents visit in video chats, admiring the kids' art and reading books together, celebrating birthdays and holidays, and sharing everyday ups and downs. From birth, children live in a seamless physical-digital environment. It is different from the world we grew up in, and we must learn from them to see it as they do.

Nearly half (46 percent) of adolescents reported that they are online all or almost all of the time that they are awake.[2] More than two-thirds (68 percent) of teens take their smartphones to bed with them, and 36 percent wake up during the night at least once to check their phones.[3] In 2021, "media multitasking," a phenomenon made plausible by mobile devices like smartphones, tablets, and portable gaming platforms, exposed adolescents to an average of eight hours, thirty-nine minutes of screen content daily—*not* including school-related use in the year when many students were remote schooling.[4]

For today's children and adolescents, interactive screen media function similarly to the Force as described by Obi-Wan Kenobi, "an energy field created by all living things. It surrounds us and penetrates us; it binds the galaxy together."[5]

In his book *Brain and Culture: Neurobiology, Ideology, and Social Change*, Yale professor emeritus and psychiatrist Bruce Wexler pointed out that even as infants, our children will want what they see that we find appealing. What captures our attention captures theirs. Brain imaging techniques have shown that "socially endorsed, repetitive use of human-made objects such as musical instruments is associated with actual changes in brain structure," he wrote.[6] "Through such means, adults influence what in the continuous stream of sensory input infants are most aware of, become most familiar with, and think most about."[7] What works with infants works throughout childhood. Children are watching us all the time, emulating what we do to manage the world and what it throws at us, watching for the results, and ultimately deciding how they are going to do things, hopefully better.

Over more than a half century of research, scientists have focused largely on individual devices, from televisions to smartphones, and on durations of screen use, measuring specific health outcomes from obesity to aggression. Given today's multiplicity of devices and their near-constant presence from the very beginning of children's lives, narrowly focused studies are helpful but of limited use for parenting today's digital natives. It is more realistic and effective to understand young people's holistic experience of screens as a digital environment. They are growing up in homes with one or more screens in every room. Their homes are smart, controlled by voice-activated digital assistants. Their parents have screens in their pockets and on their wrists. The internet of things is the internet of us.

When Nicki's mom excused herself from the examining room, Nicki looked up from her phone. "Ugh, she totally doesn't get it . . ."

"So . . . what could she do better?"

Nicki thought about that for a while. "Pay more attention to me. She is always busy."

Nicki's mother, like many parents, managed the dueling demands of workplace and family. She relied on the constant connectivity and mobility of her smartphone, tablet, and laptop, toggling from job-related tasks to scheduling her children to the news to shopping to resolving coworkers' conflicts to organizing vacation photos and planning the next one (and exploring interesting but unrelated hot links, as we all do). What had brought her to my office with Nicki were her concerns that she was "losing" her daughter—losing her to the vortex of social media and the endless online array of messaging, shopping, entertainment, and, *and*, AND! She was right—her daughter was turning away—but she was mistaken about the reasons. It wasn't just about Nicki's phone and screen diversions. It was about both the daughter's and mother's media use and a parent-child relationship that had become fraught with distraction, annoyance, mistrust, and dissatisfaction. They had both succumbed to the constant seductions of the digital environment. If we start to think about our "infosphere" as we think about our atmosphere, we can pay more attention to our "air quality" and our family microclimate. We can seek out and use that which improves our knowledge, health, and relationships, living and thriving in the digital environment together.

The 3 Ms for Parents: Model, Mentor, Monitor

Parents are their children's first and best teachers. We joke that kids pay attention to 1 percent of what we say but 100 percent of what we do. But it's true, they're watching everything: what we do, how and how frequently we do it—including using our smartphones, laptops, tablets, smartwatches, televisions, and social media. Children look to their parents to figure out how to behave in the world. We check our smartphones an average of ninety-six times every day, every ten minutes, and are on them for an average of five hours and twenty-four minutes each day.[8] Our children see that as not only normal but as a behavior to emulate as they grow up. Understanding that how our children interact with the digital environment will affect their health, development, happiness, and success, our first goal is to *be* the change we want to *see*, to **MODEL** the behaviors that we hope they will learn.

This begins, perhaps surprisingly, with the most basic way we establish expectations around how we behave in the world, and specifically in the media-infused world of our everyday lives. Do we dictate or do we discuss? I recommend expectations instead of rules because rules do not work as well as expectations. As part of normative autonomy-seeking, many adolescents (including me, back in the day) reflexively question authority and challenge rules coming from that authority. Rules are unilateral and nonnegotiable, issued from and enforced (or not) by the authority of the parent. Adolescents, especially, may hear them as suggestions and evaluate whether they want to follow those suggestions. When parents try to enforce their rules, it leads to conflict or to driving the adolescent "underground," where they pretend to adhere to the rules but continue their online lives in privacy from parents. Though developmentally different, tweens and often younger children have a similar response—resistance—and the more you shift to rigid enforcement, the more quickly you lose reasoning ground you'll want to build upon going forward. Parenting well in the digital ecosystem is a process of establishing expectations rather than laying down rules.

Expectations may cover all the same issues as rules, but they are heard and adhered to very differently. Expectations are established when you **MENTOR** your child in the use of each new digital tool and are modified as the child grows up and uses that tool in various ways. Consensus can be reached by thinking through and establishing together how healthy uses can advance your child toward their goals and how unhealthy uses can set them back. Be explicit both about the healthy and the unhealthy, adjusting for your child's age and developmental readiness. At every age, you must talk about how to be a good digital citizen. Eventually, you must talk about pornography, hate sites, and other disturbing content. This mentoring conversation is not "one and done" but the first of many usually brief and casual discussions as they grow up in an ever-changing psychosocial environment.

Expectations are suggested by the parent for the family as a collective. Expectations that family meals and sleep time are device-free, that all screens are off an hour before bedtime, and that family conversations take precedence over smartphones are based on collaboration, parents and children working together to build relationships and behaviors that benefit all. Rules are made to be broken, but expectations bind us together. And it is far worse—a potentially stronger deterrent—to feel your parent's disappointment that you did not meet your shared expectations than it is to feel their anger that you broke a parental rule.

Developmental psychologists have found four parenting styles resulting from levels of parental responsiveness to and demandingness with their children.

	High Responsiveness	Low Responsiveness
High Demandingness	Authoritative	Authoritarian
Low Demandingness	Permissive	Uninvolved

Terence Sanvictores and Magda D. Mendez, "Types of Parenting Styles and Effects on Children," *StatPearls [Internet]* (Treasure Island, FL: StatPearls Publishing), updated September 18, 2022, https://www.ncbi.nlm.nih.gov/books/NBK568743/.

Engaged, effective parents who have high expectations of their children and want to do the best by them in terms of their mental health, education, and character tend to be demanding. When we are at our best, we balance the high standards we have for them by listening to them and being responsive to their needs and opinions, practicing and enjoying authoritative parenting. But let's face it, when stressed, frustrated, and tired, we can easily fall back into authoritarian parenting—dictating rules—which, in all truth, most of us experienced from time to time as children. The goal of effective parenting (and of this book) is to move toward authoritative parenting.

How we model media use matters more than we like to think. If we yell at our children to turn off the television or stop playing video games in between checking emails on our phone, they see that as the height of hypocrisy and ignore us, either overtly or covertly. Even very young children pick up on these inconsistencies. When parents say one thing and do another, we lose credibility and authority. Children will learn and reflexively behave the way their parents behave with digital devices, just as they unquestioningly use seat belts and put on bike helmets if that is what their parents do. When we're preoccupied and constantly distracted with our smartphones and laptops, we not only shortchange our kids on important time and attention, but we also teach them the same habits. And we parents, too, derive benefits from modeling the behaviors we want to see in our children: using our digital devices in mindful, focused ways at specific times; putting down digital devices when we are together with our children; and leaving devices out of our bedrooms and family meals. Both the research evidence that supports authoritative digital parenting and the reports of parents who have put their phones and laptops away during their time with family have shown reductions in parent anxiety, listening to and enjoying their children and partners more, and even being more productive when they were online.

My friend and collaborator in ideation, Tiffany Shlain, who is an artist, filmmaker, tech innovator, and originator of the Webby Awards, has observed a "tech shabbat" since 2010. At a time of great stress, having lost her father to cancer and given birth in the space of a few days, she and her husband, Ken, a robotics professor at the University of California, Berkeley, participated in a one-off National Day of Unplugging. "And it was amazing," Tiffany said. "I got my presence back, I felt like I got my soul back." So she and her family began to do it every week, turning off all technology for twenty-four hours from Friday night through Saturday night. Through the pandemic, when all of us depended on the internet to learn, work, communicate, and connect with others, contrary to expectations, they continued to do it, and "our tech shabbats were ten times more important."[9] Her teenage daughter observed that their tech shabbats were the only day that she did not feel that the family was in quarantine—because they were together and present as they always had been.

MEDIA Rx
Dial Down Hyperstimulation, Embrace Mindful Presence with Digital Downtime

Powering down media distractions for a period of time is one of the best things you can do for your child, your partner, and yourself. A cognitive break from the hyperstimulation of smartphones, Zoom calls, and the always-on connectivity of digital life gives everyone the chance to take a deep breath and realize a social emotional boost. Time unplugged helps your child develop the habit of mindful media use and helps you grow closer as a family by spending time together without the "technoference" of digital distractions. Part of media mastery and mindful media use for your child—and you—comes down to intentionally setting aside digital devices and being truly in the moment, undistracted, together.

If possible, sit down together for least one screen-free meal a day. That means no phones or tablets at the table and no TV on in the background. Research shows that when parents are distracted by screens, they talk less to their kids and are less patient with them.[10] Use this time to talk together as a family, listen, laugh, and commiserate with each other and check in on how each of you are doing.

You, too, can observe a tech shabbat or digital sabbath and realize the benefits that Tiffany Shlain and her family did. This becomes a chosen regular time when you intentionally unplug from constant connectivity and opt instead for here-and-now connection with one another. It can be for an afternoon or for a day, but it has to be long enough to give your mind and emotions a complete break from the constant input. Your child needs that!

YOU CAN

Create traditions. Celebrate family, friendship, community, and caring. It is surprisingly easy with these three simple steps:

1. *Plan a special activity in a private setting.* Unplug at home and cook a special meal together, plan an evening of board games, or embark on an outdoor adventure.

2. *Make the most of it.* At first, it usually feels awkward, even uncomfortable, to "just be" with one another or even by yourself device-free, but science says it's important, and you will feel the difference. With each successive digital sabbath, the discomfort gives way to a sense of liberation. You are no longer on call for your friends, family, or everyone who wants to sell you something. This dedicated time for unplugged improvisation helps your kids develop brain-based skills for listening and conversation, reflection, self-awareness, self-expression, and more effective problem-solving at school and in life. And it helps *you* de-stress—all the better for your children!

3. *Stick with it.* Explore and enjoy digital downtime, and show your kids that this quality of time together is a priority. That's what they'll learn, and they'll learn to enjoy it themselves. Once you get the hang of it, powering down devices for undistracted time gets easier. It's always rewarding to put aside distractions and focus on yourself and the ones you love. Even the awkwardness in the beginning is helpful practice for similar moments that arise

throughout life. Learning the skills to defuse social awkwardness or anxiety is just one of many ways a supportive family serves as a child's first arena for socialization.

Media are not inherently malignant, but they are powerful. When all is said and done, good parenting is what it has always been: understanding the facts of child development and the ways in which their environmental exposures affect their health and development, having clear goals for your child, making informed decisions, and implementing the plan as clearly and consistently as possible.

Unencumbered by preconceptions of doing things "the right way," children are early adopters and innovators, finding uses for digital technologies that their inventors never envisioned. This open and curious mind enables children to do better than adults in some learning situations, a new study suggests. Researchers surprised the adults and four- and five-year-old children participating in the study by making information that was irrelevant at the beginning of the experiment suddenly important for a task they had to complete. "Adults had a hard time readjusting because they didn't learn the information they thought wouldn't be important," said Vladimir Sloutsky, coauthor of the study and professor of psychology at The Ohio State University. "Children, on the other hand, recovered quickly to the new circumstances because they weren't ignoring anything. I'm sure a lot of parents will recognize that tendency of children to notice everything, even when you wish they wouldn't."[11]

The gift of a naïve mind presents opportunities and risks. Digital devices, platforms, and applications are powerful tools, not toys or treats to be awarded for academic performance or confiscated for bad behavior. As amusing as it is to see what a toddler does with a tablet, unintended consequences must be considered. If that toddler sees that they make their parents proud when they show they can manipulate the tablet or that they are provided with the tablet every time they fuss, they will learn to do what it takes to get the tablet and develop the habit of using it. The long-term implications of displacing their experiences of the world and the people in it at this stage of rich and rapid learning will only be realized later in their lives.

As mobile devices like tablets, smartphones, and portable gaming devices have proliferated, parents, teachers, and others who work with children and youth have worried about kids staring at their screens, increasingly crowding out physical play, hanging out with friends, doing homework, and spending time with their families. Increasingly, after a day at school with their friends, children rushed home and turned on screens to game, gossip, and explore. When the COVID-19 quarantine lockdowns occurred and many schools shifted to remote schooling, several interesting phenomena occurred. Having little experience with using screens productively, a significant minority of children and youth did not log on to school at all, logged on without turning on their camera, or opened another window or device to game or communicate with others during the school day as they had typically done after school. And many kids stayed online after school, connecting with each other, often through game spaces like *Roblox*, *Minecraft*, or *Fortnite*. As we found in a Digital Wellness Lab pulse survey, the majority of parents felt that their schools had done a good job of remotely teaching academic subjects like math, science, and English language arts, but they felt that their children did not do as well with social emotional learning (SEL), their acquisition of "soft skills," like interacting and communicating effectively with others.[12] Unlike some academic studies, these are skills kids will use throughout their lives.

School is the first place where children learn to function as individuals and to create their community. Many educators believe that SEL is as important as, or more important than, academics. Now taught in some schools as part of a formal curriculum, SEL happens in every school on the playground, in the lunchroom, and in hallways between classes. Children live and learn (sometimes the hard way) how to behave with each other, how to negotiate, and how to build a society. Because schools could not reproduce these adult-supervised free play opportunities in the remote setting, kids created their own social experiences online. Prior to the "year of learning remotely," we saw how adept our children were with digital devices and allowed them, despite worries, as entertainment. However, seeing both that our children were underprepared to use these powerful technologies in productive ways and that there was little guidance of their social use, it became clear that a hands-off approach to parenting in the digital environment was not working.

What does work is to actively mentor our children's digital media use, introducing each powerful digital tool only when the child needs it and can use it effectively, responsibly, and with respect for themselves and others. Sitting side by side with your child, you can teach them to use interactive media, sharing the experience with them and parenting in the digital environment. This way you can observe your child's actions and reactions, guide their still-forming executive brain functions like impulse control, and help them navigate and use the internet in ways that take care of themselves and others. Remember that mentorship is a dialogue, not a lecture. You will learn as much from your children as they learn from you. Being open to their ideas and learning skills from them are the best ways to show your respect and gain their trust. Reassure them that you will always be available in the background to **MONITOR** their activities as they navigate the digital environment. Just as you guide and protect them in the physical world, you will do so as they move into the digital space. Discuss reasonable guidelines and come to mutual understandings about how they will meet that standard of self-care and consideration for others. One reasonable guideline is that nonessential play or entertainment should not precede homework, time with the family, physical activity, or sleep. Ultimately, what is best for the developing child is a rich and diverse menu of experiences, which can include screen media but not to the exclusion of the variety of life.

In talking about how to introduce powerful digital tools to young people, I often use the analogy of teaching your child to drive a car. Like digital devices, automobiles are a tool that can expand a young person's world and give them freedom but, when operated carelessly, can harm them or others. We sit white-knuckled beside the learning driver, guiding, advising, and correcting as they steer two tons of metal through the world. We help them master the art of smart, safe driving with guidance like "Stay in the center of the lane" or "Move with the traffic" rather than fearfully teaching them to avoid disaster: "Don't hit that tree!" We must bring the same competence and confidence when mentoring them toward mastering the digital ecosystem. Unfortunately, many of us feel less confident online than we do in the driver's seat. We are intimidated by both our children's digital ease and dire warnings of disaster. Well-intentioned parents have been caught in limbo, feeling unqualified to teach devices and applications that their children know better than they do.

Well before COVID-19, many parents had ceded the digital environment to their children. Then the pandemic abruptly plunged us into "all virtual, all the time." Kindergarteners, previously thought too young for digital devices, started their academic careers online; "circle time" was staring at children they didn't know in squares on a screen. Children would bounce from classroom to cartoon, lecture to social media, YouTube science to YouTube autofeed, believing that they could media multitask.

The problem is, the human brain is only capable of thinking about one thing at a time.[13] What we believe to be multitasking is actually switch-tasking from one thought, image, or sound to the next. Thinking about a lot of different things in rapid sequence may cover a lot of ideas but does not allow us the opportunity to think deeply about any of them.[14] It is only by deep thought, reflecting on concepts of math, science, or literature, that we are able to integrate ideas into our own experience, consolidate that learning into our personal library of knowledge, and build on that library to develop creative new ideas. It is this reflective synthesis of new information integrated with what we already know that generates innovation—and that suffers when we switch-task. The sudden shift to continuous screen use blindsided all of us and muted our mentoring response.

For some, digital parenting evolved naturally in response to the challenge posed by the quarantine. Children were able to demonstrate their compe-tence with digital tools, while parents were able to bring their parenting into the digital space, helping their children with impulse control, focus and task completion, and online etiquette. Ironically and fortuitously, the previously abstract concept of parenting in and out of digital and physical spaces happened organically. For other families, especially families with fewer resources, it was a stressful daily struggle of underconnection with inadequate bandwidth and devices that were too small or too slow to support parents' job needs and children's schooling.

Forced by circumstance to loosen concerns about children's total screen time during the pandemic quarantine, we serendipitously reaped some bene-fits. At the end of a remote school day, many children were sick of screens, experiencing Zoom burnout as much as their parents did. Instead of jumping to online games or social media, they wanted to go outside, ride bikes, or just hang out with friends, physically distanced but together IRL. What they couldn't hear from their parents or teachers, they discovered for themselves. Interactive screen media are necessary tools for life, not just play spaces or sources of entertainment.

ASK THE MEDIATRICIAN
How Can I Compete with Cool Media for My Child's Attention?

I feel like a poor substitute for the clever content and entertaining apps my child can find online or on a smartphone. How can I possibly compete?

You may feel intimidated by your children's comfort and capabilities online and hesitate to enter that world with them, but at a time when children are spending more waking hours on media than with any other activity, we must provide the real thing that media cannot. The solution for raising healthy, happy, and productive children in the digital age is human, not technological. Children move seamlessly between the offline and online worlds. We must move with them, parenting them the whole way.

Don't worry about trying to compete. Your role as model and mentor puts you in a lane of your own. As chief navigator, first take a step back for a clear view of the digital environment and look together for experiences that nurture, teach, and support your child and follow their interests. Think big—thankfully, the full range of media options stretches way beyond trending digital devices and platforms. Books, music, drawing, conversation, imaginative play, and the sensation-rich natural environment are all types of media—ways in which human communication is sent and received. Best of all, you are the touch screen that touches back.

Having modeled and mentored your child's use of digital media, the digital parent must monitor their use to stay in the game. Studies have shown that parents' active engagement with their children's media use, including co-viewing and having conversations (not lectures!) about content, is associated with positive outcomes in children's physical and mental health and their social, emotional, and academic development. Benefits include more and better-quality sleep, less aggressive behavior, better school performance, and stronger prosocial behavior.

No matter how smart, savvy, and stable your child may be, they will come across all manner of material and activities online, including some that will intrigue, confuse, engage, and scare them. Some content may be relatively harmless. Other forms come with serious potential risks and consequences. Case in point, the "cinnamon challenge," a food challenge in which participants record themselves eating a scoop of ground cinnamon in under a minute without drinking anything. This challenge, according to Wikipedia, the crowdsourced online encyclopedia, has been circulating since 2001, trending in waves across nearly a quarter century. One of many food challenges from hot sauce to hot dogs, the cinnamon challenge increased in popularity in 2007.[15] By August 2012, there were at least 51,100 YouTube clips of the challenge.[16] At its peak, mentions on X, previously known as Twitter, reached nearly 70,000 per day.[17] Its popularity surged, despite widespread coverage warning of the dangers, which included dry mouth and throat and the risk of aspiration—inhaling into the lungs—which can cause inflammation, lesions and scarring, and in severe cases, aspiration pneumonia. More common but sometimes severe reactions include extensive coughing, burning in the mouth, vomiting, nosebleeds, and breathing difficulty. A food challenge might seem fun or funny to a kid, but the cautionary tale is clear.

The cinnamon challenge is not the unhealthiest of online challenges or most dangerous content, but digital parents don't need anything stronger to make the point: having explored and learned the digital environment together, we must be able to monitor our children's online activities. But how? Parents don't have the time to monitor all that their children do online. And children, particularly during the late tween and early teen years, desperately seek privacy as they sort through a wave of new sensations, mind and body transformations, and often tumultuous feelings.

Parents do not have to be on guard all the time. If parental access to your child's device, platform, or app is agreed upon in advance, it becomes an integral part of their interactive media use. This is where establishing a mutually respectful relationship of supporting your children's success rather than policing them is very important. You do not need to constantly monitor your children's online activities; you need to *be able* to monitor their online activities.

This works for several reasons.

1. When children know that they might be monitored by a parent at *any* time, they behave better at *every* time, just like workers who are

subject to random drug testing. Young people are conscious that if you check on them and find problematic content or behavior from themselves or others, it would be considered irresponsible and disrespectful misuse of the device, platform, or application, and the consequence would be loss of access for a period of time agreed upon when that capability was introduced.

2. The more transparent both parent and child can be about the need for such monitoring to support their successful use of these powerful tools, the better this works. If you explicitly ask your child for permission to monitor social media and assure them that you will keep anything you see or hear confidential, you are demonstrating respect for your child's privacy and reassuring them that you are interested in them and concerned for their well-being. For monitoring to work, it is essential to maintain respect for the emerging individual that is your child. Avoid judging, shaming, revealing, or worst, laughing at what your child posts. If you do so, you lose their trust and your authority.

3. Given these conditions, it is likely that your child will consider setting up a private social media account that you do not know about. For all the fear of finstas, or fake Instagram accounts, these clandestine accounts are usually private, restricted to those who are closest and most trusted, which may not include parents. Unlike public accounts, finstas tend to be authentic and truthful rather than performative and risky—thus, much healthier for young people finding themselves.

4. Because your door (at least to their acknowledged accounts) is open, your child knows that they can bring even the cringiest stuff to you to help them make sense out of it. This makes your child feel safer, even though they may never admit it.

What about the kids who want their privacy? Tweens and early teens are biologically driven to individuate—and unclear about what they are individuating toward. All they know is that they don't want to be like their parents or show any vulnerability to their peers. They desperately seek privacy in which to work though their questioning. A generation ago teen girls kept handwritten diaries locked in their bedside tables. Today that diary is social media. There is an illusion that a social media account is secure and private, but it is not locked in a drawer; it's on a billboard. What kids post online is their digital footprint, a public representation of them that can go far, fast, and remain "sticky," in that it will probably be preserved on a server or hard drive somewhere. The edgier or more attention-getting the material, the more likely that it will grab the attention they crave—and that it will be saved, reposted, and possibly even go viral.

Monitoring your tween or teen's online behaviors will feel invasive and horribly unfair to them. But the reason for it is not an issue of justice but one of biology. They are in a hurry to grow up, to be independent, to be private. Their drive to have more than they had as children is normal and desirable. Their reach for privacy, as with many desires during adolescence, exceeds their grasp at this stage of brain development. To them, privacy means "so my parents can't see!" While privacy guardrails that will protect them into the future can be explained to them by a mentoring parent, their prefrontal cortex, which controls executive functions like judgment, is still maturing and won't be completed until their mid to late twenties. (Amusingly, before neuroscientists figured this out, car rental companies determined that it wasn't profitable to rent a car to anyone under age twenty-five because their risk of loss was greater than their chance of profit.)

Human brain development occurs on nature's schedule. Practicing tough love protects our children's future selves. The ability to monitor their online activities should be a condition of their obtaining interactive devices or plat-forms. It is important to let them know that using interactive media is not only a privilege contingent upon their behavior but a responsibility to respect themselves and others through what they post, repost, or condone by their acceptance. Although they will whine, complain, and try to hack around your ability to monitor them—and you won't have the time or energy to do it all the time—they will know that they can bring any question or concern about their online experiences to you.

The standoff between Nicki and her mother over her phone showed potential for improvement with a shared activity. This is often the case.

"What if you set your mom up with an Instagram account?" I asked Nicki.

"No . . . She would never . . ."

"What does she like?"

"Eating. And cooking. I like cooking, too. It's real peaceful."

"What about creating new recipes with her? You could take pictures of the meals and share them with her friends and yours. You know, your mother would feel a whole lot better, and I bet she would get off your back if she knew what you were looking at and posting from time to time," I suggested.

"No way. I'm not showing her that! We're just talking about boys. And what a dork Mr. Spencer is . . ."

"She might be relieved that you're not connecting with a pedophile."

"Yeah, maybe, but . . . I might try the food thing."

Mindful parenting calls upon us to draw from time-honored traditions and create new ones to give our children the best start in life and prepare them for a future we cannot accurately predict. Our challenge is to retool traditions and adapt sensible parenting for the digital age. Media literacy, or what I prefer to call *media mastery*—understanding how media work and using them wisely—is as important today as reading, writing, and math have always been. Wherever you are on that learning curve, whether you're a tech-savvy parent or not, nothing about this is beyond your capabilities or those of your child as they grow into competent and confident media users.

MEDIA Rx
Mentoring Puts You in the Flow and in the Know

It is important to be as present and involved with your child in their digital space as you are in their physical world. Mentoring them when you introduce digital devices and applications is a process of listening to them closely for what they want to do online and how they want to do it. If you stay curious, open, and nonjudgmental, you will be able to learn from them what other kids are doing online and communicate to them that you are interested in supporting them in realizing their goals.

Every medium has its strengths and limitations: books, TV, augmented reality, movies, internet, social media, virtual reality, music, video games, and apps. These inevitably change over time and with your child's age and development. But at any age and stage, your presence—your engagement—is the single most effective way to enhance the benefits and minimize the risks of the digital environment for your child.

YOU CAN

- *Reframe the dynamic.* Shift your view of yourself as an enforcer—policing your kids in a media use tug-of-war—to a supporter of their success.
- *Address issues of concern as they arise—or before they do.* Talk about them reassuringly in a matter-of-fact, calm, caring way.
- *Stay approachable.* You want your child to be confident that they can turn to you with questions or information about something they've encountered online.
- *Always ask what your child thinks or feels about the subject of your conversation.* Don't tell them that what they think or feel is "right" or "wrong."
- *Use "I" phrases and avoid "should-ing" them.* Talk about your feelings and ideas, not what you think theirs "should" be.
- *Respond thoughtfully.* If you need more information or to give something more thought, acknowledge that and make a plan for resolving it with your child. They'll see what thoughtful deliberation looks and sounds like—something they're not as likely to witness online.

Chapter 2

What Is Digital Wellness?

The Whole-Child Approach
to Healthy Media Use

Jonah was brought in for his first well-baby checkup at two weeks old. His parents were young, he was a first child, and they liked the way I talked to him when I had examined him in the newborn nursery.

"You talked to him like he was your child . . . but like he was six years old. No baby talk. I want to do that," his mother said. She told me that Jonah's first two weeks had gone pretty well. He was waking up every two to three hours to feed during the night (standard operating procedure for a newborn). He fed well and fell back to sleep. But when Jonah fed during the day, he would keep pulling off the breast, looking around, and had to be coaxed back, prolonging his feeding sessions by twenty minutes or more. "And he doesn't go nearly as long between feeds during the day," his mother explained. "I don't think he is getting as much in as he does at night."

I asked her all the standard questions about breastfeeding: "How is Jonah positioned? How do you present the nipple?"

Her answers to each was, "Just the same as I do at night."

So I asked, "What are you doing when you feed him at night?"

She guffawed. "Are you kidding? I am half asleep. I just stare at him and will him to fill his belly so I can get back to sleep!"

"And what are you doing when you feed him during the day?"

"I sit in my nice, comfy chair, latch him on, and turn on the TV to catch up on what's happening outside my baby bubble. Sometimes I call my mom to whine about life."

"What does Jonah do?"

"He looks at me for a while, then he starts looking around the room, and he pulls off."

"Try looking back at him next time and see if it changes what he does. Turn off the TV. Don't make phone calls. Let's see what happens."

<hr>

My focus as a pediatrician is first on keeping the whole child healthy, providing evidence-based preventive practices for families and communities to protect and promote children's health and development. Whole-child care encompasses not only their immediate physical, mental, and social health but healthy physical, psychological, social, emotional, creative, intellectual, and behavioral development. Body and mind are inextricably linked throughout life. Health and development go hand in hand during childhood and adolescence. Nutrition, exercise, learning, and socialization are important for optimizing overall wellness for us all, but especially for the youngest of us. While adults often have to work hard at eating right and exercising to stay well, children's natural instincts and youthful resilience help them stay well. What is wellness in this dramatically different environment, our screen-saturated world, in which today's children are growing up? *What is digital wellness?* These questions are the foundation of my work—and yours as families. The Digital Wellness Lab, where we focus on evidence-based practical parenting advice and the research and policy that support it, defines digital wellness this way:

> Digital wellness is a positive state of mental, physical, and social emotional health pursued through intentional, authentic, and balanced engagement with technology and interactive media.[1]

What does that mean for you and your child? The wider world of babies holds a universal truth for us all. If you haven't seen it, I highly recommend watching the documentary *Babies* (2010),[2] which follows infants from Namibia, Tokyo, San Francisco, and Mongolia. Rich and poor, living with highly educated and functionally illiterate parents, we simply watch (there is no narration) infants' physical, cognitive, and social emotional development over the first two years of life. Children live differently around the globe, but the keys to physical, mental, emotional, and social wellness are consistent: a healthy mix of sleep; play; nourishing food; sustaining relationships, which includes secure attachment to a parent or primary caregiver; and a stimulating environment that fosters curiosity, learning, and resilience.

Because media have such a pronounced presence in our lives, and each of these basic needs affects the others, children's exposure to media and their media use potentially affect every aspect of their health and development, most notably:

- sleep
- nutrition
- self-regulation
- imaginative free play
- brain development and intellectual growth
- language development
- social behavior and social skills
- emotional development
- strenuous physical activity
- outdoor contact with the natural world
- relationships and emotional intimacy
- mental health

The longer-term effects of media exposure and use by infants and young children will take years to establish through scientific studies as children grow and develop, but decades of rigorous research on early childhood health and development offer plenty of insights to inform our choices in today's digital environment. Reflecting a synthesis of findings, the American Academy of Pediatrics guidelines suggest too early or too much exposure to screen media may contribute over time to significant health problems, including obesity, as well as potentially hindering cognitive and other brain development, executive functions, and social and emotional development.[3]

Sleep is a vital component of health and development, yet it is one of the most common casualties of children's packed schedules—and the adverse effects of media use on sleep are well documented.[4] Research shows that media use and even passive exposure can affect children's quantity and quality of sleep, which, in turn, can affect their physical and mental health. Further, poor sleep leaves a child overly tired throughout the day and makes them more vulnerable to other health and behavioral complications, including:

- difficulties learning, listening, concentrating, and solving problems[5]
- feeling stressed and worried, anxious, or fearful[6]
- irritability with friends and family, moodiness or defiance[7]
- unhealthy eating and weight gain[8]
- lower immune resistance[9]

These aren't inevitable outcomes of media's presence in children's lives, however. They are signs of a mismatch, an imbalance, patterns of media exposure or use that aren't supporting a child's optimal health and development. The ubiquitous presence of screens in contemporary life calls for an update of traditional measures of wellness to include digital wellness—a way to account for both the benefits and risks of media use to children's health. Although we know that screen use can undermine healthy sleep, we also know concrete steps we can take to minimize those effects, and as apps for stress reduction, relaxation, meditation, soothing music, and other calming content have proliferated, they're a reminder that media are neutral; we can choose to use them in ways that support our children's optimal health and development.

Digital wellness can be adapted to each child's age and developmental stage—and will need to be updated as the child has different needs for and demonstrates responsible use of media devices and applications. You can fit these strategies into the context of media use in your home and other physical settings, family dynamics, individual health or behavioral needs, and how closely and by whom the activity is monitored.

A 2023 scoping review of thirty-five recent research studies for definitions for digital wellness reflected diverse orientations from the philosophical to the pedagogical to the practical.[10] But a common denominator was the goal of using media to maximize benefits and minimize adverse effects in psychological, social, academic, and work contexts, balancing offline and online life,[11] screen time and nonscreen activities,[12] physical play and digital play.[13] Digital wellness included "flourishing" through autonomy, mastery, purpose, and connectedness with people[14] and having resilience and critical capacities to cope with online risks and achieve online safety.[15] Most of the studies in the scoping review focused on three core domains, physical, mental, and social emotional, but Audrey Yue and colleagues proposed achieving digital well-being by adhering to a comprehensive nine-part model:

- safety and security
- rights and responsibilities
- health and self-care
- creativity
- emotional intelligence
- communication
- consumerism
- employment and entrepreneurship
- activism and civic engagement

Yue suggested a three-dimensional framework that integrates (1) crafting and maintaining a healthy relationship with technology that can be used in a balanced and civil way, (2) identifying and understanding the positive and negative impacts of engaging with digital activities, and (3) being aware of ways to manage and control factors that contribute to digital well-being.[16]

Because formal research focusing on digital wellness for young children is scant and slow, it is important to draw on the wealth of evidence-based knowledge we already have about children's developmental needs, then factor in your observations and intimate knowledge of your child to consider the media choices you make.

The Balancing Act: Our Presence and Media's Presence

As we aim for a child's optimal development and digital wellness, the first powerful evidence we have is the gaze between the newborn and their care-giver. Newborns only see in high-contrast black and white and can only focus on objects about ten inches away (the distance between mom's breast and her downward gaze).[17] The complex coordination of your baby's eyes and brain into a sophisticated visual system will take place over the first two years of life. Undeveloped as it is at these earliest stages, your baby's visual system is already their most important sensory tool for perceiving, exploring, and understanding their world. They stare intently at whatever is in that ten-inch sight line. Their gaze while breastfeeding is on their mother's face until and unless their mother's face is turned away. Breastfeeding is not just nourishing the baby's body; it is nourishing the baby's and mom's relationship—and both of their mental health. This is the first instance of many in your child's development in the digital ecosystem where what you feed their mind is as important as what you feed their body. Skin-to-skin contact, your baby's sounds, and that intent gaze between mother and child cause both mom and baby to release the hormone oxytocin, which stimulates letdown, where milk is released from the milk glands into the ducts.[18] (This is why nursing moms will often leak milk when they hear a baby's cry.) The milk letdown is important for breastfeeding, but oxytocin has critical psychological effects on both mom and baby. It is called the "cuddle chemical" because it calms both mother and child, stimulates physical caressing, talking in nurturing tones, and yes, cuddling.[19] Oxytocin, along with beta-endorphin, another hormone released during breastfeeding and skin-to-skin contact, reduces anxiety, produces feelings of happiness and calm, builds secure attachment, and appears to be protective against postpartum depression for the mom.[20] For dads who are bottle-feeding their infants, that gaze is important support for father-infant bonding, especially when feeding involves eye contact, cuddling, and cooing.[21] Although it may seem as if feeding time is "downtime" in the busy 24/7 life of a new mother or father, don't miss out on this critical opportunity by pulling out your phone to catch up on what you've missed. This is precious and fleeting time to bond with your newborn.

Jonah was able to stare at his mom's half-asleep face during his nighttime feeds, but when she was distracted by the television and phone calls during the day, his behavior suggested he felt abandoned, disconnected, and anxious. Engaged with news and emotion-laden conversations, mom's epinephrine (adrenaline) flowed instead of oxytocin. Jonah's distraction and anxiety rose with his mom's. While smartphones are smaller and quieter than, say, televisions, laptops, and digital tablets, they are no less intrusive. It is easy to pull a phone out of a pocket while doing something else, whether it be getting onto an elevator or breastfeeding a baby. But the many functions of smartphones demand arguably even more attention than a television. Come feeding time, whether breast- or bottle-feeding, it's possible now to watch the news *and* chat with your mother or friends *and* post photos of your baby *and* text *and* shop *and* . . . all from that one device. And all at the expense of your nursing baby's searching gaze.

ASK THE MEDIATRICIAN
Brexting—Mealtimes with Baby and Media in the Mix

Does texting while breastfeeding affect how a mother bonds with her baby?

This is one of the most important questions for parents in the digital age, one that will recur, in various forms, for both parent and child from infancy through adolescence: "How do we maintain human connectedness in the infinite connectivity of the digital environment?"

Parent-child connectedness—the mutual, sustained, positive emotional bond between parent and child—may be the single most protective factor in a child's life in terms of their physical and mental health and their socialization as a member of a family and the larger world. The human brain develops remarkably quickly during the first few months of life, and critical to that development is interaction with other people, particularly with primary caregivers. The simple physical contact of being held and the visual contact of the parent-infant gaze during breast- or bottle-feeding can help build that connection. Research shows that face-to-face gazing between mothers and their children can positively affect their children's moods and help them regulate their emotions. A father's focused attention provides similar benefits.[22] Even long after infancy, the parent-child gaze remains a powerful, primal source of nurture and strength for both.

Texting while feeding a baby diverts the caregiver's attention away from the child. Although constant attention is not necessary, be mindful that feeding time is a unique opportunity to spend intimate time with your child and help build this powerful connection. Staring softly at each other in silence can be calming, centering, and a great way to develop an understanding of your baby's subtle physical cues. Reading out loud and talking or singing to your infant and toddler can increase their language development while reinforcing connectedness.

Remember, the challenge for us all is to strike a balance between media use, such as texting, and our human needs. Texting isn't inherently bad—it can be an important tool for information-seeking and communicating, especially when a child is napping. Limit your texting when you are with your child so you don't miss out on the special things they do and say and so you don't model disconnected, distracted behaviors for your child. Children learn more from what we do than what we say, so let's stay connected to them and model connectedness with others and with the world.

Every parent wants to know: *What can I do to help my baby get off to the strongest possible start?* Your infant's future as an active learner, a socially and emotionally engaged and resilient individual from childhood into adulthood, results from neurons connecting with other neurons in their brain and those connections either being reinforced through use or being pruned through disuse. The stimuli for neurons to connect and be reinforced or pruned away come from the environment. So what features of our physical-digital environment optimize a child's brain development from infancy onward?

Bonding and building a secure relationship with a parent or primary caregiver is the bedrock of healthy development. What happens if a growing infant does not have warm and nurturing interactions with caregivers in the earliest stages of their lives? Without rich, complex human interaction, developing brains do not reach their potential.

Tragically, history provided us with a decades-long experiment. From the late 1960s to 1990, under the dictatorship of Nicolae Ceaușescu, Romania's totalitarian government sought to grow the nation's economy with workers. It celebrated mothers who produced ten or more children, while it prohibited contraception and abortion and taxed the childless. The result was a surge in births of children who were quickly abandoned because their impoverished parents could not support them. The government institutionalized an estimated 170,000 of these children in orphanages, where they were efficiently diapered and fed by bottles propped in their cribs. But they were left alone. They were not held. They were not spoken to. No one looked them in the eyes. No one read or sang to them. When American psychologists first entered the industrial-sized Romanian nurseries after the fall of the Ceauşescu regime, they were stunned by the silence. Infants, toddlers, and even older children were in row after row of cribs, staring.[23] One of those psychologists, Dr. Nathan Fox, observed, "The most remarkable thing about the infant room was how quiet it was, probably because the infants had learned that their cries were not responded to."[24]

Research conducted by Fox; Dr. Charles Nelson, my colleague at Boston Children's Hospital and Harvard Medical School; and others has shown that the Romanian orphans have smaller brains, with less gray matter (brain cells) and white matter (connections to other brain cells). As they have grown up, they have struggled with cognitive function (thinking), language development, and gross and fine motor skills (large and small muscle strength and coordination). Their most prominent and persistent deficits are social emotional behavioral problems and psychiatric disorders.[25] Deprived of human interaction as infants, they were found to have difficulty forming human attachment and establishing and maintaining attention. Years later, many have marked intellectual, sensory, and movement disabilities that have persisted into early adulthood and will likely be for life.

The effects of neglect are not limited to extreme situations like totalitarian orphanages, however. Studies of American children whose parents were neglectful to varying degrees have shown that some have "poor impulse control, social withdrawal, problems with coping and regulating emotions, low self-esteem, pathological behaviors such as tics, tantrums, stealing and self-punishment, poor intellectual functioning and low academic achievement."[26] Neglect is not always extreme. Having screens in virtually every physical space, in our pockets, and on our wrists is a setup for microneglect, moments of distraction that can create instant problems, such as when a driver is adjusting the GPS, or cause cumulative, incremental neglect, as when a parent is routinely texting while with an infant or toddler.

The Digital Dilemma of Distractions

The digital environment has made it increasingly complex to raise a child to be physically, mentally, and socially healthy. Decades of study by pediatricians, child psychologists, and educators have grounded us in a good understanding of the arc of normal human development from infancy to adulthood. But each child is a moving target on that arc, varying in unique ways, responding to both genetic and environmental stimuli. New parents are open and learning all the time with their first child. With their second, parents are frequently surprised and befuddled, sometimes frustrated, sometimes delighted. Thinking that they had this parenting gig figured out with their first child, they often expect their second child to follow similar patterns of behavior, learning, and growth. And they are quickly disabused of that notion. Not only is each child a unique mix of genes that predispose them to respond to stimuli in individual ways, but the stimuli they experience are different. Today the digital environment in which we live is evolving so quickly that not only are the stimuli that children experience different from what their parents experienced as children, but they are different from the stimuli that their older siblings experienced. Keep in mind that as a parent you are navigating those three moving targets: (1) the developing child, (2) the rapidly evolving digital environment that is both affecting and reflecting that development, and (3) the transformation in all of our behavior as we use our digital devices.

Smartphones, more than any other device, have exacerbated distracted parenting. It's so easy to feel we're there, supervising, when we're really only half there, pushing a child on a swing while scrolling through texts, or "watching" them (but not really) climb a jungle gym. More than 200,000 playground injuries require medical care each year, and observational research on playgrounds has shown that parents are looking at their phones instead of their children for 30 percent of the time—and that children take more physical risks when their parents are distracted.[27] Parenting is labor-intensive, requiring one's attention most of the time an infant or toddler is awake. Parents have jobs or other activities that demand thought and responsiveness. It is tempting, perhaps even essential, that they try to keep up with their many demands by "multitasking," even while caring for a child.

Our attempts at multitasking long preceded smartphones. Parents have cooked meals while helping a child with their homework, juggled work demands while keeping an eye on kids at play, and driven while talking to someone in the car with us. The brain experiences this type of juggling back and forth between demands just as a juggler keeps many balls in the air by switching focus and responding to demand as each of the balls heads toward the ground. And switch-tasking works (most of the time) for juggling or for cooking because these actions involve well-practiced muscle memory and reflexes, not reflective thinking and not the split-second response needed to catch a child tumbling toward trouble. In contrast, even the most routine email, text, or notification requires more cognitive resources. Summoning those resources requires diverting them from paying attention to a child. And much more than physical risk is at stake. The Romanian orphans were physically safe, confined to their cribs, but the damage caused by neglect was discovered to be profound and long-lasting, possibly irreversible.

We try to live our lives to the fullest, fitting in as much as possible. When smartphones and tablets were introduced, we believed that they would increase our efficiency, enabling us to get more done in less time because we could respond immediately. And we believed that this would give us more time for ourselves, for our families. But what has happened is different. Exploiting our increased efficiency as a competitive edge, we have gone home after work but kept working, into the evening, on weekends, whenever we can. Our bosses, coworkers, and competitors do the same. We've demanded 24/7/365 always-on attention and productivity of ourselves and of each other, not just in our work, but in our social interactions as well.

Research by developmental and behavioral pediatrician Dr. Jenny Radesky in 2014 found that 73 percent of the parents studied used a smartphone, tablet, or laptop while eating with their children. When parents were using their devices, they had 39 percent fewer nonverbal interactions with their children and 20 percent fewer verbal interactions. The verbal interactions they had were predominantly disciplinary, brief, and harsh.[28] Developmental psychologist Dr. Kathy Hirsh-Pasek and educator Dr. Roberta Michnick Golinkoff have studied the dynamics of early-childhood learning as learning has evolved from traditional classrooms and homes into interactive, mobile, and potentially constant screen use. In an experimental study of how responsive interaction (talking and responding) between parent and child affects language development, they had mothers teach their two-year-olds nonsense verbs describing simple actions, like bouncing or shaking plush toys. They would repeat the new word the same number of times over the same amount of time. But half of the responsive sessions were interrupted by the mother answering her phone for thirty seconds before returning to teach the child for the rest of their time. When the mothers asked the toddlers to demonstrate the actions, the children whose responsive interactions with their mothers were interrupted by a brief phone call could not do so, while those whose interactions were not interrupted could.[29]

Hirsh-Pasek re-created a variation of this experiment for Diane Sawyer's television cameras by having mothers play with their toddlers, then get interrupted by a phone call. When their mothers shifted their focus to the phone, most of the toddlers would call out for their mother's attention, showing their mothers a toy or something they were doing ("Look at me!"), growing increasingly distressed. Heartbreakingly, one girl, seeing her mother engage in a phone conversation, went to her chair and sat quietly, waiting for her mother to come back to her. For a brief moment, she was a silent baby warehoused in an orphanage.[30]

Decades before smartphones existed, Dr. Edward Tronick at Boston Children's Hospital conducted the "Still Face Experiment" with one-year-olds. Their mothers would interact with them, talking and smiling, and the babies would babble a greeting, smile, and point out things of interest in the environment. Then the mothers would turn away briefly and turn back to the children with still, expressionless faces. The babies would greet their mothers, reach out to them, point to objects of interest to see whether their mothers' gazes would follow. When their mothers' faces remained still, the babies would grow increasingly distressed, arching their backs to get out of their seats, shrieking painfully. Losing the powerful visual communication of their mothers' gazes, as they do when the mothers are watching screens, is felt as abandonment.[31]

Testing his clinical observations, child psychiatrist Dr. William Beardslee conducted a comprehensive longitudinal study of children of depressed parents. What he found was that being raised by a withdrawn, minimally responsive depressed parent increases the child's risk of depression four to six times.[32] A parent reading a text, checking a notification, or making a purchase on their phone has a still face and is as withdrawn and minimally responsive as a parent who is depressed. In our momentary digital distractions from our children, are we continually disrupting a necessary human connection that will have implications for their learning or even their mental health?

As babies become increasingly aware of the world around them, they are especially dependent on parents and other caring humans to respond to and interact with them. As they did while breastfeeding, they seek out faces for connection. They are learning how to be human by studying humans. And they are learning how to behave by observing those around them.

Connectedness Is Human, Connectivity Is Technology

Connectedness—deep, meaningful relationships with others—is as essential to human health as food and shelter. Connectivity—a measure of our digital reach in followers and likes—is quantifiable, suitable for competing with others but not for sustaining the human spirit. Our worlds are broader due to our near-infinite connectivity, but our connections are increasingly superficial, and our mental health and social fabric suffer. Despite all the ways that kids use media to stay connected with each other or the larger world—messaging, playing games, posting pics and status updates—they often choose these arm's-length connections over in-person, face-to-face interactions. Digital connectivity feels less awkward and safer to self-conscious youth, but the "cooling" effect of screens (first described by the Canadian media theorist Marshall McLuhan) diminishes emotion, and asynchronous communication can lead to disconnect, misunderstanding, and hurt.[33] Today's children and adolescents have more continuous connectivity than ever and often choose it over opportunities for meaningful connectedness to others.

The best and the worst features of our digital tools amplify the difference between connectivity and connectedness. Video chats with family and friends relieve some isolation and create new opportunities for developing friendships—even virtual dating. But constant screen connectivity can become stressful, even oppressive. We try to lessen our shyness with others by interacting on screens, but we hope, even expect, to find meaningful relationships there. Interactive screen media don't hinder our development of the social skills needed to meaningfully connect and communicate; it is how we use them that determines whether they connect us in sustaining human relationships or limit our connections to the superficial.

Your child's mental health will be an important thread as we look at child and adolescent social development, friendships, dating, sex, emotional intimacy, and self-regulation. Concerns about adverse effects of unhealthy media use are justified, but children can learn to manage their media use and develop healthy habits that support learning, satisfying relationships, rewarding social connections, and a sense of community.

Impressed by the improvement in Jonah's breastfeeding and, even more so, in his ability to self-soothe, Jonah's mom and dad completely changed their own media habits. Dad explained to his boss and coworkers that for family health reasons he could not respond to work messages after hours, and he turned off his phone when he left the office. As Jonah was weaned and grew into toddlerhood, his mom read to him during their cuddle time. When Jonah was awake they focused on family time, playing games, spending time outdoors, walking the dog, and doing projects together. They only watched television or went online when Jonah slept, his mom said, adding that an unexpected benefit was that they watched better-quality shows because they had less time for TV. At Jonah's three-year-old health maintenance visit, his mom tentatively asked whether he could watch educational television because his preschool friends were talking about Elmo. Surprised that he was not yet using screens, I described co-viewing *Sesame Street* and other educational programs with Jonah as a healthy part of a balanced and diverse menu of experiences. At Jonah's four-year-old checkup, when I asked about his screen use, his mom acknowledged that she wasn't perfect at controlling it, in part because he watched television with his friend, Eric, on playdates at Eric's house. She said Jonah "was very excited about some fighting between 'good guys' and aliens." But he often chose to keep playing with his LEGOs when he could watch at home, and he was starting to read to her during their cuddle time.

MEDIA Rx
Family Digital Wellness Checkup

Digital wellness is an ongoing work in progress, not a static set point. It is an evolving relationship with media use shaped by personal, family, social, school, and work dynamics. A child's family setting provides an environment in which to make intentional media choices, practice them, modify as children grow up, and develop healthy habits. Use this questionnaire to assess your family's current media use and identify opportunities to make intentional choices. There are no right or wrong answers—only useful information to start conversations about healthy choices.

Ask yourself these questions periodically to evolve your family strategies as children grow up.

1. What screen devices are in your home?
2. Which devices does each family member use? When and where do they use them?
3. Is watching screen media or gaming done alone or as a shared activity?
4. What screen media do you watch or play with your child(ren)?
5. Are screens turned on for a purpose and turned off once that purpose is achieved?
6. Do you have a regular family mealtime together? Are any screens used at the table?
7. Do your children use screens in their bedrooms or just before bed?
8. Do you or your child(ren) use a screen when you are talking to each other?
9. Does your child's day care or school use screens? How do they use them?
10. Does your family have shared expectations for everyone's screen use? What are they?

Chapter 3

Hungry Brains

Wired by Curiosity, Driven to Connect

Maya's birth was routine. The labor nurse was coaching loudly enough to be heard over the new mother's pushing. The new father was nervously stroking mom's hair back from her sweaty forehead. The obstetrician was quietly murmuring to her resident, then more loudly encouraging mom, then went back to teaching the resident. Mom's grunts and yells grew louder and louder. A tiny patch of wet hair appeared, then a head, then a whole baby!—and all fell silent. Dad shakily cut the umbilical cord. As the pediatric resident, I wrapped the newborn in a blanket, rubbing her dry. She took a big breath, squinting into the light as I cleaned her on the warming table, wrapped her in a clean blanket, and laid her on her mother's chest. Her mother said, "Hello, Maya . . ." Maya turned her head toward the sound and looked up at her tear-drenched parents. Her eyes opened wide for a long, still moment, then her head relaxed onto her mother's breast, her eyes closed, and she slept.

Even the most routine births are dramatic for the newborn. From warm darkness, the comforting, steady rhythms of mom's heartbeat with the occasional muffled murmur of her voice, a newborn is plunged into bright lights, a cacophony of harsh sounds and strange voices, shivering from the cold, and finally finding warmth, a familiar voice drawing her attention to gaze at her parents' faces for the first time. Flooded with new and intense sensations, she absorbs all she can—then shuts down.

In many ways this is the pattern you'll see throughout your child's life, from their early years through adolescence (and into adulthood, if you think about it). At different ages and stages of development, your child will seek sensation, take in as much as they can, and then need a break to process it all, rest up, then reengage with you and the world around them. What has always been a complex developmental journey from infancy to adulthood has been made increasingly complex in today's media environment. But with challenges come opportunities. As we navigate the challenges, it is important to feel the joy of loving our children and sharing the wonder of life in this exciting landscape with them. With that trajectory in mind, as we move through the markers of early brain development, we'll catch a glimpse of similar brain and behavioral patterns that lie ahead on the age and developmental-stage continuum. Your deeper understanding of the "why" underlying early brain development, and the 3M skills—modeling, mentoring, and monitoring—not only will help with your baby and toddler but also will prepare you for the years ahead with more confidence.

The Newborn Brain: Connecting and Pruning

When a healthy baby is born, most of her organs are small, fully functional versions of what they will become—except one. Her heart, lungs, liver, and kidneys all start doing what they will do for a lifetime, but her brain is just starting its most important stage of growth. Other mammals, like puppies and calves, struggle and, although they're somewhat wobbly, manage to walk almost immediately after they're born. The newborn human, however, doesn't walk for about a year. Even our closest relatives, higher primates like chimpanzees and orangutans, are born with brain circuitry programmed for survival—they can grasp and cling to their mother's fur for warmth and protection and move themselves to find their mother's nipple for sustenance.

Humans are born with the brain of a fetus, little more than a receiver of sensory input. Our newborns are unable to communicate anything more than discomfort. They cannot walk or grasp things. They cannot keep themselves warm or obtain food. They are helpless, completely dependent on others. Unlike animals born with brains capable of survival skills, human brains are all potential at birth.

Although this makes us vulnerable as newborns, the opportunity to build our brains in response to the stimuli and challenges of the world gives humans a dramatic long-term advantage over animals that are born with brain architecture already committed to survival.[1] We humans have many failings, and it can be reasonably argued that some animals are smarter, but only the human brain has produced spacecraft, symphonies, and super-computers. How a baby's brain grows and develops can make the difference between a scholar and a straggler. It is because human brains develop within and in response to the physical and psychosocial environment in which they will function that we end up with (arguably) the most intelligent, flexible, and creative brain in the animal kingdom.

We are born with almost all of the estimated eighty-six billion neurons that we will have in our adult brain.[2] Contrary to conventional wisdom, we don't have more neurons than other species, either in total or in our cerebral cortex, the part of the brain with which we think. The African elephant has about three times as many total neurons, and pilot whales have more than twice our cerebral cortex neurons.[3]

The human brain triples in volume during the first two years of life, not from generating more neurons, but by making useful and effective connections among the neurons we have.[4] These connections, called synapses, are how neurons signal each other. Greater numbers of synapses networked together generate more complex brain function. Reflexive withdrawal of a body part from a painful stimulus needs few synaptic connections; developing the theory of relativity requires many. Each of the estimated twenty-five billion neurons in our cerebral cortex can develop more than ten thousand synapses. At the height of neural development during the first several years of life, human brains are making as many as one million synaptic connections every second.[5]

As anyone who has spent time with very young children will observe, development of a baby's brain architecture and capabilities happens sequentially. Babies typically walk before they talk. Brain development occurs in order, with certain capabilities developing before others—and opportunities for that development closing before others. From its earliest moments, the human brain is registering stimuli from the eyes, ears, nose, tongue, and every sensory nerve ending, and those sensations trigger movement. For survival reasons—so that we can withdraw from pain—synaptic connections along sensorimotor pathways form earliest, peaking at two to four months of age.[6]

Language development follows sensorimotor pathways, with synaptic formation peaking at seven to nine months and slowing dramatically at five years of age, explaining why it is so easy for very young children and so much harder for school children to learn foreign languages.[7] Synapses involved in higher cognitive functions such as thinking, creating, academic learning, and innovating develop more slowly, peaking between one and two years of age and continuing well into adolescence and beyond.[8]

HUMAN BRAIN DEVELOPMENT

Experience-dependent synapse formation

Neurogenesis in the hippocampus

Adult levels of synapses

-9 -8 -7 -6 -4 -3 -2 -1 0 1 2 3 4 5 6 7 8 9 10 11 12 | 1 2 3 4 5 6 7 8 9 10 11 12 13 14 15 16 17 18 19 20 30 40 50 60 70

Months   Months   Years   Decades

Conception   Birth   Age   Death

Time courses for synaptogensis		
▬▬ Higher cognitive functions (perfrontal cortex)	▬▬ Receptive language area / speech production (angular gyrus Broca's area)	▬ ▬ Seeing / hearing (visual cortex / auditory cortex)

Deborah Phillips et al., *From Neurons to Neighborhoods: The Science of Early Childhood Development* (Washington, DC: National Academy Press, 2000), https://www.ncbi.nlm.nih.gov/books/NBK225562/figure/mmm00006/.

Everything Maya, as a healthy newborn, was sensing was new and intense. As I laid her on the warming table, she threw her arms outward in a Moro reflex, a startle response to the stimuli flooding her. Newborns are unable to distinguish between important and unimportant stimuli. They react to every stimulus with a startle, then try to figure out that stimulus until the next one startles them. This is normal, an indication that their sensory capabilities are far greater than their analytical skills and their life experience. As Maya grows older, the Moro reflex will disappear as her brain learns to make sense of the stimuli coming from her environment.[9] As her senses mature, their sensitivity and complexity increase. To register and respond to inputs that matter, first for her survival, later for focusing on what interests her, Maya's brain needs to develop from its newborn "startle until shutdown" state into one that can focus on what is important to her and filter out that which is not.

All said, that is the brain's task for the rest of our lives, so how it gets started, and how our interaction with media and technology affects it, is both important and fascinating, especially as it reveals the enduring power of the nontechnological force that launches it all: human relationships.

This fundamental truth about the lifelong benefits of early bonding with your child bears repeating: from birth, the mutual, sustained positive emotional bond between parent and child may be the single most protective factor during the child's life in terms of their long-term physical health, mental health, and socialization as a member of a family and the larger world.[10] The simplest interactions can have profound effects. This important connection and interaction between parent and child that begins at birth over physical sustenance—the bonding that develops in the face-to-face closeness of nursing your infant—carries forward as they grow older. The tradition of breaking bread together as a family is universal, around the world and across time. Sharing a meal and sharing undistracted time together strengthens bonds and offers a safe place and protected time to decompress and just talk with those whom you love and trust. Connectedness and communication with family have been shown to be among the single most important activities to improve and protect mental health, even among the most silent and sullen youth. Sit-down family meals without screens have been shown to improve not just healthy nutrition but overall well-being.[11] When any screen, television, or smartphone is in the room, unless it has an intentional, purposeful role to play, the positive effects of a shared meal are largely lost.[12]

Important signals stimulate synaptic formation, connecting neurons that carry the sound to others that trigger hunger, a smile, or a vocalization. Repetition of important signals reinforces the initial synaptic connections and creates others for more complex emotional responses.[13] A baby's brain needs to distinguish important stimuli like the sound of a mother's voice and filter out environmental noise like the rumble of a truck outside. While the infant brain builds sensitivity by connecting its billions of reactive but uncoordinated neurons, it simultaneously focuses its ability to synthesize its responses into sensations, feelings, and thoughts. For a baby to understand that the pattern of light and dark detected by her eyes is her mother's face, the important visual information has to be perceived and the unimportant information discarded, much in the way that we can listen to a specific human voice in a crowded, noisy environment.

Maya's developing brain gradually focused the flood of sensory input that startled her as a newborn through a process known as *pruning*. Just like pruning a fruit tree, cutting off unproductive branches to strengthen productive ones, by eliminating synaptic connections that contributed less useful signals, Maya's brain improved its ability to identify and sense important signals, like differentiating between her mother's voice and environmental noise. She still hears the noise, but she filters it out as unimportant. This is how developing human brains constantly improve the signal-to-noise ratio— the dominant signal your brain "hears" above the distracting background noise of less important or undesired signals.[14] Thus, it is essential that stimuli provided to the developing brain optimize the functions that are needed and desired for the mature brain. Perceiving, synthesizing, and responding to these stimuli make the brain stronger, more resilient, and more creative. Not using the brain in these ways risks the loss of circuits that might be needed in the future—nature's form of "use it or lose it." We'll see shortly how that plays out in the media environment. The brain Maya will have as an adult will be the result of an ongoing work in progress, the work of connecting neurons and pruning unnecessary connections that occurs most rapidly during the first days, weeks, months, and years of life.

The environment in which a child grows and develops provides the stimulus for brain development. While that potentially gives humans a competitive advantage over animals that have brain networks precommitted to survival reflexes, it also means that the growing child's environment can dramatically alter their development. Without rich, complex stimuli, brains do not reach their potential.

The current state of knowledge on human brain development points to three environmental features of early childhood that are associated with healthy, creative, and flexible brains as children grow up:

- interacting with parents, siblings, and other humans,[15]
- moving within and manipulating the physical world,[16] and
- free play.[17]

Children who feel safe and loved, surrounded by people who see and hear them, who talk and listen to them, who read to them, who sing, dance, and play with them grow up to be caring, confident, and curious. Secure or healthy attachment with their primary caregiver is what enables your child to feel they have a secure base from which to explore the world and trust they will find comfort and nurturing from you when they need it. It is the first way infants learn to organize their feelings and actions, relying on the stability of that relationship. In continuing study of the Romanian orphans after reforming the care in the orphanages, the attachment relationships of these children were tested alongside children from the community who had grown up in families. Infants between twelve and thirty-one months old entered an unfamiliar playroom with their "attachment figure," a nurse from the orphanage, while the children from the community entered with a parent. Then a stranger entered, and the parent and nurse attachment figures left. Every one of the community children, 100 percent, turned to their parent when the stranger entered and became distressed when their parent left. Among the children from the orphanage, only 3 percent showed secure attachment to their nurse. The majority of them had "disorganized" responses to the stranger in the room. Some froze while others approached then retreated—behaviors that have been linked to psychopathology later in life.[18] These research results revealed why the nurseries were so eerily quiet when the psychologists first arrived. Children who did not have human interactions in their earliest months never learned that they could seek comfort for their distress. Because they were warehoused in cribs, with little to no opportunity to move around, let alone play, their psychological development was damaged, physical growth was stunted, and fine and gross motor skills were delayed.

When these findings were publicized, Romania prohibited institutionalizing children under the age of two, and many of the institutionalized children were moved into foster homes. Retested at age three-and-a-half, nearly half of the children who had been moved into foster homes showed human attachment, and those who moved before the age of two showed the greatest improvement. Even with much more attention and compassion from staff, only 18 percent of those who remained in the orphanages had established secure attachments, likely because with many caregivers instead of one or two, children did not know to whom they could communicate and relieve their distress.[19] Although children who had established attachment continued to have lower rates of anxiety, depression, and limited empathy and affect at age four-and-a-half, 40 percent of children who were once institutionalized were later diagnosed with a major psychiatric disorder.[20] Children still institutionalized had smaller brains and profoundly lower brain activity than children who were never institutionalized.[21] The profound difficulties forming human attachments and establishing and maintaining attention as well as the marked intellectual, sensory, and movement disabilities experienced by the institutionalized Romanian children are extreme, but a spectrum of less-severe developmental issues has been observed in children who had limited interactions with consistent caregivers.[22]

Babies who grow up in a warm, complex, and stimulating environment optimize their opportunities for brain development. Infants who can explore their physical world—from shaking a rattle to grasping a Cheerio and getting it into their mouth to stacking up and knocking down blocks—have opportunities to perfect their fine motor skills. Those who can roll a ball back and forth, shake their booty to music, and climb up and jump off the couch build their strength and gross motor coordination. Free play, in which children can imagine and create, whether it be with crayons and a blank piece of paper, a sandbox, or a box of dress-up clothing, helps children make and become anything they want—in the moment and into the future.[23]

When your child uses their brain to perceive, synthesize, and respond to what they see, hear, feel, and do, they are making and reinforcing the synaptic connections of a stronger, more flexible, resilient, and creative brain. If the potential of their developing brain is not challenged, synaptic connections may not be formed. Important neural connections will not be reinforced, leaving them vulnerable to pruning.[24] It is the structure and strength of this architecture that creates the uniqueness and power of the human brain. Just as the stress of exercise stimulates growing bones to remodel themselves to be stronger, the growing brain responds to environmental demands by building more complex and sophisticated neural networks. Protecting that process in a digital environment, recognizing what the developing brain really hungers for and what is genuinely fortifying, is an essential piece of whole-child wellness—knowing when to prioritize human interaction and set aside digital interaction for another time. Especially with infants and young children, we have to use our own natural intelligence to make that choice. As the science on screen use is showing us, looks can be deceiving.

Looking Isn't Learning: The Orienting Response Snags Your Baby's Attention

Jack had been a perfect baby. He slept through the night from early on, was easy to calm, sat up at five months, and walked at thirteen months. When it was discovered during his two-year checkup that he had fallen behind in his language development, Jack's parents were worried. He had shown no previous signs of developmental delay, and they had provided him with lots of love and plenty of stimulation, from mobiles to baby videos to interactive learning toys. A thorough neurological evaluation yielded no clues.

The neurologist called Jack's language delay a normal variant, reassuring his parents that because he was meeting all other developmental milestones, his language would sort itself out in time. Jack's parents, a lawyer and a tax accountant, wanted to improve his chances, though, so they went to the library, studied everything they found, and provided him with every recommended support, including his own tablet with edutainment software. Then, a year later, Jack's preschool teacher expressed concern about Jack's limited vocabulary and asked his mother about his TV viewing as an infant. The teacher had heard that TV viewing might slow language development. Jack's mother was stunned. She thought the educational baby videos were helping Jack. To be honest, she said, she heard so much different advice from so many sources, she couldn't keep up with it. Jack seemed to watch the videos intently while she worked quietly beside him, though he looked toward her every couple of minutes. He didn't fuss, and she got her work done.

In the late 1990s and early 2000s, the most popular baby shower gift was *Baby Einstein*, a video series that promised to teach your infant language, music, culture, and more to make your baby into Einstein. Parents loved the idea. Babies were attracted to and watched the videos, full of brightly colored toys bouncing to classical music. In 2002, a newspaper article gushed that *Baby Einstein* videos were "mesmerizing babies across the country."[25] A national survey found that 27 percent of American families with infants between six and twenty-four months old had one or more *Baby Einstein* videos.[26]

Baby Einstein was a huge commercial success. Infants "watched" *Baby Einstein* videos, and their parents were able to take a shower or prepare a family meal while they were mesmerized by the "electronic babysitter." *Baby Wordsworth/ Mozart/Galileo/Van Gogh/Shakespeare* all followed, and *Teletubbies*, *Your Baby Can Read!*, *Baby Genius*, and others crowded into the lucrative marketplace on their coattails. But science was catching up to them.

In 1999, the American Academy of Pediatrics cautioned that infants and toddlers under the age of two should be discouraged from using screens in a policy statement that made the front page of the *New York Times*.[27] This was very controversial, especially among parents who had incorporated television, the only screen in widespread use at the time, into their family's daily routine. "How can I feed my family if I can't have the kids watch TV while I cook dinner?" (This, of course, begs the question of how we survived without eating until television started becoming widely available after World War II.) Although the 1999 recommendation was based more on pediatricians' empirical observations than on rigorously conducted science, neurodevelopmental research on the effects of early childhood screen use has subsequently supported this advice.[28]

There was no evidence to support *Baby Einstein*'s claims that "your child will learn to identify her different body parts, and also discover her five senses . . . in Spanish, English, and French."[29] Researchers at the University of Washington published a study in 2007 that found for every hour on average each day that babies watched *Baby Einstein* videos, they knew six to eight fewer words and scored 10 percent lower on language-skills tests than babies their age who did not watch baby videos.[30] A 2010 study from the University of California, Riverside, found that twelve- to fifteen-month-old toddlers who frequently watched *Baby Wordsworth*, a *Baby Einstein* video claiming to increase toddlers' vocabularies, showed no increases in either understanding or using words when compared to toddlers of the same age, gender, and stage of cognitive development who did not view the video. The only differences in language development found were increases in vocabulary comprehension and production in those children who had been read to the most.[31] Complaints to the Federal Trade Commission led to the removal of the word *educational* from *Baby Einstein* packaging and advertising. Under threats of a lawsuit for false advertising from a child advocacy group that estimated *Baby Einstein* owned 90 percent of the "baby media" market, Disney offered refunds to frustrated parents, costing the company an estimated $100 million before selling *Baby Einstein* in 2013.[32]

What was going on? To parents and baby video producers, it looked like babies were paying attention to the videos. How could they not be learning what they saw—learning less, in fact, than babies who did not watch videos designed to teach them? In fairness, baby video producers, like pediatricians, were relying on their observations. Babies looked at and kept looking at the videos, so baby video producers assumed that they must be learning. Pediatricians were observing developmental delays in toddlers who had watched a lot of television as infants, so they surmised that it might be related to television viewing.

In 1863, neurological physiologist Ivan Sechenov described his discovery of the orienting response, reflexive attention paid to a novel change in the environment that is not sudden enough to elicit the startle response but might require an immediate reaction.[33] Thought to have evolved as a survival reflex, the orienting response is seen in infants who turn their heads toward a visible or audible stimulus.[34] Baby Maya demonstrated the startle response at birth and then the orienting response when I came into the exam room for her two-month checkup. Babies will turn to face anything new in their environment, using their senses to determine what it is and whether those images or sounds represent either a threat or potential benefit, but when it is no longer novel, they will become habituated and turn away.[35] Baby videos do not hold infants' attention; rather, they keep grabbing and regrabbing the orienting response by constantly introducing new stimuli with rapid cutting, sound effects, and scene changes. Observing this through adult eyes, it appears as if the babies are watching the screen. It is tempting to conclude that the baby is engaged with and learning from the content. Unfortunately, all that they may be learning is to stare at the stimulus provided by screens.

Video grabs the attention of babies and toddlers even when the content on screen is not aimed at or interesting to them. Pioneering work by Dr. Daniel Anderson at the University of Massachusetts Amherst showed that when toddlers were offered a variety of toys, their play was spontaneous, continuous, and concentrated, providing cognitively rich opportunities for imagination, problem-solving, and world-creating. But when a television in the background was turned on to an entertainment channel, their attention was distracted and play was interrupted. They would look up and glance at the television for a few seconds, abandon a toy mid-play, and restart play with another and another, never fully engaging or completing play.[36] Television disrupted the child's play—and distracted parents from the child.

Seeing the dramatic increase of screen use in ever-younger children, media companies are trying to penetrate younger and younger markets with their products. They know that they must convince their consumers— parents—that their child is learning from the companies' products. Given the educational successes realized for preschool children with evidence-based and rigorously evaluated programming such as *Sesame Street*, developmental psychologists and educators have been actively exploring how very young children perceive and respond to screen media.[37]

A critical first question that must be answered is at what age and developmental stage very young children are able to decode that two-dimensional images on a screen represent the three-dimensional world. Dr. Georgene Troseth and Dr. Judy DeLoache demonstrated that two-and-a-half-year-old children could find a toy that they had watched being hidden on a video screen, but two-year-olds could not. Although their experimental results came after the 1999 AAP recommendation discouraging screen use before two years of age, they offer support to the notion that children under two may be distracted by but are not learning from watching a screen.[38] Since screen learning does not appear to teach infants and toddlers the way it teaches preschoolers, how can we enrich early childhood in a world where we cannot avoid screens, where we now use them for virtually every life activity? Three activities known to build strong, flexible, creative brains—interacting with caring humans, physically exploring their sensory world, and free play—are notably missing or weakly imitated on digital screens. We can do better than defaulting children's brain development to screens.

Building and Nurturing Human Relationships Is Job #1, Best Done One-on-One

Reading to a baby is more than the story that can be shown on a screen. Just look at how babies view videos, strapped securely in a seat, frequently while their parent is busy elsewhere. Your baby's attention is grabbed and regrabbed by the screen, but they are distracted from building and enriching their relationship with you. Even when you are there, the screen hijacks *your* attention too. Research has shown that when a TV is on, adults speak far fewer words to their infants and toddlers, from half as many to no words at all.[39] Contrary to the claims that baby videos encourage parent-child interaction, this can explain why children exposed to TV as infants have a higher prevalence of delayed language development and attention problems.[40]

Because a cool, flat screen showing a story cannot compete with a warm lap, encircling arms, and a familiar voice reading that story, digital media for very young children are often embellished with features that tablets can do and books cannot. Touch the cartoon of the lion and it roars; touch it twice and it will show you a video of a real lion roaring. When a book is read by a loving adult, they point at the lion, they say its name, they roar—and teach the infant to roar. This engages the child in imagining and taking ownership of the idea of a lion rather than handing them a prepackaged image and sound of a lion.

The bonding that occurs when reading together gives greater value to what is learned because of whom the child learned it with. The roar produced when they touch the lion picture does not unleash giggles by roaring in increasingly loud or silly ways. When a parent does that, the child learns to make it happen again and again with increasing glee, building memories of not only what a lion is but what a parent is as well. Reading together from a tablet can be as effective as a parent reading from a book—as long as the tablet is treated as a book.[41] The lap is more important than the app. When the child is being held, talked to, cuddled, looked at, and listened to, a full-body social and sensory experience releases oxytocin in both parent and child, laying the groundwork for learning and human connectedness that kids will seek and experience throughout their lives.[42]

The power of human connection gives rise to a positive use of interactive screens with children under two—video chatting with known loved ones. Infants do not pay much attention to video chats with those they have not met in person. Once your baby knows and has established an in-person relationship with grandparents, family, or friends who cannot be present, brief audiovisual interactions with them, while not as enriching as being together in person, are enjoyable on both sides. Even interactions with those they know are best limited to the infant's attention span—so it is good to observe when your child's focus shifts (and not let it hurt Grandma's feelings). Interestingly, it remains unclear whether the child is decoding the visual image as a symbol of Grandma or recognizing her voice and the child is just staring at the color patterns and movement on the screen.[43] Such interactions are emotionally valuable to the adults on either side of the screen, and the warmth and happiness of human connection they model is absorbed by the child.

The Developing Brain and Body Seek Sensation

Unlike adults, who can learn through abstract concepts, young children learn concretely, through what they experience. The primary developmental tasks of infants and toddlers are to master their five senses and use them to understand the world and their place in it. The interwoven development of brain, mind, and body relies on direct experience—that hands-on sensory immersion in the physical world. Sensory learning energizes curiosity, creativity, and joy of learning.

Early childhood is a time when children are powerfully drawn to but wary of new sensations. They are building their knowledge of the world and how to behave in it from sensory experiences of their environment. We have seen how the sensory component of hearing a loving voice reading a story while feeling a warm lap, smelling a familiar body, seeing pictures, and even tasting a board book is richer than seeing and hearing that story on a digital screen. Children can be told that their plate is hot but will still touch it more often than not. While many children resist trying new foods, an evolutionary artifact perhaps of avoiding illness, when they get involved in preparing the food, they are more likely to try it and frequently discover they enjoy the flavor of apples, carrots, and even spinach, but maybe not liver.

While your child can draw with millions of colors on a digital tablet, they will lose interest fast, but when they finger paint with just primary colors, they are unconstrained from having to function by the rules of the device, learning about mixing blue and yellow to make green, smelling (sometimes tasting) the paint, and feeling it squishing between their fingers. They also discover, to their delight, the interesting response they get from both their parent and their baby brother when they paint his hair. An environment rich in stimuli for all five senses builds minds that are open, inquisitive, and brave.

Infants and toddlers are just learning that they have a physical body. They are discovering its boundaries and capabilities. As they learn to live in this incredible biological machine called the human body, they discover its parts—eyes, nose, mouth, fingers, feet, genitalia. What parent hasn't enjoyed their infant's delight in discovering their toes or their newfound dexterity to shake a rattle? Or who wasn't mortified when their toddler showed their discovery between their legs to the relative or friend most offended by it? What parent hasn't marveled to see their young child struggle to learn a playground skill, then bring that confidence to the next challenge? This is how they explore and celebrate their bodies. All this physicality is deeply interwoven with brain development.

As children develop greater physical capabilities, from sitting up to crawling to cruising to walking to running, they naturally want to pursue each new skill until they master it, then move on to the next physical challenge. Physical play, where they test themselves, increases their abilities and their self-confidence, setting the foundation for good body image and self-respect built on what they can do rather than how they look. Risk for this age group has to do primarily with the risks necessary for learning—learning to walk, falling down, trying again and falling again until they finally succeed. Trying tasks and trying again and again will be a pattern that repeats throughout life. And it's OK for them to get bumps and bruises in the process. That's how they learn. We want our children to learn. What they need is a safe environment in which to try things, and—especially for the younger child—to know that they have Mom or Dad to rescue them when they fall down.

For the young child, this is a wonderful time to get them outdoors, lying in the grass, looking up at the clouds and trees, crawling through the backyard, and stooping to stare at birds or bugs. As they start to walk, it is safer and more fun to fall into autumn leaves than a coffee table. They will get muddy, and we will hose them off. They will learn that the earth is not a dangerous or dirty place but their home. It is a place where they can be, if only for a moment, wild and free. Not only does nature provide endless opportunities for physical exploration and imaginative play, but your child will learn to value and preserve their earth from the beginning. They will climb trees, and some may fall; some may even get hurt. But a broken arm can be fixed. A broken spirit cannot.

Free Play Nurtures Curiosity, Creativity, and the Joy of Learning

Infants and toddlers are learning how to learn and learning to love learning. Few facts that your child learns during their first few years will persist in a meaningful way into their school years and beyond. What will persist in later life is a fearless willingness to meet challenges, solve problems, work with others and be persistent, imagine, and create the new. As we have observed with both digital and analog early-learning programs, rote memorization and repetition will allow any precocious toddler to mimic what she has seen or heard—but can backfire if they come to dislike drills, resent being treated by doting parents as a trick pony, and end up resisting education in any form.

Children live in the present, with little awareness of the future and, thankfully, limited memory of the past. They are naturally playful, experimenting and fooling around with the people and places they experience. While recent discoveries have shown that Aristotle was wrong—nature does not always abhor a vacuum—children always do. When told to sit still and be quiet, children will invariably begin to play with each other and even by themselves, talking, singing, and getting physical, often to the chagrin of parents or teachers. They seek sensory stimuli, and if they don't find it in their environment, they make it. They just play! Their play has no predetermined rules, but kids learn to develop a structure that makes sense—and fun!—out of their play. Unlike adult-created games or organized sports, there is usually no goal to achieve, conflict to win, or end point to free play. It is the process of play for play's sake that draws children in and from which they learn.

The most important way to support your young child's learning and growing is to nurture their curiosity, creativity, and joy of learning. Make it an adventure to have new experiences, and help them feel they are safe to take necessary risks. They need the time and space to explore their world and figure things out on their own. Instill in them the security that you really care what they think, feel, and understand and that you are there to listen, see, read, and genuinely appreciate what they create. This is a great time to get kids involved in making media, whether by putting a piece of paper and crayons in front of them when they are looking at a mountain or by listening to music and handing them a drum. Making the connection between consuming and producing media—in the broadest sense of the word—will teach them that media are a means of communication between people.

MEDIA Rx
Brain-Building Strategies for Babies and Beyond

At every age, from birth through adolescence, healthy brain development draws in vital ways from your child's direct, face-to-face, physical interaction with people and the natural world. Their exposure to and use of media can promote healthy development or get in its way.

To create a nourishing, possibility-rich environment for your child's mind and body, tap the senses in loving, playful ways.

YOU CAN

- *Hug your child.* Research shows that school-age children whose mothers nurtured them have brains with a larger hippocampus, a key structure important for learning, memory, and response to stress.[44]
- *Talk to your child from birth.* Research has shown that when babies hear speech sounds, especially when face-to-face with the speaker, their brains rehearse speech mechanics well before their first birthday.[45]
- *Nurture creativity with low-tech, tactile toys.* Simple dolls and plush animals, dress-up costumes, musical instruments, and blocks that can be built up and knocked down enable your child to create and rebuild imaginary worlds.
- *Stimulate your child's senses.* Offer meals that explore taste and texture. Play visual games from peekaboo for baby to "I spy" on car rides right through adolescence. Sing (even off-key—they will remember *that* forever), dance, and make rhythms.
- *Take your child outdoors.* Being in nature challenges, educates, puzzles, and calms kids, building self-awareness and reflective thinking.

- *Turn off background media to decrease visual and auditory distraction.* Children will hear the subtle, ambient sounds of home, nature, and street life and will learn to enjoy quiet.
- *Help your child learn to calm themselves.* Read, rock, and play music to them *before* they go to sleep, but then turn everything off and let them fall asleep on their own. Avoiding screen use before sleep may be painfully obvious, but even the most soothing music or crib mobile actually stimulates the brain's arousal centers and impedes sleep. You do not want your child to need media to sleep, as it may establish an arousal-sleep battle for many years.
- *Walk, run, and play tag.* Physical activity refreshes brain cells and supports growth and resilience.[46]
- *Avoid using screen media as an electronic babysitter.* Share with rather than exclude your child from your activities. Sit your baby in their bouncy seat to watch the water trickle down the shower curtain. Sit them on the floor and give them a spoon and a bowl while you make dinner. Their senses will be more finely tuned.
- *Make time for your child to be bored.* Boredom is where imagination and innovation grow, not just because it is empty space in their consciousness but because that space is uncomfortable and needs to be filled. Encourage them to fill it with the new rather than media.
- *Tell stories and build brains.* Storytelling builds integrated neural networks for memory, attention, reflection, integration, and comprehension.[47]
- *Encourage your child to create in a range of media* from clay to video, text to music, and share it. Give your child the tools, a safe space to create, and an appreciative eye or ear when and if they choose to share.
- *Model and establish a habit of purposefully enjoying screen media and music and turning them off when done to focus on the next activity.*

From Startle to Sustained Focus, Attention Develops from Birth Through Early Adulthood

Five-year-old Charlie was rambunctious, restless, inattentive at preschool and disruptive at home. Thirteen-year-old Suzanne was quiet and well-behaved in class but began failing academically when she started middle school. Seventeen-year-old Walter was hyperfocused, intense, and impossible to interrupt. Attention problems like these are among the most common worries that parents bring to me. "Why does she drift off whenever I am talking to her?" "His teachers say he is unmanageable, getting up and walking around the room during class!" "No matter how many times I tell him something, it just never seems to stick. It is literally in one ear and out the other." Confronted with a child's attention challenges, parents feel ineffective at home. Hearing concerns from teachers, they worry that their children are failing at school. Kids feel lost, both academically and socially. They try, they fail, their anxiety builds, and they act out.

Building a child's attention span by increasing their ability to absorb information, process it in their working memory, and complete tasks is a critical developmental task of the growing brain. Sustained attention is important as children grow older, attend classes, do homework, and eventually work and build a career. An estimated 6.1 million children in the US ages two to seventeen years old have been diagnosed with attention disorders, and their number continues to rise.[48] For most, their distractibility impairs academic performance; for many, it also impacts social interactions because they have difficulty following conversations.

It may not be that the number of young people living with attention disorders is actually rising but that these behaviors are being recognized earlier and in more children. A teacher may bring concerns to the attention of a parent, who then consults with their pediatrician, and often the child is diagnosed with attention deficit hyperactivity disorder (ADHD). In my clinical experience, attentional struggles vary in severity and behaviors, from Charlie to Suzanne to Walter. I see ADHD not as pathology but as a variant of normal, one that can be addressed effectively with strategies at our disposal. This characterization allows young people and their parents to be more accepting of their diagnosis and of themselves. But how do I explain ADHD as part of the spectrum of human behavior when it is so dysfunctional in the classroom, family, and social life?

Not so long ago in evolutionary terms, when we humans were hunter-gatherers, distractibility was a critical survival skill. The ability of the human brain to be hypervigilant to all the stimuli in the environment enabled our ancestors to crawl out of the cave each morning, hunt for their family's next meal, and avoid becoming the next meal of a predator tracking them while they were tracking their prey.[49] Our distractible ancestors survived and reproduced, passing those survival traits down generation after generation. But when you put that effective survivor into a classroom and demand that they sit still and ignore distractions, they don't do so well. The environment we inhabit today requires sustained focus, frequently on less stimulating components of the environment, but many of our brains maintain our formerly protective hair trigger of distractibility. A study of two indigenous tribes, one in Arizona and one in Kenya, found that traits that conferred a survival advantage in earlier environmental conditions became a vulnerability when the environment changed patterns of animal migration and food sources.[50] In our media-rich digital environment, with an endless stream of stimuli, distractibility has become a vulnerability, the brain's Achilles heel.

All children can have trouble focusing and behaving at one time or another. A child's ability to pay attention is on a continuum that varies with the child's age and developmental stage, as well as day to day or moment to moment, depending on their environment. It is only when their attention cannot be engaged by a teacher or parent or when their attention difficulties impair their function at school or home that a diagnosis of ADHD and possible treatment is sought. Extreme distractibility and a short attention span are hallmark characteristics of ADHD. A growing body of research is expanding our understanding of ADHD in children, adolescents, and adults, how attention disorders affect the brain, and how media use and repeated disrupted attention affect executive functions.[51] A child with ADHD might:

- act impulsively
- squirm or fidget excessively
- talk too much
- forget or lose things frequently
- make careless mistakes or take unnecessary risks
- have a hard time resisting temptation

- have trouble taking turns
- have difficulty getting along with others

Not all distractible kids have ADHD, so it is important not to rush to a diagnosis and medication that may not be needed. But there are also kids with ADHD who are not diagnosed or treated, so it is good to be alert to their behaviors and seek help from a pediatrician or psychologist who can make an informed diagnosis and, if warranted, treat your child. Many children who struggle with ADHD instinctually find work-arounds for academic demands in school but may struggle socially, frequently ostracized as "annoying" or "weird." The hyperactive kids who are most disruptive tend to be diagnosed during the preschool years. Children with ADHD who are distractable but not hyperactive often stay quiet and don't "out" themselves by asking questions or discussing ideas, so they may fly under teachers' and parents' radar. Many ADHD diagnoses are made at points in a child's schooling when academic demands outstrip their abilities to compensate: when they learn to read (first grade), when they read to learn (fourth grade), and when entering middle or high school, where curricula ramp up toward college. A few make it to college before they crash and seek help. A significant number of people with ADHD make it to adulthood, undiagnosed and untreated, struggling to hold a job or maintain social relationships. The hyperactivity, vigilance, impulsivity, and distractibility that were adaptive for hunter-gatherers can lead to educational failure, substance use, and even criminal activity in today's world.

What Is Attention?

Attention is the process by which the brain receives, processes, and acts on incoming stimuli. Sound, smells, visuals, and other sensory stimuli, along with our own thoughts and feelings, compete for attention in the brain. If you're excited by seeing a friend across the street, your impulse to rush across can easily override your attention to traffic if you haven't yet developed the executive function to prioritize what you attend to and to control your impulses. Executive function, the brain's "air traffic control" of information, occurs in the prefrontal cortex, the part of the brain that does not fully mature until our mid to late twenties.

The ability to pay attention and ignore distractions affects a child's development at every stage. To bond and thrive as an infant, to develop language and engage in conversation, to have and to be a friend, to show empathy, to be resilient, to use working memory to complete tasks and work toward goals, to read a situation, to learn from mistakes, and to solve problems—all require focused attention. A key component of a child's developing attention and executive function skills is working memory, the limited amount of sensory, perceptual, and increasingly language-based information that can be held in the mind at one time to apply to cognitive tasks. Children's working memory starts in the earliest stages of life as they improve their signal-to-noise ratio through synaptic reinforcement and pruning. Free play as an infant and throughout childhood is an important way to build working memory because, with no predetermined rules or objectives, it must be structured in real time by the players. As they play, kids must make decisions, develop rules, and adhere to and modify them as circumstances demand. No external authority is judging or measuring this play. There is no Right Answer. Free play has a random quality to it, but as a learning process, it is not random. The power of free play is that it is "unimportant," that it is not achieving a goal, but it is play for the sake of play. Free play happens in an alert, unstressed frame of mind. The child must pay attention. They are free to fail, free to take risks, and free to quit at any time, so they try things. This is the best state of mind for learning, for creating the new, and for developing working memory.

ASK THE MEDIATRICIAN
Does Watching Screens Make Kids Inattentive?

Our seven-year-old son struggled to sit down long enough to learn to read in first grade. We just got back from a two-week family camp where there were no electronics, and he is a different child. He is calm, wants to play outside, builds things with his dad—he even pulled out a book. He is asking for the TV and his video games, but we wonder whether they are what made him inattentive and hyperactive. What should we do?

You are right to be concerned that your son's screen use may be affecting his ability to pay attention. The media environment of games and videos is persuasively designed to hook and hold your son's attention with little cognitive effort on his part. Research shows that while screen media use can contribute to symptoms of attention deficit and hyperactivity, they are not necessarily the cause of attention disorders.[52] Cross-sectional research from the University of Washington found an association between hours of television watched at ages one and three to be associated with attention problems at age seven.[53] Does this mean that using screen media causes attention problems? Not necessarily. The association between early television viewing and school-age attention problems could just as easily be due to the fact that children who had problems with attention and hyperactivity at ages one and three were put in front of a screen to distract and calm them down. And it could be a vicious cycle in which a distractible toddler is furthering his inherent distractibility by his increased use of screens.

Because your son's attention and activity improved during and after your electronics-free camp, he and you will likely benefit from thoughtfully reintroducing screens to his routine. Whether he has intrinsic attention problems or not, he benefitted from a screen-free break that lowered his hyperstimulation. But staying screen-free is neither possible nor desirable at this point in history. Screens are used to teach as early as preschool, and he will need to use them effectively to excel in school. And his friends will have screens that they will use together if he does not have access at home. The best choice is to mentor his screen use, introducing devices and content he will need to master in school. Use screens together in durations that match his attention span, then move on to playing outside, exploring the natural world, reading books, and eating dinner with you, talking about his day.

Observe how your child acts before, during, and after screen use. Do you see behaviors that worry you? Is it difficult for him to settle down after watching a show? Does he ask constantly for more screen time? Does he behave more aggressively after he has watched or gamed? Talk openly with him about what you observe, and discuss with him what changes can be made to improve his overall wellness. Listen to him thoughtfully and respectfully, without judging him, and support his success in using media in healthy, smart, and civil ways. He is more likely to adhere to a plan that he owns because he developed it with you.

Dialing Down Distraction—Together

We are all distractible. Scientific evidence now shows that when media use continually interrupts our thought processes—or we're distracted in anticipation of the next buzz or ping—the brain shifts into an oscillating, split-tasking mode that fragments our focus.[54] Distraction undermines listening, learning, self-regulation, and behavior. It's like static in the brain, even when you can't hear it.

In one study, researchers from the University of Texas found that the mere presence of a smartphone may induce "brain drain" by using cognitive resources needed for attentional control. In the study, brain drain occurred even when users chose not to respond to the device. The effort to actively ignore their phones split their attention and came at a cognitive cost.[55]

A recent study of adolescents, media use, and ADHD symptoms found that the more teens checked social media and streamed video, the more likely it was that they might develop symptoms of ADHD. Tracking 2,587 students in ten high schools across Los Angeles County, California, for two years, this is considered the best study so far on the connection between screen use and attention. However, the study does not show or even suggest that media use causes ADHD, only that teens who use devices frequently throughout the day are more likely to develop behaviors that are common with ADHD.[56] It is our experience in the Clinic for Interactive Media and Internet Disorders that interactive media environments like social media or online games can reveal ADHD that has been subclinical or compensated for in the classroom or at home.

It is ironic perhaps that long before the dawn of the digital age, we have used *pay*, a term of economics, for applying attention. We are now living in an attention economy. The digital ecosystem has monetized, paid for, and profited from our attention. The internet has provided access to new and exciting information to explore and leveraged it to obtain information about us that they can sell to others. For most of us, this has been a mixed bag. The algorithms characterize us as consumers and as citizens. They calculate what they think we will be interested in and send us information about products, services, or public policy that probability shows we are most likely to buy. But because the algorithms characterize our interests so effectively, we can be led down rabbit holes of information that at best become a time suck. At worst, those rabbit holes can lead us to buy products or "buy" ideas that can harm us or our fellow humans. (More on that in part 2, "So What?") We give away for free what major corporations pay high prices for.

What Could We Do Better?

A question I ask of my adolescent patients when their parents have left the room is, "What could your parents do better?" Almost always the first answer from these young people, whose parents complain they never talk or share their lives, is, "Pay more attention to me!" As parents, we must be conscious that our kids feel they're vying with our devices for our attention. We are preoccupied with other concerns, always ready to interrupt and ask them to wait while we respond to an "important" text or call. Our interest in them appears conditional, less valued than our work or social demands. Children don't need our undivided attention at all times, but we need to offer them our openness, our listening ear, to make them feel safe and that their thoughts, feelings, and dreams will be heard. Our attention is as valuable to them as we feel their attention is important to their homework, chores, and family time. When we pay more attention to our phones and laptops, not only do we seem to prioritize those over our children, but they see our concerns about their digital device use as hypocritical. Their social media is just as important to them as our boss's urgent email is to us. They may not listen to us, but they are always watching us. We are modeling for them how adults behave, and that speaks far more loudly than our complaints about their gaming.

In today's world our attention is highly valued by those who seek to monetize it. We can, from the beginning of kids' lives, value attention as a finite resource and spend it by paying attention wisely. We can choose how we guide our children's attention and time toward the most challenging and enriching activities, including allowing them to become bored enough to think of the new. A finite amount of time is all we have in this life. We value it most, and we teach our children to value it, when we attend to each other and our world.

MEDIA Rx
Value Your Attention and Nurture Theirs

We can all, parents and children alike, learn to be aware of, respect, and strengthen our attention.

YOU CAN

- *Put away your phone, tablet, and laptop when you are with your children.* Not only are you modeling the behavior you want to see in them, but you are being present with and enjoying them.
- *Build self-awareness.* Notice what you're paying attention to in the moment. Use everyday activities or moments to recognize whether your attention is focused or fragmented. Is your attention turned outward to the world and those in it, inward to your own thoughts and concerns, or elsewhere to whatever is online?
- *Take charge of your attention.* Own it. When you pay attention, you're investing your thoughts. Are you paying attention to something or is your attention being distracted? Your attention is valuable. Don't give it away easily or cheaply. Corporations pay billions to capture and hold your attention—value it and invest it wisely!
- *Choose focus over fragmentation.* Attention is a finite resource in the moment, and it is yours to invest. The human brain, no matter how smart, is incapable of multitasking. When the brain is switch-tasking, the mental resources for attention are spread thin. Cognitive tasks will take longer, have more errors, and will not be retained as well as when one focuses.[57] Prioritize what needs your attention, and focus more fully on it—one thing at a time.
- *Focus with purpose.* When you choose to pay attention to something, it can help you stay focused to complete what you set out to do. Intention drives effective attention.

- *Train your brains.* Ask your child what they want to do with you. (They *love* doing things with parents, which can even persist into adolescence when you establish this early.) The activity could be working on a project, walking the dog, reading, drawing, playing a board game or a video game, taking a walk, or playing outside. Plan it with clear starting and ending times, mark it with a mental Do Not Disturb sign, and focus your attention on the activity and the person with whom you are doing it. You will find that kids pay better attention, you will enjoy and get to know them more, and together you will build a habit of focused attention, collaboration, and companionship.

Chapter 4

Lonely Hearts

Social and Emotional Development in the Digital Age

Melissa was always put together, wearing the trendiest fashions and sporting the latest makeup looks. She was aiming to be a fashion influencer on social media once she got into college and her parents could no longer insist that she do her homework and get to sleep on time. Confident that I would keep her "secret," she would clue me in on music, fashion, and what kids were doing that would affect their health but that their parents and the school didn't know about. When she showed up for a just-scheduled urgent care appointment, I was surprised and concerned to see that her hair was disheveled, eyes were bloodshot, and mascara was smeared, and she didn't have her ever-present AirPods in her ears.

"What's up, Melissa?"

"I'm tragically unhappy. I don't get it!" She said her life had fallen apart overnight. "No one's talking to me . . . but everyone's talking *about* me!"

When Melissa said talking, she meant texting. Usually a bubbly, intentionally edgy fifteen-year-old, Melissa seemed to have weathered the transition from the neighborhood middle school to the much-larger suburban high school well. She had added to the friend group she had known since kindergarten and fallen away from some. Her grades had suffered as her focus turned more to social relationships and her social media presence than books. Her parents had decided that her smartphone was the problem. When her midwinter report card arrived, with Bs that had turned into Cs and a D, they took Melissa's phone away that evening. After the argument spiraled into screaming in frustration and slamming doors, Melissa had retreated to her room, locking the door and refusing to do homework, eventually falling asleep. She woke up on her own the next morning, got dressed and did her makeup behind her locked door, refused breakfast, and walked to school—where her friends, old and new, weirdly kept their distance. As she approached, they would turn their backs to exclude her from the conversation or walk away. What was going on? Melissa was stunned.

So much about friendship is as old as time. Our need for friends and a sense of belonging in a social group is fundamental to human nature. In isolation, we suffer. Being social is more than a pleasure; it is survival. Animals that communicate well and develop trusting relationships protect each other. It's in our DNA. Chimpanzees and bonobos are the higher primates most closely related to humans, sharing 98.7 percent of our DNA, and although human ancestors split from the ancestors of chimpanzees and bonobos more than four million years ago, we share many traits. Male chimpanzees aggressively compete for the best mates by trying to kill young males before they reach puberty and become a threat. Female bonobos' sensitivity to social cues allows them to form alliances and protect each other's young from aggressive males.[1] Since aggression is unproductive for bonobo males, survival of the fittest has evolved into what professor of evolutionary anthropology Brian Hare and research scientist and journalist Vanessa Woods have coined "survival of the friendliest."[2] Simply put, social bonding, deep connection, and collaboration among individuals provide the protection of a strong community. Strength in numbers, especially social strength conferred by emotional bonding, is even more protective than a large brain or opposable thumbs. Humans' proclivity and ability to be social may be why we have survived many animals that were stronger, faster, and more dangerous.

There is a flip side to social bonding, however. Animal mothers that nurture and protect their young are fiercely aggressive when their young are threatened. They are constantly vigilant for threats from those perceived to be "other." In humans, this protectiveness and vigilance translates into an almost ironic (if it were not so tragic) inability to connect with, communicate with, or hear those whom we decide are "other"—other races, other genders, other-language speakers, other religions, other sexualities, other cultures, other "tribes." All of this plays out in social behavior in the digital realm, where old-fashioned tools of exclusion like cliques, gossip, snobbery, and bullying find new applications and power to punish.

This brings us back to Melissa. When her parents confiscated her phone, they disrupted a complex network of interdependent connections weaving through her teenage tribe. As with most teens, Melissa was engaged in nearly constant exchanges of texts, photos, memes, and reposts with her friends, a boy she was flirting with, and her Dungeons and Dragons group. The disruption created an overnight gap in communication between Melissa and the others. Disappointed and frustrated when Melissa didn't respond promptly to repeated texts, not realizing that it was because her phone had been confiscated, one of her BFFs posted that Melissa was ghosting her. This triggered an avalanche of posts that were sympathetic to Melissa's "heartbroken" BFF and increasingly snarky about Melissa. Meanwhile, at home, exhausted from her meltdown with her parents, and with her phone confiscated, Melissa had slept soundly, unaware that her reputation was being piled on. When she went to school the next day, she said "Hey!" to the first friend she saw—who responded by silently turning her back and whispering to the girl at the next locker. Silent stares and whispers followed her down the hallway to her algebra class, where she found "Lissa = Beyotch" written in red marker on the whiteboard. Melissa was devastated. She turned and went straight to the school nurse, complaining of an upset stomach. The nurse found nothing wrong and told Melissa to go back to class. When Melissa said she couldn't, the nurse said that Melissa needed a note from her parents or a doctor to be excused from school. So she came to our clinic for that note.

Social drama has always been a part of teen life, especially during those tumultuous peripubertal years when surging hormones drive rapid physical, mental, and emotional changes. *Who do I like? More importantly, who likes me? Why do I feel this way when I'm around them? Is everybody staring at that pimple on my chin? What did that side-eye mean? They are cute; I wonder if . . .* The questions and preoccupations of adolescence may seem superficial to parents, but they reflect vital dimensions of social and emotional development at this stage: the wondering, curiosity, uncertainty, excitement, and angst—and the terrible awkwardness of it all. Navigating the shifting moods and passions of adolescence has never been easy, but the interactive media environment has accelerated the pace of the already-frenetic journey toward individuality and adulthood. Not only do our kids feel pressured to keep the warp-speed pace that technology sets, but appealing shortcuts ultimately shortchange them by making it easy to avoid awkward situations that serve as essential developmental stepping stones.

Over the last decade the interactive media environment has subsumed fundamental experiences of direct human interaction. Texting, social media, and image-based apps have replaced face-to-face interactions. Interpersonal communication has been reduced to taps, emojis, and three-letter acronyms (IDK, LOL, OMW). Digital shorthand is easier and quicker, and its asynchronous nature allows the sender to avoid feeling exposed. But what is lost is the textured, nuanced, deep learning about others and oneself—including how to cope with awkwardness—that is needed for the developing brain, body, and psyche to mature. Deeply felt explorations of life and love that once happened intermittently over days or weeks and directly, in person or on a landline phone, now unfold in hours, even minutes, via interactive media. What has been largely abandoned is the experience of meeting someone new face-to-face, making conversation, finding common interests, learning to read another's facial expressions and body language, and expressing oneself authentically without embarrassment. We have given up opportunities to learn how to listen deeply, show compassion, and develop the self-regulation and coping skills to interact even when we're tired, hungry, stressed, surprised, or in the grip of big feelings.

Relationships are announced and ended by posting status updates on our online profiles, avoiding messy, emotional breakups. The strength and meaning of relationships are gauged by how—and how quickly—the other responds. Image-based social media couples the apparent immediacy of face-to-face interactions with the variable, sometimes lengthy response time of the handwritten snail-mail letter, frequently resulting in the worst of both worlds. Opportunities are rife for missteps and misunderstanding. The sender lobs a witty text. Will the joke sent be received as a joke? Is the edgy comment or photo clever or potentially hurtful? The unpredictable gap between Send and Reply only adds to the potential for confusion or hurt on both sides. The message may catch the recipient in an inconvenient moment or mood to reply;

in a group chat, the message catches everyone at different times. While the nature of asynchronous communication, untethered from the here-and-now of a real-time exchange, would ideally assume that a reply might come at any time, even days later, texting's implied requirement is to respond right away if you value the relationship. Little time is allowed for reflection, nuance, and mindful responses. With image-based communication, it is difficult, and with text-based, it is impossible to read facial expressions, body language, tone, or other social cues to gauge the emotional valence of the message. Finally, the more people who are engaged in a group thread or chat, the greater the potential for misunderstandings and emotional misfires as the volleys continue. Reaction without reflection is always a recipe for mishaps. As adolescents, they will need about a decade or more to develop the executive function of impulse control and the governing mechanisms to calm their limbic systems from emotional overdrive. Until then, the risk of sender-receiver mismatch between adolescents in the digital environment is high.

The speed of communication afforded by the digital ecosystem has created new challenges, expectations, and human behaviors. These are what tripped Melissa up, as they do for so many, with teens (and increasingly, tweens) being especially vulnerable. Today many relationships among young people are initiated and developed online. With 97 percent of adolescents online daily and 46 percent online "almost constantly,"[3] youth have developed expectations around the nature and rapidity of responses to their communications and posts.[4] A delayed response raises questions about the value and importance of the relationship to the responder. No response, or ghosting the sender, is read as the end of the relationship. No response from Melissa when she did not have her phone was interpreted as ghosting, and her BFF and many others instantly turned against her.

Social Media Socialization Starts Sooner than You Think

While parents' and society's worries about online activity, particularly social media, peak during the tween and teen years, the role of digital screen use in children's social and emotional development starts much earlier. After all, socialization begins at birth, with the newborn's search for connection with parents and family; as we saw in a previous chapter, the hungry brain constantly seeks nurturing connection. As we've also seen, children's earliest social experiences with media usually are not simply video chatting with Grandma. A YouTube video viewed nearly a quarter of a million times captures an all-too-typical use of screen media in early childhood. An infant, unsteadily sitting up, stares at a glowing smartphone, clutched in her chubby hands. Giggling, the mother removes the smartphone, and the baby throws a tantrum, arching onto her back and screaming.[5] Mother sits the baby back up, but the screaming continues until she hands the smartphone back, to which the baby responds with a resentful look and returns to staring at the screen in silence. Many infants' first contact with screen media is with mobile screens that are frequently used to distract and quiet them by engaging their orienting response to the light and sound.[6] When babies discover that they can make things happen by swiping at the screen, some parents are quick to applaud a seemingly precocious learner. But the truth is that the baby's behavior doesn't reflect precocious smarts. Nearly every baby can do that. What we're really witnessing is how smart Steve Jobs and his product designers were in creating the intuitive transparency of a touch screen to link the searching eye, pointing finger, and inquisitive mind with the digital ecosystem. Only later would concerns arise about health implications when the inquisitive mind might belong to a young child in the earliest, most sensitive developmental stages of not only brain development but social and emotional development.

Acknowledging that this easy interface with interactive media had transformed the toddler screen use experience from television's passive viewing to active engagement and citing research showing that children can learn from screen media when interacting and co-viewing with parents starting at about fifteen months, the AAP modified their recommendations to discourage use of screens before the age of eighteen months, with the exception of video chatting.[7]

Unfortunately, the nuances of the limited scientific evidence behind the loosened recommendations were lost, and boundaries faded quickly. Babies were introduced to their grandparents at birth via live streamed video. Infants and toddlers began to watch and interact with screens as their parents, comforted by the belief that their child was learning, used tablets and smartphones as mobile electronic babysitters. Online play spaces featured brand-name plush toys for very young children, with product placements building brand loyalty early. Cartoonlike avatars allowed interacting and communicating with other players in the space, blurring the lines between play and social media.[8] The behavioral norms and expectations of the algorithmically driven digital media culture have begun to shape those of the home and family environment. To take back control of our children's social and emotional development, we must intentionally scaffold and reinforce a daily schedule and family culture that nurture them to be their best selves.

Timeless Tasks, Bigger Stage

How children and teens learn to interact with others has always been a complex dance on the developmental stage. From the curiosity of infants and parallel play of toddlers to the pal-ships of school-age children and more complicated relationships of adolescence, they follow social and emotional cues from within, naturally experimenting and discovering through trial and error how to relate to others. The choreography of growing up has always defined children's social and emotional development and continues to do so today, now with interactive media adding new layers of complexity. To understand how all that plays out in the digital ecosystem, it helps to remind ourselves of every child's developmental tasks and tools.

In many ways friendship has always been a fraught factor in child and adolescent development, as clinical psychologist and author Michael G. Thompson and his coauthors wrote in *Best Friends, Worst Enemies: Understanding the Social Lives of Children*.[9] The core challenges of children's social development still revolve around friendship, the power of the group in children's lives, social cruelty, and how kids manage conflict, betrayal, and reconciliation—all challenges that kids confronted face-to-face before social media replaced the playground, shopping malls, and analog phones.

There isn't a lot of opportunity in childhood to take charge of things, but children naturally discover their budding powers, noted Thompson. "As normal, happy children grow up they exercise their powers—their command of language (including bad language), their mastery of cognitive problems and academics, their brand-new muscular powers ('I can run faster than you!') and their social powers," he wrote in an email exchange.

What are those social powers?

"All children have the ability to show love, to demonstrate empathy, to offer respect and support to other children," Thompson said. "Children also all have more or less charisma, magnetic powers to draw other children toward them. But every power has its dark side. Children also all have the ability to hurt each other's feelings, to act in ways that are mean, and ultimately to reject one another. And they do it very particularly when they are trying to form their own identities. As children grow up, they exercise these powers on one another, showing love and affection ('Do you want to have a sleepover?') or rejection ('We don't want to play with you')." Long before the internet and social media became their social space, kids flexed their social power this way, in effect friending and unfriending one another. It just wasn't called that.

"It has always been around," Thompson said. But social media has amplified the experience. "There is just something so final about seeing something in print online, or having your former friend suddenly block access to their social media site, or having other kids witness that you have been unfriended. These online rejections hit kids really hard—harder than in the old days, when your friend might suddenly avoid you, not want to play with you, and seem to be turning their attention to someone new." Before the digital age, nothing went viral. Missteps had a half-life in memory; damage control was more feasible.

"There is a certain irreducible minimum of social cruelty in childhood," Thompson said. "It turns out that that is true in person and on the internet. I don't know how to compare the pain of the two rejections, one in person and the other online, but what they have in common is that basically it hurts, and part of growing up is learning how to recover from a social wounding."[10]

Screen Play Can Be Social Too

While parents, schools, and communities play a large role in social emotional learning during childhood, as young people enter the autonomy-seeking tween and teen years, TV shows (easily viewed and binged on digital devices), movies, video games, popular songs, and social media begin to influence how children and teens believe they should behave.[11] Even in the days before social media, what children and youth learned from screen content was very powerful. But these were still "pull" screen media, meaning that viewers had the freedom to choose what to watch and their access was limited to broadcast schedules and movie showtimes. The internet and social media have enabled "push" media, which use complex algorithms, the invisible hand of the digital age, to profile each user and direct to them customized programming and products to which they are likely to be attracted. At its best, we enjoy the consumer experience of getting more of what we like. But the flip side is the algorithmic echo-chamber effect that narrows and amplifies favored patterns to the exclusion of the more diverse world of ideas, people, and opportunities to learn and grow beyond what we already know and like.

Although what we call *social media* have been the primary source of parental worry and target of policymakers, the definition of social media and the boundaries between it and other interactive screen media are increasingly unclear. Gaming, for example, once viewed as a solo screen-based recreational pastime, has become a social space more familiar than playgrounds and neighborhood malls to many young people. As we've seen, youth have migrated to massively multiplayer online games (MMOGs), like *Roblox*, *Minecraft*, and *Fortnite*,[12] and social media sites dedicated to gaming,[13] like Discord and Twitch, to connect and interact with their peers.[14] Parents worry about how their kids behave and especially how they talk to each other, swearing into their headsets, while they game. When asked about their MMOG experiences, youth did not talk about gameplay or whether they won or lost but about "hanging out with my friends."[15] These digital environments have become what the mall was to an older generation. There is no question that social media and MMOGs are commercially driven, but so was the shopping mall. Kids spent money there (mostly at the food court), but it was a place where they could gather as the independent individuals they were becoming—and the ones they aspired to be. Today social media and gaming sites where youth gather offer these important advantages to tweens and teens stepping out of childhood into an uncertain future.[16]

It is important to be aware of what fertile environments the internet and social media are for key developmental tasks of young people. They seek:

- **Experience.** They can instantly connect with anyone, anywhere in the world, at any time. They explore other places and cultures; interact socially with others, known and unknown; and share themselves with the world.
- **Independence.** As they become individuals distinct from parents, teachers, and other authority figures, they have a direct, private channel to send, receive, and experience for themselves.

- *Social consciousness.* Looking outward, they see injustice and wrongs that they want to right—climate change, political division, animal cruelty—and become activists and change agents online.
- *Identity.* Searching for and building their personal identities, they find characteristics of role models near and far that they wish to emulate (and those they want to avoid), building their identities like a mosaic, tile by tile. This is particularly important for LGBTQ+ (lesbian, gay, bisexual, transgender, queer/questioning, plus others), neurodiverse, and other nonconforming youth, who may be marginalized and bullied in their physical communities but can find online an accepting and supportive community of peers.[17]
- *Connection.* All of these critical objectives come together in their drive to be connected, accepted, and feel a sense of belonging. These are fundamental human desires, but for adolescents, the stakes feel higher as they seek to build a cohesive inner self and outer persona amid the swirling uncertainties of both worlds.

Social media has become more than the evolved watering hole on a digital frontier. Social media is now the most populous "nation" on earth, where citizenship is fluid, borders are porous, and trends hop from one platform to another to the physical world and back.

Digital gathering places provided by social media and MMOGs proved especially popular and important during the COVID-19 lockdown, enabling researchers an unprecedented opportunity to capture real-time data on adolescent development interrupted. A Digital Wellness Lab pulse survey in March 2021 found that:

- At the height of the pandemic, 59 percent of children and adolescents increased their video gameplay and 45 percent increased their social media use.
- While nearly half of the parents reported that the frequency of arguments about their kids' media use increased, those arguments were mostly about how long the kids were using screens, not about the content on those screens.
- Forty-five percent of parents said that their children's screen use was helpful for their mental health while only 19 percent felt it was harmful.

- Fifty percent felt that family relationships were better and 56 percent believed their children's friend relationships were helped by their interactive media use.
- While 52 percent reported that reading skills and 48 percent reported that math skills were helped by online schooling (far more than the 14 percent and 18 percent who reported these skills were harmed), only 39 percent felt their children's social skills had improved, and 32 percent believed that their children's social skills had suffered.[18]

ASK THE MEDIATRICIAN
Who's Who in My Son's Online Community—Should I Worry?

My twelve-year-old son plays an online role-playing game with a group of his friends, mostly kids from school plus some from places around the world. But a few people I don't know have joined his guild over the past year or so. One of them, who seems to be an adult woman, has taken a leadership role in their quests and battles. As they game, they chat a lot about school, sports, friends, bullies, and their parents. I can't hear what she is saying because of my son's headphones, but recently he started calling her "Mom." I got angry at him. He's got a mom! But he said it was no big deal; that was the name she chose in the game. Is this OK? Is there something I should do?

Role-playing games (RPGs) are especially popular with tweens and teens because they allow young people the opportunity to invent and reinvent themselves at a time when their development is fluid and they are looking forward to what they might become. While your son's initial instincts to play with his school friends were good, the introduction of unknown others, particularly an adult, is a reasonable concern. While there are certainly many adults who play RPGs, it is unclear why this person (who may not be what they present themselves as) would want to play with children. Without knowing the person's identity or motives, playing with vulnerable youth is of concern in and of itself, but asking the boys to call them "Mom" is a red flag. It may be innocent, perhaps a lonely person seeking connection with anyone who will accept them, but frankly, the benefits your son and his friends get from the game is not worth the risk of potential harm to their mental, or even physical, health.

Apologize to your son for getting upset. Explain that you were scared for him, not angry at him. Sit down with your son to talk about your concerns together. Ask him directly what "Mom" does for the game and whether he and his friends could have as much or more fun just among themselves. Help him understand that they have no way of knowing who this person actually is, where they might be, and what they might want from the boys. Don't scare him; empower him—to take care of himself and his friends. With his permission, reach out to the other kids' parents to let them know how you are handling the situation without drama. Each family will likely handle it differently, and he and his friends will certainly discuss what they want to do. They deserve to have fun without worry. The goal is for them to decide to play their game the way they want to with each other and the people they know.

You can also use this opportunity to talk with your son about the issue of being authentic online—not deceptive or manipulative in how you represent yourself—while protecting your privacy. Being authentic does not mean sharing your identity, address, school, or any personally identifying information. Those who would take advantage of young people can be quite adept at obtaining information like their name, address, school, interests, and daily travel patterns. And their target doesn't have to give this information voluntarily. Metadata, sometimes hidden to the eye, such as the location where a photo was taken, can be discovered. An FBI briefing to a health-care group revealed that even a child's photos of their kitten on the couch were able to lead a registered sex offender to that child's door, where he was arrested. The point in sharing this is not to scare your son (or you). It's to give him some fact-based intel so he and his friends can think it through for themselves and take it into account as they make choices about their online interactions.

Being present in your child's digital life is not only advisable, but it should be an expectation, both for your child and for you. If you would not let them go alone to the house of a friend they have never met, whose parents you do not know, and you have no idea who else will be there or whether alcohol, drugs, or weapons will be present—don't let them go by themselves to the 24/7 house party of the internet. Many games, especially role-playing games, capture potential gamers' attention by being edgy, hypersexualized, and violent and inciting fear and hatred of the "other," whether that be women or people of other races, ethnicities, languages, or cultures. The risk is not that your child will be physically harmed but that fear and hatred are normalized, even glamorized, for the gamer. Ask your child to give you tours of games and social media sites that they wish to be part of, and decide whether you want your child to become desensitized to and potentially adopt the attitudes and behaviors portrayed there. Ask them how they would feel about behaving that way rather than telling them not to behave that way. If they say that they know it's not real, that they would never behave that way, ask how they would feel about a younger sibling or friend playing the game. Even when they do not believe they are affected, they will frequently see a problem for someone who they feel is more vulnerable.

It may be difficult to imagine how your ten-year-old's proud success as a team leader in a fantasy kingdom fighting an evil empire will help them develop transferable skills that will be valued at school and eventually in the workplace. So-called "soft skills," social and emotional competence, that are now viewed as critical to effective leadership have traditionally been learned and implemented in person.[19] However, in the "next normal," they are being implemented in hybrid school and work environments. Social competence is the ability to form and maintain respectful and effective relationships. Emotional competence is having the self-awareness to recognize and manage one's feelings and to have empathy for the feelings of others. Achieving these competencies begins with social emotional learning during childhood and adolescence, learning that now occurs in a continuous physical-digital environment, including online get-togethers on MMOGs, where kids are talking to (and sometimes swearing at) each other. These social emotional skills are fundamental components of digital wellness:

- Effective communication
- Active listening

- Respect for others
- Emotional intelligence
- Empathy
- Adaptability
- Problem-solving
- Stress management
- Negotiation
- Mentorship
- Gratitude
- Optimism

Many young people have been developing these skills online all along (and maybe you did, too, when you were that age). We just haven't noticed and appreciated that aspect of their online social experience. Research done with 14,564 college students just before the pandemic found that those who used social media proficiently demonstrated greater social emotional competence than those who did not.[20] As we model and mentor these soft skills for our children and teens, they not only learn the basics we can offer but build upon those. And as we've seen through the evolution of social media platforms, kids soon become our mentors in the changing digital environment.

Protecting the More Vulnerable in the Social Commons

In 1998, when what was to become social media was primitive online sites where personal profiles could be exchanged, Congress borrowed from the motion picture ratings system to pass the Children's Online Privacy Protection Act (COPPA), restricting the collection of personal data from those under thirteen.[21] As social media expanded beyond its early use for networking among college students and rapidly reshaped the broader social commons for us all, child advocates, legislators, and the public scrambled to manage it. Attempting to comply with COPPA, social media companies developed "age-gating," requiring users to report their birth dates before admitting them to the platform. Unfortunately, COPPA did little to constrain children who, with or without their parents' help (yes, many parents helped), faked their ages to find their way onto social media and gaming sites that attracted global users in the millions.[22] Efforts to restrict children's access to the forbidden fruit of social media made it all the more attractive to young people, who are doing everything they can to grow up fast.[23] Although COPPA made obtaining truthful data from underage users difficult, a 2021 survey by Common Sense Media found that 38 percent of eight-to-twelve-year-olds were on social media, with 18 percent using it every day.[24] Several states have introduced legislation to require parental consent and oversight of social media use by their children under the age of eighteen.

Not only have age boundaries broken down, but the defining boundaries of social media have become largely meaningless, further eroding efforts to create and enforce safeguards. Everybody talks about social media, but no one really knows what *social media* is anymore. TikTok and X clearly are, as are Instagram, Snapchat, and Facebook, but YouTube identifies itself as a broadcast medium. In practice, however, YouTube is functionally a social media platform where people of all ages are posting videos and commenting. Posting videos is usually started for fun, but some who post attract many comments, followers, and advertising dollars as social media influencers (now the number one career goal among youth[25]).

Online gaming is a social arena, one that has always offered a social interface with virtual camaraderie, but especially for young people in pandemic lockdown.[26] Harsh language or disturbing online dynamics of some players have made some MMOG communities toxic, especially for beginners; in other communities, especially those that have a creative component to them, users encouraging game or video development by others can be supportive. For parents who wonder and worry about specific social media sites, it is important to recognize that all interactive online media are already or have the potential to become social—and that it is the social element that supercharges the breakout success of products like *Fortnite* and TikTok.[27] Attractive as it is to youth, the social element is also where risks lie.

A Wiser Way to Navigate Social Media

Dawn's dad didn't like the amount of time his sixteen-year-old daughter was spending on her smartphone. She was a socially anxious kid who had always had trouble making friends, but in the past six months, she seemed to have made a group of friends online. She spent all her free time scrolling and sending and receiving messages. She would smile, laugh out loud, text furiously, and then stare at the phone for a response. But she also had become more anxious and, most recently, dark and edgy. She was extremely private about her texting. At times her dad would overhear her talking with someone, always in tense, hushed tones. She was up at all hours, falling behind academically, exhausted and withdrawn. When her dad tried to talk to her, she would snap at him to stop bothering her. She seemed to be in an emotional tailspin.

Dawn always had her phone clutched in her hand. Finally, one night her dad got fed up and tried to take her phone from her. Dawn flew into a fury, punched him, and yanked the phone back. As he backed away, Dawn threw the phone at him, hitting him in the head. Her brother called the police. By the time they arrived, Dawn had retreated to her room and locked herself in. The police asked her dad whether he wanted to press charges for assault. He declined, in shock that it had come to this, and chose to bring her to the Clinic for Interactive Media and Internet Disorders.

In our first conversation, Dawn described a typical day (and night, we learned) for her on social media. It followed a familiar trajectory. An exchange might start as casual banter but often escalated into a volley of images, comments, memes, and increasingly edgy rapid responses. In addition to the group's messaging, she would often be texting with one or more of them separately as they reacted privately to one another's posts. At times when there was a pause in their replies, Dawn imagined—no, she just knew—that they were saying snarky things about her to each other. And there were other friends, other groups, other chats, all underway at all hours.

"Just the usual teen drama, right?" she said bleakly to me. She was right. Overwhelm on social media has become a new rite of passage for adolescents. Dawn had gotten in over her head. She wanted to make friends, and she wanted to be a friend. But the online social scene became overwhelming. She wasn't happy, but she was involved, engaging in a volley of dialogue that she couldn't end unless she was willing to let one of her online friends have the last word. She usually wasn't.

But the reason Dawn had been so desperate to hang on to her phone was that she had a friend, several time zones away, who was struggling with her own sadness. Dawn's friend felt alone and hopeless. She talked about how much she hated herself, how the world would be better without her, and how it would not even notice if she were gone. Her friend's suicidal talk scared and fascinated Dawn. The friend would text whenever she felt low, and Dawn felt she was the only one who was trusted, who could help. Dawn felt needed—and needed to be available 24/7.

Dawn's dad didn't understand why she attacked him. Dawn felt that he was trying to stop her from being a friend—and placing her friend's life at risk. She was frantic to keep her phone. Her instinct to help was admirable, but her judgment was faulty, a shortcoming of her still-developing executive function. Dawn was caught up in the drama, but she had neither the professional training nor the emotional distance to actually be of help. Once she revealed the reason she was so "pangry" (panicked and angry) about her father trying to take her phone, we could share her concern and help her friend get the intervention she needed.

The American Psychological Association (APA), in a 2023 health advisory on adolescents and social media, recommended that before teens use social media, they should get training in social media literacy that equips them with "psychologically informed competencies and skills that will maximize the chances for balanced, safe, and meaningful social media use."[28] With the objective to increase the frequency of positive interactions online, the recommendations suggested that although more research is needed, "emerging science offers preliminary support" for the effectiveness of a digital citizenship and digital literacy curriculum to "increase the frequency of positive interactions online." Additional competencies the APA suggested included:

- questioning accuracy and representativeness of social media content
- understanding tactics used to spread mis- and disinformation
- limiting "overgeneralization" and "misestimation" errors that lead users to incorrectly estimate others' behaviors or attitudes based on social media content or reactions to content
- recognizing signs of problematic social media use
- knowing how to build and nourish healthy online relationships
- knowing how to solve conflicts that can emerge on social media platforms

- knowing how to refrain from excessive social comparisons online
- knowing how to better understand how images and content can be manipulated
- knowing how to recognize structural racism and critique racist messages online without engaging in "comment wars"
- knowing how to safely communicate about mental health online[29]

Dawn was both relieved and scared to realize how she might have felt responsible if her friend did harm herself in some way. Dawn hadn't urged her online friend to reach out for professional help. She hadn't shared her friend's situation with an adult, and she hadn't reached out to an adult on her own behalf to say, "Can someone help me with this situation?" When Dawn's anxiety and depression were recognized and treated, she acknowledged that suicidality and self-injury are issues that need to be dealt with acutely by trained professionals who can assess the risks and intervene, not by friends who have emotional skin in the game.

Given the adolescent mental health crisis in the US and the extent to which teens use social media as their preferred mode of communication with peers, as Dawn's experience so painfully showed, learning how to safely communicate about mental health online has the potential to be lifesaving, both for those sharing their pain as well as those attempting to hold it with them, as friends do.

ASK THE MEDIATRICIAN
Conflicted About Show Depicting Teen Struggles with Life—and Death

My fourteen-year-old daughter wants to watch 13 Reasons Why. *Although she read the book, I haven't allowed her to watch the series, given the controversy surrounding its depiction of suicide. I'm thinking that it might be OK for her to watch now that she is in high school. I've read that it is paired with resources and encourages teens to seek help if they are struggling. I'm still conflicted about her watching something that is so graphic that it is rated for mature audiences. Is it OK for her to watch?*

It's wonderful that you and your daughter openly communicate about media that interest her and that you are thinking this through together. You will want to do this with any content that deals with sensitive or disturbing subject matter. Realistically, if your daughter wants to see this or any other show, she'll figure out a way to watch it, if not at home, then most likely at a friend's house or at school. My suggestion to you is to talk with her about why she wants to watch *13 Reasons Why*, share with her your concerns, and then agree to watch the show together. Keep these points in mind for processing what you see together:

- Co-viewing, or watching together, will allow you to discuss the show with your daughter and address her concerns or questions. See this as an opportunity to model and mentor key media literacy skills. Help her deconstruct the message. Don't be afraid to pause the show when you think further discussion is needed or if something is clearly disturbing your daughter. Ask her questions like, "What is happening with these characters?" "Do you think that situation is realistic?" and "What isn't being shown here?"
- Reviewing the show's companion website and reading episode descriptions can help you both prepare to talk about the difficult topics the show covers.
- Identify and discuss with her the trusted adults in her life to whom she can turn should she need immediate help, such as a school counselor, teacher, coach, or relative. Use this as an opportunity to combat one of the many fictions of the show: that most adults, even mental health professionals, cannot be trusted or are too preoccupied with their own lives to be bothered to help.
- Discuss with your daughter the critical truth of suicide that is not adequately explored in *13 Reasons Why*. Depression is the usual reason for suicide, not what others have done to the person. Because depression is internal, the signs that the person is at

risk—loss of pleasure, feelings of hopelessness and helplessness—
are not always obvious. Adolescence, with its normative mood
swings and poor impulse control, makes depression even harder
to detect and suicide harder to predict. It is always better to ask
the person how they are and if you can help or get help to them.
It is always better to be blamed for violating their privacy than to
attend their funeral. If the person is acting erratically, threatening to harm themselves or others, you can call 911 to have them
evaluated and possibly brought to an emergency department for
professional care.

Use watching *13 Reasons Why* as an opportunity to connect with
your daughter and talk frankly with her about depression, anxiety, and
mental health. Remind her that you are there, no matter what she or her
friends are dealing with at school or at home. Maintaining and modeling
open communication with her so she can safely share whatever she is
thinking and feeling is the most protective strategy for preventing self-
harm or suicide.

Safe Haven for Some, Lightning Rod for Others

Social media has become a lightning rod in the trending conversation about child and adolescent anxiety and depression. It's easy to point a finger at smartphones and social media as the cause because young people's digital technology use and mental health issues have appeared to rise together, both statistically and experientially.[30] The more time teens spend on a computer, the higher their risk of experiencing anxiety.[31] Teens who spend more time using computers on the weekend are at a higher risk for depression.[32] However, tweens whose parents establish and follow through with rules regarding time spent on social media report better mental health.[33]

While it is reasonable to observe these phenomena and consider whether using social media may influence youth mental health, we have to remember that many factors affect mental health, particularly for adolescents. Chasing a singular cause of mental health problems means that other contributing factors get ignored or deprioritized. Adolescent anxiety and depression preexisted smartphones and social media. Many young people who struggle with anxiety and depression use smartphones and social media, but many more young people use these devices and platforms without problems. If we were to get rid of smartphones and social media, anxiety and depression would not disappear. And the reality is that we will not get rid of smartphones and social media because of their economic and human benefits. Devices and platforms are already evolving into technology that is easier, faster, and even more immersive—which, if we are smart, persistent, and collaborative, we can grab as an opportunity for improving our wellness in the digital ecosystem. This includes access to telehealth visits with clinicians, support communities, and programs that provide prevention materials and other resources. These may not cure the nation's mental health crisis, but they can make accurate information and therapeutic resources accessible to more people.

Depression is among the most common chronic illnesses in America among adults, and many people are anxious, not just teens.[34] Until recently, mental health issues were deeply stigmatized and not openly discussed. Today public awareness is changing. More people understand the prevalence of anxiety and depression and the importance of talking about it, recognizing the signs and symptoms, and getting professional help. Development and broad acceptance of effective and safe medications such as selective serotonin reuptake inhibitors (SSRIs, such as Prozac and its relatives) have made it safer and more acceptable to acknowledge these conditions as common, treatable illnesses than it was when such treatments did not exist. Because of the shift in public awareness, it is hard to determine whether there are more cases of depression today or if it just seems as if there are more because we talk about and treat them more openly.[35]

Adolescence can be a time of emotional lability. Mood swings that are normal in adolescence can look very similar to depression, anxiety, and even bipolar disorder in other age groups. Many teens talk about being "depressed" and "stressed out," terms that have become part of their everyday vocabulary. What they are experiencing, however, typically does not meet the criteria for a diagnosis of clinical depression or anxiety. And because so much of adolescent interaction takes place via text and social media, some of the drama that makes them sad or stressed plays out in social media, which can, due to its algorithms, accelerate and amplify the drama. We lost a lot when *friend* became a verb in digital-age parlance, bringing the speed and ease of the internet to forming and ending human relationships with a click.

In his 2021 advisory "Protecting Youth Mental Health,"[36] US Surgeon General Dr. Vivek Murthy reported a 40 percent increase in high school students reporting persistent feelings of sadness or hopelessness, a 36 percent increase in those who had seriously considered suicide, and a 44 percent increase in those who had a suicide plan.[37] Suicide rates rose by 57 percent between 2007 and 2018.[38] More than 6,600 young people ten to twenty-four years old died by suicide in 2020.[39]

There were three major US social media sites in 2003, a year before the birth of Facebook. Friendster was the frontrunner, with 3 million monthly active users; MySpace and Second Life had just launched.[40] By 2020, 288 million Americans (98.6 percent of the population ten years and older[41]) were using a plethora of social media sites.[42] The surgeon general's 2023 advisory "Our Epidemic of Loneliness and Isolation"[43] reported that during the same 2003 to 2020 time frame in which social media grew from nothing to everything, Americans' social engagement with friends decreased an average of twenty hours per month, and our social isolation increased twenty-four hours per month.[44] Research showed that loneliness more than doubled our risk of depression.[45] In his "Social Media and Youth Mental Health"[46] advisory, also in 2023, the surgeon general explored the relationship between the simultaneous increases in social media use, anxiety, and depression in teens.[47] In 2022, 97 percent of American teens reported using the internet daily, with 46 percent using it "almost constantly."[48] The surgeon general found research evidence and broad agreement in the scientific community that adolescent social media use had potential for both benefit and harm to their mental health.[49] The benefits and harms of adolescents' use of social media appear to be related to *how much*, *when*, and *how* they use social media rather than whether they use.

In terms of benefits, majorities of teens report that using social media helps them feel more accepted (58 percent), connected to friends and their lives (80 percent), and supported by others when they are struggling (67 percent), and it also provides a place to be creative (71 percent).[50]

The harms found were significant. A study of 6,595 adolescents ages twelve to fifteen found that those who spent more than three hours a day on social media had double the risk of anxiety, depression, and other mental health outcomes.[51] Limiting social media use of depressed college students to thirty minutes per day for three weeks improved their depression scores by more than 35 percent.[52] Harms have been attributed to content viewed on social media, ranging from racist and other hate-based content[53] to risky challenges[54] to self-harm and suicide-related information.[55] Social comparison on social media ("compare and despair") has been associated with body dissatisfaction, depression, and eating disorders.[56] Asked how they felt about their bodies after using social media, 46 percent of thirteen-to-seventeen-year-old females felt worse; only 14 percent felt better.[57] Cyberbullying on social media, disproportionately targeting adolescent females and sexual-minority youth, has been consistently associated with depression.[58] Problematic use of social media (more on this in chapter 11) has been linked to poor sleep quality and duration, sleep disorders, and depression.[59]

Because social media are so thoroughly integrated into contemporary life, especially for adolescents, and the data show that positive and negative outcomes are related to how social media are used, the surgeon general called on researchers, technology companies, policymakers, parents and caregivers, and the young people who use social media to work together to

- rigorously investigate social media spaces and behaviors that lead to help or harm,
- empower users with digital literacy,
- recognize and address harms promptly and transparently, and
- share information on characteristics of the social media environment that promote or threaten digital wellness.

In response to this challenge, on June 20, 2023, the Digital Wellness Lab proposed an aspirational Inspired Internet Pledge to all stakeholders in the social media environment.[60]

Youth have already started to learn to live well with social media. According to a Pew Research Center survey of US teens ages thirteen to seventeen conducted April 14 to May 4, 2022, "teens themselves paint a more nuanced picture of adolescent life on social media," in which most "credit these platforms with deepening connections and providing a support network when they need it, while smaller—though notable—shares acknowledge the drama and pressures that can come along with using social media."[61]

There are clearly features of social media and, frankly, of the internet at large that make superficial, exploitative, and asymmetrical human connections easy. The algorithms that profile social media users in order to target them for marketing frequently steer them into echo chambers of like-minded users where they only hear and see what they already agree with. Special interest groups can form and evolve into less healthy places through these algorithms. What can start with an interest in dance can take the user from being healthy to losing weight to anorexia nervosa as a lifestyle choice. It is easy to see how adolescent curiosity and the desire to connect with others can be highjacked by an unhealthy belief system. But it is also too easy to blame social media for our behavior. Social media is not going to go away, and legislative and technological fixes will be incremental and slower than the evolution of our behavior in the digital ecosystem. Calling out problems and seeking help from policymakers and tech corporations will help change things for the better for the next generation, but it will not help us or our growing children today. We have to live and raise children now, in the admittedly flawed digital ecosystem we have. We must develop a fuller understanding of that ecosystem and bring positive parenting to it, engaging with the idealism of youth and embracing the positive affordances of digital tools while remaining aware of, preventing, and mitigating negative effects.

We cannot approach this challenge with fear and by playing defense. The fact that children and adolescents are deeply and almost constantly engaged with interactive media must be seen as an opportunity for digital wellness. Teens seek each other, as well as music, videos, gaming, and seemingly directionless explorations of the internet, doomscrolling when they feel anxious or sad. Seeing a scary movie, playing a violent video game, or witnessing a terrorist attack reported in near-real time can easily contribute to a teen's feelings of anxiousness and sadness. But research also shows that hopeful, optimistic media content can calm and focus youth after a long day at school, and watching videos such as cats riding robot vacuums can cheer up adolescents when they feel sad.[62] Media are powerful tools—it is how we use media, the content we choose, and the contexts in which we use those media that can help or harm us.

Not all young people respond the same way to media. In their landmark work on media effects, Dr. Patti Valkenburg and Dr. Jessica Taylor Piotrowski at the University of Amsterdam have advanced and tested the "orchids and dandelions" theory that children's susceptibility to different media effects varies child to child. Some, like orchids, are sensitive to the slightest disruption of their media ecosystem, and others, like dandelions, are so hardy that they are barely affected, if at all, by their digital media use. The violence in news, entertainment, and gaming that may traumatize or desensitize one child may help others cope with stress because they were able to master that content vicariously.[63]

Learning nuanced social cues and the skills for authentic human interaction, friendship, and emotional intimacy is a vital part of growing up. While many media can help strengthen and sustain the connections children and teens make in real life, they can also limit the formation of deeper, meaningful friendships and other relationships that emerge from shared real-life experiences. In the virtual environment, "likes" and friends can feel real, then be fleeting, rising and falling in a viral instant. Online gathering places vanish like desert mirages. Friends become ghosts. The popularity of any particular platform may be fleeting, but the impact on young people of drama shared there can travel fast, spread far, and become sticky as attention-grabbing content is saved and posted forever forward.

Tweens and teens are particularly vulnerable to hurting others or being hurt by their online behaviors. They are doing anything they can to be accepted by others but neurodevelopmentally remain a decade or more away from achieving impulse control and other executive functions.[64] Before their prefrontal cortexes are fully developed in their mid to late twenties, the potential for missteps and mistakes is significant, but so is the opportunity to educate and empower them to be authentic and kind on social media, building relationships that support rather than compete.

Once we identify how a child's media use behaviors and exposure to content may be contributing to their distress, we can take steps to address those issues. Used mindfully, media (including social media) can be another useful tool to help a child develop healthy coping mechanisms for stress and emotional turbulence, a sense of agency that counters helplessness and hopelessness, and opportunities to engage in ways that contribute to genuine connectedness with others instead of settling for the easy but superficial connectivity that social media enable.

MEDIA Rx

Model and Mentor Responsible, Respectful, Healthy Social Media Use

Help your child start and continue to use social media in healthy ways.

YOU CAN

- *Treat social media as the power tool that it is.* Much as you will when your child learns to drive, sit down next to them and set up their social media accounts with them. It is a good idea to set them up on only one platform at a time, allowing them to learn and become adept with its features before deciding that they need the capabilities of another platform.
- *Set clear and complete expectations for using social media.* Friend them, know their passwords, and let them know that you'll be monitoring the accounts from time to time. If all goes well, as it most likely will, you won't need to do much monitoring. Just the fact that you *can* will change their behavior.
- *Use social media with your child.* Encourage them to keep you informed about what they are seeing and hearing and with whom they are interacting, and reflect with them on how they feel while and after using social media. They will certainly teach you things you did not know. And you will have the opportunity, as a co-user rather than the media police, to talk with them about using media mindfully to connect with others in authentic and responsible ways that are respectful of themselves and others.
- *Talk about cyberbullying and its many forms*—all of them unacceptable—across different platforms and devices as your child gains access to them. From gossip, teasing, taunting, and subtle microaggressions, which they may think are harmless, to intimidation and outright threats that they recognize as clearly wrong, make sure they know what to do if they are bullied or if they see bullying of others in social media or gaming chat rooms. Encourage them not to engage with a bully in any way. Regularly review what your child does and with whom they interact online.

Teach them how to block and report users who are harassing them on social networking sites.

- *Establish social media use as a tool to communicate purposefully, not to lurk or doomscroll.* Model using it in the right context so it does not displace sleep, homework, exercise, family meals, or other important activities.
- *Help your child manage the time they spend using screens.* Balance social media use with other activities, including going outdoors and having face-to-face time with friends. Structure schedules around all activities, not just media use, so that your children and you have a rich and diverse menu of experiences.
- *Hold everyone (including yourself) accountable for meeting family expectations.* Research shows that children are more likely to abide by media use rules when they are held accountable.[65]
- *Teach your children to think critically about media, to question the motivations behind different media depictions of relationships.* Encourage them to think critically about the relationships they have both online and offline and what it truly means to *be* a friend, not just to friend.
- *Cultivate open conversation about both online and offline social behavior.* This establishes that you're calm, approachable, reasonable, and transparent in how you think through social complexities. When your child is upset by social drama playing out in texts or posts or runs into disturbing content online, you want to learn from them about their experiences, be a nonjudgmental support, and help them figure out their own responsible and mindful behavior on social media. Better that you hear about your child's worries or missteps from them rather than hearing it first from the school principal or the police.

Authenticity, Activism, and Social Good

Most of us use social media the way corporations do, to market ourselves to the world. Among adults, social media can be like a 24/7/365 high school reunion. Adolescents, desiring to make connections and find acceptance, often post only their best—their beach vacation, the great party they were invited to, or their hot new boyfriend or girlfriend. One problem with this curated presentation is in the eye of the beholder. Such postings trigger social comparison by others who, knowing the whole of their own reality, may feel "less than." The other problem lands squarely on the individual posting their curated life. The relentless pressure to keep impressing an unseen audience can bring them down too. And it is really hard, especially for adolescents who are at the peak of self-consciousness and insecurity about venturing out into the world, to even know, let alone broadcast, the whole truth about their authentic selves.

As Surgeon General Murthy wrote in *Together: The Healing Power of Human Connection in a Sometimes Lonely World*, "To be real is to be vulnerable, and this takes courage, especially if we believe that others will like us more if we hide or distort who we truly are. Technology can promote this belief by making it easy to pose online as someone braver, happier, better looking, and more successful than we really feel. These poses, in fact, are a form of social withdrawal. They may let us pretend that we're more accepted, but the pretense only intensifies our loneliness."[66] Due to the discrepancy between appearance and reality, the receiver compares and despairs and the sender feels like a sham, unworthy of connection.

As I see it—and share with my patients when talk turns to their life challenges—social and emotional authenticity are the scaffolding for healthy adolescent development, from defining yourself to yourself and to others, to making good friends and being a good friend, to living a life that aligns with your core values and aspirations. As teens have become savvier about the negative effects of the easy superficiality and artificiality that pervade social media, the idea of genuine friendships and authenticity as a personal value is gaining ground.

True friends are not those who appear perfect but those who are real. Meaningful, sustaining relationships are built on our limitations, not our strengths, on our need to be accepted just as we are and to accept another just as they are. True friends accept and compensate for our shortcomings—and they need and depend on our acceptance of and compensation for theirs.

If we can learn to use social media as our authentic selves, we can start to build friend relationships based on truth. If we can extend that authenticity and generosity of spirit to those with whom we interact around the world, social media can become an instrument of peace.

Some of the most inspiring uses of social media are coming from young people speaking out and organizing broader activism on behalf of human rights, the environment, social justice, public health and safety, or individuals in their community who need a helping hand.[67] Social media can provide a link from seeing to doing and connecting with others, whether the inspiration comes from travel, science and nature explorations, musical performances, or tutorials for arts, crafts, and household DIY projects. Social media has been a source of positive, even life-saving connection for some children and teens who struggle to find acceptance or support closer to home. Altruism and passion are timeless hallmarks of youth, but young people's reach and power to effect positive change now are unprecedented.

Developmentally, social media serves the function that communal campfires, landline phones, and hanging out at the mall once did for older pre-digital generations. When kids are in middle school and sorting out how to establish themselves as autonomous beings, their sexuality, their likes and dislikes, and those things that make them individuals distinct from their parents, social media is perceived as a comparatively safe place to explore those issues. There they can broach a conversation with people they might never muster the courage to speak to directly at school. Social media can serve as a valuable transition zone where teens can start to overcome their anxiety about being awkward or rejected, face their fear of social intimacy, and gain confidence to talk face-to-face. Problems arise if young people get stuck in social media and don't move toward comfortable face-to-face interactions and eventually to the increasing emotional intimacy of friendships and romances.

Media change the way we connect with others; they can help maintain and deepen relationships or, in some cases, distract us from being in the moment with the people who are physically with us. Social media can be a Trojan horse. Beneath the appealing features are other influences that call for a critical eye and careful screening, something our kids aren't fully equipped to do. It's up to us to teach them. The sprawling connectivity and the industry algorithms that create click-based viewer communities can create echo chambers of content and conversations, some of which are troubling. And underlying it all are commercial interests that profit from the data and dollars your child's social media use generates.

ASK THE MEDIATRICIAN
My Child Won't Stop Asking for a Cell Phone—What Can I Do?

All of my eight-year-old daughter's friends have cell phones, and she begs me endlessly for one of her own. I'm stalling as long as I can because I don't want her to become a teenage zombie staring at her phone. What can I do—other than just give in?

Cell phones, specifically a smartphone, which is undoubtedly what your daughter wants, have become a must-have for younger and younger children. Your daughter's desire and your confusion are fed, directly and indirectly, by the wireless companies seeking to expand their market. Smartphones are constantly adding capabilities, games, mobile platforms, and engaging apps, making them more attractive and easier to use for children. The world seems to be getting more dangerous with school shootings and kidnappings, so parents may feel that children who have phones to call home are safer. And to make it even harder to say no, smartphones are less and less expensive, sometimes even free with a wireless plan, because the companies make their money on that plan.

The phone your child is asking for is not a phone. It is a pocket-size supercomputer five thousand times faster and more powerful than the vaunted Cray supercomputers of the 1980s, capable of guiding 120 billion *Apollo 11*s to the moon and back. This is a powerful tool.

Any powerful tool, from a chain saw to an automobile, can be incredibly efficient. That efficiency can be helpful when used correctly and harmful when not. Treat a smartphone as a powerful tool. What does this tool do? Does your child need the tool for their daily tasks and activities? What are the positives and negatives of the tool's capabilities? Can your child manage that tool safely and responsibly?

Ask your daughter why she wants it. If the answer is "Because everybody else has one," she sees it as a toy or status symbol, not as a power tool. Would you give her a chain saw because everyone else had one?

Do not give your child a smartphone or any interactive media device, platform, or application as a reward for good behavior or take it away as a punishment—this will undermine their respect for its power to help or harm them and others. Here's a step-by-step approach:

- When your child asks you for a phone, don't say no right away. Listen to them, and involve them in the decision. (With an eight-year-old, this will likely be a discussion that happens over years.)
- Ask, "What do you want to use for it for?" Listen to and discuss their answer. "How will it help you do what you need to do? How will it fit into your day?" Their answers and subsequent discussion can help you determine whether they are ready for a phone. If they aren't quite there yet, discuss what steps they can take to show you that they can responsibly use a phone of their own and when you believe they will be ready to continue the discussion.
- Determine through these discussions when you believe that your child can handle a phone with responsibility and with respect for others and for themselves.
- When you believe your child both needs and is ready for a phone, offer a flip phone first. They will almost certainly say "No way!" But this makes it clear that, at least at the beginning, you expect them to use the phone for talk and text only. And if they use it in other ways, you will replace a smartphone with a flip phone.
- Discuss what they will use the phone for. Talk explicitly about the fact that beyond talking and texting, virtually all of the apps available for smartphones are for entertainment and distraction. There is nothing wrong with entertainment, but it can easily displace more productive activities, like school, face-to-face interactions with family and friends, sports, or other physical activities. Some apps like Snapchat are for communication with friends, but when using any image-based communication, they must be mindful of what the images show and how they might be interpreted.
- Discuss explicitly what they will *not* use the phone for. This is arguably the hardest part for parents to do well because it should be framed as giving your child the skills to protect and take care of themselves, not as a dire warning. You want them to feel safe

coming to you when they stumble upon potentially harmful content (and they will).

- Decide with your child what the consequences of smartphone missteps should be. *Before* they get the phone they want, your child will volunteer (or, at the very least, accept) giving the phone up for a week or two if they misuse it. While confiscating the phone should not be used as punishment for misbehaving in other ways, it stands to reason that irresponsible or unhealthy misuse of a tool should be responded to with temporary loss of using that tool, with time to consider using it more wisely.

- Tell them not to share any personal information online, especially with someone they do not know IRL. This includes their name, age, address, school, any other information through which they can be found, and any financial information like credit card or Social Security numbers. They can create any fantasy name they wish and then share it only with their closest and most trusted friends.

- Advise them to be very careful about posting photos of themselves or others online. Remind them that anything they post can be reposted by strangers and could be used to find them.

- Tell them about hate sites, pornography, scams, and phishing. If you are not ready to talk openly about pornography, racism, fraud, and more online, you are probably not ready to give your child a smartphone. As uncomfortable as it is to talk about the dark side of humanity, you are modeling digital wellness here too. You want your child to be able to talk to you about upsetting experiences, so you must show them how.

- No matter how close they are to friends, they should never, *ever* share passwords. This may be the most uncomfortable part of the conversation, but it must be done, and it must lead into the discussion of consequences.

As hard as this conversation is, it builds a solid foundation for healthy smartphone use by your child and your effective, transparent, and supportive parenting in their digital and physical domains. As with everything in digital parenting, present these not as rules but as expectations that everyone, including you, lives by.

Insist on the "Second Bottom Line"

The Digital Wellness Lab works with stakeholders in our digital ecosystem—youth and their families, the tech industry, entertainment, and health care—to rethink and redesign that ecosystem by adding a "second bottom line" of individual and societal wellness to business models. Bringing the complementary and necessary skills of all of these disciplines to bear, we seek to understand how young people are affected by the media they use and how they use them, translate those findings into practical action steps that empower youth and their families to engage in preventive strategies, support early intervention with young people who struggle with media use, and feed all of this information back to the creators of devices, platforms, and content to be integrated in their product development.[68]

The needs of children and adolescents around social and emotional development will inform that work. But parents can't wait. Our kids live in the now, and from their earliest days as social beings, we're tasked with their socialization as guides to help them learn to successfully navigate the here-and-now social landscape. Social media can provide important stepping stones for social and emotional development as children and adolescents figure out how to interact with each other and the world. The goal is to help your child understand and use social media not as a destination, but as a bridge to fuller, deeper relationships.

MEDIA Rx
Kid-Friendly Reminders to Protect Privacy
and Avoid Social Media Pitfalls

Privacy, to a child or young teen, simply means that their parents can't see what they're doing. It doesn't occur to them that comments and pics they post online could have serious consequences later when they apply to colleges or for jobs. How do you help kids recognize where to draw the line on what they share online and offer some tips on how to do it? Keep it simple and developmentally optimal. Three rules of thumb that kids tell me are useful are:

- *Remember: far, fast, sticky, and tricky.* This is the idea that anything you share on social media can travel far beyond your intended recipient, faster than you can say "viral," and it remains out there in the digital universe forever, for anyone to find at any time. Far, fast, sticky, and tricky means that the choices you make now about sharing will travel instantly beyond your control and can still be saved somewhere by someone seeking to embarrass, make fun of, or harm you. Keep posts kind. Think about the different ways that people could feel about what you are posting—and save anything that might be misinterpreted for face-to-face conversations.
- *Follow the "Grandma Rule."* Don't post, repost, text, tweet, retweet, or otherwise share any words, sounds, or images online that you wouldn't want Grandma (or some other beloved and respected adult) to see or hear. For kids, Grandma brings immediate awareness—someone they love and respect and whom they want to love and respect them. Save the goofy, snarky, and raunchy stuff to share with your friends in person—the immediate laugh you get will be much more satisfying anyway.
- *Push Pause, not Send.* Big emotions can make for big trouble when you communicate via messaging or social media. Recognize when you feel angry, hurt, or offended, and give yourself time to process those emotions and move past the high-voltage urgency of the moment before you send anything.

Chapter 5

What's Love Got to Do with IT?

Virtual Connection, Physical Intimacy

S*he* asked *me* if I wanted to go out for pizza!" Tim bounced into the clinic room before I even greeted him.

"Who did?"

"Carrie! The girl I was crushing on!" I was still lost. "You know, the one who didn't even notice me . . . with the long, dark brown hair."

"The one you were talking about last year?"

"She asked me out!" Tim, who had been struggling with social anxiety since kindergarten, went on to detail how he sat two rows behind her and to her left in his freshman math class, staring at her more often than he did at the board but never talking to her. He was sure that she would want nothing to do with him. But she posted a comment to a video he had posted on social media—a spider skittering across its web to wrap a struggling fly. Not knowing who it was, Tim responded, "Pretty morbid. Do you like spiders?" She countered, "I don't mind them. I just like the way the sun shone on the dew caught on the web. Are you a professional photographer?" Tim went on to describe how they started a social media conversation about art, nature, where they went for vacation, some of the silly things they did over the summer and some of the embarrassing ones. Carrie took to calling him Photo Pete, and he called her Spider-Woman.

"Hey, Photo Pete, send me a selfie! If you send one, I'll send you one . . ." Spider-Woman texted.

Tim did. She responded almost immediately to Tim. "Don't I know you?"

"I don't know . . . (Pondering face emoji) Do you? Hey, where's your selfie?" She sent it.

"Didn't you sit behind me in Ms. Parker's math class last year?" asked Spider-Woman.

Tim was gobsmacked. Embarrassed. Terrified. Excited. Spider-Woman's text appeared: "Hey, are you still there?"

"Uh, yeah . . . I didn't think you noticed me." (Laughing with the water-falls of tears emoji) "You usually scooted out of class so fast. Before I even picked up my books." (Jogging female emoji)

"But I thought you were cute," Spider-Woman replied. "Want go get (pizza emoji) sometime?"

Tim and Carrie played out a courtship as old as time in a new way on social media. Even though he had spent a year pining for her from a distance, Tim couldn't—at least, he didn't—muster the courage to approach Carrie. The relative anonymity of social media had allowed him to be himself, to talk about his interests, nerdy as they might be, and even his worries with no self-consciousness or awkwardness since he thought he was connecting with a stranger.

Early adolescence is a difficult, confusing time as young people start to feel romantic attractions but have no idea what to do with them. They see other kids coupling up, even briefly, and they feel left behind and utterly alone. But on social media, identified only by their handles with no idea who they are interacting with and where they might be, awkward youth can be themselves, if they choose. Not all do; some choose to be bolder versions of themselves or experiment in other ways with the persona they choose to project, a charade that can backfire on them later, as we'll see.

But Tim and Carrie were just being themselves, connecting over a shared interest and a friendly vibe. They got together for pizza, and eventually their friendship moved beyond social media. Buoyed by the confidence and comfort zone they had developed through texting and sharing videos and photos from their days, they were able to build on that easy back-and-forth when they met in person. They grew to trust and care for each other. Now their relationship included texting and social media along with in-person time together, where they discovered they could be authentic, open, and vulnerable with each other, the hallmarks of genuine friendship and emotional intimacy. Experience communicating on social media allowed Tim to feel more comfortable in his own skin, less socially awkward and anxious, and excited to be in a trusting relationship with Carrie.

Conversations among parents—and questions from parents to clinicians

—about budding romance between adolescents are frequently brimming with alarm and discomfort. They focus on risks—of forced sexual activity, pregnancy, sexually transmitted infections, and worse. Adult fears have been amplified by sexting, sextortion, revenge porn, online grooming by pedophiles, and shaming gone viral. But for every sensational tale of exploitation, there are hundreds of stories like Tim and Carrie's, stories in which texting and social media support their coming of age. Whether serendipitous, as it was for Tim and Carrie, or intentional, young people have overcome the shy self-consciousness of youth by tentatively reaching out via the digital stepping stone of social media. It is both ironic and encouraging that the technologies that create consternation among adults are the same tools young people are using to successfully navigate developmental challenges and connect as evolving adults.

Adolescents are curious, sensation-seeking, creative, and risk-taking. It has traditionally been the approach of parents, clinicians, policymakers, and society at large to fear for and fear adolescents, protecting them and prohibiting them from taking risks. Practicing adolescent medicine and public health with adolescents, I have learned time and again that their natural drive for autonomy will lead many of them to challenge any protection or restriction that adults try to enforce simply because it is limiting them. I have found that it is far more effective to nurture and encourage their strengths than to avoid their risks. Their natural instincts are to be healthy, happy, and connected, and we must trust them. They will make mistakes, and we may need to provide a safety net from time to time, but we must let them stumble so that they learn to pick themselves up and try again, bloodied but unbowed. I never learned from something I did right the first time.

Have you noticed how teen movies become hugely popular at a moment in time and that moment is crystallized in pop culture for those who were teens at that time? It is not because the films are masterpieces of cinema. It is because they resonated with the issues youth were struggling with—from initiating romance to taking dares to drinking and doing drugs to being excruciatingly embarrassed by one's parents. When I taught the adolescent health course at Harvard T. H. Chan School of Public Health, I assigned not only readings of health research but viewings of a teen movie each week. Yes, it was fun to watch *Napoleon Dynamite*—but not so much fun to watch *Precious* or *Boys Don't Cry*. It was as important to watch these movies as it was to read the scientific literature because to understand adolescents, one needs to (1) understand how the adult world perceives and treats adolescents and (2) recognize that from teen movies and other cultural touchpoints, teens learn how to flirt and how to fight, how to stand up for others and how to kiss; in short, teens learn how to be teens. I asked students to choose one of the films and write a paper describing what the filmmakers got right about adolescents' life experiences, behaviors, and feelings and where they were not true to what the science showed about human development.

If we are to understand how using screen media might affect child and adolescent development, we need to do just that: understand what *is* normal and healthy development in adolescence. What do young people need to develop the social and emotional foundations for intimacy? How do they themselves think about sexuality as part of their emerging identity? By looking objectively at how media use might help, hinder, or hurt them, we can help them safely navigate this exciting and tumultuous developmental passage in the physical-digital environment.

Just an Old-Fashioned Love Song

Timeless themes of trust, vulnerability, loyalty, longing, and curiosity unfold on the developmental stage, as they always have, not as teen movies or love songs but as embodied experience. Culture creates norms and shapes expectations around gender roles and sexuality that infuse a child's environment, from romantic fairy tales and kindergarten crushes to hushed tones and cautionary tales of those who strayed from the script. But cultural norms and family expectations are often swept away by the tsunami of surging hormones, the ultimate influencers that trigger the metamorphosis of adolescence across physical, psychological, and emotional domains.

In literature, both fictional and scientific, coming of age is cast as the defining quest of seeking personhood: a young person's search and struggle to form their own identity, which includes fundamental biological aspects of gender and sexual orientation, how their uniquely wired brain interprets their experience of the world, and the core values they choose to embrace and those they choose to reject. From Homer's *Odyssey* to *The Breakfast Club* to *Barbie*, across all genres of art and life, the stories are centered on:

- personal growth and change
- identity development
- unexpectedly and sometimes reluctantly bonding with an "other"
- risks and trials that test one's inner and outer worlds
- insight, epiphany, revelation, and transformation

While the final test of the hero who has come of age may be explosive action, their personal growth happens in the still moments of self-doubt evolving into determination, kindling the emotional fire within, that is shared in dialogue with kindred spirits. How do children and adolescents navigate this complex and delicate developmental journey in a fast-moving, infinitely connected digital ecosystem given the critical importance of reflection, emotion, and dialogue in our coming-of-age archetypes?

The immediacy of texting appeals to young people's urgency, spontaneity, and yet-to-develop ability to defer gratification. The asynchronicity of social media allows more open and vulnerable communication to happen in a space perceived as private. Used in healthy ways, these features can support and promote authentic human connection and communication. But confusion and conflict frequently arise because of what is missing in the immediacy and asynchronicity of interactive media, particularly in more personal, emotionally intimate communication. Texting and social media make the exchange less intimidating but are not able to transmit the emotional nuance that comes so naturally in conversation. Digital technology cannot duplicate the physical context of dialogue. Senders and receivers can't see each other's body language and facial expressions, hear tone of voice, or feel the back-and-forth rhythm of the exchange. They are missing the face-to-face opportunity to try out and practice social skills, to make and correct errors of interpersonal communication, to grow. The problem with uneven timing between messages and responses—the gaps between when a message is sent, when it is read, and when the recipient replies—is complicated enough in everyday social interactions, but these gaps create even greater potential for miscues and misunderstandings in the context of crushes, flirting, and romantic forays.

Desperate to grow up, preteens and teens are curious, aspirational, and drawn to adult lifestyles. When one becomes aware of it, the amount of romantic and sexual content infused in our entertainment is amazing. From toddlerhood, children have seen and heard fairy tales of beautiful princesses being rescued by strong and handsome princes. More than 70 percent of television programs contain sexual content.[1] Gender stereotypes abound. Thematic analysis of seven popular children's TV programs found that boys objectified and reduced girls to their worth based on their appearance—and girls reciprocated with self-objectification; that is, they didn't treat boys as objects so much as they turned the male gaze on themselves and perpetuated the role that boys established for them.[2] Romance and sexual innuendo are staples of culture, from teen magazines to swoon-worthy novels, from pop music to advertising for beauty products, alcohol, and entertainment.

Casual and risky sex is often glamorized in media, which can lead children and teens to believe that these practices are normal and free of consequences. Children see behavior in media with which they have little to no personal experience. If unchallenged, they accept these behaviors as how adults act and seek to emulate them. For some very young children, sexual content can be, at best, boring because it is incomprehensible. But in many cases, sexual behavior can be confusing, scary, or teach them by example how to attract attention and affection. It is important to be conscious of implicit as well as explicit sexualized content in movies, video games, and television and to be aware of who else is in the room and may be viewing it as well. Limiting your very young children's exposure, even ambient exposure, to sexual content can help ensure that they are not learning unhealthy sexual behavior from movies, video games, books, magazines, and TV shows. Sex can be a part of healthy life, and developing an interest in sex is natural for adolescents, but exposure to adult sexual behavior is not developmentally optimal for young children.

As a culture we are primally attracted to yet morally conflicted about sex. So we reflexively try to limit what children see with movie, TV, and video game ratings. Does content-based age-gating protect children from establishing risky sexual attitudes and behaviors? A meta-analysis of fifty-nine rigorous studies representing 48,471 adolescents and young adults investigated whether exposure to sexy but nonexplicit content in mainstream movies, television, videos, video games, and music influenced their sexual attitudes and behaviors.[3] They found that most media portrayed sex as prevalent, recreational, and risk-free, resulting in significant effects on young people's sexual attitudes and behaviors. Exposure to sexy mainstream media was associated with permissive sexual attitudes, greater acceptance of myths around nonconsensual sex and rape, and inflated perceptions of peers' sexual experience. These attitudes were associated with earlier ages of sexual initiation, higher levels of risky sexual behaviors, and greater sexual experience. These effects were twice as strong for adolescents as for young adults (who presumably had more real-world sexual experience), stronger in males than females (who were more likely to be condemned for sexual activity), and stronger among White Americans than in Black Americans (who identified less strongly with the predominantly White characters in mainstream media).[4]

The overwhelming predominance of White cisgender (those who identify with their biological gender at birth) heterosexuals in screen media content presents a twofold problem of available role models. First, LGBTQ+ and other sexual-minority groups who are represented in media stereotypically or not at all are also seeking to find themselves, understand the world, and learn how to behave in it.[5] Second, focusing on White cisgender heterosexuals as a norm, even an ideal, promotes a limited view of sexuality and gender diversity that narrows everyone's understanding and tolerance of healthy norms in the world as it is.

Human development accelerates and broadens dramatically as children approach and go through puberty. While preschool and school-age children get taller, gain weight, and expand cognitively at a steady, gradual rate, many parents feel that puberty is a moment when a child goes to bed and a whole new person wakes up the next morning. Adolescents' heights and weights rapidly increase, usually not symmetrically, so middle school classes have tall girls with developed breasts and tiny girls without and short, heavy boys with squeaky voices and gangly ones with caterpillars on their upper lips. Girls shoot up first and are briefly taller than the boys, but the boys will catch up and pass them by the end of the decade. Girls grow moody while boys fall silent. And all of them, as the pubertal pulse of estrogen and testosterone hits them, are trying to figure out sex and their sexuality.

The quest for informative sources and peer conversations about this intimate landscape is a natural expression of adolescent curiosity about their own bodies, their own development. That aspect of human nature obviously predates the internet, but we can look for the familiar measure—how much indirect media exposure has replaced direct experience—to understand how media content and access to it has had such an impact. Young people, seeking independence from parents and attention from peers, see behaviors rewarded in media, imitate them, and may make them their own. Young people lose out on important growth experiences when media imagery, content, and online chat replace direct, grounded experiences of social and emotional dialogue, exploration, and authentic relationships.

So how do they figure out their sexual development through online dialogue? Despite national goals set by the US Department of Health and Human Services' Healthy People 2030 initiative, sex education in the United States varies widely.[6] Only twenty-nine states and the District of Columbia require formal sex education, and there is great variation in required content at the state, district, and individual school levels.[7] The most recent data from 2015–2019 showed that

- 81 percent of female adolescents and 79 percent of male adolescents had been taught about saying no to sex
- 67 percent of females and 58 percent of males were taught about waiting to have sex until marriage
- Only 48 percent of females and 45 percent of males had learned where to obtain contraception while 55 percent of females and 60 percent males learned how to use a condom

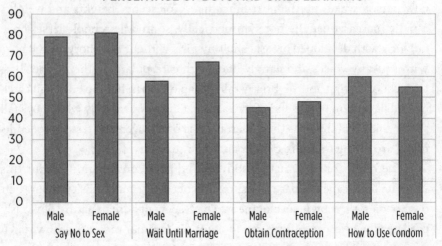

PERCENTAGE OF BOYS AND GIRLS LEARNING

Guttmacher Institute, "US Adolescents' Receipt of Formal Sex Education," February 2022, https://www.guttmacher.org/fact-sheet/adolescents-teens-receipt-sex-education-united-states#.

Compared to two decades earlier (1995), 26 percent fewer females and 22 percent fewer males had received formal sex education on birth control methods. Since most adolescents reported receiving sex education in ninth grade or later, less than half (43 percent of females and 47 percent of males) had received it before having sexual intercourse for the first time.[8]

"Pornification" Hijacks Normal Curiosity and Sexual Socialization

Marla, fifteen, had been my patient since she started middle school. She had been really embarrassed when her mom brought her in after having her first menstrual period, so I was prepared to be cautious with my questions at this visit. As soon as her mom left the room, Marla said, "I've been sexting with this cute guy, and I'm not sure whether to take it further."

Sexting, the use of the internet to send sexually oriented images or text, "is no big deal," Marla said. Seeing my look of surprise, she smiled with amused satisfaction and explained, "It's how you show them you're interested. And it's safer than actually doing something." She revealed that last year, as a freshman desperate to fit in at high school, she was dared to send a topless photo to a popular senior boy she didn't know. When Marla sent it, he threatened to "slut-shame" her on social media by circulating the photo if she didn't send more explicit ones. Slut-shaming is basically sexualized cyberbullying or, as it is described in research literature, a form of sexual stigmatization perpetrated by others through rumors, criticism, and ostracism that imposes "severe negative effects both on self-identity and interpersonal relations."[9]

"He was acting weird, so I blocked him. He sent the picture to one of his teammates, who told him it was against the law and that if he didn't delete it, the teammate would report him. I don't know who it was, but I owe that guy." Marla had taken a big risk in shutting down this attempted sextortion without telling an adult in a position to act on it. That image could still be out there somewhere. Because she wasn't immediately hurt, Marla had come to believe that sexting was harmless. When the soccer player she was crushing on asked her for a nude photo, Marla sent it. She was hoping that he would sext back.

Sexting is a phenomenon of the digital age, but the sharing of sexual material is as old as human history. One of the oldest known sculptures,

Venus of Willendorf—a woman's body with pronounced breasts, buttocks, and pubic area—is thought to have been portable erotic art for our Paleolithic ancestors twenty-five to thirty thousand years ago.[10] But sexting is not just more portable but rapidly transmissible and infinitely reproducible, and its subject is often known or easily identified. For many teens who are in a hurry to grow up fast, sexting is cool. Like smoking cigarettes was in the '50s and '60s, sexting is edgy adult behavior popularized by celebrities and illegal for children, which adolescents no longer want to be.

I could appreciate Marla's casual confidence, her ease with her developing sexuality and desire to explore, but what she didn't realize was that sexting is more than just "adultified" texting. She and her peers might think of it as flirtation, but on the internet, it is more accurately a high-risk, high-stakes setup for exploitation with potential criminal consequences for the sender as well as the receiver. Until the teammate shut her tormentor down, Marla was unaware of the legal ramifications of everyone's behaviors, hers included. I told her about a fourteen-year-old girl who sent a sexy selfie to a boy she liked—and was charged with felony distribution of child pornography in 2018.[11] And that was just one of the thousands of teen sexting cases investigated by police over the past several years. Your child needs to know that it is illegal to send (and resend) explicit images of anyone under the age of eighteen, even if the underage child pictured was the person who sent the image. In Marla's case, I was more worried about the implications of her choice to pursue a sexual relationship this way—how her readiness to objectify herself for attention affected her self-esteem and her expectations of sexual or romantic relationships. While Marla was sexting as a way of flirting and seeking intimacy, boys frequently pressure girls for sexy selfies to demonstrate their masculinity to other boys. But society has a double standard about sexting: girls who do it are typically shamed as sluts, while boys are celebrated as studs.[12]

We've seen the age-gating firewall between children and adolescents and sexually graphic content on the internet and social media platforms erode as loopholes become apparent and kids (sometimes with the help of their parents) devise work-arounds to age requirements. To further complicate the picture, teens themselves are among those using social media to post sexualized versions of traditional teen gossip fodder. In one infamous case, popular girls at a top-ranked New Jersey high school posted a Facebook "slut list" with ratings of younger girls based on their alleged sexual activity and promiscuity, but they flipped the meaning of a slut list to celebrate, not shame, those on the list.[13] The episode, which played out in 2009, still reverberates among parents and others who see such uses of social media as upending any protective norms that may once have been in place.

In Marla's experience, sexting was common among her peers: "It's our second base!" Marla's casual attitude toward sexting is a reflection of what social scientists have called the "pornification" of popular culture over the last fifty years.[14] Sex has long been used implicitly to sell everything from perfume to cigarettes to fast food, but advances in home video technology in the 1970s allowed pornography to migrate from seedy downtown movie theaters into suburban living rooms. Home VCRs made it possible to sell sex itself to a much, much bigger population of consumers. VHS tapes in plain brown wrappers, cable television, and increasingly large screens circumvented movie ratings systems and obscenity laws by moving adult entertainment from public spaces to the privacy of any home. The emergence and rapid adoption of the internet provided accessibility, affordability, and anonymity for children and adolescents to access a wide range of sexually explicit internet material with only a click.

In September 2022, a national survey of US adolescents ages thirteen to seventeen years old showed:

- Nearly three-fourths (73 percent overall, 75 percent of cisgender boys, 70 percent of cisgender girls) had viewed pornography, with 52 percent of boys and 36 percent of girls viewing it on purpose.
- Twelve was the average age of first seeing pornography, with 15 percent having seen pornography by the age of ten, a proportion that increased to 54 percent by the age of thirteen.
- Among those teens who used pornography intentionally, 59 percent had viewed it in the past week, with 34 percent of them viewing it three or more times in that week.
- More than half (52 percent) of all teens who had viewed pornography had seen violent, aggressive pornography, including rape, choking, and painful sex. Only one in three (33 percent) had seen someone asking for consent. In fact, nonconsensual sex is a subgenre of online pornography.

- Only 27 percent believed that pornography portrayed sex accurately, but 45 percent felt that it provided them with useful information about sex. At a time in their lives when adolescents are figuring out themselves and how they will behave with others, most pornography portrays sex as physical, carefree, for personal gratification, and transactional rather than affectionate, trusting, and relational.[15]

For youth who are underrepresented in mainstream screen media, pornography may play a larger role in their sexual socialization. Sixty-six percent of LGBTQ+ teens, the largest proportion of any group using pornography intentionally, used pornography to "find out what arouses and excites them."[16] Pornography use is more prevalent, viewed more frequently, and viewed at younger ages by LGBTQ+ females, but they have no greater negative outcomes than their heterosexual peers.[17] LGBTQ+ youth appear to be using pornography not only for sexual pleasure but to explore their sexuality and develop their sexual identity. Often LGBTQ+ youth start their explorations with pornography and make connections with others on social media, allowing them to share experiences before intentionally searching out dedicated sexual health sites.[18] The internet offers youth who are questioning and sorting out their sexuality, young people who are often marginalized, ostracized, and even bullied where they live, an opportunity to find a community of supportive peers online.

ASK THE MEDIATRICIAN
Am I Overreacting to "Teens Will Be Teens"?

I hear about instances where kids on social media have ranked other kids for their alleged sexual exploits—like the "slut list" story in the news some years ago—and it's all so disturbing. I worry that this could be happening in my daughter's social circle and I'd never know it. She's thirteen. Maybe I'm overreacting, but I want to talk to her about this. What should I say?

You are wise to assume your daughter may be encountering these kinds of trending news stories and sexualized gossip in her in-person social circle and social media. American media use sex to promote everything from cosmetics to fast food because sex, like violence, is a universal primal drive that can be harnessed to sell. But the superficial sex used to sell does not tell the truth, and it makes sex attractive in ways that are unhealthy. On TV, in music videos, and in celebrity culture, girls are shown as sexy at younger and younger ages.

So why do these teens *want* to be on the slut list? Perhaps because they see this type of behavior the way media portray it—as empowering and attention-getting. At this age, their brains haven't yet developed the executive function and future thinking to take care of their own well-being.

As a parent, you can help provide the reflection and perspective that your teen daughter doesn't yet have. How? By asking her open-ended, nonjudgmental questions. This way you can ask her about what is going on for other girls instead of about her personal experience. This is a safer way for her to discuss these issues with you, and if you respond with curiosity and openness rather than horror or disapproval, you position yourself as supportive and caring and are more likely to get somewhere useful in the conversation.

For example, share what you read about the slut list in the news, and try asking your daughter how she feels about this story, why she thinks girls wanted to be on this list, and whether she thinks sexual behavior is a way of determining popularity. Even if she says something like, "Oh, Mom, you're so old-fashioned—everyone's doing this," you can teach her to think critically about the way things are by questioning it yourself. Keep asking questions you truly don't have the answers to, like, "But why do they do this? Can you explain it to me?" In this way, you encourage your daughter to reflect on how others see people who are on this list, how those who are on it might feel, whether this is an "honor" that will serve them well into the future, and whether they actually wanted to do whatever they needed to do to get on that list. Additionally, you are teaching her to consider what defines *her*. Is it her clothes? Her sexual behavior? Something else about herself? This experience of introspection, critical thinking, and building self-respect is a lesson that will benefit her for the rest of her life.

Pornography Is "Easier" than Awkward Reality

Although the majority of CIMAID's patients are brought to us by worried parents, Miles, nineteen, came to CIMAID on his own. He stood out in the clinic waiting room, wearing a jacket and tie among the hoodies and T-shirts. He followed me down the hall to the exam room and sat down tentatively.

Miles was nervous, shifting in his seat, looking up at me, down at the floor, and up at me again. "I'm not sure this is the place I should be," he began. "I heard from a friend that you can help people having trouble with the internet."

He was in the spring term of his freshman year in college. Away from home and on his own for the first time, he had been doing well academically but was unhappy. "I'm not having the college experience."

When I asked what that is, Miles revealed that while his roommate was out virtually every evening and often asked Miles to leave the room because he was bringing a girl back, Miles had not even gone out to parties. "I just feel awkward. I don't know how to talk to people, I guess."

He went on to describe that his fear of embarrassing himself paralyzed him. Asked how long he has felt this way, Miles answered, "Forever. High school, middle school even."

"Are you attracted to girls, boys, or both?"

"Well, I don't know. I get . . . horny. I don't know if that's appropriate . . . You said what we talk about is in confidence?"

Assured that, as an adult, he controlled both his medical information and his care, he went on.

"Gaming gets pretty raunchy at times. Hot women with nice boobs and tight butts." He glanced up for signs of disapproval, then continued. "There are even games where you play having sex. And they link to porn sites. Once I discovered porn, I was gone. I liked it way better than gaming. It feels like I spent my high school years jacking off to porn.

"I never really went out with other kids. I never dated anybody. I didn't need to," Miles told me. When he got to college, he tried to connect with girls but felt awkward and unattractive, so he retreated. "Porn is easier." After several visits, Miles finally related the incident that brought him to CIMAID. "This one girl was kind of into me, I think. She came back to my dorm room because my roommate had gone home for the weekend. We started making out, taking our clothes off, and. . . . well, she was going slow, so I don't know how into me she really was. She was sexy and all, but I couldn't get it up. What's the matter with me?" he asked, tears of shame welling in his eyes.

With puberty comes the emergence of sexual interest and curiosity, occurring at the same time that adolescents are acutely self-conscious about their physical appearance and behaviors. Sexual socialization, the awkward dance of overcoming anxiety to meet increasing but not yet well understood sexual needs, is never easy for anyone. It is especially difficult, often lonely, for those young people who are unsure whether they fit into cisgender, heterosexual roles. For many young people, social media has served as a safer-feeling space in which to try out connecting with romantic interests. It is easier to message than to talk to someone face-to-face. The possibility of rejection or apathy feels less threatening in the apparent privacy of social media, especially on messaging apps like Snapchat in which messages disappear after they are read. For some, like Miles, fear of the vulnerability required for intimacy felt too daunting for even his sex drive to overcome. Online pornography was easier.

Pornography allowed Miles to avoid confronting his fear of intimacy and stalled his sexual development. Pornography is fantasy, a fictional portrayal of perfect sex predominantly from a heterosexual male perspective. Most bodies are incredibly fit, super-endowed, and often enhanced by plastic surgery. In pornography, everyone always wants and enjoys sex in a wide variety of acts and positions and never says no (but are rarely asked). The pornography user has total control of the fantasy partner, relational setting, sex acts portrayed, and the rhythm of arousal and completion. Confronted with the potential of sex with a real person with real emotions and needs, Miles sensed the imperfections of both of their bodies, the tentativeness of his potential partner, and his own anxiety, resulting in a loss of libido. Because he had not ventured beyond the perfect fantasy of pornography to meet his needs, Miles was stuck in his sexual development.

Interestingly, the percentage of US high school students who have had sexual intercourse fell from 47 percent in 2011 to 30 percent in 2021.[19] At the same time, adolescents' smartphone ownership increased from 20 percent in 2009 to 88 percent in 2021.[20] Could it be that other adolescents had, like Miles, deferred sexual activity by meeting their needs through easily available pornography? This brings up an interesting question: Since delaying first sexual activity is recommended to reduce the risk of unplanned pregnancies and sexually transmitted infections, might online pornography actually contribute to improved public health?

Social learning theory proposes that we learn social behaviors from observing others, either in person or through media. Behaviors that are rewarded are more likely to be learned; those that are punished are more likely to be rejected. A recent content analysis of 4,009 heterosexual scenes from two large pornography aggregation sites found physical aggression in 45 percent of one site's scenes and in 35 percent of the other site's scenes. Men were the perpetrators in 76 percent of the spanking, gagging, slapping, hair-pulling, and choking scenes, and women were the targets in 97 percent of them. The women's responses to violent sex were neutral or positive, rarely negative, implying that these behaviors are normal, accepted sexual behavior.[21] Hentai, the Japanese anime pornography that Miles was consuming, tends to portray female characters who are childlike but have exaggerated breasts and genitals that are fondled and penetrated by human or monster male characters. In 2022, the year that the British Board of Film Classification found that compared to adults, children six to twelve years old were "disproportionately exposed to pornography sites specializing in non-photographic content," *hentai* was the most popular search term on one of the largest pornography aggregators.[22] Miles was attracted to a girl, but his sexual expectations were skewed by the sexual behavior he was observing. His desire to connect with her was stymied because he didn't want to hurt her. Remember that for today's youth, there is no border between what those born before the internet call the "real world" and the "virtual world." Young people move constantly and seamlessly between the physical and the digital. Miles's empathy, sex drive, and genuine interest in a relationship came into conflict with the patterns of sexual relationships that hentai had established in his mind.

The digital ecosystem in which we live and raise children provides both positive affordances and negative health risks—and pornography is no exception. Pornography use that allows young people to meet their sexual needs while avoiding the awkwardness of meeting in person makes sexual satisfaction a commodity and sexual behavior a transaction. One is paying for an orgasm on pornography, whether it is by giving attention and time to advertising on a "free" site or subscribing to a paid service. For adolescents who are simultaneously self-conscious, peaking in their sex drive, and sorting out who they are and what they like, this commodification of sex is an easy work-around for the hard work of relationship building. This plays out in a variety of ways, from college students who pay their tuition with their earnings on OnlyFans, a site that includes DIY pornography, to those who seek a friend with benefits (FWB) they can abandon if they "catch feelings." Achieving sexual satisfaction with someone who only wants sex can be attractive and easy, however short on emotional intimacy. In terms of developmental gain, it's more on par with playing basketball or sharing a pizza. There's the gain of practical experience and perhaps (though not always) pleasure, but it bypasses the opportunity for establishing emotional intimacy and sustaining human relationships.

ASK THE MEDIATRICIAN
Are Dating Apps STI Traps?

I was at my son's high school and overheard two older teen boys in the hallway talking. One was looking at a dating app, intending to "hook up" with a girl, and the other said he'd better be careful about picking up a sexually transmitted infection from partners found through that particular app. How can I talk about this with my son so he's cautious in this dating scene? What's your advice about using dating apps?

First of all, most dating apps are age-restricted to age seventeen or older and tend to have better enforcement of the limits. While there are youth seventeen and older in many high schools and some of them may be trying out adult behavior, it is likely they are in the minority and that your son is not among them. But if you heard it, you can bet your son has, so it is worth talking honestly about it with him.

Let's break down the science regarding risk. The risk of contracting a sexually transmitted infection (STI) has less to do with how people meet and more to do with their behavior before and after they have met. There hasn't been a study that conclusively finds that people who use certain dating apps are more or less likely to have an STI than those who use others—at least not yet. What we do know is that the risk of contracting an STI is greater when a person engages in sexual contact

- without using a barrier method, such as a condom
- with multiple partners

- with a partner who has multiple partners
- with a partner who is older
- while under the influence of alcohol or other substances
- with a partner whose sexual history is not well known
- with a partner who has symptoms of an STI

Safer sex practices, including obtaining and sharing regular testing for HIV and other STIs as well as using barrier contraceptive methods, help reduce the risk of contracting and spreading STIs, rather than using some dating apps and avoiding others.

However, a reminder here is important. Certain dating apps have a reputation for being focused on finding hookups for casual sex; they are online tools that facilitate sexual activity with low personal investment. As a result, the probability of meeting someone who has had many sexual partners about whom they know little is higher with these apps. It is important to discuss expectations and set boundaries with any person met through a dating app. Casual sex with a veritable stranger—whether met through a dating app or in person—can increase the risk of contracting an STI.

For anyone thinking about using a dating app to meet potential partners, I want to remind them that when using any media, you need to engage your critical thinking skills and use them mindfully for what they do well. For example, think about *what* you are looking for when you look on a dating app, just as you might think about what you are looking for when you go out to college dances, parties, or a singles bar. If you are looking for a meaningful relationship, know that a hookup app isn't designed to provide that. Choose apps, websites, and real-life activities that are designed to help you make the kinds of connections you'd like to make.

Dating apps have disrupted human mating rituals. They have transformed the process of selecting romantic partners from meeting through known social circles to the equivalent of online shopping. During the COVID-19 lockdown, traffic on the most popular apps increased significantly while many popular singles bars and in-person meeting places shut down.[23] Since then, dating app use has continued to grow, and public meeting places have been sluggish in returning. Apps have increased the information people have about each other before meeting, but that objectifies potential partners further. Many profiles start with a picture that can be selected or not. This leads to scrolling quickly through many photos, swiping left or right, like shopping for shoes. Users read profiles of another person's interests and activities, so all that awkward getting-to-know-you talk is taken care of. Although the photo and résumé of interests seem to add a level of verification both before and during the first date, there remains a "buyer beware" caution. How true to life and recent is that profile photo? Is their list of interests and activities exaggerated or accurate? How honest do you expect someone to be on a dating app? How honest is your own profile? What will you do if someone's profile proves to be bogus? This is a good conversation for a teen to have prior to using a dating app.

One in five of all US internet users and more than three hundred million people worldwide are currently using dating apps. More than half (54 percent) of US online daters believe that those relationships are just as successful as relationships that started in person; another 5 percent believe they are more successful. LGBTQ+ users are twice as likely (55 percent) as their heterosexual, cisgender peers to use dating apps. Nearly all (98 percent) of online daters claim to "always" or "often" be truthful on the app, yet 71 percent believe that others lying to appear more desirable is very common. More than one-quarter (26 percent) of dating app users do not want a commitment, and 19 percent have connected with eleven or more potential dates at once. Despite appearing to be another commodification of sex, dating apps continue to gain popularity, and over 13 percent of online daters have gotten engaged to or married a person they met through an online dating app.[24]

However, dating apps are not without health risks. Dating app users are twice as likely to have unprotected sex, and a high prevalence of HIV was found in gay men who use dating apps.[25] Women using dating apps are twice as likely as men to be threatened with sexual violence, and dating apps that feature geolocation, allowing users to choose others who are nearby, have allowed unwanted cyberstalking.[26]

Murky Waters, Danger Zones: Catfishing and Other Sexualized Scams

Dierdre, a funny, quirky, and instantly friendly teenager, came into my care at age seventeen not for issues with technology but for help losing weight. She had always been overweight but had recently decided that she was tired of being the DUFF for the group of girlfriends she had been with since elementary school.

"What is the DUFF?" I asked ignorantly.

She looked at me disdainfully. "Really? Don't you go to the movies? Designated Ugly Fat Friend!"

"That's terrible! Who calls you that?"

Making air quotes, Dierdre replied, "My 'friends.'" She patiently explained to me that she hung out with a popular group of attractive but catty girls at her high school. "You've at least seen *Mean Girls*, haven't you?" I nodded. "Well, we have been together, one way or another, since kindergarten. They let me hang around because I make them laugh and I don't threaten them. They trade hot boys around and bitch to me as the DUFF about how awful the other girls are." Her eyes lit up. "But I have a secret, and that's why I am here!" She went on to say that she had a boyfriend of her own and she wanted to lose weight so he would be happy with her. She met him online. He lived in Georgia, and they had been exchanging texts and pictures for several months. They wouldn't be able to meet in person until the summer, five months away. "And I can't have him seeing me like this!"

"First, we need to talk about the pros and cons of meeting people online. How do you know that he is who he says he is?"

"We FaceTime or Zoom. He says that I have a pretty face. He's taken me on a virtual tour of his house, shown me his bedroom, and introduced me to his mother. I'm not stupid. When he comes, I will meet him at my home when my parents are around."

"How do your parents feel about you meeting him this way?"

"They didn't say much at all. They're just happy I met someone. They're not too savvy about social media. But I insisted that they be home when he shows up."

"One last question. It sounds like he likes you the way you are. Why go changing things now?"

"You are asking me this? You, the guy who has told me I needed to lose weight at every visit for the last five years? You should be happy that I want to do this at all, even if I am doing it for what you will call the wrong reason."

"I just want to help you be as healthy as possible. And I don't want you to get taken advantage of by a stranger."

"I can take care of myself."

We worked with a nutritionist on Dierdre's weight loss plan. The first ten pounds came off quickly, but she needed to lose forty more, and those didn't budge. As the summer approached, Dierdre grew increasingly anxious. "I'm gonna tell him not to come."

I tried to reassure her, "He likes you! And you have lost ten pounds!"

Dierdre pulled her phone out of her back pocket. "He is in love with this!" She showed me a picture of a younger, thinner version of herself in a beautiful summer dress. "Not this!" she gestured down at her body. Bursting into tears, she confessed, "I catfished him—with a picture of my little sister. If he comes up here, he will fall for her!"

Catfishing, a scamming phenomenon made possible by our digital ecosystem, involves using a false online persona to lure someone into a relationship, which might be romantic, sexual, or friendly. In Dierdre's case, she used a photo of her sister. Deirdre didn't think of herself as a scammer. She was a lonely teen who did not feel good about herself trying to connect romantically with someone. When she realized it was impossible to continue the deception, she confessed to the boy. Although it was painful for her and a shock to the boy with whom she was connecting, she was able to resolve it by making a video call and stepping back from the camera so he could see her whole body and meet the real Dierdre. "He was not mad; he was sad that I lied to him," she told me. "We are going to keep in touch, but he's not coming up here to visit."

As embarrassing and hopes-dashing as her experience was, Dierdre was lucky. Other catfishing cases have not been so benign. Hearts have been broken, reputations have been damaged, and in the worst cases, children and their families have gotten caught up in extortion, murder, and suicide. The common thread in all cases is a lonely individual who is targeted online by someone who seeks to exploit the person's desire to connect in order to take advantage of them financially or sexually or to gain social control over them.

Middle-aged men have pretended to be teenage girls and posted provocative selfies to attract teen boys to meet them—and some have. Online predators, often from outside the US, have monetized catfishing for financial extortion or sextortion, using sexy selfies of attractive nude females to encourage teen boys to sext them back. When the boys send the requested "dick pics," the catfish asks for $500–1,000 or they will send the boys' explicit pictures to their entire contacts list. More than seven thousand sextortion cases with over three thousand victims had been reported in the US as of December 2022.[27] Most victims are fourteen- to seventeen-year-old boys, but some cases have involved children as young as ten.[28] More than a dozen teen boys, feeling trapped by sextortion schemes that demanded amounts of money they could not pay, have committed suicide, sometimes within hours of initial contact by the sextortionist.[29] Their parents had no idea of what was happening to their sons because the boys, embarrassed and ashamed, did not share their digital lives.

A fifteen-year-old girl developed an online relationship with someone she believed to be a seventeen-year-old boy. The catfish, a twenty-eight-year-old police officer, obtained her personal information and drove from Virginia to her family's home in Riverside, California. Confronted by her mother and grandparents, he killed them, set the home on fire, and kidnapped the girl. When cornered by police, he killed himself, and the girl was rescued. "If something like this can happen here, in our neighborhood, it can happen anywhere," said the girl's aunt.[30] "Please, parents! When you are talking to your children about the dangers of their online actions, please use us as a reference. Tell our story to help your parenting. Not out of fear, but out of example of something that did happen."[31] Riverside Police Chief Larry Gonzalez put it bluntly: "This is yet another horrific reminder of the predators existing online who prey on our children. If you've already had a conversation with your kids on how to be safe online and on social media, have it again. If not, start it now to better protect them."[32]

A few weeks after the Riverside tragedy, Robin Abcarian, a columnist for the *Los Angeles Times* who was raising a then twelve-year-old niece, wrote that she and other parents remained deeply shaken. "I am spending a lot of time these days pondering how to balance my niece's privacy with the lengths to which I need to go to keep her safe. . . . I have decided to be a hard-ass.

Her iPad belongs to me, I remind her. I have the passwords to her accounts, and I look at them regularly to keep tabs on her online activities." When her niece asked indignantly whether Abcarian was looking at her messages, she said, "Yes, I am," adding, "I probably will until I feel confident that you understand that bad things can happen to kids who are too trusting online. You aren't there yet."[33]

As intrusive as it may seem, your continued mentoring and monitoring of your child's activities in the digital ecosystem remains important. Parents may resist the idea because they don't have the time to monitor all of their children's activities. Children fight it because they don't want to be spied on. But if a precondition of having these powerful devices and apps is that their parent has the capability of randomly checking in, and that condition, like seat belts and bicycle helmets, is nonnegotiable, children will accept it. Keeping the door of communication and oversight open will encourage your tween or teen to behave online in ways that will preserve their access to digital devices. It will also allow them to tell anyone seeking contact after hours or pressing them for photos, for information, or to meet up that their mom or dad (or other adult) monitors their social media. And you'll have the advantage of staying engaged with the whole of your child's life during a stage when many parents and their teens adrift apart.

ASK THE MEDIATRICIAN
How Can I Block Sexual Content from My Fifteen-Year-Old's Devices?

What is the best way to block websites with sexual content that appear in web searches on my fifteen-year-old's devices? The built-in controls are a blunt instrument and block too much or all content. I want him to be able to use the internet, but I am freaked out by what he is accessing.

As you're finding, software controls aren't very effective at blocking sexual content. They may allow unwanted sites that are creatively named while blocking healthy sites about, say, breast cancer awareness. Even if the software were more effective, if your son wants to get around it, he will. That's why the best "software" for protecting your son is the knowledge in his head, knowledge that you can help him acquire.

First, know that it's natural and healthy for him—and girls too—to be curious about sex. But as you have found, the world of sex online can be a minefield. The images there are likely to be unrealistic and dehumanizing, treating sex as a commodity—as something to buy and sell rather than an intimate expression of love and trust. That can affect a child's understanding of sex and sexual behavior.

That's where you come in. As a parent, you can direct your son toward online information that will support him in developing positive sexuality (check out scarleteen.com). You can also help him interpret the negative portrayals he sees online by having a candid conversation with him. Ask questions like, "What is really going on there?" "How do you think that makes her feel?" and "Is that the kind of relationship you want to have?"

Video games and online gaming communities offer an excellent basis for conversation along these lines, as they typically feature characters with hypersexualized physical features and the dialogue often targets female players or characters with sexually aggressive moves or comments. Research on the psychosocial impact of this environment on players has been limited and yielded mixed results. The consensus that more and better research is needed underscores the importance of your child recognizing that their personal experience is what matters most. They alone know how any online or social media experience makes them feel and think about themselves—and about others, both in the gaming environment and in real life.

Approach this as an opportunity to parent your son in his seamless physical-digital world. The more that his sexual education is part of an ongoing, open, and nonjudgmental conversation with you, the better the chance that he will grow up to be an adult who is able to have a respectful, committed, mutually caring, and trusting relationship with a significant other.

MEDIA Rx
Make It Safe to Talk About Sex and Sexuality, Gender, and Relationships

We can no longer afford the luxury of squeamishness or denial. Since sex is a dominant feature of today's media landscape, especially for adolescents (and the preteens who aspire to adolescence), we need to shift our focus from trying to shield our children from all negative content (impossible) to teaching them how to best handle the content to which they are inevitably exposed.

- The best "software" for protecting your child against harmful content is between your child's ears.
- The best "hardware" is your dining room table, where they can go online while remaining present in the family circle.
- Model, mentor, and monitor them well. Be present in their digital life, and keep the lines of communication open.
- Your proactive digital parenting can trigger outsized reactions from other kids' parents, especially if you ask them what media the kids will be using at the other house.
- Be an effective advocate for your child and others with a more reasoned, compassionate response that understands the strengths and limitations of their developmental stage. These conversations need to be had, and had frequently, as your child grows up and the digital landscape evolves.

Relax. You can do this. While many families have different values regarding sex, it is best to build this conversation on what we know about how exposure to sexual material in media affects children's knowledge, attitudes, and behaviors around sex. Your values and moral standards can be introduced once you have your child's trusting ear. Leading with negativity, warnings, and fear will shut down the conversation and, ironically perhaps, make that which you are warning about much more attractive to your child. Do your best to avoid embarrassing your child or yourself. Our society has a double standard when it comes to sex. We are intrigued by and attracted to sex so much that it is a commonly used advertising tool—but we also feel that it should be hidden away and treated as shameful.

YOU CAN

- *Talk with your child about relationships and sex early, often, and in a matter-of-fact way.* Children are curious about their bodies and ask where babies come from as young as their toddler years. Respond to their questions openly and in a scientifically matter-of-fact way. If you talk about sex and sexuality as a normal, healthy human activity before it has become eroticized for them, you make yourself approachable to discuss relationships and their developing sexuality as they grow older.
- *Be alert for your child's questions or concerns.* Keep an eye on your child's media use for developmentally optimal content. If they see or hear something they didn't expect or that upsets or confuses them, talk with them about it right away. This allows you to define how they manage and interpret the content.
- *Help your child develop a critical eye toward sexualized content.* It's important to help your child identify, deconstruct, and challenge sexual content as it is portrayed by screen media, from children's television to video games to sex in popular movies to online pornography. By helping children see that on-screen relationships and sexual behaviors may be unrealistic, disrespectful, or unhealthy and often ignore the consequences of these behaviors, they will be less likely to accept what they see or hear as a model for how they should behave.
- *Watch what you're watching—because your child is.* Be aware of what *you* are watching and/or playing when your child is present, and make sure that they can manage the content. Know that even if your child may not understand it, the sexual information may still influence them. Many music videos, song lyrics, TV shows, video games, and magazines contain glamorized, stereotypical, or unhealthy sexual images and behaviors that may negatively impact their views on sex, love, and relationships.

- *Pay attention to the attitudes and behaviors portrayed in the screen media your child uses and the music they listen to.* Be open-minded, not judgy, or they will shut you down. They will make fun of you, and that is OK, because secretly they are pleased that you are paying respectful attention to them and their interests. Talk with them about what they see and hear when it comes to relationships and sex. Co-viewing or listening together can often jump-start discussions with your kids about media portrayals of sex and consequences of sexual behavior. Remember that one of the best times for these discussions is when you are in the car, alone and together with no interruptions (phones off) and belted in so you do not have to look at each other.

- *Talk about issues of privacy and the fact that privacy does not exist on social media.* Anything they text or post can be shared instantly and publicly—and may be used to humiliate or exploit them or others. Talk about respecting themselves and others online and what they can do when they see hurtful behavior by others.

- *Talk explicitly about pornography, scammers, catfishing, and sexploitation.* No one wants to be manipulated—including your child. Kids need to be aware of the sophisticated ways that people intent on exploiting them will continue to get around measures designed to safeguard kids. This now includes AI-generated nude images incorporating elements of real kids' digital photos and used to create graphic sexual images for porn sites or personal exploitation.[34] Kids have got to protect themselves—and that begins with keeping you in the loop and keeping a tight lid on their personal information and images. Assure them that you understand how they might be sexploited and that you will not ever be angry with them but will do everything you can to protect them, no matter what the image is that is being used to shame and manipulate them. Keep up-to-date with and share with them the fact-based information available on the Digital Wellness Lab site (digitalwellnesslab.org) and other resources listed there.

- *Know what they are creating and sharing online.* Teach them that they are creating a digital footprint that represents them to the outside world. Remind them of the "Grandma Rule"—don't post anything online that you don't want Grandma to see.
- *Facts matter.* When they are ready to hear you, provide factual information about safe sex and emotionally healthy relationships from reliable sources. Tap reliable online sites for materials that you can view together.
- *Use media content as conversation starters.* Portrayals of relationships, sex, sexuality, and gender diversity can be springboards for discussing difficult subjects about other people in a way that is less uncomfortable than talking about oneself.
- *Keep the lines of communication open no matter what.* You want your child to know that they can come to you with any questions or concerns about puberty, sex, sexual orientation, pregnancy, STIs, contraception, or sexual assault.

Ultimately, what is most important is that you do everything you can to support and guide your child to grow into a healthy and whole adult. Sexual curiosity is a normal part of development, and it's how they will figure out healthy adult behavior when they're ready. Finally, remember that what you do is even more important than what you say, so if you are in a relationship, be sure to model a healthy, mutually respectful romantic relationship for your child, the kind of relationship that you want them to have when they grow up.

The Coming-of-Age Quest—To Be Continued

The internet's accessibility, affordability, and perceived anonymity make it a natural place for adolescents to go with their curiosity about sex and explorations of relationships. Driven by strong emotions and powerful hormones relatively unconstrained by executive function, teenagers need enough freedom to venture beyond the known in relative safety. Learning to live in the physical-digital world is a critical passage toward successful adulthood.

Staying present as their parent and role model is the single most important key to their learning.

In the iconic 1985 teen movie *The Breakfast Club*, five high school students are assigned to detention for a day. In close quarters, the teens' angsty conversations and gradual emotional disclosures change the way they see themselves and each other as their stereotypes and assumptions crumble, replaced by greater authenticity. In an assigned essay to the principal at the end of the detention, they push back against stereotyping. "You see us as you want to see us, in the simplest terms, the most convenient definitions," they write, "but what we found out is that each one of us is a brain, and an athlete, and a basket case, a princess, and a criminal."[35]

Our kids need to experience that authenticity with one another and with the wider world. To the extent that their media use supports their efforts to take first steps and then develop and maintain more authentic relationships, it serves them well.

Social media is not inherently toxic. Used in mindful and authentic ways, social media can serve as an important transitional space as your child learns how to express their romantic or sexual interest in someone. But online interaction is something that is healthy to move *through* and not live in forever. Interactive media can make reaching out to another person, being open to them, and showing affection more comfortable—but it's not the final stop. It's a way station on their journey to a more intimate and meaningful relationship.

Chapter 6

The Teachable Moment

All Media Are Educational—What Is Your Child Learning?

I t was *awesome!*"

"It was anything but!"

"C'mon, Mom! I completed the 900 and almost landed it! That jerk Serge just talks about it, but he's never even tried it."

Mom just sagged into the chair beside the exam table in the hospital's emergency department. Will kept talking a mile a minute about his skateboarding exploits. "That's why everyone calls him 'Won't'! The opposite of me! 'Cause he just talks smack and never does any of the challenges! And I"—he puffed out his chest even as I was trying to suture up the muscle layer of his calf—"Will!"

The fourteen-year-old was talking about the challenges that his friend group, all skateboarders, had learned from a popular video game. Will had always been something of a daredevil. He broke his leg jumping off the back of the couch as a two-year-old. At nine, he had gotten sick to his stomach in a worm-eating contest. At twelve, he skied off the roof of the log cabin in Maine where his family went for winter vacation. Now he and his friends were totally into skateboarding. When they weren't perfecting their tricks, they were playing a skateboarding video game—and trying the tricks from the game the next time they went out. The problem was that when they wiped out doing the more extreme tricks from the video game, there was a quick splatter of cartoon blood, then their avatar jumped back on the board to try it again. It didn't work that way in the vacant lot where they skated. When Will missed his landing on the board, it shot out from under him, flipping him upside down, and he landed on a partially collapsed chain-link fence, lacerating his calf.

In pediatrics, we often speak of the "teachable moment." When a child falls off their bike and scrapes their knee, we take the opportunity to encourage wearing a helmet. Children are most likely to learn prevention when they seek treatment for the preventable. In pediatric practice, we don't just respond after an injury. At each annual wellness checkup, we include anticipatory guidance, looking forward with the child and their parent to their next stage of development and how to stay healthy—car seats and safe cribs for infants, seat belts and bike helmets as they grow older, sleep and balanced nutrition throughout. Pediatricians are good at anticipating and preventing physical harm. But even when we see boys hurt themselves practicing wrestling moves or girls starving themselves to look like fashion models, we are less likely to help them avoid behavioral health problems by becoming critical of what they view on screens.

Why is that? Because our culture draws a false distinction between education and entertainment. We believe that children learn important skills and useful information in school, so we invest significant public and personal resources and focus our attention on schools. We see the screen media that children and adolescents consume for most of their waking hours as entertainment, relaxing downtime for their brains. That's not wholly true. Relaxing, perhaps. But the learning brain doesn't take time off. Children are constantly learning about the world, how they fit into it, and how they should behave. For them, every moment is a teachable moment.

And the screens in our world are powerful teachers. We do not even need to be paying attention to them for us to learn from them. Screens are everywhere—in almost every room of our homes and public spaces, in stores and on billboards, in our pockets and on our wrists. Screens are the backdrop to everyday life and often in the foreground with our attention fixed on our phones and computers. With the emergent metaverse, the online interactive space negotiated by virtual reality (VR) and augmented reality (AR), the boundaries of the screen dissolve and media content becomes even more present, constant, and immersive. For VR and AR, you wear an audiovisual headset that covers your eyes and ears to deliver an immersive three-dimensional "reality" that in the case of VR is entirely created and in the case of AR is a blend of the created with the physical world. As you turn your head and look up and down, the image and sound move with you as if you were in that altered reality. While these immersive screen experiences are still in their awkward and expensive infancy in the first quarter of the twenty-first century, they will evolve quickly and be succeeded by as-yet-unimagined audiovisual technology. Whatever technology is delivering our information stream, screen media portray select curated images and sounds of the world beyond our direct experience, shaping our perceptions of that world and setting expectations of the ways that we should behave in it. In a time when screens are so ubiquitous in our lives that it is difficult to determine the number of hours we are engaged, it is important to pay attention to *what* we are watching and how that might be influencing our behavior.

━━━━ ━━━ ━━

Both of Larry's parents accompanied him to his annual physical the summer before his freshman year of high school. Always very involved with their children, they were excited about this new phase of his life. Larry had good grades in middle school and was looking forward to greater choice and difficulty of courses as he prepared for college. He thought he wanted to be an architect or engineer. He had really gotten into building things since his computer science teacher introduced his class to *Minecraft*, the massively multiplayer online game. A soccer goalkeeper, Larry had been asked to start practicing with the varsity team two weeks before school started. Asked whether they had any concerns about Larry's health, his parents couldn't think of anything at first. But when we were wrapping up so I could talk privately with and examine Larry, his dad, as he was leaving the room, said, "I don't know if this is anything, but Larry has stopped walking the dog. I know it's just an annoyance that I have to do it, but he loves that dog and has walked her since he was eight. He started resisting it, sometimes really aggressively, about four months ago and now we can't make him do it, even when the dog really has to go!" Once the door closed behind them, I looked at Larry, who looked away.

"What's going on?" I asked.

"Nothing."

"So is it true that you won't walk your dog?" I asked, indicating that he should take off his shirt and pants and climb onto the exam table.

"Yeah, but Dad does it."

"Why did you stop?"

"I don't know. I had school activities or soccer practice or was hanging out with my friends."

"Even when you are at home in the evening?"

"Then I have homework."

"But you had homework when you were walking the dog before."

"Yeah, but I was kind of naïve then. I wasn't aware of the danger."

I put my stethoscope in my ears and started listening to his chest.

"It seems like everyone carries a gun and there's a shooting every day," he said.

"In your neighborhood?"

"Somewhere."

Larry stopped talking so I could hear his breath sounds. When we resumed conversation, he revealed that he was increasingly anxious about his safety and when he walked the dog, especially after dark, he felt that he was in danger. Our conversation drifted to other subjects, such as what he had been doing this summer and what he did for fun.

"The usual stuff—going to the pool, hanging out with friends, playing video games."

"Oh, what games do you play?"

"*Minecraft* still. *Roblox.* And *Fortnite.* My friends and I hang out there now."

"When did you start playing *Fortnite*?"

"Last spring when everybody else did."

That was shortly before Larry stopped walking the dog. In *Fortnite*'s most popular free game, the player is dropped onto an island with as many as ninety-nine others. As in *The Hunger Games*, the goal is to be the last person alive. It's kill or be killed. While there has been much focus on whether violent video games can contribute to aggression in youth, in Larry's case—playing a game where danger could be lurking behind every bush or building—it triggered anxiety.

And it is not just games; any screen media, especially television news, can increase our anxiety. One of the lessons of 9/11 was how profoundly our sense of security and safety was rocked by watching commercial airliners flown into and bringing down the Twin Towers of New York's World Trade Center. Concerned about how children would respond to what we had all witnessed, I and several colleages at Boston Children's Hospital offered counseling to families in our community. What we found was unexpected—immediately comforting, but in the long run deeply concerning. For the most part, children were not as fearful and traumatized by the televised horror as their parents were. From cartoons to movie ads, they had seen worse on television. Even very young children were desensitized by screen violence. It was feeling their parents' fear that had built the children's anxiety.

Today, videos of mass shootings from schools to supermarkets to bowling alleys repeatedly traumatize children, families, and communities. Now these events are captured by people with smartphones on the scene, people just like them who happened to be in the everyday place where a terrifying event occurred. And now children and adolescents are not seeing these events at home, surrounded by their family, but alone, on their smartphones, in near real-time and very similar locations. This brings the terrifying potential closer and ratchets up their anxiety. From Little Red Riding Hood in Germany to Lon Po Po in China, there have historically been cautionary tales of the danger that befalls children who stray. Now, just as children who are cyberbullied can never feel safe, today's parents and children have become helpless witnesses through ever-present screens to constant breaking news stories of a proverbial "wolf" just around the corner from any child, regardless of their behavior. And our response is to become more vigilant, more attentive to the news, accelerating our vicious cycle of anxiety.

The Educational, Entertaining "Elsewhere"

More than a decade before television became the electronic hearth of American homes in the 1950s, E. B. White wrote, "Television will enormously enlarge the eye's range, and, like radio, will advertise the Elsewhere . . . it will insist that we forget the primary and the near in favor of the secondary and the remote."[1] Indeed, more than a half century later, 9/11 happened not just to New York City, but to the world—as we watched live.

In 1938 when White wrote this, television broadcasting was still experimental, limited, and sporadic. Television sets were not yet being sold to the public. By 1962, when nearly 90 percent of American homes had one or more of fifty-two million televisions,[2] Newton Minow, chairman of the Federal Communications Commission (FCC), assessed "Television and the Public

Interest" in his first speech to the National Association of Broadcasters.[3] "When television is good, nothing—not the theater, not the magazines or newspapers—nothing is better. But when television is bad, nothing is worse. . . . Keep your eyes glued to that set. . . . I can assure you that what you will observe is a vast wasteland."[4] It seemed that with the explosive growth of commercial television in the US, White's pessimistic view had prevailed.

The 1960s were a decade of great change in the US, and television reflected and affected that change. Congress aggressively debated taxpayer-supported public television as an alternative. On May 1, 1969, Fred Rogers (whom we know affectionately as "Mr. Rogers") testified to the Senate Subcommittee on Communications. Speaking gently to the self-described "tough guy" chairman, Senator John Pastore, Mr. Rogers shared how he bade farewell to child viewers in signing off from his bare-bones show: "You've made this day a special day, by just your being you. There's no person in the whole world like you, and I like you just the way you are."[5]

To the committee, he continued, "I feel that if we in public television can only make it clear that feelings are mentionable and manageable, we will have done a great service for mental health."[6] Those words resonated powerfully with the hard-bitten politician. "It's the first time I've had goosebumps for the last two days," Pastore said.[7] Those words resonate as strongly today. In the tumultuous and conflict-filled 1960s, Fred Rogers gently confronted racism, war, divorce, and death in ways that helped children feel safe and loved while acknowledging hard realities. "Always look for the helpers," he said. "You will always find people who are helping."[8] Mr. Rogers taught us that lessons in how to be human can, with courage, start early and never grow old. And he did it through a television screen.

Just six months after Mr. Rogers secured funding for public television, content took a new turn down *Sesame Street*, where children always found a "sunny day, sweeping the clouds away."[9] This now iconic educational program had been in development for several years, supported by foundations, but public affirmation and government support allowed *Sesame Street* to be realized in a pilot episode. Where Mr. Rogers, a minister and musician whom many have described as a modern-day saint, connected directly to the hearts of children, *Sesame Street* was the product of years of deep research in child development, education, and psychology. Joan Ganz Cooney, an Emmy-winning documentary producer, teamed up with experimental psychologist

Lloyd Morrisett to develop a television show aimed at preschool children that would "master the addictive qualities of television and do something good with them."[10] Realizing that 95 percent of American homes had televisions and that engaging commercials had children singing beer jingles, they believed that television could use its unique draw to educate the many young children who did not have access to preschool.

Advised by Dr. Gerald Lesser, a professor at Harvard Graduate School of Education (and one of my mentors), developmental psychologists, scriptwriters, and educators worked with puppeteers to create another childhood neighborhood where kids learned letters, numbers, and most robustly, about living in a diverse and imperfect community with tolerance and understanding.[11] The Children's Television Workshop, as it was then called, did formative research to create programs intended to teach specific lessons. Once the programs aired, the Children's Television Workshop educators did summative research to see whether and how well they taught what was intended.[12] *Sesame Street* was a neighborhood of adults, children, and puppets of all colors, sizes, ages, and abilities who worked together to understand and solve problems that ranged from sounding out a word to recycling to resolving conflicts.

ASK THE MEDIATRICIAN
Is It OK for My Toddler to Binge on a *Sesame Street* Movie?

What are the consequences of my child watching the same children's movie over and over? It's a Sesame Street *movie, and it's only about one hour long, so it's not commercial television or a computer. But my daughter is two-and-a-half, and she would be happy to watch this twice a day! We usually watch it together and sing and play along, so it's not passive watching. But still—is all this repetition OK?*

Your daughter is right at the age at which she can really start to learn from watching television and videos. Do not worry; it is developmentally normal for her to want to watch the same movie over and over (and over and over) again—that's how she masters the material. The scenario you described is probably working well for your daughter for a few reasons:

1. *Sesame Street* content is developed to support prosocial learning. Part of what your daughter is seeking to master is an understanding of how communities function and how people interact within them. *Sesame Street* portrays a community where people and puppets from different religions, cultures, races, and species have formed a successful, dynamic society. And in fact, research has found that many children who watch *Sesame Street* exhibit gains in prosocial behavior and self-esteem, as well as in academic readiness and achievement.[13]

2. You are watching with your child. She learns from what she watches not only by processing what she sees but, more importantly, by processing it with you. You help her make sense of the content in ways that are unique to her and what interests her.

3. You are interacting with the material. By dancing and singing along with the movie, you help your daughter's learning move beyond skills and drills and to reflective thinking and complex communication. You are using the movie as a catalyst for the kinds of interactions and lessons you want her to learn.

In short, you are co-viewing developmentally optimal programming with your daughter in ways that encourage her to interact with the material and with you—and that is likely to have a positive effect on your daughter's academic and social skills. Just remember to make sure that it doesn't keep her from the other important activities in her day, like sleep, meals without screens, and free, unstructured play.

Parents often ask me about educational programming: What is good and what is bad? My answer starts with a simple clarification. The idea that media are either good or bad, education or diversion, is a false dichotomy. It ignores two essential facts. First, children are learning all the time and from everything they encounter. Second, content that connects with their minds and their hearts as well as their senses will hold their attention and be remembered. Once their brains have developed enough to decode what is happening on-screen, children learn as much from the media they watch and listen to as they do from formal education. They learn from all the media they consume—not just programs or products labeled "educational." In fact, the concept of educational media is redundant. *All* media are educational. The only difference is what they teach and how well they teach it for the developmental stage of your child.

Fred Rogers understood this. Within the imaginary home and neighborhood of the studio, he welcomed preschool children into his living room with songs, visited and chatted with neighborhood friends, took his young viewers on field trips to farms or factories, performed simple science experiments, and created playful craft projects. Mr. Rogers would look directly out of the screen at children, speaking softly and gently in a deliberate and slow-paced cadence. This technique allowed him to model caring social behavior and to tackle issues that children struggle with, like how to deal with anger, disagreements, or the death of a pet. When the evening news featured deadly battles in Vietnam and a motel owner throwing acid in his swimming pool because Black people were using it, Mr. Rogers invited Officer Clemmons, a Black man, to cool his feet side by side in a wading pool, drying the policeman's feet with his own towel.[14] Mr. Rogers understood that young children are not little adults but unique individuals whose developmental tasks are to become social beings, to channel their primal instincts, to get along with others, and to build the world of the future. *Mister Rogers' Neighborhood* may have been deadly boring for adults, but it was hugely popular with children, who felt safe, respected, and cared for. And they remembered the lessons learned into adulthood. Fred Rogers was asked by many former viewers, on graduating college, to give their commencement addresses. What he offered, more than forty times, was the same message he had given them nearly two decades earlier. "It's not the honors and the prizes, and the fancy outsides of life which ultimately nourish our souls. It's the knowing that we can be trusted."[15]

All media intended as learning tools should be evaluated by how well they help your child learn what they need now and develop both knowledge and soft skills for the future. Only a few "educational" videos, apps, and games have done rigorous research to evaluate what and how well they teach. There are key questions for parents to ask about media labeled as educational. What is it teaching your child about the world and the relationships among those who inhabit the world? About how to relate to others? About how to be the best version of themselves?

ASK THE MEDIATRICIAN
How Can I Find Quality Television Shows for
My Seven-Year-Old Granddaughter?

My daughter has been frustrated by the shows my granddaughter currently watches, as she believes the female characters treat each other cruelly. My daughter is starting to see my granddaughter becoming competitive with and critical of her friends. She's concerned about how these "mean girl" portrayals affect her daughter. How can she guide her daughter to choose healthier shows, and how can she influence what is presented on television?

These questions are ones with which many parents struggle when searching for developmentally optimal content that features positive, inspiring role models with whom their children can relate. The issue becomes more apparent when specifically looking for positive portrayals of women and girls in children's media, as female characters have historically been underplayed or portrayed as weak, sexualized, mean-spirited, or competitive with other females. Research has repeatedly shown that these portrayals of female characters can negatively influence how girls view their bodies and gender roles, yet even today, these negative stereotypes persist in many movies and television shows.[16]

You and your daughter are not alone in wanting to guide your granddaughter toward media that will be enlightening, empowering, and uplifting for her. There are many practical steps you can take when seeking and selecting media for your granddaughter:

- *Look for regularly updated resources.* Check out sources such as A Mighty Girl (amightygirl.com), which provides users with descriptive listings of media that bolster girls' self-esteem and intelligence and foster their curiosity to learn.
- *Ask an expert—and go local if you can.* Many local libraries have DVD sections. Children's librarians can be a valuable resource when it comes to choosing a television series or movie that will best fit your granddaughter's needs.

- *Do your research and choose girl-positive shows.* Read reviews, get advice from other parents and caregivers, and explore the "Kids" guidance from streaming services, such as Netflix, Disney+, Hulu, and Apple TV+. Assess what a program's typical content might be: Stereotyped cartoons? Catty sitcoms? Positive, empowering stories? Choose to watch shows and networks/streaming services that make conscious choices to support children's social emotional learning as part of their mission, such as PBS Kids.

In terms of the current content your daughter is finding, remember that broadcast and streaming video is a business, and businesses depend on consumers to survive. Your daughter and granddaughter represent those customers. Broadcasters and streaming services are selling either subscriptions to viewers or viewers' attention to advertisers. Either way, their business depends on consumers to view their programming and come back for more. If there are shows that your daughter believes may harm your granddaughter, she (and you) can write to the producers, distributers, and broadcasters to say, "We will not be watching this show anymore." Believe it or not, very few people write to creators and providers of television content, so even a single letter can make a difference.

Your daughter can follow up by discussing, respectfully and compassionately, with your granddaughter her concern that watching those shows may harm the child's developing brain (just as she might explain why her daughter shouldn't drink alcohol at age seven). When we watch any show, we are not just condoning but actively encouraging producers to make more shows like it. Your granddaughter's understanding of how she is affected can make her an ally with her mom, ensuring that she will avoid viewing shows that diminish her at home and anywhere she goes. And she will spread the word to her friends, and they will spread the word, and so on. Producers will follow the market, so the best way to stop unhealthy media content is to increase their cost with pushback via letters and decrease their earnings because your daughter, and other parents like her, will just turn it off.

Media-Based Learning Put to the Test

Watching high-quality educational television can help children with their ability to reason, perform tasks, plan, and solve problems.[17] Preschoolers who watch evidence-based educational programming develop more pre-reading and pre-math skills, are more ready for school, and are more tolerant of others when they begin school. Studies of teens who had watched *Sesame Street* showed that they read more, had higher grades, placed more value on achievement, were more creative, and were less aggressive compared to peers who watched entertainment programming during their preschool years.[18] It must be acknowledged that, in this case, watching *Sesame Street* as a preschooler likely did not cause these outcomes but rather is one marker of a host of parental decisions that exposed the child to learning opportunities through their lives.

Because *Mister Rogers' Neighborhood* and *Sesame Street* have been trusted and effective teachers for more than fifty years, television producers and later software developers realized that if they labeled their content as educational, parents would feel that they were helping their children by providing it to them. The success of *Sesame* Street has resulted from their rigorous before-and-after research and their understanding that effective education includes both academics and social emotional learning. In the 1990s, when the Children's Television Act required broadcasters to air three hours of educational programming each week, producers scrambled to label a wide variety of their existing and planned content as educational. Some programs, based in educational science and developmental psychology, were done well. Many more labeled themselves as educational in an attempt to cash in on parents who wanted to feel less guilty for using television as an electronic babysitter.[19] But few programs delivered the educational value they claimed. Commercial "educational" programming frequently had product marketing embedded in the content, whether through branded toy characters, brand placement, or portraying consumer behaviors or preferences that encouraged sales. Content producers discovered that parents did not need research to convince them of the program's educational value; they would take the producers' word for it. While there are educational television shows, apps, and other media that have been well-researched and do, in fact, help preschoolers learn, be aware of "educational" marketing claims, as these claims are unregulated and often not supported by science. Remembering that children are always learning, how well children learn from screen media is not the only factor parents should consider. *What* they learn matters even more.

After several decades in which *Mister Rogers' Neighborhood* and *Sesame Street* were joined on the airwaves by dozens of shows targeting early childhood, psychologist David Walsh demonstrated the immediate effects of viewing a television show on young viewers' behavior. He filmed a class of preschoolers watching *Barney and Friends* and then *Power Rangers*, now classic children's shows that first aired in the early 1990s. *Barney* was all about friendship, fun, and warm fuzzies—a virtual celebration of prosocial behavior. *Power Rangers* was superhero action featuring youth with superpowers battling evil forces. In Walsh's study, after watching *Barney*, the children marched and sang together, keeping rhythm with maracas. After *Power Rangers*, the same children exuberantly pushed and kicked each other, hitting each other with the maracas.[20] The concept of using violence for a good cause was missed. Instead, they learned the visceral excitement of violence. The dramatic short-term influence of these two shows on preschoolers demonstrated how children watch and learn. They learned to sing from *Barney*. They learned to prevail through force from *Power Rangers*. Since behaviors appeared to change in positive and negative ways after viewing *Barney and Friends* and *Power Rangers*, the big question that we need to ask is: Can harmful or risky behaviors be learned from screen media?

ASK THE MEDIATRICIAN
How Do I Manage a Rough and Rowdy Boy?

I am a second-grade teacher who has seen my share of rowdy, rambunctious seven- and eight-year-olds. I love their energy, but what I don't love and don't quite know how to deal with is one boy whose behavior scares me. He is big, has a lot of energy, and is quite creative in his play scenarios. His classmates are drawn to him on the playground, but he throws them to the ground again and again, sometimes jumping off the playground equipment on top of them. It does not seem to be bullying because they jump up laughing and rush at him again. I am worried someone will get hurt. When I met with this child's parents, they said they had never seen similar behavior with his younger siblings. "He's too tired to do anything when he comes home from school. Most of the time he curls up on the couch and watches TV with his dad." When I asked what they watched, his father said, "The Three Stooges. *Professional wrestling." Am I right to be concerned about this boy's rowdy behavior?*

You are right to be concerned about your student's unsafe behavior with his classmates. You are also right in sensing that this is not necessarily bullying because the smaller boys appear to enjoy the attention, but it may be culturally learned toxic masculinity. One research study found that even well-behaved elementary school students became more violent, even imitating unique moves, after watching wrestling on TV.[21] Another found that children learn that cheating and verbal intimidation are acceptable and effective problem-solving techniques from watching pro wrestling.[22] Research has shown that adolescents who watch professional wrestling are significantly more likely to be involved in fights and dating violence; to carry, threaten, or hurt others with weapons; and to engage in risky behaviors, from substance abuse to sex.[23]

Dramatic moves like throwing someone to the ground are show-pieces of dominance and swagger in professional wrestling. While your student is likely demonstrating his dominance, his classmates appear to enjoy it. (Don't expect them to think about power dynamics or anticipate the risk of injury.) Professional wrestling and slapstick comedy like *The Three Stooges* present violent behavior as entertaining and funny. Violence combined with pleasurable feelings, such as swagger, sex, or laughter, has been shown to have the greatest influence on viewers' learned behaviors.[24] The ability to distinguish fantasy from reality does not develop until the age of seven or eight, the age of your students. Kids younger than that will say they know it's only make-believe, but they cannot readily distinguish risk-free, fun, fake violence from real violence that can hurt them. When violence is portrayed in media as exciting or funny, as it is in professional wrestling and *The Three Stooges*, it is seen by children as normal, even desirable, human behavior, which it is not.

Seeking to engage young viewers more actively in learning from screens, programs like *Dora the Explorer* and *Blue's Clues* ask questions of their young viewers rather than serving them predigested answers. Even though they are on the receptive-only television screen, these programs were not designed to be passively consumed but rather ask the children to answer questions and solve problems. Children enthusiastically shout out their answers to the unresponsive television, but these early forays into interactive edutainment laid the groundwork for educational technology.

Enthusiasm for learning with interactive media coincided with the trend toward increasing recreational screen time that had been underway since the turn of the millennium.[25] With the introduction of mobile devices like tablets and smartphones, total screen time for children of all ages increased for three reasons:

1. Small devices, intuitively controlled with touch screens, made it possible for even toddlers to independently view and play, so interactive media use was initiated earlier in life. Instead of circumscribed television viewing times controlled by parents, very young children could go online to watch videos and play games. Relieved parents took advantage of their child's self-sufficient abilities, using mobile devices as a pacifier of tantrums and a convenient distraction while waiting for meals.[26] Unfortunately, research has shown that these short-term behavioral solutions have long-term implications.[27]

2. Separate, portable screen devices that young people used to switch-task between two or more screens simultaneously increased their cumulative screen exposure. Kids could watch television with distant friends while talking to each other via text or do homework while watching a sporting event and listening to music. As we've seen in earlier chapters, multitasking is a myth. Switching from one idea to another takes cognitive energy and time to recover what we were thinking previously. Each time we switch, we add to the overall time that each task takes, we suffer losses in interrupted trains of thought, and because we are skating over the surface of each idea instead of thinking deeply about it, we do not retain or learn all that we could. Research from college students shows that media multitasking can negatively affect a variety of academic outcomes, including GPAs,

test scores, recall of information, comprehension, and note-taking abilities.[28]

3. Smartphones were rapidly adopted by children and teens as an essential accessory of growing up. Wireless companies were delighted to bring their products to younger and younger customers, and whether as a reward for good behavior, a distraction, or a safety measure, parents were quick to respond. Ownership of smartphones increased rapidly; in 2019, 69 percent of twelve-year-olds had their own smartphone.[29] It became commonplace for everyone to carry a smartphone everywhere and to expect that everyone else was carrying one too. Not only did this increase the time available for using screens to twenty-four hours a day, but it completely changed how we use screens. No longer did we sit down to just watch television news or entertainment programs. Led by the children, our behaviors have evolved rapidly, moving from the physical to the digital and back again. We read and responded to texts whenever they came—and we expected that everyone who cared about us would do the same. We Slacked, we tweeted, we Insta'ed, and we YouTubed, filling every moment. With screens on many walls, elevators, and grocery carts, in our pockets, and on our wrists, we were constantly available, and everyone and everything was constantly available to us.

In part because mobile devices allowed for screen viewing in pauses between other activities, downtime while traveling or in an elevator, or even (to many teachers' chagrin) during lapses of attention in class, short-form videos have become extremely popular recreational viewing among children and teens. They have proven to be very effective marketing tools, both because the ratio of screen time between commercials and programs is nearly even and because brand placement in short forms effectively transforms the program material into infomercials. While many students have been distracted by instant gratification and constant opportunity for external stimulation, pragmatic researchers and creative teachers have found educational value in short-form videos. Given the well-publicized concern about the effects of image-based social media on body image, a recent study evaluated the effect on adolescent females of viewing a single five-minute video from an edutainment series about the diversity of female bodies and appearance-related internalized racism. Significant increases in acceptance of appearance diversity were found among all girls, and Black girls experienced significant improvements in appearance-related internalized racism.[30] Another study found that using a short-form video platform as a teaching tool with college students created an engaging learning environment, increased motivation to learn, and encouraged the development of curiosity and creativity.[31] A sub-community dedicated to books on a popular short-form video platform has been shown to build informal, out-of-school reading for fun among teens, revealing to them "the power in reading, the power in communities, and the power that teenagers have to imagine new worlds where literature is central to their identities and day-to-day lives."[32]

Encouraged by the capabilities and increasing affordability of digital technologies, and the promise of personalizing learning through digital analytics, many school systems bought in to the promise of possible cost savings. They were largely supported by parents interested in preparing their children for the twenty-first century. Laptops or tablets replaced notebooks and pencils in many classrooms. Children learned keyboarding rather than penmanship. They learned to use online search engines instead of the library's card catalog.

Digital programs focused on teaching and practicing skills like touch-typing, and DIY videos on everything from painting landscapes to making home repairs have provided all of us unprecedented opportunities to explore our curiosities, acquire needed skills, and learn individual special interests. Online programs that delve deeper into academic subjects from astrophysics to zoology, augment classroom learning of STEM disciplines, or prepare students for standardized tests like the SAT are increasingly popular, even though their effectiveness is highly variable, depending greatly on how the learner uses them.

In the formal schooling environment, it was soon discovered that digitally mediated education could not replace the highly relational space of learning. Computers were not teaching machines that could replace teachers. While some exclusive schools boasted "a tablet for every student," research showed that two or three students per device led to experimentation, discussion, and more effective learning as children worked together to figure out the questions posed in math, science, or language arts.[33] Conscious of the ease with which children adopted and used digital technology, many teachers felt unprepared. Some were unwilling, while, similarly unprepared, others were only too willing to work with computers.[34]

Without close instruction and supervision, many students found themselves distracted from their studies by the many attractions of the internet. Educators observed disturbing trends. Spelling deteriorated (no need with autocorrect). Students did not bother to learn facts of history and science because "I can Google it" and were thus left without the building blocks of new ideas. Children and adolescents had little experience with reflective thinking about literature or art because synopses, critiques, and even college-level essays were freely available online. Gamified teaching tools were shown to be helpful with the skills-and-drills learning of math and other subjects involving memorization, but some children had difficulty building on this knowledge and transferring it into applications.[35] In a 2015 global assessment of digital skills by the Organization of Economic Cooperation and Development (OECD) titled *Students, Computers and Learning: Making the Connection*, it was noted that "even countries which have invested heavily in information and communication technologies (ICT) for education have seen no noticeable improvement in their performances."[36] Practical experience was supported by research showing that teachers were needed as much as ever to supervise, ask provocative questions, and guide the students' learning.[37] Critical to its effectiveness is *how* educational technology is used by both teachers and students to support and enhance the learning experience. Educational technology was not the panacea that was promised.

ASK THE MEDIATRICIAN
Can My Child Use Digital Technology to
Supplement What She Learns in School?

My ten-year-old daughter got really interested in geology on a class field trip to the San Andreas Fault. She wants to learn more about fault lines, earthquakes, volcanos, and the shifting continents. I'm concerned about just letting her roam online to do this. How can I keep her in a safe zone as she explores?

What a terrific opportunity for your daughter to learn how to put online resources to their best use. Resources available on the internet range from texts and reference works to self-taught and instructor-led courses that can enrich and extend children's learning in many school subjects like science, history, and literature. There are effective programs to develop academic skills in everything from reading to keyboarding to creating in a variety of artistic media. Kids can practice foreign languages, even participate in virtual travel experiences in other cultures. Many teachers provide sources of supplemental information that they have vetted, so reach out to your daughter's teacher or media specialist for suggestions. However, especially as this is a new experience for her, it is important for you to evaluate all programs that claim to be educational by checking reviews from credible educational experts or institutions and, as with other online activities, explore those programs before and when introducing your child to them. Not only will this allow your daughter to dive deeply into subjects she wants to learn more about, but you will be spending time together, modeling and mentoring digital literacy skills by seeking out, comparing, and contrasting multiple sources and different perspectives on the same subjects.

Education was in flux during the second decade of the twenty-first century. Some schools, concerned about the loss of fine motor skills without training in cursive writing or teaching research strategies beyond asking Google, pulled back from educational tech. Going even further, the Waldorf schools advocated for screen-free childhoods, both in school and at home. Other schools, recognizing the inevitability of adopting digital tools, invested in rethinking their curricula and training their teachers to teach effectively with technology.

In November 2022, the public release of ChatGPT, an artificial intelligence (AI) chatbot that scrapes the internet to generate a large language model (LLM) of the world's accumulated text-based knowledge, created another challenge for educators. Using mathematical probability to predict the most frequent groupings of words on any subject, ChatGPT demonstrated remarkable facility for creating competitive college essays, achieving respectable Bs on MBA exams, and passing medical boards and legal bar exams.[38] While some educators decried ChatGPT as automated plagiarism and sought ways to expose offending students, others saw it as a challenge to raise the level of learning, developing strategies for using AI's remarkable research power to shift their students' efforts toward higher-level conceptual work. When AI is used to do the mechanistic operations of research just as a calculator does arithmetic calculations in math, it, too, can liberate the learner to reflect on that knowledge in deeper, more complex ways. Of course, there will always be attempts by some to use AI as a cheat to get through school. But what happens when they get their first job with a freshly minted degree but have no applicable knowledge or skills because their schoolwork was executed with AI? I believe, and fervently hope, that AI can actually reverse the tide in higher education so that instead of finding the path of least resistance for getting a passing grade and a degree, students demand to be challenged by their teachers and do the work necessary to enrich their knowledge, capabilities, and skills.

Of growing consideration with the use and application of AI in schools will be the much more complex (and rarely discussed) issue of cognitive atrophy—the loss of neurons and networking synapses due to disuse as AI takes on more analytical and critical tasks. As best stated by Dr. Philip McRae of the Alberta (Canada) Teachers' Association, "Technologies should be employed to help students become empowered citizens rather than passive consumers. Innovations are needed in education that will help to create a society where people can flourish within culturally rich, informed, democratic, digitally connected and diverse communities. We should not descend into a culture of individualism through technology where our students are fragmented by continuous partial attention."[39] If we over-rely on AI for determining what is right and what is wrong, we run the risk of moral passivity in our individual decision-making and our societal behavior. AI can organize massive amounts of data but lacks key components necessary to utilize that information in the lives of humans—emotional intelligence, empathy, and the ability to reflect and have insight on those data, then build on them strategies for living well.

MEDIA Rx
AI Is Ours to Use Intelligently and Responsibly

Like all of us, you may be approaching AI with a mixture of fear and excitement. Remember that it is a tool, perhaps the most power- ful interactive and generative media tool yet. It is a tool created by humans, based on how we learn using neural nets, so it will carry the strengths and the inherent biases of those who created it. Think of it as a lightning-fast reference librarian whose personal history, beliefs, and psychology are unknown to you. Learn it together with your child as critical thinkers. Think about the way facts are presented and the lens through which they are seen. History is particularly sensitive to bias. Imagine the history of the war in Vietnam, for example, as told by a US general, a Swedish diplomat managing peace talks, a Vietcong guerilla, a US Army draftee who did not want to be there, and a Vietnamese villager. AI would gather some but not all of those stories. It would consolidate them into a single seemingly comprehensive but distinctly biased story. Use AI to collect information, but use the tools of digital literacy to find the inevitable biases and blind spots. Do not accept any information without questioning and deconstructing its parts. Challenge your own preconceptions with counter-narratives. Seek to fill the gaps with alternative logical perspectives. With the research done by AI and the counter-research done by you and your child, find the most logical narrative. In presenting that narrative, be transparent, acknowledging when and why you choose to focus narrowly on a particular perspective and exclude others.

YOU CAN

- *Reframe your thinking.* AI and other emerging technologies can feel invasive and put you on the defensive, determined to contain and control both the technology and your child's attention to it. Instead, consider yourself on the learning curve together. Trade your protective stance for one aimed at learning how to help your child best use the tool to enhance learning and their mental and physical health. Ask yourself, *How can I help my child use this this tool well?*

- *Be mindful.* Set fears aside and focus on the positive potential of AI. As with all advances before it, you'll learn as you go. But you'll have to be open and proactive. Doing so allows you to take control of the narrative around it, as opposed to being driven exclusively by fear. When utilized properly, AI will be a tool like the calculators we rely on routinely.

- *Mentor and monitor.* Learn about AI alongside your child, and take a proactive role in their technological abilities. Let them share what they're discovering and experiencing while sharing your insights and learnings. Turn AI program testing into a family game—ask your generative AI tool for a weekend meal plan or recipe, and then shop for the ingredients together.

- *Make integrity transparent.* Teach your child to acknowledge and cite the tools used in every aspect of their work. Use multiple AI tools to obtain different angles on the information. If your child must cut and paste a phrase or more from a source, make sure they use the original source, put quotes around it, and fully reference it in their endnotes and bibliography.

- *Use AI as a resource, not a substitute.* Encourage your child to use AI as a tool. Like using a powerful search engine, it's an efficient way to gather information, and it adds a novel aspect to work. But using it as a substitute—writing a paper with the click of a button, for example—denies your child an opportunity to learn, think about and share their perspective, and develop new and diverse ideas. They can get through school riding the back of AI, but they will have little to show for it—and potentially serious consequences for representing it as their original work. Demand better of them and teach them to demand better of themselves. They should see using generative AI to do their schoolwork as the height of self-disrespect.

In 2019, the same year that more than two-thirds of seventh graders had personal smartphones, schools were still figuring out their love-hate relationship with interactive media. Children under eight years old used recreational screen media an average of two hours and twenty-four minutes every day, tweens ages eight to twelve for four hours and forty-four minutes, and teenagers for seven hours and twenty-two minutes.[40] Online learning had been implemented with children who, due to disability or distance, lacked access to a traditional learning environment, and it was used to augment traditional learning for advanced or struggling students.[41]

Concerns about the impact of increasing screen use on kids' social and emotional development as well as academics were front and center in the increasingly heated debate over screens in schools. Those who expressed concerns were dismissed as old-school alarmists by those who insisted that screens were the future of learning and socializing. The polarized energy generated a standoff that was both pedagogical and practical, drawing educators, parents, and child development experts into the fray.

Then COVID-19 struck, and the pandemic pulled the plug on the either-or debate. School shutdowns, remote instruction, and social isolation made screen-based life the new normal. By necessity, we were all online for dramatically longer durations than previously.[42] The pandemic did not create children's problems using interactive media; it served as an accelerant of ongoing trends. For some young people, especially for adolescents, the rapid increase in screen use duration proved to be a problem. For others, it was not the use of interactive media but the isolation that was the most serious problem. For teens, whose primal developmental drive is to move away from the nuclear family, establish an independent identity, and connect with peers, the lockdown with family, isolated from friends, was torture.

Reflecting on survey findings that about half of parents believed their children did better with remote learning, educators felt that remote schooling democratized the classroom so that the majority of students in the middle got the same amount of attention as the students who were excelling or struggling. Unfortunately, children of lower-income families with slow or small-screen devices and limited or no broadband connection, for which they competed with working parents, struggled with underconnection.[43] In the spring of 2020, more than 20 percent of Boston public school students never logged on during the pandemic lockdown, functionally dropping out.

During 2020–21, "the year of learning remotely," 42 percent of Boston students were chronically absent.[44]

In much of the United States, the pandemic caused children to lose three years of normal school. It was particularly difficult for the children and teens for whom those years crossed transitions, like advancing to middle or high school, relocating to a new community, and major milestones like senior prom and graduation. While losses in academic learning were considerable for some, it was children's and teens' social emotional learning that suffered more.

Arguably more important than academic facts and skills, social emotional learning occurs in school as children and teens act as individuals figuring out who they are, how to behave, and how to build a community from diverse individuals. It occurs in the classroom but also on the playground, in the lunchroom, passing in the halls, and after school. Essential to adult success, these complex and nuanced soft skills will serve them well or trip them up throughout their lives. As hard as educators worked to make their academic teaching effective in the remote setting, there was little done for social emotional learning. Young people found it themselves, using social media, online games, and interactive platforms as the new hanging-out space, where they could get together, without adult involvement or interference, to be themselves while they figured out who they were.

Power Tools, Powerful Teachers

How can screen media have such a powerful effect on behavior? We experience the world and others through our senses, but our five basic sensory systems are not equal. Marshall McLuhan, who famously stated, "The medium is the message," defined media as technological extensions of the human body that allow humans to connect and communicate. McLuhan theorized that the ratio of perception among the senses affects the power of media to communicate. Because of the specialized complexity of the eye and the distances at which it can receive a stimulus, seeing is predominant. Hearing was a close second when we were hunter-gatherers and storytellers, but seeing became even more important when the written word surpassed oral history.[45] Touch, smell, and taste, so important for many animals, are less important for humans. Our sight and hearing develop early because they are critical survival tools. These senses are how infants first observe and try to understand human behaviors. Coupling them with the emotion-generating limbic system helps infants tell the difference between nurturing and threatening behaviors. *(Are they smiling or frowning? Singing or shouting?)* We learn by sensing—and we remember what we have learned suffused with the emotions we felt at the time.

Think back to your earliest memories. They are primarily visual for me. My first conscious memory is the image of my newborn sister being brought into our home, an event that was powerfully charged for my twenty-six-month-old self. Instantly, I lost being my parents' sole focus, but I gained a companion, one whom I believed I could shape and control with my nurturing or threat. Memories are emotionally laden moments that are recalled visually. We don't have full recall from our childhood, but we remember experiences associated with feelings: the loss of a pet, moving from a known home to a strange new one, making a friend, even cooking a meal with family and making a mess. Conscious memories are just a small part of what we have learned, the tip of the iceberg. Beneath those conscious memories lies an accretion of everything we have experienced, layer upon layer, shaping how we see and understand ourselves, others, and the world.

Screens use visuals to elicit feelings. We go to the movies, watch television, and play games to be transported into another reality. We laugh, cry, get scared, or feel triumphant. Interactive electronic games are arguably the most effective educational technology yet developed. They create an environment with certain conditions, they reward certain behaviors and punish others, and they incentivize repeating and rehearsing those behaviors over and over and over again. What is learned can be playing basketball, flying a plane, designing a city, killing terrorists, or virtually any human activity.

Children learn by watching, observing which behaviors result in positive outcomes, imitating the actions that are positively reinforced, and, if the behavior works for them, making it their own.[46] That's how they learn to feed themselves, get along with others, and perceive the world around them. Children absorb, assess, and integrate what they experience into schemas, mental constructs that help organize our understanding of ourselves and others. Schemas are the mental shorthand the human mind uses to make sense of, neurologically encode, and conceptualize the essentials of what it learns. It's how we recognize that cats are distinct from dogs and how we recognize a cat that we've never seen before *as* a cat; it shares key characteristics with cats we have seen before.

We create such schemas for everything we are exposed to, whether it's something concrete, like a cat, or abstract, like anger. We use schemas to structure what we know about the world and how to behave in it, including in the digital space. This is useful but can become problematic when schemas become rigid, when we aren't flexible enough to accommodate new information and reach a new understanding.

Increasingly, screen media are children's first and most frequent exposure to many experiences, behaviors, and beliefs. As children grow older, screens play an increasingly important role in shaping the schemas by which kids organize their experiences. Produced and presented thoughtfully, screen media can help children develop more diverse, flexible, and tolerant schemas. Or media can contribute to narrowing, stiffening, and concretizing their understanding of themselves and their world. McLuhan proposed that mechanical technology, from the printing press to the steam engine, allowed us to learn about, connect with, and experience other cultures, languages, and belief systems, effectively detribalizing us. Having seen the masterful manipulation of radio and motion picture technology by Joseph Goebbels and Adolph Hitler, he warned that, unless we are self-aware, critical thinkers, electronic technology can retribalize us.[47]

The media we see and hear every day can be a powerful part of the cultural messages that affect us all in deep, long-lasting ways. When schemas become fixed stereotypes about those who speak other languages or worship other deities, people of color, those of different genders, or virtually any identity group, we make them "other," and we are diminished. The assumptions and expectations that are established in our culture, on television, through music, in video gameplay, and on the internet and social media shape our perceptions and expectations of the world and of each other.

Children are *always* learning about themselves and the world, but they perceive and learn differently at different developmental stages. What you think your child is learning may be quite different from what your child is actually taking away from the experience. Effective educational programming, music, computer software, and websites introduced at developmentally optimal times can expand your child's knowledge and experiences in ways that will benefit them through adolescence and into adulthood.

MEDIA Rx

Shaping Your Child's Screen Curriculum

You know your child best. Especially with very young children, view some of the screen media you are thinking of sharing in advance. If your gut tells you that your child will be able to learn from it, view it with your child and watch their responses closely. If their face shows fear or confusion, pause the video and talk about it. Explain to them why you paused: "You looked upset." Listen to their concern and answer their questions. As we learn and grow, there are unpleasant realities of history and humanity that we must learn when we are able so we can prevent them and protect ourselves and others. "Those who cannot remember the past are doomed to repeat it."[48]

But your child may be upset by and unable to learn from what they see on screen. In that case, turn it off, but don't leave them alone with those feelings. Help them understand that they are safe with you and apologize for showing it to them. Some children will want to view it again, either immediately or after a while, so they can try to master those feelings. Model for them how to understand and master experiences that are confusing or upsetting and how to learn from them. This is not to desensitize them to terrifying, enraging, or demeaning experiences but to model and mentor how you understand unpleasant experiences, learn from them, and seek better experiences.

YOU CAN

- *Be sure that the perspectives and behaviors portrayed in your child's media are what you want them to learn and incorporate in their life— because they will.* Exposure to media content that disturbs, distracts, or desensitizes your child (without your moderation) can teach them that the world is a scary, selfish, objectifying, and ultimately cruel place in which they may have to fight to survive. If, despite your efforts, your child comes across media content that you feel may teach them harmful lessons, process it with them by asking, "How do you think that character felt? How would you feel if that happened to you? How would you feel if you did that to someone?"

- *Avoid relying on media rating systems to replace your parental judgment.* Movie, video game, and television ratings are designed to protect the business interests of media producers, not the well-being of the children and adults who use the media. They are determined by raters whose qualifications may be that they are or have been parents. They are not experts in child health and development, so they are not asked to determine what may be harmful or helpful to a *child*; they are rating what they think may be objectionable to *parents*. As a result, media ratings tend to be measures of shifting social values. Research has shown that motion picture ratings have shifted to be more permissive at a rate of one rating level every eleven years.[49]
- *Model responsible, mindful media use.* Choose media that you believe will teach you or expand your experience in some way, talk openly about your decision process, and invite others to share the experience. When you teach by example, the lesson sticks.

Thinking back to our earliest memories, are they of screen experiences? While my earliest non-screen memory was from age two, my earliest memory of any screen experience was from age ten when I got in trouble for watching Abbott and Costello movies on television instead of going to Sunday school. And even then, what really stuck in my memory was my laughter being interrupted by Mom's reprimand and the flush of shame I felt—the television was instantly in the background. While media effectively harness the power of our senses and emotions to engage us, those created experiences are less powerful than those we experience directly. When thinking about children's screen media, always consider alternatives: What else might they be doing and experiencing? How they are affected by what they experience on screen is usually less important, meaningful, and potent than off-screen opportunities they displace.

Tell stories, take walks, make meals, laugh when you can, and cry when you must. Make memories! Let those be the teachable moments you and your child carry for life.

Part 2

So What?

Chapter 7

Insidious Influencers, Consuming Passions

When Persuasive Messaging and Personalities Turn Toxic

didn't see Lisa at first when I called for the eleven-year-old. She didn't immediately respond. When her mother stood up and walked toward me, Lisa reluctantly followed, head bowed, barely missing a beat with her frantic texting on her glitter-encased smartphone. I had looked right past her because, at first glance, she looked seventeen or eighteen. She was wearing stylish jeans, furry boots, and a lot of artfully applied makeup. When she and her mother sat down to meet with me, Lisa completely ignored her mother's admonition to put the phone away, and she did her best to ignore me. Her perfectly manicured fingers just kept texting. Her mother revealed that she was bringing Lisa in because she was worried about her. This was her typical behavior: withdrawn, noncommunicative, uncooperative.

"I don't understand it," her mother said. "Her father and I ask so little of her—to do as well as she can in school and stay out of trouble. She has everything she wants." At this point Lisa looked up to glare at her mother, who excused herself to sit in the waiting room.

Once her mother was out of the room, Lisa finally talked to me, slipping the phone into her jacket pocket, where it insistently signaled notifications with the sound of a squeaky door opening.

"She thinks I'm depressed, but I'm just bored. School is boring, my friends are boring, and *she* is especially boring."

"What do you enjoy?" I asked.

"I don't know, hanging out, shopping . . . but I don't have enough money to *really* go shopping."

As we spoke further, it was clear that Lisa was right; she did not have any of the diagnostic signs of depression. She was dissatisfied. Her parents both worked full time to support a comfortable lifestyle. She didn't have to worry about where her next meal or next pair of shoes were coming from, but Lisa was constantly on her parents' case to buy trendy clothes and a new phone.

Like her friends, Lisa had had an iPad since kindergarten, a smartphone since first grade, and a laptop by fourth grade—the year before—with few to no restrictions. She was never offline and spent her free time engrossed in fashion websites, YouTube makeup tutorials, and social media.

"How do you feel when you're on your phone?"

"I don't know . . ." Surprised by the question, Lisa finally said, "Meh."

"How do you feel when you get off the phone?"

"Bad. So I get back on. Or I never get off at all."

Lisa's self-worth was determined by how she looked and what she had. The competitive marketing culture that pervaded the digital ecosystem in which she lived had put her in a constant state of discontent. A healthy sense of self-worth, for any of us, at any age, is grounded in our intrinsic value as human beings—attributes that define the quality of our character, our way of being in the world. When children feel loved, accepted, and celebrated for who they are in that most basic sense, they have a solid foundation of self-worth. Counterinfluences, from a distant or distracted family to broader cultural messaging of being not quite good enough, amplified in media and advertising to increase sales, can chip away at a child's self-worth. Especially in the tween and teen years, advertising and social media—which has become a "superpeer"[1]—sway a young person's sense of self. Social media influencers pack a special punch, combining the persuasive force of a personal friend who understands you with the sophisticated messaging of targeted marketing.

Consumer product companies and their advertisers leverage the fact of human nature that people buy when they are discontented. After three minutes of looking at a fashion magazine supported by advertising for cosmetics, clothing, and weight-loss products, women were more likely to feel depressed, shameful, and guilty.[2] Children and adolescents, immersed in interactive media and unconstrained by the realities of incomes and credit scores, are particularly vulnerable. Not only are they receiving endless messages about how their inadequacies could become strengths with various products, but children and adolescents are emotionally open to manipulation and a decade or more away from developing effective impulse control.

"Everywhere we look we are offered false excitement, pseudo intensity," media critic and documentary filmmaker Jean Kilbourne wrote in *Can't Buy My Love: How Advertising Changes the Way We Think and Feel*.[3] "Not only does this inevitably disappoint us, it also contributes to the general feeling in the culture that every moment of our lives should be exciting, fun, that sex should always be passionate and intense, education ceaselessly entertaining, that anything less is *bo-ring*."[4]

Kilbourne wrote that book twenty-five years ago, galvanizing attention on advertising's negative effects, especially on youth and in particular on girls. Things have only gotten worse, she said in a more recent online interview with Rachael Berman of thehumanist.com. "I actually think advertisements that sexually objectify and stereotype women are worse than ever," she said, citing the shift of advertising to the internet and the impact of that as young people spend so much time immersed in online and social media environments. "This changes everything because it makes it possible for advertisers to target people much more individually because they get so much information from Facebook and other social media platforms." Photoshop and other image-editing software tools have made things "infinitely worse," she said, "because it's now possible to show people as completely flawless." The only way that things have gotten better, she added, "is that there is more attention to this issue now."[5]

It is good business strategy to exploit adolescent self-consciousness and underdeveloped impulse control to sell products to youth who have more disposable income and freedom to spend it than ever in history. But good business for the corporation is not always healthy for the consumer. Adolescents are developmentally driven to step away from parents and do whatever they can to be attractive to others, but the influence of the interactive media environment starts well before the teen years and promotes more than consumer products.

Early Buy-In, Lasting Buyers

As children have greater access to screen media at younger and younger ages, those who sell ideas, attitudes, and behaviors have been eager to engage them early and often. Previously advertisements were limited to TV commercials for sugary cereals and toys between Saturday morning cartoons when Mom and Dad were still asleep. The advent of touch screen tablets opened 24/7 access to very young children. Marketers are aware that children are always learning (sound familiar?), and they apply sophisticated developmental psychology to meet children at each age and stage. Targeting parents, they create schemas that buying their product is the way to meet their child's needs.

Jean Piaget, one of the pioneers of developmental psychology, structured child cognitive development into four stages—and marketers have figured out how to reach children at each stage so they can build long-lasting schemas and brand loyalty.[6] During the sensorimotor stage (birth to two years), infants figure out the world by coordinating sensory perceptions (what they see, hear, feel, taste, and smell) with their physical activities.[7] So if they see a brightly colored piece of sugared cereal, pick it up, put in in their mouth, and it tastes sweet, they learn to pick up the next piece. Between four and seven months of age, babies come to understand that they are distinct beings separate from the world and develop object permanence, the awareness that objects exist even when they can't directly see, hear, or otherwise perceive them. As early as four months of age, before they develop object permanence, infants' attention will be drawn to a screen.[8] Children start to see images of brightly colored cereal and fuzzy toys early and often on screens. At eighteen months, toddlers start to decode the images they see on screen into symbols of attractive foods and toys and to connect them with product logos. Now able to connect what they see in an on-screen commercial or product placement and what they see in the store, children start to ask for what they want—and we are off to the races![9]

A very young child has an *experience*—Mom offers a fuzzy toy, and the child reaches out and grasps the toy, creating a schema for what to do when a toy is offered. When Dad offers a toy, the child accesses that schema and grasps the toy, using the remembered experience to *assimilate* to the new experience. When the child squeezes Dad's toy, it squeaks—and the child *accommodates* this new experience as a variation of the schema, building an enriched understanding of how to interact with people and objects. Understanding that children learn about the world and how to behave in it by experiencing, assimilating, and accommodating, marketers socialize new consumers by reaching out to children at the earliest age possible.

Children between the ages of two and seven years, in what Piaget called the *preoperational stage,* are prime targets for marketers because they can connect what they see on screens with what they see on store shelves, but their brains are still developing and cannot yet understand the persuasive intent of advertising.[10] Unable to reliably distinguish between media portrayals and reality until they are seven or eight years old, they perceive the advertising they see as one and the same as the program material and believe that the nice people on television are offering them the same fun that is happening on screen. The toy metal detector in the commercial is a great way for them to participate in the treasure hunting they see in the program. Commercialism is even harder to distinguish when specific products are embedded in the program and used by the characters the child admires and seeks to emulate. Children now realize that they are independent individuals, with their own ideas, needs, and desires. They are able to think about things that are not right in front of them, which means they can want things they do not have. The tantrums of the "Terrible Twos" are frequently about the realization that things they want to do or have can be stymied by the parent, who is still in control. This is the stage at which children become increasingly independent screen users, particularly of television and tablets, often because parents need a break and put them in front of a screen for a moment of calm.

Ethan's two-year-old annual medical visit was unremarkable. He was eating and sleeping well, meeting all of his developmental milestones. But he had an interesting finding in his otherwise completely normal physical exam: a pattern of tiny, pinpoint scabs covering his forehead. When I looked up at his mom quizzically, she blushed.

"Oh . . . We were in the toy store buying a birthday present for his cousin, and he saw . . ."—she silently mouthed the words *Thomas the Tank Engine*— "And he stared at it for the longest time. He asked for it, and I explained that that we were there to get Danny his present. He continued looking at it while I made the purchase, and I had to drag him away by the hand. When we got out on the sidewalk, he got down on his hands and knees and started banging his forehead on the concrete. He wanted that toy!"

"So . . . what happened?" I asked.

"I lifted him up so he couldn't bash his head anymore, took him by the hand, and walked him straight to the car."

"Good for you!"

She had set limits for Ethan, kept him from hurting himself, and did not acknowledge the drama. Ethan quickly forgot about it, though his forehead would take a little longer to recover.

Preschool children are drawn to cartoons, puppetry, and other imaginative content (great for *Mister Rogers' Neighborhood* and *Sesame Street*, but also good for selling action figures and other merchandising).[11] They develop parasocial relationships, one-sided love for and bonding with Elmo or Daniel Tiger. They want everything to do with those characters, from toys to pajamas, and may melt down if they see them in a store and are not allowed to have them. The nag factor, advertising designed to encourage children to nag their parents for a product they want, is a recognized tool in marketing. National advertising industry meetings have been dedicated to understanding, teaching, and implementing the nag factor. A study conducted with mothers of three-to-five-year-old children who shopped for groceries with their children found that nagging, especially manipulative nagging, increased as the child grew older. Thirty-six percent of the mothers recommended limiting commercial exposure, and 35 percent suggested explaining to children why they are buying or not buying certain products.[12]

ASK THE MEDIATRICIAN
How Do You Explain Advertising to Young Kids So They're Not Pushovers?

My five-year-old son really looks up to professional athletes and gets excited when he sees them in commercials and advertising. How can we help him understand that using these products is not the secret to being great like them?

Today many star athletes accept endorsements from companies that require them to integrate recognizable brands in their gear or perform in commercials. This is a question that every one of us can use the answer to—we all fall prey to ads at one time or another. The critical problem for all children your son's age and younger is that kids under age six haven't yet developed the cognitive capacity to understand persuasive intent—that is, they don't understand that the purpose of advertisements and brand integration is to persuade viewers to buy that product. While you and I as adults can recognize how silly it is to show a highly trained athlete guzzling a beverage loaded with sugar and caffeine, your son does not, and instead he draws an immediate association between the athlete and the drink. This challenge and opportunity presents itself to every parent and child, so I'll offer these suggestions for all.

YOU CAN

Talk to your child directly about the ads they see. This is why it's important to co-view media with young children.

- *Ask why the commercial caught their attention.* Was it the colors, music, famous person, or funny cartoon?
- *Ask how the ad made them feel.* Did it make them feel happy, excited, or like they wanted something they saw?
- *Figure out together what the ad is selling, whether your child would want the product, and why or why not.*

Breaking down advertisements together will help your child develop critical thinking skills, which will help them deal with not only commercials but any information they receive. By engaging a child early in scrutinizing ads, you're laying the groundwork for them to be a critical thinker about the media messages they will see in the future.

I also want to make note here that even though you may break down each ad and discuss all the reasoning behind it, a child may still want to emulate their favorite athlete or celebrity. In your situation, your son will still probably want what his favorite athlete drinks and want to buy it when the pop-up ads appear as he plays his favorite game. There isn't a perfect solution, as every five-year-old and even adults will still be attracted to advertised products—even when they are educated about persuasive intent.

In *Can't Buy My Love,* Kilbourne pointed out that "much of advertising's power comes from this belief that advertising does not affect us. The most effective kind of propaganda is that which is not recognized as propaganda. Because we think advertising is silly and trivial, we are less on guard, less critical, than we might otherwise be. It's all in fun; it's ridiculous. While we're laughing, sometimes sneering, the commercial does its work."[13]

So make sure that your end goal is to have your son begin to assess, on a case-by case basis, who is creating the advertised message and how they want us to change our behavior. Reaching for this goal will help your son acquire early media literacy skills that he can build on throughout his life.

By the time children reach school age, they have received millions of messages, not only for products but for ideas and perspectives on the world and other people. While there is concern for their manipulated attraction to junk food or toys that will be quickly broken or forgotten, they have also been exposed to gender and racial stereotypes, images of what makes people attractive or ugly, sexualized or antisocial behaviors that are used to win, and glamorized (or just normalized) portrayals of substance use and other high-risk behaviors. Tweens, seven to twelve years old, are in Piaget's concrete operational stage, when their thinking and logical structures are developed.[14] They have their own opinions and see them as distinct from the opinions of others. Their ability to distinguish fantasy from reality is better than when they were younger, but by no means is it consistent. They enjoy fantasy books, movies, and games, both physical (*Magic: The Gathering*) and electronic (*Fortnite*). At the same time, they are more aware of what is realistic and more critical of what is not. Because they are avid consumers of media and fluid thinkers forming their own ideas and opinions, this is an ideal stage to consciously build children's media literacy.

ASK THE MEDIATRICIAN
Are There Homeschool Media Literacy Programs for Seven-Year-Olds?

We are a homeschooling family who has decided to exclude media from our daughters' lives until they turn seven. Our daughters have never watched television and have never seen an advertisement, movie, YouTube clip, and so on. Our eldest is turning seven in June, and we want to introduce her to media though a media literacy curriculum or activities. Can you direct us toward a quality program?

Your impulse to introduce media literacy at the same time that you introduce media is a great one! At whatever age kids start using media, whether it be as a preschooler or a tween, it's essential for them to learn to think critically about the stories, images, and ideas they see and hear.

And your decision to introduce screen media at age seven is supported by developmental psychology research, which has shown that it is around this age that children develop the cognitive ability to recognize persuasive intent—that commercials are trying to get them to buy a product—and to distinguish fantasy from reality in what they see on screen.[15] As they initiate their screen media use, it is really important that you watch with them, observe how they respond, and discuss the issues that are brought up, teaching and, perhaps more importantly, modeling critical thinking for them.

Make sure that any media or digital literacy program you use focuses on critical thinking and can be applied to all media (like books, video games, social media sites, magazines, movies, and more). Look at these online sources for some ideas:

- MediaSmarts[16]
- Media Power Youth[17]

Use these sources for educational strategies as you teach them to become literate, prosocial digital citizens. This is not dramatically different from what you are already teaching them; it is just transposed to the digital environment. Although they have not yet been exposed to electronic screens, they are already experienced consumers of media. The books and magazines they read, billboards on the highway, and advertisements emblazoned on their own or their friends' clothes can be a useful entry point for talking about messages that they will see on screen media. Ask them to identify messages in their environment that are designed to persuade them of something, then ask how they respond to those messages—first immediately, then after they have thought about them for a while.

Make it a game to identify overt and covert messages in their environment and together deconstruct those messages by asking the five key questions of media literacy:

- Who created this message, and what did they want you to do?
- What techniques are used to attract your attention?
- What lifestyles, values, and points of view are represented?
- How might different people interpret this message differently?
- What is omitted from this message?

Once your daughters have experience with messages they already know, they will be better prepared for the screen messages they experience in the future.

Media Literacy Makes Kids Savvy Media Users

When I am asked when children should start becoming media literate, I say, "When they start using media." That may sound glib, but it does not mean that you need to teach them formal media literacy skills when they are toddlers video chatting with their grandparents. What it does mean is to introduce each device—whether it be television, a tablet, or a computer—as a powerful tool (not a toy or a pacifier) when the child needs and can benefit from that tool. Model its effective use for the child, and use it with them, especially at the beginning. Observe how they respond to the screen, and talk about it with them. Even if they are not able to become fully media literate in the sense that they cannot deconstruct media messages, they can start to achieve fundamental digital literacy as new devices and applications are introduced. They can use the five Cs of digital literacy to guide them at the beginning: Critical thinking, Cultural understanding, Communication, Collaboration, and Creativity.

As children grow older and are using the online space with greater freedom, the co-viewing and discussion between parent and child that occurred earlier in life can evolve into more sophisticated and thoughtful media literacy training, either at home or school, ideally both. Media are the many and evolving means of communicating with large numbers of people, some known but most unknown to the sender. Media are everything from newspapers and magazines (remember those?) to television in its many forms to music to social media to any verbal, visual, or audio communication beyond direct, face-to-face conversation.

Media literacy is the ability to access, analyze, evaluate, and create media. Not so long ago, when television and movies were our screens, most people's contact with media was as a receiver of professionally created content. Then the emphasis of media literacy was on analyzing and evaluating what we saw, heard, and read. But today's digital environment is dramatically different—a fast-moving two-way street in which virtually every user is both receiving and creating. This has yielded remarkable opportunities but has presented new risks as well.

To enjoy media and use them wisely, staying healthy, smart, and kind, we must start with understanding and communicating to tweens and teens these key concepts of media literacy:

1. All media are constructions, creations crafted with the intention of communicating an idea or feeling to the receiver. Media literacy deconstructs the messages to determine how they are made and what the intended response might be.
2. Media portray alternate realities, regardless of whether source material is factual or fictional. Media creators choose the story they wish to tell, the perspective from which to see it, what to include and exclude from the whole facts, and the attitudes, interpretations, and conclusions to be drawn from the story. Because they give us what E. B. White called "the new opportunity to see beyond the

range of our vision," media provide most of the observations and experiences from which we develop our understanding of the world, how it works, and how to behave to be successful in it.[18]

3. Each person chooses media and perceives the reality they present differently. Each of us views what we experience through our own lens of personal interests, attitudes, needs, anxieties, mood, family and cultural background, and moral and political beliefs.

4. Media communicate overt and covert commercial, ideological, social, and political messages. Understanding that much of our sense of reality is constructed through our experiences, which include messaging of all kinds and from all sources, media literacy builds awareness of media ownership and control, recognizing that a relatively small number of individuals with financial or political power control what we see, hear, and read in the media. Media can shape profound individual or societal change, in positive or negative ways, by giving us an intimate and personal sense of national and global concerns.

5. Each medium has a unique aesthetic form, grammar, and techniques for encoding reality. Television communicates differently than social media, poetry differently than journalism. Within that aesthetic form, media are more or less enjoyable, more or less powerful. Form and content are linked in media messages. Remember, as McLuhan noted, the medium is the message.[19] Different media, even the same medium created by another producer, will reflect a different reality of the same fact.

The advent of interactive media, first as created by professional game designers to be played on individual computers or consoles and now online and created by anyone, has followed and completely changed these key concepts. Media remain constructions, but instead of being created and controlled by the few, they are created by the many and controlled by none. The filter bubble algorithms of social media, designed to profile consumers and direct personalized advertising to them, have created echo chambers of public discourse, feeding media users more of what they already believe.[20] Media choice then enters a vicious cycle of seeking out information that is self-validating with no opportunity for alternative perspectives that might call one's beliefs (or sources) into question. Media still have immense power to influence, especially when an image or story goes viral online. That influence is still, in many cases, wielded by those in financial or political power but has also been commandeered by the common people. Even there, a profit incentive now drives some of the content, either financial (influencers) or social capital/power. Interactive media online has an aesthetic all its own and, unlike earlier media, is constantly evolving as we enter what some call the *metaverse*, an immersive three-dimensional online interactive space navigated by VR and AR.

Matt came in with a painfully swollen ankle. He had turned it while running to catch Greninja, a character in *Pokémon Go*. He had collected the cards when he was younger but had lost interest until he went to high school. Everybody was following a YouTube influencer who was streaming his *Pokémon Go* play. Matt dug out his four binders of Pokémon cards and joined the chase and the online conversation. His ankle was sprained, not broken. He had to temporarily suspend the chase, but he continued the conversation with a growing following because of his depth of Pokémon knowledge and his wealth of cards offered for sale or trade.

The adolescent years (twelve and up) are Piaget's final stage of cognitive development, the formal operational stage.[21] Now capable of abstract and critical thinking but still developing impulse control and other executive functions, teenagers gravitate even more strongly toward peer and parasocial relationships. So while they are aware and often hypercritical of advertising, they remain avid consumers of products and ideas.[22] They follow favorite celebrities of popular culture, who are now joined, if not superseded, by social media influencers, who combine the parasocial value of fame with the perception that they are the adolescents' all-powerful peers.

Not only are young people receiving commercial messages from influencers and corporations that they could be more attractive if only they . . . (fill in the blank), but the wide-open environment of online social media tantalizes them with the promise of personal stardom and riches. To make themselves feel better, they are creating media, performing, and representing themselves to the world while they are still figuring out who they are. The pressure to develop a personal brand expressed in a curated online persona is the incessant demand of the social sea in which teenagers swim (or just try to tread water). Before the advent of social media, this desire played itself out in a smaller, more private arena—obsessing over what to wear to a party or whether one's crush even noticed. Now these desires and anxieties play themselves out on a fast-moving global stage. Insecure adolescents buy and do whatever they can to be attractive, presenting only the best of themselves on social media, then watching how many looks and likes they get in how much time. Not only does this amplify their anxiety, but it makes them vulnerable to trolling by peers or strangers, further fueling their discomfort.[23]

MEDIA Rx
How to Boost Your Child's Awareness of Influencers and Manipulation

Advertising is the easiest media with which to develop and on which to practice media literacy because ads are overtly trying to sell products or principles. They are a great target for adolescents to deconstruct. Kids hate to be told what to do, scolded, talked down to, or manipulated by their parents or anyone else. One of the most successful public health campaigns in history has been the Truth initiative, which harnessed adolescents' strong sense of social justice and staged everything from "die-ins" in front of tobacco company headquarters to prank calling tobacco executives. When youth realize that their attention and personal data are being sold by social media companies, many are as outraged as they were at Big Tobacco—but not as many have acted on that outrage. Avoiding smoking is much easier than giving up their constant feed of social connectivity.

How you talk with your child about influencers—toy ads from an early age, but more sophisticated messaging and messengers as they move more widely in the media environment—can deepen over time as your child is able to have a more complex understanding of the dynamics of persuasion and how marketers target them to make money. If you're concerned that your child or teen is being influenced in unhealthy ways by the media they use, share your concerns in a nonjudgmental way. Stay on their side. Don't make it about their media use but about how *you* hate to be manipulated, fooled, or taken advantage of. Tailor the following tips to address the behavior that has caught your attention. Demonstrate to them how marketing works—how we are all targeted with messaging designed to hook and hold our attention, to capture our buying power, or to profile us as consumers and sell our personal data for a profit. In essence, we are all being played by marketers. Once your child understands how that works, they may gain more insight about themselves—enough to want to be more critical and value their attention and time as much as marketers do. Their willingness to recognize your concerns as valid and their developing ability to critically view and question media will empower them to see the current situation more clearly and protect themselves, both now and into the future.

YOU CAN

Empower your child with these questions to spark their critical skepticism:

- *Follow the money.* Who made this commercial or program, and how do they want me to respond? Who stands to profit from my attention—or the data they will collect from my digital footprint? How does their profit motive affect how I think about the message?
- *What's the hook?* What techniques have they used to attract my attention? Celebrity endorsers or online influencers? Game-like play or other interactive features?
- *What are they trying to get me to do?* What actions, values, or points of view does this message represent or promote? Does that reflect what I really believe? Who I want to be? Do I want to follow their lead?
- *What's the potential downside for me?* What are the risks of my behavior? Are they downplaying the risks to me? Does it affect how I feel about myself?
- *What's in it for them?* Are they selling me a product? An idea? Using me to enhance their image? Expanding their reach or boosting their metrics?
- *What is left out of this message?* Is the information provided fact-based and complete? Can I check sources? Might missing information change how I feel about the message?

- *Evaluate a program or favorite website together.* Make it fun! Play a "Catch the Marketing" game. Co-view with your children and pause the program whenever anyone hits the buzzer. Discuss what you are seeing. Once kids see how advertising and marketing target them—that it's easy for anybody to be played by marketers—they are frequently angry about being treated as if they were stupid. Help build a critical skepticism about products and ideas being sold to them.

Always show your respect for your child or adolescent and their capacity to be open to new information and think through these issues. Their anger and their developing critical thinking skills will empower them to protect themselves, both now and into the future.

I didn't see Lisa again for six years, when she showed up for a routine physical exam the summer after she graduated from high school. She was dressed for the weather in jean shorts and a tank top. It took me a moment to remember her, but Lisa greeted me like an old friend and spontaneously caught me up on her life. She was working as an assistant in her aunt's veterinary practice. When I asked what she was thinking of studying in college, she said that originally she was thinking about fashion. "You were deep into it back in the day," I awkwardly interjected. But now she was contemplating pre-vet. "I took this job because it's good pay, but I like the animals so much that I think I'd like to try for vet school," she said with a hopeful smile. I tentatively asked Lisa how things were going at home. She paused, with a quizzical look, then broke into a big smile. "That's right! You haven't seen me since middle school. I was miserable. And I made everyone else miserable, especially Mom. We're good now. She likes the videos of kittens and puppies posted online." I was glad to hear that things were better at home and that she was creating, not just scrolling online. "That just got boring," she said. "I have better uses for my time."

Chapter 8

A More Perfect Me

Body Image Through a Glass Darkly

Tara slumped into the seat, shapeless in her black hoodie and sweatpants. Her stringy blond hair fell forward like curtains, masking both sides of her face. She tensed up as her mother followed her into the exam room. Tara hadn't been my patient previously, but her mother brought her to see me on the recommendation of Tara's pediatrician.

"Her pediatrician says she is underweight. It happened so gradually that I just didn't notice it." At sixteen, Tara weighed seventy-eight pounds. The report from her pediatrician showed that she had not had a menstrual period for more than two years, her heart rate was dramatically slowed, and recently she had fainted several times when she stood up quickly.

"What I did notice was that she was always on her phone, always on social media." Mom paused, looked at Tara, and her face softened. "She just wanted to be healthy and do better in gymnastics, but then she went out of control." Tara sat silently while her mother revealed that Tara had been dieting the past four years, first counting calories, then cutting out fats, then carbs, then red meat, and now she was vegan.

"How can I help?" I asked Tara, but she just scowled. Her mother went on: "She hasn't eaten dinner with us for I don't know how long. And even then she just cuts her food up in tiny pieces and pushes it around her plate and—" Tara glared at her mother. "I'll shut up now. And I will leave the room!" When the door closed behind her mother, Tara slowly relaxed. I sat back and waited quietly. Tara peered at me through her hair.

"She has no idea; she doesn't know a thing about me!"

I listened as Tara told me how much she had hated her body for ten years. She had been pudgy in elementary school. The kids called her "Tara Tots" and pushed her around on the playground. She made no friends. When financial straits and family tensions prompted her parents to move them to a more affordable neighborhood, she saw it as a fresh start and was determined to be popular at her new school. She began exercising religiously, doing as many as six hundred abdominal crunches a day, and watching what she ate, counting calories, avoiding fats, and training herself to eat as little as possible. At her new school, she made friends, forming a group of girls who hung out on social media, got together for sleepovers, shared gossip, and talked about boys. Tara read teen magazines and followed dozens of online teen influencers. The fat-shaming of others rampant on social media was all the reminder she needed to stick to her weight-loss regimen and to join in on fat-shaming others. She took diet pills on and off when her weight loss would stall. Then, at one of her sleepovers, a friend taught the others to purge. It disgusted Tara, but she and her friends all did it, vomiting their dinners into a shared toilet bowl.

Tara remained deeply entrenched in her belief that she was eating and exercising in healthy ways. She became angry and withdrawn, distrusting of her parents, clinicians, and teachers, especially when they urged her to eat. She still went to school but came home and locked herself in her room until she left for school the next day. She communicated with friends online and made new friends who followed a "pro-ana" website. Pro-ana, short for "pro-anorexia," sites are usually created by people struggling with anorexia nervosa who advocate for this condition as a lifestyle choice rather than a health problem. Tara would scroll through the "thinspirational" messages and tips for how to dress so people wouldn't notice, avoid medical care, and maintain the lifestyle. When the pro-ana site was shut down by the internet service provider, Tara turned to an image-based social media platform where she posted daily entries to share her "journey" and developed a gratifying following of like-minded friends.

Tara scoffed at her mother's description of her being out of control. She saw herself as anything but. For once in her life, she felt absolutely in control. She considered her rigid approach to diet and exercise and her thinspirational social media image a tribute to self-discipline. She felt she was attractive and admired—and she had the fans to prove it. Like Tara's mother, most people have a hard time understanding disordered eating behaviors. For a parent, who is biologically, psychologically, and culturally programmed to nurture their child, it is confusing, terrifying, and guilt-provoking to watch your child starve themselves. Desperate to fix the problem, many seek a straightforward solution by finding a single cause, in this case, social media.

Our societal drive for thinness finds its recent origins in the cultural changes of the 1960s when the voluptuous ideal of Marilyn Monroe was replaced by the ultra-slim look of Audrey Hepburn. Thinness was equated with success—Wallis Simpson's adage "A woman can never be too rich or too thin" became an aspirational goal of that era and beyond—and with health at a time when obesity was rising dramatically in the US. The cultural focus on thinness as attractive was latched onto by marketers selling all manner of appearance-improving products, from weight-loss programs to clothing to cosmetics. Fashion magazines featured articles on thinness as the way to look and feel your best—and placed advertising for products to help right next to the articles.[1]

Body image disturbance and eating disorders, as well as concern about the influence of popular media on them, predate the rise of social media. The incidence and prevalence of eating disorders in children and adolescents has increased significantly in recent decades, with a striking uptick during the COVID-19 lockdown that forced us all online.[2] A 2016 *Journal of Pediatrics* study of children ages nine to fourteen found that over half of girls and boys were dissatisfied with their body shape. Children were asked to select pictures representing their perceived shape and the shape they desired or wanted to be. Half of the girls wanted to be thinner, while the boys were divided: 21 percent wanted to be bigger and stronger and 36 percent wanted to be thinner.[3] Other studies show that children as young as three fret about being fat, and by age five, some children are already developing body image issues.[4]

ASK THE MEDIATRICIAN
Will Conversations About "Skinny" Media Images Scare My Girls?

At what age should I teach my daughters about the ways media idealize thinness and objectify beauty? I want to reach my girls before their opinions are shaped by media influences, but I don't want to alarm them about something that doesn't seem to bother them yet. They're in fourth and fifth grades now, and I feel like, even if I choose my words carefully, talking to them about healthy body image could inadvertently inspire worries about dieting and other unhealthy eating habits. How and when should I be having this talk?

You have good reason to be concerned about how media images of beauty affect your daughters and us all. Studies show, for example, that the increase in dieting by girls as young as five may be related to influences from the media to which they have been exposed.[5] You may not be facing the influence of media messages with your daughters now, but helping them build a healthy body image and sense of self-worth independent of their appearance can be a constant challenge.

To help tweens navigate their media environment, you can help them focus their attention on things you do want them to notice and value:

1. *Focus on who women are and what they do, not on how they look.* Research shows that by directing even critical attention to media images of beauty and weight with your girls, you could accidentally send the message that looks are most important.[6] Instead, focus on who a person or character is and what she does—like whether she's a good team player, a loyal friend, or a talented artist. Introduce them to media that aim to do the same (like *New Moon Girls* for tweens and *Teen Voices* for adolescents).

2. *Take cues from your daughters.* When they do start commenting on an actor's appearance, redirect their focus to who the characters are. If they comment on how pretty someone is, you can say something like, "But what does she do that makes you like her?"

3. *Be conscious of how you talk about yourself.* Again, focus on who you are and what you do rather than on how you look. Then when and if you do comment on your own appearance, keep it positive. Say things like "I love how I feel after a hike" rather than "I wish I could lose a few pounds." Wherever you focus your attention is where they will learn to focus theirs.

Your daughters are already exposed to and affected by unrealistic and unhealthy images in media. You can help increase and emphasize the positive messages they see, limit the negative ones, and be a voice and a role model who gives them a healthier, more positive way of seeing themselves and the world.

Internalizing Malignant Messages About Body Image

Research on the relationship between media use and eating disorders suggests that early and consistent exposure to images, stories, and stereotypes that equate thinness with attractiveness results in some girls and women internalizing the thin body ideal that contributes to disordered eating.[7] Expectations that women be attractive result in some girls objectifying and judging themselves against a cultural ideal of small-breasted, narrow-hipped, ultrathin models. Girls, whose natural pubertal changes move their bodies away from that stick-thin ideal, can become distressed and depressed when they see media images. Playing off this insecurity, the majority of articles in magazines aimed at teen girls focus on improving their appearance—how to be thinner, sexier, and more attractive. Intentional or not, the editorial strategies of these magazines make their readers feel inadequately attractive or successful, preparing them perfectly for the cosmetics, clothing, exercise gear, diet programs, and weight-loss pills they advertise.

The societal norms portrayed by media affect boys as well as girls but in different ways. Cartoon superheroes and comic book characters have evolved into bodybuilder looks with six-pack abs and huge arms and shoulders. Action figures have gotten increasingly muscular and jacked like bodybuilders since the 1960s.[8] Consistent through children's programming, themes of hyper-muscular males continue into adolescence with manga, anime, and video game characters. In parallel with fashion magazines, male magazines feature articles about building muscle and reducing fat coupled with advertising for exercise gear, clothing, and nutritional supplements. In contrast to girls, boys' pubertal changes move them *toward* the muscular male ideal, so they're at risk for developing more narcissistic body concepts—pushing natural male attributes to the extreme. Some develop what has been dubbed the "Adonis complex," in which boys go to great lengths to achieve physical perfection.[9]

The pursuit of the male ideal leads some adolescent boys not only to restrict eating and purge but also to hyperexercise and abuse bodybuilding supplements, including anabolic steroids. A recent study focused on adolescents and young adults found that 55 percent of males were using protein powders or shakes, and consuming protein powders or shakes was associated with a significantly increased risk of using steroids as a young adult.[10] Of particular concern is the dangerous practice of "dry scooping"—taking powdered supplements without recommended water before working out—which is promoted on social media as a way to boost the effects of the supplements.[11] The dangers of dry scooping the highly concentrated powder include "choking, accidental inhalation, overconsumption, injury, and death," according to a 2022 *Pediatrics* study of dry scooping and other pre-workout tips trending on social media, collecting more than eight million likes.[12] A study of more than 2,700 Canadian adolescents found that 21.8 percent of men, 14.2 percent of women, and 8 percent of transgender/gender-nonconforming participants had dry scooped in the past twelve months.[13] "Participants who reported weight training, greater time spent on social media, and clinically significant symptoms of muscle dysmorphia were more likely to report dry scooping."[14]

Seth had always been the smallest boy in class, always the last one chosen when dividing up teams on the playground. When he got to high school, Seth went out for wrestling, competing in the lowest weight class, one hundred and six pounds. Finally, his size was an advantage! He worked out and consumed protein supplements from the health food store to convert his body fat into lean muscle. Determined to succeed, Seth watched coaching videos and ran two and a half miles each evening. Before matches he would run and work out in a neoprene "sauna suit" to drop water weight so he could make the one-hundred-and-six-pound limit. Seth did well his freshman year, placing second in the state tournament. When he came in for his preseason physical during his sophomore year, Seth was worried that he had grown and would not be able to compete in the same weight class. While I was examining him, Seth said, "I've lost my six-pack. I don't get it. I'm doing more and getting worse results." I asked him what he meant by doing more. "I added creatine to my pre-workout. I am running four miles daily. Added sixty extra crunches, but I'm not cut anymore. No definition. A senior on my team, one of the tri-captains, said I should try steroids." He was watching my face and knew how I would respond. "But I don't want my balls to shrivel into raisins." Taking his blood pressure, I noted that it was higher than it had been in previous visits. I asked Seth whether he ever fainted. He had once, in the shower after a run, and acknowledged that he had "browned out" several times when standing up. We talked. He knew how I would advise him about steroids and reassured me again that he would not go there. I explained that his elevated blood pressure and increased water retention that obscured his six-pack could be due to the addition of creatine. "But it's bulked up my arms and chest." Seth had decisions to make.

The struggle between appearance and performance becomes the dark side of athletic striving for both boys and girls when discipline, control, strength, and endurance turn treacherous at the competitive edge—even when the competition is with themselves and their "personal best." From dancers and gymnasts to runners and swimmers, from the community ballet studio and soccer field to the Olympic arena, the pressures to be sleek and strong at any cost can take their toll via eating disorders. Often these begin young, when a child's athletic drive or their focus on appearance is greater than the impulse control and critical thinking required to balance commitment with sound health practices.

Children, especially adolescents who aspire to more adult content and behaviors, are surrounded by a media culture of curated perfection. Historically, children and teens developed their knowledge, attitudes, and behaviors related to appearance and health in a heterogeneous environment of peers and adults with a wide variety of sizes and shapes. Today, however, they spend more time with superpeers on television and the internet who attractively and easily displace real-life role models. According to the Dove Self-Esteem Project, eight out of ten girls with low body esteem (ages ten to seventeen) are so concerned with the way they look that they opt out of social activities.[15] Seven out of ten girls report putting their health at risk by not eating or not going to visit the doctor when they don't feel good about the way they look.[16] Australian girls say that body image is one of their top worries in life.[17] From swimming to visiting the doctor, going to school or playing sports, anxiety about their looks can keep girls and boys from living healthy, active lives.

The introduction of the iPhone in 2007 exploded onto the teen scene, selling one million of the powerful, mobile, internet-connected computer/music player/camera devices in the first seventy-four days.[18] It quickly became a must-have accessory for adolescents, who used it for staying in constant contact via text and taking endless selfies. Adolescent life was rapidly transformed from hanging out in person to hanging out online via smartphones, exchanging countless posed images of themselves with or without text. For many, this led to documentation of every activity, from travel to social events to lunch, and a sense that if it was not documented with a selfie, you didn't do it.

The smartphone and social media synergized to transform adolescence and adolescents. Many young people became minor stars (and some became millionaires) on social media, gaming, and vlogging sites, sharing content from yoga to designer drugs, makeup to pro-ana, gaming to cooking. Social media can be a powerful influence on children's body image because it starts with what's real and digitally enhances it with lighting and filters, even product-specific digital makeovers. Highly edited, perfected selfies have become accessible to all, playing on normal adolescent insecurities and stoking unrealistic and unhealthy expectations. Comparing their realities to the enhanced representations of others, many young people become competitive, anxious, and depressed. A few, like Tara, seek to chase perfection and get caught up in anorexia nervosa, the psychiatric condition with the highest death rate. A 2018 study of pro-ana content on image-based social media analyzed 7,560 images from Instagram with hashtags #ana, #starve, and #fasting, finding they fell into nine categories. Those categories included image and text memes (26 percent) with aphorisms like "Hunger hurts, but starvation works" and thinspiration images (25 percent) of underweight female bodies with protruding collarbones, ribs, and pelvises.[19]

Ten percent of the images analyzed were associated with tips, like "The Thin Commandments" for maintaining one's eating disorder: concealing it from parents, teachers, and clinicians by eating and weighing oneself in private; wearing baggy clothes; and avoiding gym classes, clinical visits, and other opportunities where they might be weighed.

Thin Commandments[20]

1. If you aren't thin, then you aren't attractive.
2. Being thin is more important than being healthy.
3. You must buy clothes, cut your hair, take laxatives, starve yourself, do anything to make yourself look thinner.
4. Thou shall not eat without feeling guilty.

5. Thou shall not eat fattening food without punishing thyself afterward.
6. Thou shall count calories and restrict intake accordingly.
7. What the scale says is the most important thing.
8. Losing weight is good; gaining weight is bad.
9. You can never be too thin.
10. Being thin and not eating are signs of true willpower and success.
11. If you are thin, you will be loved and accepted.

Unique to the social media environment were gamified and interactive challenges (4 percent), like "name a food, and I won't eat it for a month" or offers to do ten sit-ups for each like, twenty for each comment, and one hundred for each shout-out.[21]

Among these posts targeting others living with eating disorders were selfies (6 percent) that showed only faces, not bodies; memes linking disordered eating with depression (3 percent), such as "Depression is living in a body that fights to survive with a mind that tries to die"; as well as self-harm and suicide (6 percent). Eight percent of the posts promoted recovery; urged seeking professional help; showed healthy, balanced meals; and expressed hope for the future.[22] Interestingly, posting selfies and memes about disordered eating, pro and con, challenges the stereotype of being secretive about one's eating disorder and brings the underlying pain to the surface and into the mainstream. By bringing eating disorders and the pain that drives them into the open, it is possible that image-based social media may encourage acknowledgement of that pain, care-seeking among those suffering, and a prevention message for other youth. Indeed, a study of pro-ana videos on YouTube found that the many pro-ana videos found were surpassed in likes and positive comments by videos opposing them and promoting help.[23]

Worry about the influence of social media on disordered body image peaked in 2021 when whistleblowing former Facebook engineer Frances Haugen revealed to a Senate subcommittee and the public that Facebook had done research showing that 32 percent of adolescent girls with poor body image felt worse after using Instagram.[24] Among the thousands of internal documents Haugen shared with lawmakers were surveys of teen girls showing that 17 percent in the US reported their eating disorders got worse after they used Instagram and 13.5 percent said they had more frequent suicidal thoughts after they started using Instagram.[25] These findings from corporate market research needed to be verified by rigorous, unbiased scientific investigation, but Facebook did not report them, raising questions about whether they were concerned about the health of the young people who were at that time the majority of their users. At the "Facebook Papers" hearing, Senator Richard Blumenthal challenged Facebook, saying they "exploited teens using powerful algorithms that amplified their insecurities" and asking "whether there is such a thing as a safe algorithm."[26]

But is there added risk of disordered body image and eating disorders from using social media? A recent meta-analysis of sixty-three independent research studies representing 36,552 adolescents from Asia, Australia, Europe, and North America found a significant but small increase in body image disturbance among those who spent more time using social media.[27] That this link was statistically significant was not a surprise, given young people's frequency of social media use and the intensity of their social comparison when using it, but the small size of the effect was unexpected. In fact, the association between social media use and body image disturbance was significantly smaller than the small-to-medium effect sizes on both females and males of using print and screen media. This may be because traditional media have been more likely to feature idealized content of celebrities, usually with image enhancement, while social media show a broader range of people with less (or less sophisticated) image manipulation.[28] Browsing general content on Facebook for ten minutes had no effect on body dissatisfaction in one study, while another study showed less weight and body shape preoccupation after twenty minutes.[29] However, body image dissatisfaction was greater for users of image-based, appearance-focused social media and for younger users.[30] Greater body image disturbance among younger social media users is consistent with their more self-conscious developmental stage and with the fact that negative body image diminishes with age—a good reason to adhere to the US surgeon general's 2023 recommendation to limit social media to those older than thirteen.

Just as media literacy has been shown to be protective of youth in relation to consumerism, the corrective lens of critical viewing—being able to recognize unrealistic, altered images; the equation of thinness with attractiveness and appearance with self-worth; and the promotion of appearance-enhancing products—has helped many young people develop a healthy, critical response to unhealthy messaging and ideals around body image. Social media, by virtue of its open-to-all, instantaneous feedback dynamic; its algorithms that channel users' interests and curiosity; its perceived reality due to being produced by real people; and its blurring of commercial and user content, presents unique challenges, particularly when issues like body weight are discussed indirectly. Key concepts of media literacy become very unclear with social media. These include how to identify the content creator, their targeted audience, point of view, and intent and, most importantly for body image, the information's accuracy and completeness and the reliability of the source. Social media literacy can be protective but requires a more complex and nuanced assessment of messages that focuses primarily on discerning the content creator and their goals (Likes? Reposts? Attitude or behavior change?) and the effect of the social media platform's algorithms on the audience that receives the messages.[31]

In 2022, at a time when TikTok was one of the most popular social media platforms among youth, researchers conducted a content analysis of one thousand videos from ten popular nutrition, food, and weight-related hashtags, each with over one billion views.[32] Ninety-seven percent of the videos presented a "weight-normative" view of health, that health is only possible at a specific weight, weight and disease are directly related, and one has a personal responsibility for meeting healthy weight expectations.[33] Not only will these explicit and implicit messages reach well beyond those who seek out information on body image to anyone interested in personal health, but they are a setup for self-doubt, anxiety, and depression for those who do not fit into weight-normative guidelines, as well as potential body-shaming and cyberbullying by others.

In caring for young people with eating disorders, one of the risks we face in hospitalizing them is that they will learn from other patients strategies for hiding and perpetuating their unhealthy behaviors. Generative AI, powerful research tools that can rapidly search billions of pieces of text or image data and generate responses to virtually any question, can provide and promote the dissemination of these dangerously unhealthy strategies even more effectively than social media. A 2023 study by the Center for Countering Digital Hate tested six popular AI platforms, three chatbots and three image generators, by asking twenty prompts, questions that vulnerable young people curious about losing weight might ask. In response to a total of one hundred and eighty prompts, the AI platforms provided 41 percent harmful eating disorder content. Two of the three chatbots generated 23 percent harmful information, while one produced none. But when jailbreaks, prompts designed to circumvent safety features, were used, all three chatbots produced 67 percent harmful content. This content ranged from tips for hiding food to manually inducing vomiting to smoking ten cigarettes a day, swallowing a tapeworm egg, or using heroin. Image-based AI tools responding to twenty prompts like "thigh gap goals" and "skinny body inspiration" generated 32 percent of images glorifying extremely low-weighted women with pronounced rib cages, protruding hips, and cachectic, or severely wasted-away, legs.[34] Generative AI's ability to search the web for unhealthy information encouraged and supercharged vulnerable youths' quest to be thin.

Tara nearly died from malnutrition. After medical hospitalization for nutritional resuscitation and an extended stay in residential treatment for anorexia nervosa, Tara met a therapist who asked her to keep a selfie photo diary for their work together, taking her own full-body picture each day and writing about it. Although the illness distorted what Tara saw, the camera did not. Each day she looked at an image—not an image of an idealized ultrathin model but of herself. At first, this nearly skeletal teen tried to maintain her claims that she was fine—healthy but still a little overweight. After all, she'd been following a thinspiration influencer for several years. But between looking at the images each day (which were subtly changing as she was re-fed), writing about the images in her diary, and talking about them with the therapist, she gradually came to grips with how devastatingly underweight and unhealthy she had been. "It was like I had torn myself down to almost nothing and had to rebuild," she told me in a later medical checkup. "Not only did I finally recognize how I had hurt myself, but I learned to accept, maybe even like, the me I rebuilt."

Tara is better today. She has achieved a normal weight and completed college and graduate school. She recently married and hopes to have a child. But when Tara is stressed, she still feels the strong pull of her eating disorder. Like alcoholics in recovery, she has had to acknowledge the constant and unchanged possibility that she might backslide into pathological behaviors that she may never totally exorcise. When Tara senses that she is vulnerable, she pulls up her recovery album from her digital folder, and the selfies and journal entries bring the work of therapy back to mind—her reality check. She remembers where she has been and does not want to return.

MEDIA Rx

Set the Stage for Health—and Watch for Red Flags

Your roles as model, mentor, and monitor are vital in the effort to push back against malignant messaging about body image and to support healthy nutrition and exercise, as well as character- and capability-based measures of ourselves and others.

YOU CAN

- *Eat a healthy, balanced diet, and exercise regularly and within reason.* Remember that bodies of growing children look different and have different needs than your adult body. Even if you are trying to lose weight, don't talk about dieting. Instead, talk about healthy eating and being active.
- *Ditch the diet talk. Don't encourage or allow a growing child or teen to diet or fast.* If your child is a vegetarian, is vegan, or adopts another prescribed diet, make sure that it is with medical guidance or a consulting nutritionist. Avoid demonizing entire food groups, such as fats or carbohydrates. Both, in their most nutritious forms, are essential ingredients of a balanced diet; it's just a matter of how much and in what proportion to other parts of the diet.
- *Bring clarity and compassion to the table.* If your child is in the grip of an eating disorder or a struggle with negative body image, they're likely to be defensive and in denial, so you'll need to bring clarity and compassion to any intervention. They will try to avoid eating together, but a sit-down family meal every day both provides nutrition and supports mental health. It is more important than ever if your child is developing an eating disorder. Stay aware of their eating behavior. Are they pushing their food around their plate? Cutting it up into tiny pieces? Do they ask to be excused to the bathroom and stay long enough to throw food away or throw food up?
- *Believe your eyes.* Pay attention to your child's eating and food-related behavior. Never justify or explain away changes in eating patterns or weight loss or gain. Because you see your child all the

time, changes may be gradual. Parents are frequently the last to notice when a child's weight has changed, particularly if the child does not want you to know. Watch for perfectionistic tendencies and a persistent preoccupation with thinness or appearance beyond what feels reasonable and healthy. A child or teen with an eating disorder can find plenty of online support with dieting tips and tricks to avoid detection by caring parents, teachers, counselors, and doctors. If you are worried, trust your instincts and seek medical care.

- *Use your ears.* Listen to the way your child talks about their body or appearance that may suggest a developing or existing problem with their body image. Constant references to their appearance, as if that's the most important thing about them; persistent dissatisfaction or use of negative language to describe their body or aspects of their physical appearance; negative comparisons to people they know or see in the media; or generally depressive, sad, or harshly judgmental comments about their looks are your cues to act.

- *Talk with your child in a caring, nonjudgmental way.* Many signs are subtle, especially in the early stages of a developing body image disturbance. If you have any concerns, talk with your child using "I," not "you," phrases. "I've noticed . . . I feel . . ." Identify what you have seen or heard that concerned you. Your child may not realize that certain attitudes about weight and eating, negative body image, patterns of food consumption, or exercise behaviors can be serious health concerns. They may be in denial about the signs you see clearly. If they do have an eating disorder, they may insist it is not a problem but a lifestyle choice and make greater efforts to hide it from you.

- *Contact your child's physician with concerns about disordered eating behaviors or changes in their weight.* Ask their doctor to evaluate what is going on medically and psychologically. Seek recommendations on best steps to address the issue with nutrition, healthy activity, and changes in media use.

Chapter 9

Wirelessly Wired

Media Influence on Tobacco, Vaping, Alcohol, and Other Substance Use

M ax came to me one afternoon late in August, feeling ill after what sounded like a typical long summer weekend for a beach-going fourteen-year-old boy. He'd spent most of the past four days out in the sun and each day had grown weaker and sicker. It seemed likely that he'd gotten dehydrated, so I sent him to the ER for IV fluids. My next call was from the intensive care unit. Max had indeed been dehydrated, but the IV fluids went straight to his lungs and flooded them. Max nearly died, drowning in his own fluids—and we did not know why his lungs were so damaged.

When I saw him weeks later for his annual health maintenance exam, I asked Max the usual questions about alcohol, smoking, and substance use that he had previously denied.

"I did start vaping right at the end of last school year, but it was no big deal," he volunteered. He had thought it was safer than smoking—and the device was cool. Over the summer he had continued vaping nicotine and added THC cartridges. He had bought all of this online simply by checking the box next to "Are you twenty-one?" Inhaling the solvents in which the vape nicotine and THC were dissolved had damaged Max's lungs.

The tobacco industry has a problem with its business model—they must replace nearly half a million American and more than seven million global customers who die every year of illnesses related to tobacco use.[1] The campaign to reduce tobacco smoking has been one of the biggest successes of public health in the United States. In the early 1960s, 42 percent of all Americans smoked cigarettes, each lighting up an average of 4,345 cigarettes in 1963. Almost 90 percent of adult daily smokers started as teenagers, some even as younger children.[2] There were cigarette ads on TV and radio. Billboards, newspapers, and magazines highlighted celebrities, even doctors, recommending certain brands.[3] Quitting smoking was hard. Not only is nicotine powerfully addicting, but smoking was deeply ingrained in the habits of individuals and the fabric of social interactions from work breaks to social drinking to post-sex. Eighty-seven percent of regular smokers had smoked their first cigarettes by their eighteenth birthdays, and 95 percent had started smoking before turning twenty-one.[4] So anti-tobacco campaigns focused on preventing smoking. In schools, health teachers cut open "black lungs" from lung cancer victims. Ironically, the danger and the focus on limiting tobacco to adults made smoking even more attractive to youth seeking the freedoms of adulthood.

In 2000, public health advocates harnessed youths' independence-seeking and engagement with screens with a subversive campaign by the anti-smoking Truth Initiative, broadcasting truth-telling prank calls from youth to tobacco executives and videos of young people piling body bags in front of company headquarters. By pitching youth against the corporate machine, they made smoking uncool. Researchers found the Truth campaign to have prevented 450,000 youth from starting to smoke in its first four years and saved $1.9–5.4 billion in health-care costs in its first two years.[5] But Big Tobacco is not easily beaten. As impressive as the Truth-related health savings over two years were, they were dwarfed by tobacco marketing. In 2019 alone, tobacco corporations spent $8.2 billion marketing tobacco and tobacco products.[6] Continuing to sell cigarettes to vulnerable populations, they pivoted to high-tech vaping products to engage new consumers. Big Tobacco disingenuously presented the vaporization of nicotine (or any other substance) as a healthier solution that would help smokers wean themselves off nicotine. Vaping devices are small, sleek, and tech-sexy, attractive to youthful early adopters of tech and easy to use surreptitiously, even in a classroom. The tobacco industry aggressively courted new vapers with "e-juice" in a variety of attractive flavors, from berries to butterscotch, cookies to cotton candy, melon to marshmallow to milk. They packed e-juice with even more nicotine and steadfastly insisted that vaping was only for adults who sought to quit smoking.

Max's experience revealed two media phenomena that landed him in harm's way. The first is a long-established advertising tactic for many products, but especially for products that are restricted to adults or potentially harmful. Tobacco and other products are not advertised on their merits but instead tell a story of who you will be if you use them. Marlboro cigarettes, still far and away the most popular among adolescents and adults, dramatically shifted their advertising strategy in the 1960s as the public began to realize the negative health effects of smoking tobacco.[7] In 1958, before there was widespread public awareness about the health effects of smoking, advertising emphasized the flavor and quality of the product. One typical ad of the period depicts a suave, suited man-about-town with a flower in his lapel—and a cigarette to his lips. The text read: "More to like than ever" and "Marked improvement in Marlboro filter does not disturb Marlboro flavor."[8] By contrast, in 1981, in one ad not only did they not talk about the product at all, they simply showed the "Marlboro Man," an independent, masculine cowboy on the open range, who is not even smoking a cigarette.[9] Such tactics appeal to our feelings rather than our logic. Emotions are primary in human decision-making, driving snap decisions while logic follows later to reconsider and most frequently cement final decisions. Dale Carnegie, one of the historical grandmasters of persuasion, wrote in *How to Win Friends and Influence People*, "When dealing with people, let us remember we are not dealing with creatures of logic. We are dealing with creatures of emotion, creatures bristling with prejudice and motivated by pride and vanity."[10] Reacting to perceived and imagined stimuli, emotions arise from the unconscious mind and usually overpower slower-moving and less motivating logic. All of us, but youth in particular, tend to choose the self-image of the rugged individual over the boring numbers nerd. Sexy beats cautious—especially for young people whose visual centers of the brain are at least a decade more mature than the prefrontal cortex and its executive functions of impulse control and future planning.

Interestingly, the second media phenomenon that affected Max seemed to be speaking to his logical thinking, reassuring him that vaping was safe. Misinformation is inaccurate or incomplete information, as distinguished from disinformation, which is fiction intentionally disseminated as fact in order to mislead others. Vaping was disingenuously introduced as a means to help tobacco smokers quit, like a do-it-yourself weaning from nicotine that previously had been the purview of physicians with prescription nicotine gum and patches. What went unmentioned were the child-friendly flavors;

the attractive, cutting-edge devices; or the fact that a user could be exposed to higher doses of addictive nicotine even more quickly than they could achieve with cigarettes. Promotional information on vaping focused on adults quitting smoking. Unlike disinformation, this was not an intentional fiction. It was just a small sliver of the truth. What it omitted was the larger part of the story—that there was now a sexy, must-have electronic device from which you could get a buzz without a nasty taste or getting caught. In 2022, over three million—more than one in ten—middle (5 percent) and high school (17 percent) students were using tobacco products, over two and a half million were using e-cigarettes, and almost one million were smoking cigars and cigarettes.[11] One in four of the students using e-cigarettes were vaping daily, and nearly 85 percent were using flavored vape products.[12] Earlier generations smoked cigarettes because it made them look and feel cool. Then the Truth campaign and public health education made cigarettes uncool—kids who smoked were seen as victims of old people (like their parents!) who ran corporations. Now vaping had claimed cool—it was what the young and tech-savvy did.

ASK THE MEDIATRICIAN
Should I Be Concerned About My Kids Seeing Smoking and Vaping Scenes in Movies?

I've seen news stories about the dangers of kids seeing smoking in movies. I'm a bit confused, as I thought smoking was no longer really an issue, especially in kids' movies (G, PG, PG-13), and that smoking in general is on the decline. Is this something I should still be concerned about when I take my kids to the movies or watch one at home?

You are right to be concerned about your child seeing smoking in movies because the US surgeon general concluded that the research shows a causal relationship between portrayals of smoking seen in movies and the initiation of tobacco use among young people.[13] Numerous research studies have shown that when all other factors are controlled for, seeing portrayals of smoking in the movies significantly increases the risk that a young person will start using tobacco.[14] Smoking is often used by filmmakers as narrative shorthand for rebelliousness or sexiness or just to make a scene look cool with backlit smoke. Tobacco use in a movie by any character, good or bad, normalizes it as acceptable behavior and, because it is being done by a star, conveys attractiveness and glamour to intensely self-conscious youth yearning to be accepted.

Despite our knowledge that screen media are now the strongest motivator of smoking initiation among youth, 31 percent of all youth-rated movies had tobacco incidences in 2018, and tobacco incidents increased 120 percent in PG-13 rated movies from 2010 to 2018.[15] Public health initiatives like Smokefree Media have actively worked for nearly two decades to prevent the initiation of smoking among young persons by reducing movie portrayals of tobacco use.[16] Because of these efforts, the six major motion picture production companies now have policies to reduce tobacco imagery, which they have publicized well, thus your impression that it is no longer an issue. The good news is the number of films portraying tobacco use decreased 61 percent from 2018 to 2020, but fewer movies were released that year, likely due to the COVID-19 pandemic. With the rise of video streaming services, it will become even more important to ensure that media on those platforms to which youth are exposed are not normalizing tobacco use.[17]

Because fewer tickets are sold to R-rated movies, the ratings board of the Motion Picture Association (MPA) has not agreed to demands that smoking in a movie receive an automatic R, thus leaving those too young to legally buy cigarettes unprotected from the tobacco industry's most effective marketing tool. We cannot rely on the rating system or the assurances of movie studios to protect children from the powerful influence of smoking in screen media, but *we* can protect them with mindful media consumption.

YOU CAN

- *Choose movies using research-based, health-focused resources as well as film reviews.* Websites such as Smokefree Media provide information on smoking references for theatrically released and streaming movies and shows. The Digital Wellness Lab offers information on the health effects of substance use portrayals in media.[18]

- *Read the descriptor in small type under the MPA movie rating.* Although the rating may not reflect it, smoking and images of any substance use should be listed here.
- *Most importantly, talk to your child.* Watch movies with your child when possible and talk about them afterward. Ask questions such as, "Why do you think that character was smoking?" "How do you think their smoking affects them?" and "What do you think about that choice?"

Ultimately, your children's knowledge and common sense are their best protection. Rather than accepting it as the norm, you can help them see smoking as an unhealthy, unattractive, and stupid habit. While poor health may be dismissed by adolescents as a distant potential, no young person wants to be seen as unattractive or stupid. Empower them with knowledge—the most effective anti-smoking campaigns, like Truth, have been generated with and for youth. Having open, honest, and regular discussions with your children will help them make informed, healthy decisions for themselves, despite what they see on their screens.

Development Stokes Experimentation

Adolescence is a time of rapid physical, psychological, cognitive, and emotional growth. It is also a time of mismatches. Teens grow tall and strong but are clumsy and easily get hurt. They fall head over heels in love but do not recognize when they are not loved back. They act confident but are deeply insecure and desperate to fit in. Venturing out of the nuclear family on their own, they seek new experiences, sensation, and respect. They feel powerful and invulnerable, which makes them uniquely predisposed to try not only tobacco products but substances from alcohol to cannabis to designer drugs and beyond.

Two normal development drives of adolescence, sensation-seeking and the desire to be seen and treated as an adult, lead many young people to experiment with substances. Legally restricting products that give a buzz to adults makes them more attractive, the forbidden fruit to a young person anxious to experience the world and be seen as an adult. Our culture and media portrayals make alcohol, cannabis, and other pleasurable substances that children are denied doubly attractive to adolescents. Like tobacco, alcohol and the emerging cannabis industry leverage adolescent sensation-seeking and "adulting" to engage young people before they are of legal age, building brand loyalty and weakening the deterrent effect of the law even for illegal use of substances. Just as they have done with cigarettes and vaping products, underage users will find access and will face health risks. Like Max, they often don't notice immediate consequences, and they are certain that they can always stop using if they do. While many youths will experiment with tobacco, alcohol, and cannabis and eventually abandon them, some will develop long-term health problems. Tobacco addiction, problem drinking, alcoholism, and substance abuse and dependency affect millions of adults, resulting in decreased quality of life; prolonged, debilitating illnesses; and a drain on personal and public resources.

Planning, prioritization, and long-term cause-and-effect thinking are executive brain functions controlled by the prefrontal cortex, which will only be fully developed in the mid to late twenties. Preventing chronic health conditions is only part of the big picture. Substance use can have damaging effects on a brain that is still developing.[19] There are immediate risks to address when alcohol or cannabis is the substance in question. Motor vehicle crashes are one of the leading causes of death among fifteen-to-nineteen-year-olds in the US, a quarter of which involve an underage drunk driver.[20] Unlike alcohol, we do not yet have a reliable roadside test for drivers high on cannabis. Alcohol remains the most commonly used drug among twelve-to-seventeen-year-olds; 20.9 percent of fourteen-to-fifteen-year-olds say they've had at least one drink in their lifetime.[21] In fact, underage drinking accounted for $17.5 billion in sales revenue in 2016, 7.4 percent of the total sales revenue for alcohol.[22] Media influences on young people to start drinking are not so different than those to start smoking or vaping.

What this translates to is alcohol advertising directed at a young, undecided population. Indeed, many key advertising venues, whether online or through more traditional media such as magazines, billboards, bus signs, and sports programming, reach large numbers of adolescents. In addition, most of the major distillers brand and promote "alcopops," soft-drink-like malt liquor beverages that are designed to build early brand loyalty to the liquor. The packaging, colors, and attitudes associated with many of these starter beverages are unique, interesting, and engaging. The commercial face of these beverages in advertising, from tailgating beer to fruit-flavored vodka, often features irreverent attitudes, rock music, and animal mascots such as dogs, frogs, and lizards presented in a way that makes alcohol consumption appear to kids to be both fun and risk-free. What happens when an impressionable child or adolescent, who is trying to understand how to be cool, watches movies, listens to music, or reads popular magazines where drinking, smoking, and substance use are presented this way? What do they make of their favorite idols using these products in movies, music videos, or celebrity news?

The influence of entertainment media on substance use starts early and has a delayed response. Of G-rated animated feature films released between 1937 and 2000, assumed to be safe for children, 47 percent portrayed alcohol use and 43 percent portrayed smoking.[23] Only 4 percent of the films contained any message about the risks of smoking, and there were no messages about the risks of alcohol use.[24] Research has found that adolescents who watch more television are more accepting of alcohol consumption than those who watch less.[25] Substance use of various kinds is deeply integrated in our culture as an enjoyable, low-risk *adult* activity, an irresistible siren song to many young people who aspire to be adult. Tobacco and alcohol corporations are spending billions to reinforce this message, even in their ads that encourage adults to "drink responsibly."

Media Literacy Can Lower Gullibility and Vulnerability

The good news is that media literacy training has been effective in reducing risk for substance use as well as consumerism. Programs implemented in North Carolina public schools have shown dramatic reductions in both brand consciousness and desirability of alcoholic beverages among elementary and middle school students who received training in how to understand and deconstruct media messages.[26] With conscious, critical awareness of how media can influence them, children were able to protect themselves and prevent the changes in alcohol-related attitudes and behaviors that have been observed in children without such training.

Public health measures incorporated into media presentations can give all viewers the ability to protect themselves from negative effects as well. For example, inoculating moviegoers with a short trailer revealing the health realities of tobacco use before a feature film that portrays attractive, hip stars smoking cigarettes has been found to completely eliminate the persuasive effects of the tobacco product placement in the movie on young viewers. Some kids actually had a more negative attitude after the reality trailer and the movie than they had before seeing them.[27] Effective efforts to guide children and teens to make healthy choices before starting are vital because messaging that normalizes or glamorizes risky behaviors compounds the risk of beginning to use an addictive substance, and some kids who stumble never fully recover.

Unfortunately, the tobacco industry understands the protective power of education and peer pressure—they also understand who is less protected. Their products are disproportionately used by socially and educationally vulnerable middle and high schoolers. In 2022, 11 percent of all middle and high school students used tobacco products, but they represented 27 percent of failing students; 18 percent of those reporting psychological distress; 17 percent of transgender students; 16 percent of lesbian, gay, or bisexual students; 14 percent of Native American students; and 13 percent of students of low socioeconomic status.[28]

MEDIA Rx
Five Reasons to Monitor Media Choices and Start the Conversation Now

Sophisticated strategies in advertising and marketing are designed to sell even young children on the idea and the image first, then the product and the brand. Develop a habit of conversing with them to help them make informed choices as they move into adolescence and out on their own.

- Alcohol, smoking, and drugs are often glamorized in entertainment media, which can lead children and teens to believe that everybody is using substances and having fun.
- Movies and TV shows usually do not show short- or long-term consequences of substance use, which can lead to children believing that these activities are risk-free.
- Alcohol and tobacco advertisers make their products look appealing to children and teens, especially when marketers use celebrity endorsement, cute animals, and attractive models.
- Despite laws against paid product placement in movies and television, companies that own a variety of businesses can put their products in the hands and mouths of popular stars on-screen by bartering giveaways to the entertainment producers.
- Children and teens who are exposed to media showing substance use may be more likely to use tobacco, alcohol, or drugs.[29]

In a tale of two ballers, basketball teammates who met as fifth graders, Daniel and Nate first tried smoking cigarettes under the gym bleachers in middle school. Nate was a patient of mine, and at his annual physical, he acknowledged that he had tried smoking tobacco but didn't like how it made him cough. Daniel kept smoking, while Nate took up vaping. Like many young people, Daniel, Nate, and their high school basketball teammates partied together. When Daniel and some of his other friends started smoking blunts—cigars refilled with cannabis—and drinking beer, Nate just drank beer. Sensation-seeking, Daniel and Nate engaged in several health-risk behaviors, one after the other. With each risk behavior, the next became easier—and more dangerous. Research shows that once youth are involved with one health-affecting activity, they are at much higher risk for engaging in others.[30] The reason for that is not physiological or chemical but rather attitudinal. When using a psychoactive substance is normalized and acceptable, it becomes not only easier but also more desirable. Some adolescents, seeking to fit in with others and to increase the thrill, want to top what they have done before.

Nate and Daniel were at a party junior year. Daniel passed out. Nate, figuring that Daniel had drunk too much, lifted him from the floor onto a couch but noticed that Daniel was really out of it. "He's breathing funny!" Nate said to the party's host, who responded, "Get him outta here! I don't want my parents to find out!" Daniel's blunt-smoking friends moved away from them, unwilling to help. Not knowing what else to do, Nate called his parents, and they told him to call 911. The ambulance took Daniel to the emergency department of a local hospital, but Nate was not a family member, so he could not accompany Daniel. When his parents came to pick Nate up, he persuaded them to call the hospital, only to find that Daniel was admitted to the intensive care unit and on a ventilator to support his breathing. It turned out that Daniel had been snorting OxyContin and the cannabis he smoked had been laced with fentanyl. Daniel was stabilized medically then admitted to a psychiatric hospital detox program.

Nate's parents, shocked at what had happened to a young man they thought they knew, and at the realization that Nate had been vaping and drinking himself, prohibited Nate from connecting with Daniel at all. They did not allow Nate to obtain a driver's license until after he graduated high school, provided that he stayed clean and sober. Scared straight by Daniel's brush with death, Nate did stay clean and sober, but he secretly kept in touch with Daniel by text. Nate went on to college, where he was so concerned about the unrestrained alcohol use there that he started a blog about it. He tried to share the realities he had experienced in the hope that others would not have to learn the hard way. He has not yet been able to quit vaping, although he does intend to quit "someday." Daniel, returning home from his detox, did not do well; he eventually slid back into using OxyContin and then, because OxyContin was too expensive, started snorting heroin. He dropped out of touch with Nate sometime during Nate's sophomore year in college.

Addictive behaviors often remain a lifelong challenge and play a role in a wide range of other health issues, both physiological and psychological. However challenging treatment for physical or psychological conditions may be, underlying chemical dependencies make them even harder. Prevention and early intervention on addictive behaviors can save lives. While efforts like the Truth campaign will continue to do what they can to improve the prevailing cultural narrative about substance use, entertainment media and advertising will most likely continue to glamorize and normalize it. The narrative must be changed from "adults only" to "healthy versus unhealthy," unsafe at any age. We must bring Nate's voice and those of other youth and parents to the public conversation and, in our own homes with our own families, model, mentor, and monitor media use to prepare our children to make healthy choices.

MEDIA Rx
Talk Truth, Consequences, and the Power of Personal Choice

It's hard to find popular media that don't glamorize substance use or depict it as the norm, but you can limit your child's exposure and bring a reality check to those they see.

YOU CAN

- *Say something when you see something.* Children learn from what they see in media, whether it is in advertising or programming. When you see substance use, point it out to them as unhealthy, not normal. Saying nothing condones or accepts it.
- *Model positive, healthful behaviors.* Talk openly and honestly about substances, from tobacco to alcohol to illegal drugs, starting early in your child's life. This is neither to scare your child nor to desensitize them to the risks but to be realistic. Substances do make most people feel good in the moment, which is the attraction, but the risks they present usually happen afterward and are much more serious, long-lasting, and potentially life-threatening.
- *Be aware of what you watch and/or play when your child is present.* Know that even if the content seems to be OK to your adult eyes, even casual exposure to substance use as normal can affect children's and teens' attitudes and behaviors.
- *Co-view or keep an intermittent eye on incoming media.* This is in part to "change the channel" if you don't want your very young child to be seeing something and in part to be able to use those depictions to open discussions with school-age and older children about the health, social, and legal consequences of substance use. Many music videos and lyrics, TV shows, video games, and

magazines portray behaviors that may influence their views on alcohol, tobacco, and drug use.

• *Make sure your child knows the facts.* As the alcohol and tobacco corporations understand, focusing on an adults-only aspect of substance use only makes it more enticing to kids. Explain to your child why substance use is unhealthy for anyone's current health and for their long-term brain development. If someone in your family or extended social circle drinks or smokes, explain to your child how drinking, smoking, vaping, and using drugs recreationally can create a chemical dependency that makes it increasingly hard to quit once the habit is established. Be prepared to explain why an occasional glass of wine or alcoholic beverage might be safe for some adults under certain circumstances but never for a growing child.

• *Dump the trendy branding.* Do not buy or allow your child to have tobacco or alcohol promotional materials like gym bags, jackets, or coolers. There is a strong relationship between youth owning such items, brand loyalty, and future drinking initiation.[31]

• *Raise a cynic.* Pay attention to the alcohol advertising in sports events and during commercial breaks. Skip the ads or talk with your kids about them. Deconstruct the messages and the hidden health risks they intentionally overlook. Critical thinking allows children to question the motivations behind different media depictions of substance use and how accurate they are. By teaching children that substance use in the media is frequently unrealistically positive and can be detrimental to their health, children will be less likely to accept what they see or hear as a model for how they should behave.

• *Show them the money.* Talk about the profit motive behind the cigarette and alcohol industries and call out product placements, smoking, and drinking portrayed in screen media. Do the same for recreational use of cannabis. It's the new big business. Just because it's now legal in many places doesn't make it healthy or safe for kids. Aside from having a parent who smokes, viewing smoking in screen media is one of the biggest risk factors for young people to start smoking. Even though we've done a remarkable job of getting overt tobacco advertisements completely out of youth-facing publications, now the most potent marketing effort is brand placement. From direct advertising to product placement, making their products look trendy and appealing in the media boosts someone's bottom line.

- *Take a cue from your child's music.* Pay attention to song lyrics and music videos, and discuss with your children references to drinking, smoking, and other substance use.
- *Use your consumer voice.* Complain to the Motion Picture Association, individual studios, stations, online platforms, or publishers about portrayals that you think exploit or harm your child. You would be astonished to know how few consumers communicate with them. A single voice can carry a lot of weight. They need customers and will listen to your concerns.

Chapter 10

Lessons in Fear and Loathing

Violent Media, Aggression, and Anxiety

I was examining the abrasion and bruise over the energetic four-year-old's left cheekbone, just under his eye, as his distraught mother explained that Dylan had been in a fight in preschool.

"Well, it really wasn't a fight," his mother said. "His teacher called me very upset. She says he's really smart and he's usually pretty good, but this time he just lashed out. I guess they were building with LEGOs. He and his friend made guns. I would never let him have a toy gun; you know me . . ."

I did know her. Her fourteen-year-old daughter, Sierra, had been my patient for years. Dylan's mother and her husband worked in a food co-op and described themselves as "old hippies" or "refugees from the sixties."

"They were shooting at each other and his friend got too close," Dylan's mother said to me. Then to him: "I really don't want you playing with him. He plays too rough!"

"Jack Bauer will never let him kill the hostage!" Dylan intoned.

"Jack Bauer?" I asked him. Jack Bauer is a fictional character, a counter-terrorism agent in the TV series *24*.

"You know, the guy that protects his family from bad guys," Dylan explained.

"How do you know about Jack Bauer?"

"It's on sometimes when I'm playing at my friend Ethan's house."

Violence has dramatically changed the lives of American children and the parents who love and want to protect them. From Sandy Hook Elementary School to Marjory Stoneman Douglas High School to Michigan State University, mass murder in schools, once a safe and secure place of learning and nurturing, has become horrifically commonplace. Children as young as nursery schoolers have regular shelter-in-place, lockdown, and evacuation drills with their hands clasped over their heads. Many are being taught the "Run. Hide. Fight." response to a mass shooting or if any shooter is on the loose. Parents wonder and worry as their child boards the school bus each morning. In each of the last three years, there have been more than six hundred mass shootings (four or more fatalities or injuries excluding the shooter) in the US, a rate of nearly two each day.[1] Firearms are now the number one cause of death in children ages one to nineteen, surpassing motor vehicle deaths.[2] Violence is central to the top three causes of death among teens and young adults: unintended injuries, suicide, and homicide.[3] For parents and for our society, violence is a critical public health concern in today's world. It is not the escalating statistics, so terrifying to parents, that bother the kids. What they see on screens—bloodshed and anger, near and far—is their everyday, in their backyards, their supermarkets, their music festivals, their bowling alleys. Mass shootings occur in the most mundane of places and at the most unremarkable of times. They feel deep, visceral vulnerability.

Concern about the influence of screen viewing on children's aggressive behavior was the first health effect of viewing media to raise public concern, extending back to and before the earliest days of television. Quaint as it might seem now, Congressional hearings were convened in 1952 and 1954 to bring psychologists, educators, and television executives together to assess whether media violence in programs like *Gunsmoke* was contributing to what was then called *juvenile delinquency*. Although those hearings resulted in no substantial changes, they revealed that although clinicians, educators, and others who worked closely with children and adolescents were deeply concerned, there were plenty of strong opinions but little scientific evidence to support those worries. The hearings became a debate between opposing opinions about whether children could learn violence from screens, and the debate ground to a standstill. Unfortunately, those Congressional hearings set the stage for a societal stalemate between protecting the health and safety of children and defending our constitutionally guaranteed freedom of expression, a polarized deadlock that has persisted to the present. Fortunately, Congress's lack of action motivated serious scientific research on whether and how screen viewing might influence the mental health and development of children and adolescents. Serious investigation of the effects of media violence on young people has now been pursued for seven decades.

Early experiments by Albert Bandura at Stanford University showed that three-to-six-year-old children who watched a film of an adult hitting an inflatable Bobo doll were more likely to hit a Bobo doll in a playroom full of toys than children who had watched a film of nonaggressive play or those who had not watched either film.[4] These experiments supported social learning theory, which says that human social behavior is learned by observing and imitating others.[5] But they were criticized for lacking ecological validity (not being an accurate representation of a child's life experience) and for only testing children's behavior immediately after the film viewing but not again after an interval of time to see whether the learned behavior was sustained.[6]

To determine whether and how the laboratory-tested effects apply to the realities of children's lives, the relationship between media exposure and violent behavior needed to be studied in the real world. Although less controlled than experiments, epidemiology can examine real-world relationships among screen media exposure and aggression, other factors that might be at play, and how much that exposure increases the risk that a young person will behave violently. A 1960 survey of 875 eight-year-olds in New York found that the more children viewed violence on television, the higher their level of physical aggression.[7] Ten years later, the researchers reinterviewed more than half of their original research participants and found in the boys a strong relationship between the level of media violence viewing at age eight and a history of aggression at age nineteen.[8] This correlation was consistent, even when the child's IQ, social status, parental aggression, social and geographic mobility, church attendance, and baseline aggression level were controlled. In fact, the boys who at age eight were rated as "low aggressive" but watched a lot of television were more aggressive at nineteen than those who at baseline were rated "high aggressive" but did not watch violent television.[9] Twelve years after that, in 1982, repeat interviews of then thirty-year-old study participants and review of criminal justice records revealed that individuals who were more aggressive at age eight had more traffic violations at age thirty while under the influence of alcohol, disciplined their children more harshly, and had been convicted of more serious crimes as adults.[10] While such "natural laboratory" studies of children's lives can begin to address the shortcomings of controlled laboratory experiments, they have been criticized for measuring correlation but not proving causation. Just because an outcome of interest changes in parallel to a change in conditions, it does not mean that the change in conditions caused the change in outcome.

This is true and it is an essential truth of public health research—we can observe the results of controlled but artificial experiments in the laboratory and we can measure real-world correlations with epidemiology, but humans and their behaviors present many potentially confounding variables. Causality can never be proven. Indeed, we have still not proven that smoking cigarettes causes lung cancer, because there are smokers who never get lung cancer and there are lung cancer sufferers who never smoked. What we do have is hundreds of scientific findings that have shown a significantly higher relative risk of getting lung cancer among smokers than nonsmokers. Because the overwhelming weight of the evidence points toward increased risk of heart disease, emphysema, and lung and other cancers, we recommend that people do not smoke. And because evidence also suggests that even second-hand smoke poses risks for children, we urge avoiding their exposure to it.

When many research papers investigating the effects of viewing violent movies and television were analyzed together in a meta-analysis twenty years ago, the increase in aggressive attitudes, thoughts, and behaviors found was stronger than the correlation found between calcium intake and bone mass, between lead ingestion and lower IQ, between not using a condom and becoming infected with HIV, and between secondhand tobacco smoke and lung cancer.[11] The relative risks of each of these exposures are enough for clinicians to make recommendations and for society to avoid them to prevent undesired outcomes. We have yet to develop a public health strategy regarding media violence even though the relative risk of aggression and anxiety is greater among those who have had greater exposure to screen violence.

Combining the findings of hundreds of research studies done in more than a dozen different disciplines from psychology to education to public health, scientists have developed a General Aggression Model, which proposes that human aggression arises from a combination of personal characteristics (hostile traits, rapid physiological arousal, poor anger management) and situational variables (victims of abuse, poor adult role models, exposure to media violence).[12]

In media, it is not violence itself but the context in which it is portrayed that can make the difference between learning about violence and learning to be violent. Violence is a reality in our world and must be learned about to prevent or intervene on it. Thoughtful explorations of human violence in plays like *Macbeth* and films like *Saving Private Ryan* treat violence as what it is—an all-too-common human behavior that causes suffering, loss, and sadness to both victims and perpetrators. Arguments that media violence has no effect on actual interpersonal violence have cited the level of extreme violence in Japanese movies and the very low level of violent crime in Japan. However, a 1980s study of Japanese media violence showed that those who suffered from violence and loved ones who experienced their loss were portrayed as much or more than those who prevail.[13] As in *Macbeth* and *Saving Private Ryan*, the experience viewers are left with is tragedy, not triumph.

Unfortunately, most entertainment violence is leveraged for immediate visceral thrills while portraying little or no human cost. In their efforts to obtain a much more commercially desirable PG-13 rather than the restrictive R, movie producers will frequently limit or eliminate blood and gore. While it is usually successful in scoring a PG-13 rating, showing less blood may actually increase the likelihood of aggressive thoughts and behaviors as it sanitizes and reduces the apparent suffering from violence.[14] Slapstick violence played for comedy and violence against sexy women, from Bond movies to video games like *Mortal Kombat*, can be particularly powerful, because they associate positive feelings with attacking and hurting others.[15]

ASK THE MEDIATRICIAN
Does "No Graphic Gore" Make Violence in Games Less Harmful?

Can you please offer guidance on Fortnite? *It seems to be all that kids eleven to fourteen years old are doing these days. I do not allow my children to play, but I saw my godson play and was horrified—the guns all look real, but the deaths show no blood. As a person who grew up in a hunting family and with firearms, I find the game to be irresponsible and addictive, but I was surprised by the seemingly positive review of the game from Common Sense Media. Please advise!*

Thank you for your question and for including your personal note about coming from a background of gun ownership and hunting. The huge popularity and number of hours children play *Fortnite*'s fight-to-the-death *Battle Royale* has raised many parents' concerns. Your knowledge of guns and the seriousness with which they must be handled brings an added understanding to the implications of children playing this game. It has been encouraging to receive and respond to questions from knowledgeable gun owners who are concerned about media violence featuring firearms.

Fortnite is considered both a third-person shooter game, where players' avatars are visible on-screen, and a sandbox game, where players are allowed to roam a virtual environment and choose to partake in different tasks. While the primary thrust of the core game is to build structures and collect supplies in order to survive a zombie apocalypse (think survivalist *Minecraft*), the most popular gameplay is in *Battle Royale* mode where up to a hundred players are airdropped onto an island and fight each other with the goal of being the last one standing. Once they are killed or prevail, they are immediately dropped into another conflict, so their quest for victory—and adrenaline level—never drops.

When comparing *Fortnite* to other popular shooter games, such as *Halo*, *Grand Theft Auto*, and *Call of Duty*, *Fortnite*'s player avatar graphics indeed seem cartoonish, showing less graphic carnage and gore when players kill others. Interestingly, the level of detail is amped up when it comes to the weapons players can win and use, from battleaxes to assault rifles. What is concerning is *Fortnite*'s combination of weapon glorification and cartoonish violence as the player sees the world through a lens that values weaponry but minimizes with cartoons the human damage those weapons cause. Each bloodless death of another player's avatar, not just a computer-generated NPC (non-player character), is just one step closer to winning, not the tragic loss of another child's representation.

Do not allow yourself to be misled by marketing messages (and even reviews) that seem to say, "It's not graphically gory, so it's not harmful." Research shows when activities such as smoking or drinking are shown without consequence and watched repeatedly, some teens are *more* likely to try them.[16] Experts warn that the same may be true when children see repeated acts of violence that are bloodless and unpunished. When violence is coupled with pleasure, such as comedy or sexiness, or a means to a victorious end, violence is more attractive.[17] The player focuses on the good feeling of prevailing, rather than negative emotions such as loss, remorse, or guilt for the "life" lost. As an experienced owner and user of guns, you know what it means to actually take a life. *Fortnite* does not re-create that experiential knowledge; it subverts it.

As an engaged and caring parent, you were right to try to understand *Fortnite* better, especially once you saw the intensity with which your godson played. Multiply his experience by the millions of children playing. While game reviews can be helpful, understand that they are not based in science, but are reviews by gamers, or in Common Sense Media's case, parents of gamers. What you bring to the table is your experience both as a parent and as a hunter. You know guns and you know your children. Explain to them what firearms can do and how to responsibly use them, as well as the difference between using a weapon in real life versus in a video game. And above all, whatever they do to have fun, ingrain in them the value of their lives and well-being—and the lives and well-being of others.[18]

After the Sandy Hook Elementary School shooting, opponents of gun control pointed to violent video games as the problem, not easy access to guns. In reality, this is not an either-or situation. The prevalence of firearms in violent screen media desensitizes users to both guns and violence. An experimental study randomly assigned eight-to-twelve-year-old children to watch a PG-rated movie clip with or without guns or play an E-rated (for "Everyone") video game with or without guns. Moved to a different room with toys and games and a file cabinet with a randomly assigned real but disabled 9 mm handgun hidden in a drawer, almost all of the children found the gun. Those who had viewed film or played a game with guns were more likely to handle the gun and pull the trigger, including while pointing the gun at themselves or a friend.[19] Increased portrayals of gun violence on television between 2000 and 2018 has been associated with more gun-related homicides involving fifteen-to-twenty-four-year-olds as both perpetrators and victims.[20] These findings parallel research demonstrating that visually portraying the means of suicide increases the likelihood of those means being used in suicide attempts.[21] Suicide accounts for the majority of all firearm deaths (54 percent), while homicide accounts for 43 percent.[22] The normalization of guns in media, including youth posing with them on social media to appear powerful, makes it more likely that youth who feel vulnerable will carry weapons.[23]

Interactive Games Make Powerful Teaching Tools

Video games appear to be even more powerful teachers than passively viewed media like television and movies.[24] While witnessing violence appears to desensitize viewers, violent video games do more, making children active participants in a violent narrative. Video games provide behavioral scripts for players, a specific set of behaviors that will be rewarded with points and opportunities for more complex and interesting play.[25] Whether the game is soccer or fighting your way out of a hospital for the criminally insane, the behavioral script will be played over and over and over again as your child improves their skill and progresses farther in the world of the game.

Video games create an opportunity for a young person to learn, rehearse, and perfect the central task of the game. What better teaching tool? Pilots who play video games have higher levels of visual attention, making them able to detect and process many more visual inputs in a broader visual field.[26] Surgeons who played video games more than three hours per week demonstrated improved eye-hand coordination and dexterity.[27] Likewise, studies have shown that, over time, young people learn from the violent media they consume; they develop a hostile attribution bias, which means that they are more likely to assume that the statements or actions of another are of hostile intent.[28] This changes the dynamic of interactions with others, tilting the interpersonal balance toward a conflict that must be won rather than resolved.

The relationship between violent games and aggressive thoughts and behaviors is especially troubling when you realize that nine out of ten bestselling games reward players for doing violence to others.[29] Research has shown that heavy users of violent video games exhibit fewer prosocial behaviors and poorer academic achievement.[30] These findings raise concern about what this highly effective teaching tool is actually teaching. Research from China examining the relationship between playing violent video games and cyberbullying found that, consistent with the General Aggression Model, greater violent video gameplay correlated with greater bullying and cyberbullying and that this association was stronger among those gamers with high trait aggression and weaker among those with high moral identity.[31]

Unfortunately, even morality as a moderator can be hacked if the violence is seen as justified, done by the "good guy" against the "bad guy." Observational research showed that violence that appeared to be prosocial and justified was more likely to be imitated.[32] Functional brain research with eighteen-to-twenty-two-year-olds has shown that violence portrayed as unjustified or "wrong" activates the part of the brain that responds to scary or repulsive events, while violence done to protect the helpless or avenge wrongs triggers the brain's reward centers.[33] Such distinctions between "bad violence" to be rejected and "good violence" to be emulated become problematic when non-Whites are disproportionately represented as "bad guys" and women are disproportionately victims of violence.[34]

ASK THE MEDIATRICIAN
How Can I Talk to My Husband About Media Violence?

I have eight- and ten-year-old daughters and a six-year-old stepson. My new husband thinks that PG-13 movies and violent video games are fine for all of our children, even his six-year-old. But I have never let my daughters use violent media because as a school guidance counselor, I am well aware of the dangers of media violence for children. How can I educate my husband on this issue?

You and your husband are not alone; many sets of parents disagree with each other about media violence. From what I see in my clinical practice, opinions usually fall along gender lines: moms tend to be concerned and dads tend to think that it isn't a big deal. Why is this long-standing debate not yet resolved? Because it focuses on values-laden beliefs like "I really don't like watching all that shooting" and "I played video games as a kid, and I turned out OK"—instead of on scientific evidence of how media use actually affects kids and on parents' awareness of their child's temperament and vulnerabilities.

Focus your conversation on facts rather than opinions. Avoid opinion and value judgments like "the dangers of media violence." Calmly explain to your husband that scientific research shows that children who use violent media are more likely to

- become fearful or anxious about the violent situations they see and hear about,
- become less sensitive to the suffering of others, and
- become more aggressive in their thoughts and behaviors.

The child who is upset by violent media is learning that the world is a dangerous, scary place; the child who is not upset by it is learning that violence is the way to solve problems. Parents aren't likely to want either of these outcomes for their children.

In your conversation with your husband, focus on the positive. Since it's a fact that kids learn from media, talk about what you *do* want them to learn. What kinds of behaviors do you want them to see, hear about, and emulate? Then brainstorm with your husband for examples of movies, TV shows, and music that provide positive models they can learn from. If you focus on what kinds of media you want to share with your children, you can find common ground.

If the conversation with your husband does not resolve the issue and the kids continue to use violent media, discuss openly as a family what they are seeing and how it makes them feel. This will give your kids an opportunity to discuss images that might have scared or confused them, help you and your husband understand what your kids are seeing and learning, and give you an opportunity to reinforce how you do want your kids to behave.

Meta-analysis of studies representing 15,386 gamers has shown violent video gameplay to be correlated with greater physical aggression over time, with the strongest effects on gamers between thirteen and sixteen years old.[35] Another meta-analysis of research involving more than 17,000 gamers found that the strongest association between violent video gameplay and aggression was found in White gamers, less strong but significant among Asian gamers, and unreliable among Latinx gamers, suggesting that desensitization to violence resulted in lower empathy among those who felt more socially powerful.[36] Although violent video gameplay has been associated with less prosocial behavior overall, recent experimental research has found increased prosocial behavior among nine-to-twelve-year-olds after co-play (partnered with another gamer) of *Fortnite Battle Royale* compared to co-play of a neutral pinball game and to solo play of either *Fortnite* or the pinball game.[37] This may be due to a sense that violence in defense of another is prosocial, helping behavior and that effects of gameplay on behavior may be moderated by moral identity as identified in the Chinese study.[38]

ASK THE MEDIATRICIAN
Why Do Different Kids Respond Differently to Media Violence?

My boys, now fifteen and seventeen, are so different. I've noticed that they can watch the same violent programs together but they respond differently. Is it true that after viewing violent programs, some children will behave more aggressively while some children become more fearful? If yes, can you explain how that happens? Any chance that some children are not affected at all?

Different kids will absolutely respond differently to different material, and there are many reasons for these variations, not all of them easy to identify. Some reasons have to do with age, some with temperament, and some with what else is going on in a child's life, but on the whole, there are three effects to watch for:

Desensitization (coming to accept violence as a normal part of life). The most universal and pervasive effect of exposure to violent media—one that affects us all, regardless of our age, education, or sophistication—is that the more we see, the more desensitized we become to violence and to the suffering that results. When we see a lot of violence, whether it's in the media or in real life, our understanding of the world shifts. Humans are adaptable organisms. If we live—and particularly, if we grow up—in an environment that is violent, we adapt to it. The more violence we see, the less out of place it seems.

Fear and anxiety. This may happen more in younger children. Seeing violence all over the news, in movies, and in video games can lead kids to believe that the world is a very dangerous place and they are potential victims every time they leave their homes.

Increased aggression. This is the least common effect but the one that is most worried about. In entertainment media, violence is often used to resolve conflicts. Furthermore, the negative consequences of this violence are not often shown. Seeing this over and over again, some kids may have increased aggressive thoughts and learn to solve problems using physical violence.

You also asked whether there are kids who aren't affected at all. In general, no, and frankly I would likely worry even more about a child who appeared completely unaffected. Humans relate to each other in positive and negative ways. As undesirable as aggressive interactions are, a child who cannot connect enough to care and feel empathy for those who are hurt is deeply worrisome.

Unfortunately, there is no good way of predicting which kids will be affected in which ways by their exposure to violent media. That makes prevention tricky. But given that most children will experience at least one of these three main effects, reducing exposure to media violence can only help. When your kids do encounter violence on the news or in entertainment media, teach them how to think critically about what they have seen and heard from the side of the aggressor and from the side of the victim. Imagine what they might do in a similar situation. And, as Fred Rogers learned from his mother, think about the helpers of those who are hurt.

Preventing Is Better than Unlearning Violence

At the end of World War I, US military leaders were shocked to discover that more than half of all the battlefield fatalities had died without firing their weapons. Analyzing this concerning phenomenon, psychologists concluded that because the fresh recruits had been trained to shoot at paper bull's-eye targets, the first time they drew a bead on a young person like themselves, they paused. The brief moment when they confronted the reality of killing one of their own kind was enough to let the other guy shoot first.[39] Military leaders recognized that this instinctive resistance to killing another human had to be overcome if soldiers were to succeed on the battlefield. For World War II, they trained soldiers to fire at plywood silhouettes of enemy soldiers—and battlefield losses with unfired weapons were cut in half.[40] Techniques for creating ever-more-realistic training scenarios have evolved with each military action. Today both the military and police academies train recruits on first-person shooter video games to enhance their vigilance and visual attention, improve their eye-hand coordination, and overcome their instinctual resistance to killing another human.[41] At the same time, importantly, recruits are drilled in military discipline, trained to shoot and stop shooting on command, and taught to respect the power of their position and of their weapons. The concern of Colonel David Grossman, a retired Army Ranger and professor of psychology at West Point who has studied the act of killing and its psychological effects, is whether children and adolescents who play those same first-person shooter games without counterbalancing discipline and respect may be desensitized to killing.[42]

In 2013, the *New York Times* featured an article titled "Unlearning Gun Violence," which discussed the work of an epidemiologist who, after a decade of fighting TB, HIV, and cholera in Africa, returned to a life-threatening epidemic in his hometown of Chicago—gun violence. He used the same techniques that worked for infectious diseases in Africa, identifying sources and patterns of contagion, connecting community peers with shooters and victims to interrupt the deadly cycle of violence, and going to the hospital to intervene on revenge when someone was shot.[43] Such secondary and tertiary prevention is effective—but it can only be done after violence has occurred. So that no more need to die, we must move beyond unlearning violence to practicing primary prevention. We must never learn violence.

That same week, a research report published in *Pediatrics* detailed the dramatic increase in gun violence in PG-13 movies, tripling over the last three decades.[44] Movies that any child can watch (hopefully, but not necessarily, with parental guidance) were now more violent than those that were restricted to those seventeen or older unless accompanied by an adult. One day later, I was asked to present research in support of a bill in the Massachusetts State Senate that would appoint an expert commission to study whether and how violent video games and other interactive media influence and teach their users.[45]

The video game industry has forged dramatic financial success and transformed our society not only by surpassing movies, television, and other media in revenues but also by leveraging young people's involvement with these virtual experiences into formal education. Encouraged by the software manufacturers' assertions that gamified curricula are the secret to engaging young learners and teaching everything from science to citizenship, we have invested billions of dollars in devices and software for our schools. At the same time, the video gaming industry has argued to legislative bodies that their entertainment products do not teach kids or influence their behavior in any way. I have testified at those hearings that the science shows that children are learning all the time. They are constantly building their fund of knowledge about themselves, the world, and how they should behave in it. Movies and television mirror the world, portraying a variety of human choices and the outcomes of those choices. Video games create virtual environments in which players are rewarded for making the correct choices, practicing over and over activities from sports to killing.[46] Both scientific research and common sense support the media industry's assertions of their products' potential and power to teach. But at the beginning of the first school year after the tragic shootings at Sandy Hook Elementary School, a school year that saw *Grand Theft Auto 5* capture nearly $1 billion in its first three days of sales, the industry was arguing to the Massachusetts State Senate that we did not need to understand what and how well these games teach our children.[47]

Knowledge is power—the power to make choices, as individuals and as a society, with full understanding of the risks, benefits, and potential outcomes of those choices. If video games can teach, they can teach calculus and they can teach killing. In addition to supporting the secondary and tertiary prevention of helping our fellow citizens unlearn gun violence, perhaps we should consider practicing primary prevention and never teach violence in the first place.

ASK THE MEDIATRICIAN
Does Torture Up the Ante in the Effects of Depicted Violence in Games?

My sixteen-year-old son loves role-playing games on the internet. We recently became concerned, though, when we found out that the games' plots often involve torture. We wonder why he is attracted to this kind of play and if there are any long- or short-term risks we should know about. We wonder if we should totally restrict his internet access but realize that this is not a realistic option. We do our best to keep the lines of communication open, but we need some guidance as to how to talk about our concerns with him.

Seeing your child engaged in this kind of play can certainly be alarming, and your impulse to talk to him about it is right on—but your discussion needs to be driven by reason rather than emotion or it can backfire. Understanding what might be going on can help.

Kids are often drawn to media violence not because they like violence but because it scares, upsets, or alarms them. In returning to it, they are attempting to master the troubling experience. But children who repeatedly engage with violence until it doesn't bother them can become desensitized not only to virtual violence but to psychological and physical violence as well. Part of the problem with exposure to media violence is that it makes violence seem more common than it actually is and changes our beliefs about what is normal.

Another contributing factor may be your teen's big feelings, which may include anger and vulnerability. His interest in these games may be driven partly by a need to explore those feelings. However, engaging in simulated torture is not the healthiest way to do that. Short-term effects could include signs that he is more on edge, such as increased anxiety, sleep disturbances, and irritability. In the long term, he may see violence against others or himself as a way to resolve his conflicts.

It sounds like you've already set the groundwork for open communication about media messages, and talking about the issue of torture need not be very different. Still, there are some particular approaches that may be helpful in addressing this issue:

- *Help him find a way to explore the big feelings.* Restricting internet access won't make the feelings go away. That's why it can be helpful to have him work with a therapist to find a different, more therapeutic outlet for them, like sports or martial arts.
- *Keep the computer in public space,* like the dining room table. That way he can play in areas where you can see what he's doing and discuss it with him.
- *Open conversations about his game by playing with him or sitting beside him while he plays.* Ask him to teach you about the game and to explain what's going on in it, how he feels playing it, and what he finds enjoyable about it. Seeking to learn from him is showing your respect and love for him and your interest in understanding his engagement with the games, not judging or reprimanding him. Listening to him can help you learn what needs this game is meeting for him and can open the door to brainstorming other ways to meet those needs.
- *Set limits on content.* It may be difficult to be reasonable rather than emotional at this point, but try saying something like, "As your parent, just like I won't feed you junk food, I don't believe you should practice hurting others. I see that you find it exciting, and I know that your rational mind understands it's only make-believe, but getting used to even simulated torture changes anyone. I don't want you to change that way." Then work with him to find games that excite him but don't include torture.

Remember that his media interests can offer a window into what he's processing internally, so a combination of setting limits on the content and helping him find another way to explore and process the feelings should serve the whole family well.

Dylan's mother brought him in for a runny nose on a very cold winter day shortly after he turned eight. As they were leaving, his mother said, "I'm not sure whether this is appropriate to ask you, but is it normal for him to be wetting his bed still? It isn't often, but it's often enough that I have a plastic mattress cover." Dylan was healthy and normally developed. There was no family history of urinary problems. They had cut off all fluids after dinner and made sure that he urinated before going to bed. "But every so often I hear him yelling or crying deep in the night," she said. "When I go in there, his bed is soaked in urine, but he's sound asleep."

Although parents worry about children learning to be violent from violent media, far more children learn to be afraid, as Dylan's nightmares and bedwetting suggested. When children spend as much time with media as they do, screens become a major source of information about the world and how they should behave in it. And because violence is primal, language-optional (unlike romance or character development), viscerally grabbing, and less expensive to produce than other audience-engaging plot elements, it is the surest bet for media producers who want to improve their chances of making a profit. As a result, there is a high prevalence of violence in the media used by us. All of us. And media need to keep exceeding their last effort to remain edgy and re-grab our primitive attention.

Most violent TV portrayals found by the National Television Violence Study in the 1990s were found in children's programming.[48] Of course, that included a lot of cartoons, and many would say that kind of violence is different than, say, an Arnold Schwarzenegger action film or "torture porn" like the *Saw* films. And they are right. The content is different. When Wile E. Coyote falls to the bottom of a deep canyon or gets crushed by an anvil, the violence is more stylized and clearly make-believe—to adults. But for young children it's different.

Cognitive psychology, which studies how and when the human brain develops specific abilities, has shown that children under the age of about seven or eight cannot clearly distinguish between reality and fantasy.[49]

What this means is that, for a young child, there is little difference between seeing a shooting in the street and seeing a shooting in a cartoon.

The point was brought home to me powerfully when I was asked to serve on a hastily organized task force to assess and respond to the psychological trauma experienced by children who witnessed 9/11. There was a deep concern that we would need to respond to mass post-traumatic stress disorder among children who watched images of planes crashing into buildings, collapsing them over and over again during that chaotic and terrifying day. In the weeks after 9/11, parents were distraught, afraid, tearful, and insecure—but, to the surprise and relief of many, their children appeared mostly unscathed. When children were asked about it, many shrugged: "No big deal. I've seen it before." To them, the violence they saw on screen was just as real as *Power Rangers* or *Looney Tunes*.

Increased Anxiety in a World That Feels Dangerous

When children, particularly young children, see violence on television or play violent video games, they learn that the world is a violent and threatening place. It is a logical conclusion to draw when their major experience of the world beyond their homes is the entertainment they watch and the games they play. Witnessing virtual violence can result in increased anxiety, fearfulness, and sleep disturbances.[50] At a time when more and younger children are on psychiatric medications for anxiety, attention deficit/hyperactivity disorder, depression, or sleep disorders than ever in history, perhaps we should consider whether we can prevent or reduce their symptoms by reducing their exposure to anxiety-provoking experiences. Although concern for the effects of violent media has focused almost exclusively on whether exposure makes some children violent, increased anxiety among many more children and desensitization of us all has a more widespread effect on our society and the health of our children.

I had not seen Dylan for nearly ten years. Then he came to the clinic at age seventeen with a man who introduced himself as Dylan's counselor. The Department of Youth Services needed a recent physical and immunization history of Dylan because he was now on probation. I was surprised. All of his issues while growing up had seemed to be within the normal range of rebelliousness and risk-taking. Dylan was a nice kid. He had a wonderful, supportive family and a great education. He grew up with everything he needed or wanted. He had no issues with drugs or alcohol.

"What is going on?" I asked.

"Assault and battery," his counselor related. I looked at Dylan quizzically.

"It was a stupid thing," he said. "I know that now." After glancing at his counselor to check whether it was OK to talk, Dylan related that he and three friends had been arrested for "happy slapping." They had dared each other to attack a random stranger, video it on a cell phone, and upload it to the internet. One of his friends had seen videos of happy slapping on YouTube and thought it was pretty funny. The older brother of the student they'd attacked did not think it was funny, and he called the police.

What about media ratings and media made especially for kids? Even G ratings or the wholesome Disney brand do not protect children from violent media. Every feature-length animated film created between 1939 and 1999 contained portrayals of characters perpetrating violence on others.[51] Among video games rated E in 2001, 64 percent were found to involve the game player in violent behavior.[52] It is important to understand that media ratings systems for movies and video games were developed and are implemented by the media industries themselves, not by the government or an independent organization dedicated to optimizing child health and development. The MPA movie rating system was implemented in 1968 not to protect children and guide parents but to free creative filmmakers from the tight restrictions of government censorship so they could honestly portray the social ferment of the times. The game-rating Entertainment Software Rating Board (ESRB) was similarly created in 1994 by the video game industry to avoid governmental oversight of their products after the public and Congress grew concerned about increasing violent and sexual content.[53] Age-based ratings are assigned in similar ways by both groups. Several trained raters whose qualifications are that they are or have been parents review the proposed release version of a movie or a written description and video of selected scenes from a game. The raters are asked to determine for what age of child a parent is likely to approve the product. Resulting ratings reflect the social values of the time more than what is best for child health and development. This has resulted in ratings creep in motion picture ratings.[54] ESRB game ratings have been criticized for not including questionable content in the game videos submitted for ratings review. Because the ratings systems are overseen by the industries themselves, there is an understandable business incentive to seek the least restrictive ratings and push the limits of those ratings to attract viewers and players. Because of this, child advocates have an equally understandable skepticism of the industry ratings. Now that the majority of screen media are consumed in homes rather than movie theaters, motion picture ratings are unenforceable, serving only as effective marketing tools advertising mature content.

From my perspective as a pediatrician and parent, prescriptive, "age-appropriate" ratings are inherently flawed on three counts: (1) no matter how unbiased by business considerations, oversight organizations cannot reliably prescribe media for children they do not know as well as their parents do, (2) every child of the same age is not at the same developmental stage, and (3) content that is appropriate for one family is inappropriate for another. Media ratings remain largely based on social values rather than developmental effects. For a media rating system to be truly effective at supporting healthy child development, it would need to be a descriptive system that outlines what kind of content will be encountered in a movie, television program, or game. Information on screen content would allow decisions to be made on what is developmentally optimal, not just for the normal variations among children of the same age but for a range of neurodiverse kids of any age, allowing the parents to determine what they deem optimal for each child. Finally, cultural and religious beliefs vary widely, so description rather than prescription would allow families to assess what they feel is appropriate for their children. To their credit, both ratings systems are now including content descriptions with their categorical ratings.

Media ratings will never be perfect. Content that confuses, upsets, scares, or grosses out a child will get through even much-improved ratings. Ultimately, it is through modeling and mentoring your child to be a critical viewer and critical thinker, sharing media and media experiences openly, and always keeping communication open for discussing, answering questions, and helping them process these experiences that your child will develop the media literacy necessary to optimize their development and their physical, mental, and social health.

Media Violence Echoes in Bullying and Cyberbullying

Shari was the quintessential queen bee. She'd been practicing since third grade, when she first earned her reputation as bossy, directing the play of her friends at school and playdates. On the playground she maintained control by announcing each day who her best friends were; they changed with her whims. By fifth grade Shari dominated the girls' clique and used slights and snubs to flex her social power, make some girls miserable, and ensure the others lived in fear. The next year her parents gave her a smartphone for making honor roll at school. Shari instantly weaponized the phone as a tool for expanding her reach and capacity for social aggression. She took embarrassing pictures of others and posted them on social media, spread gossip, made mean comments, and worst of all, responded to texts with long silences that left her targets squirming.

Shari was brought to our Clinic for Interactive Media and Internet Disorders after being suspended for three days during her freshman year of high school. Shari had shot a video of an overweight classmate, Maddy, dancing wildly in her pajamas at a sleepover. Shari posted it as a meme on a popular image-based social media site with the caption "HippoMaddymus dancing the Butt-Ugly," and it went viral, getting over 150,000 views overnight. Mortified, Maddy stayed out of school for a week. When the school called her parents, Maddy said she couldn't go back to school because everyone there hated her but wouldn't say why. When her mother reached out to Maddy's friend since kindergarten, the friend revealed what Shari had done. Because she violated the school's zero-tolerance rule on bullying, Shari was told by the school that she needed to participate in anti-bullying counseling before returning to school.

Once both Shari and Maddy were back at school, the school social worker conducted several restorative justice meetings where Shari could publicly make amends, Maddy could explain the hurt, and their classmates could discuss how they might have been complicit bystanders to bullying. As these discussions evolved, it was revealed that Shari had been cyberbullying Maddy and several other students since middle school and that cyberbullying was common in the freshman class. At the third and final restorative justice meeting, Shari broke down and revealed that she had been bullied since they were in middle school together by a girl now in the junior class—but Shari refused to name her.

Bullying, as has been practiced throughout recorded history, is the systematic use of threat or force by the more powerful to coerce, hurt, or harm the weaker or more vulnerable. Bullying can lead to school and behavioral problems, such as poor grades and acting out, for both bullies and victims.[55] Frequently occurring as an extension of in-person bullying, cyberbullying is the willful use of online digital technology to repeatedly humiliate with name-calling or embarrassing images, spread malicious untruths, ostracize, stalk, threaten physical harm, or send unwanted explicit images to or of a targeted victim.[56]

Smartphones and social media opened new opportunities for bullying. The ease of posting casual cruelties and the speed with which they travel to a worldwide audience transformed bullying into a digital-age spectacle. In a case eerily similar to Dylan's, a fourteen-year-old girl was physically assaulted by another girl in her school's hallway, and a video clip of the assault was posted to TikTok. Her father told reporters after she died by suicide that his daughter had lamented, "I don't want to be that girl who gets beat up on video and made fun of."[57]

Research has shown that those who are bullied at school are frequently bullied online, and those who bully at school often bully online.[58] In 2022, 46 percent of US youth reported being cyberbullied.[59] Although reduced from the 59 percent reported in 2018,[60] when half of a school community are victims of bullying, the social culture is permeated with threat. Forty-one percent of bullying victims confess that they believe they will be bullied again.[61]

Cyberbullying usually occurs between children or teens who know each other. In a survey of UK tweens and teens, only 1 percent reported that they were bullied solely online.[62] While physical bullying is more prevalent among boys (for example, the big ones giving wedgies to the little ones on the playground), cyberbullying is almost three times as prevalent among girls, whose psychological forms of bullying are easily transposed into the digital realm.[63] Fifteen-to-seventeen-year-old girls (54 percent) are more likely than fifteen-to-seventeen-year-old boys (44 percent) or thirteen-to-fourteen-year-olds of any gender (41 percent) to have experienced cyberbullying.[64] As with in-person bullying, a power differential is exploited in cyberbullying, with the socially entitled targeting the socially marginalized. Black youth are nearly twice as likely to be victims of cyberbullying (21 percent) because of their race or ethnicity, compared to Latinx youth (11 percent), and more than five times as likely as White youth (4 percent).[65] Youth who identify as LGBTQ+ are almost twice as likely to be cyberbullied as their straight peers.[66] There is a large overlap between the 58 percent of youth reporting having received and the 53 percent reporting having sent hurtful messages online.[67] Because identities are less clear online, cyberbullying has empowered the victim-bully, cyberbullying victims who then bully others, even those who bullied them.[68]

Teens who have been victimized report that cyberbullying often begins in person as repeated microaggressions, constant snarky comments, disrespectful interactions, social exclusion, or behaviors that put someone down, socially isolating them and ignoring their feelings. Then a hurtful message from an unknown sender is received and felt in isolation. The remote connection and the time lag between send and receive protects the sender from seeing the harm they have done—and makes the receiver feel terribly alone. The speed and spread of the digital ecosystem rapidly escalates the hurt, and it goes viral. Perceived anonymity and online mob psychology encourage piling on of cruel comments, so the victim feels that, as one patient cried, "The whole world hates me!"

These characteristics of the online space can make cyberbullying more damaging to the mental health of individuals and to the culture of a school or community than in-person aggression. Spoken words and flying fists are less deeply painful and inflicted injuries more transient than online shaming, hurtful rumors, and demeaning, hateful images that will linger forever. Increasing majorities of children and teens are continuously connected with their peers via smartphones. While this connectivity can facilitate positive social engagement, it also facilitates cyberbullying to be perpetrated twenty-four hours a day and accessed anytime from anywhere. Victims cannot escape to the safety of their homes the way that they can escape in-person bullying. Cyberbullying can affect the mental health of victims, leading to anxiety, anger, frustration, low self-esteem, depression, suicidal ideation, and a variety of other emotional and psychological problems.[69] Victims often feel alone and helpless and are at much higher risk for suicide.[70]

When cyberbullying was first identified as a mental health threat, schools argued that because it occurred off campus and after hours, cyberbullying was not their problem. That perspective has radically changed. In 2023, the EdWeek Research Center surveyed educators and students to assess what had negatively affected student mental health in the past year. Seventy percent of educators pointed to online bullying, making it their number one concern; only 11 percent of students cited cyberbullying, making it their number fifteen.[71] In reality, a majority of cyberbullying victims do not report their victimization to an adult.[72] This is not because they lack a caring, trusted adult in their lives but because they believe that the adult would try to protect them by taking their phones and cutting off their access to the online space. What parents or caregivers see as the vector of harm, youth see as their early warning system, shield, and weapon of retaliation. Victims sometimes strike back. When school shootings have been investigated, the shooters have almost universally been found to have been ostracized and victimized by bullies in the school's "power elite."[73] The negative effects of being cyberbullied can be even more severe than in-person bullying, and the effects of any form of bullying can last into adulthood.[74]

Research on the psychology of bullying has shown that three components are needed for bullying to occur: a bully, a victim, and accepting, sometimes encouraging, bystanders.[75] These human behaviors map exactly on the three outcomes that have been consistently linked to media violence exposure: increased aggression (bully), fear/anxiety (victim), and desensitization (bystanders). So is violent media "enter-training" our children to identify in one of these three groups from an early age?

MEDIA Rx
Defusing the Effects of Media Violence on Children's Aggressive Thoughts and Behaviors

Violence can be found in many forms of popular media, from television news to cartoons. Understand that children are always learning from the media they watch, play, and listen to—and from the way we respond to it. If they see parents or friends consuming violent media, they will learn to accept it as normal and enjoy it as entertainment. You know your child, with all their personality traits and sensitivities, better than anyone on earth. Limiting their exposure to violent media is part of your task. It is equally important to help your child process the violence they inevitably see to guide them to learn *about* rather than learn to *do* violence. Help your child learn that violence is not normal, socially acceptable, or, in real life, an effective way to solve problems.

YOU CAN

- *Use media with your child as much as possible.* Look for opportunities to share a good time, learn from them, cheer them on in a game, or hang out together as you each do your own screen thing.

- *Read summaries of books, movies, TV, music, and games before offering them to your child.* Many feature characters who solve conflicts with violence and are treated as heroes. Children may see favorite characters' aggression as justified and internalize that to mean aggression is acceptable for them as well.

- *Place home computers in a common area*, like the dining or living rooms, to discourage your child from viewing excessive violence or engaging in cyberbullying. Make sure that all internet-connected devices such as tablets and smartphones are left in the living room or kitchen to charge overnight. By keeping these electronics in a common area, you can monitor their use much more easily and be aware of any violent media or cyberbullying.

- *Observe your child's response to media they are using.* Are they afraid or excited? Do they shrink away from or imitate aggressive acts they see on screen?

- *Co-view movies or TV, co-listen to music, and co-play (or at least observe) video games* that you don't know and observe your child using them. Discuss openly your observations and questions to help your child make optimal media choices.

- *Understand media rating systems* for movies, TV, video games, and music from the entertainment industry and advocacy sites like Common Sense Media. After you have seen a movie or TV program with your child, read various reviews and ratings and calibrate what you read there to your child. Use your own personalized rating to guide what your child will actually see and hear.

- *Model and mentor being a critical viewer.* Encourage your child to notice and think about the victims as well as the perpetrators of violence and how they might avoid becoming a victim or a perpetrator.

- *Model and mentor your child to be respectful and considerate when communicating with others online*, to think whether their words, images, or actions could feel hurtful to someone else. Explain how microaggressions hurt others and can be a form of bullying, whether online, at school, on the sports field, or elsewhere.

- *Notice and talk about potential problems while online together.* Take particular notice of snarky, mean-spirited, or even joking put-downs or teasing in their communications with others. Talk about how these might be negatively interpreted. It is better to have your child laughing at you for being silly or uptight than to let potential first steps toward disrespect or harm go unnoticed.

- *Be aware of violent content in videos or games* that you and older siblings are watching and/or playing when younger children are present. Even if your very young child may not understand the content, the sights and sounds of violence can still disrupt their play and increase their anxiety.

- *Be aware of your child's ambient exposure to violent media and help them avoid becoming desensitized.* When children see media violence as normal, they are not upset when they see it and are less likely to try to avoid or stop violence when they see it happen in the real world.

- *Reduce the risk of a child becoming a cyberbully or a victim of cyberbullying by setting expectations, mentoring, and monitoring your child's online activities.*[76] This is especially important when introducing your child to a new interactive device, application, or platform. At that time, it is critical to explicitly describe cyberbullying as deliberately threatening physical or psychological harm, name-calling, ostracizing, spreading false rumors, stalking, or sending unwanted explicit images to or of a targeted victim.

- *Have regular open and honest conversations with your child about what they are seeing and doing online.* Ask them specifically about cyberbullying and if they have or a friend has experienced it. Be sure your child knows that you are always there for them. Just knowing that they can safely tell someone they are being bullied lessens the negative psychological impact cyberbullying can have on them.
- *Reassure your child that if they share with you that they are being bullied, you won't yank their device, game, or social media access.* Tell them that you are always there for them, and encourage them to talk about anything they see, hear, or find themselves doing online that confuses, upsets, or weirds them out.
- *Encourage them not to engage with a bully in any way.* Regularly review what your child does and with whom they interact online.
- *Remain alert for signs of your child being cyberbullied,* such as becoming hypervigilant online, hiding their phone screen when you walk by, being awake and online in the middle of the night, losing interest in school, feeling sad or depressed, or withdrawing from friends and family.
- *Notice any concerning behaviors by your child,* and if your child agrees, seek help from a school counselor or therapist who may be able to provide other supports to help stop and prevent cyber-bullying from occurring.
- *Teach your child how to block and report users who are harassing them on social networking sites.* Children and youth are much more likely to block than to report cyberbullies because they don't want to tattle. Motivate your child to report by pointing out that they are not tattling but protecting other kids from harm.

Chapter 11

Virtually Hooked

Problematic Interactive Media Use (PIMU)

Patrick was barely twelve when his parents brought him to CIMAID. He was scared and confused, feeling that he was being punished. When I asked what brought him to CIMAID, he evaded, eyes downcast: "They did." That made me smile. Patrick didn't smile back.

"How can I help?"

"Ask them!"

I looked to his parents. Dad looked down at the floor. Glancing nervously at Patrick, Mom recounted his transformation in less than a year from an amiable, athletic, social fifth grader to a reclusive, uncommunicative sixth grader, a change that they attributed to "the F-word"—*Fortnite*. Patrick had withdrawn into his room, tablet on his lap, gaming. He lost interest in soccer and dropped off the team. He hacked his school-issued Chromebook to play while appearing to take notes; each time the teacher approached, Patrick covered his game environment with an essay he was working on. He stopped hanging out with friends. When asked to come down for family meals, he would say, "Just a minute!" Not just a minute, but thirty, sixty, ninety would pass, and he would still be in his room. When he was with his family, Patrick was nervous, edgy, irritable. The family stopped including him in meals and activities because he made everyone miserable.

Dad described Patrick staying up deep into the night, even all night. If he was forced to go to bed, Patrick would wake up to play after his parents were asleep. When they cut off his internet access, Patrick would simply continue with games he had downloaded to his devices. Each time his parents would try to redirect him toward homework or sleep, he would resist. When they pushed it, he would fly into a rage, slamming his bedroom door to keep them out.

Patrick was gaming when his grandparents and cousins arrived for their annual summer reunion. He had been in his room all weekend. His mother insisted that he take a shower before they all went to dinner at their favorite Italian restaurant. While Patrick was in the shower, his father found his gaming tablet. Getting out of the shower, Patrick announced that he did not feel well and could not join the family for dinner. His grandparents and cousins tried to convince him to come, but Patrick was adamant that he felt really sick. Finally, they gave up and all climbed into his grandfather's van without Patrick, his father taking the tablet and the internet router with him.

Once they were gone, Patrick, anxious to return to his gaming, looked in vain for his tablet. Convinced that his parents had locked it in the family car, as they had done before, he searched frantically for the car's remote key. Frustrated, he tried to open the mechanical door locks with a screwdriver. Finally, Patrick took a hammer from his dad's workbench and smashed the windshield and a side window to break in, denting the hood and gouging the doors. He searched the car in increasing distress. When his family returned, they found Patrick sitting on the floor of the garage, furious and in tears. Irate about the damage to the car, Dad confronted Patrick, who bolted from the garage, disappearing into the night.

After two hours of mounting worry, his parents were preparing to call the police for help when Patrick strode into the house. He went straight to the kitchen, grabbed a chef's knife, and held it to his own throat, declaring, "If you don't give my tablet back, I'll kill myself." Terrified, his mother dialed 911. The police came and disarmed Patrick, and paramedics took him to the hospital emergency department.

The emergency department staff had to determine whether Patrick was in danger of harming himself or others. Patrick, still furious at his parents, refused to "contract for safety"—to promise he would not harm himself or others—so the emergency mental health team admitted him to a psychiatric hospital. Once he was transferred by ambulance to a locked psychiatric ward, Patrick's rage turned to fear. His parents could not visit but only talk to him on the shared hospital landline phone. He apologized again and again, begging to be taken home. The psychiatrist explained that she had to make certain that he was safe. Patrick promised that he would not hurt himself or his parents, but the psychiatrist said that it would take some time to be sure. She started Patrick on a medication to help him with anxiety and depression.

He was allowed to game on the shared patient computer, but it did not have Patrick's favorite game. He tried other games, but they weren't as much fun—and his gaming group was not there. He gave up waiting for his turn on the computer. Observed for ten days and determined by the psychiatrist not to be a danger, Patrick was released home. Humbled and scared by his own out-of-control behavior and by the fact that medical professionals took it seriously, Patrick agreed to the hospital's discharge plan of following up at CIMAID.

"The draw of this game was just . . . unbelievable," his mother continued. Patrick's frantic search, loss of control wrecking the car, and explosion in frustrated rage looked to his parents, police, and paramedics to be the behavior of someone in the grip of drug addiction.

"We should have come here much earlier," Patrick's father admitted. "He's addicted. And the irony is that I introduced him to gaming when he was really young on a website. You probably know it—Addicting Games."

Addiction?

In therapy and other personal-growth settings, there's a saying—*name it, claim it, tame it*—that refers to the importance of naming a challenge or problem and taking ownership of it as the first steps toward effectively addressing it. Naming matters because it identifies the true nature of the challenge you face as you claim it and take steps to tame it. *Addiction* is a word commonly used to mean an intense, persistent urge to use a substance, such as alcohol, cocaine, or opioids, that is pleasurable but unnecessary for life. Use causes measurable, reproducible physiologic changes desired by the user. Use continues and usually increases to get the same level of pleasure, despite negative consequences to relationships, productivity, and overall well-being. Withdrawal from use causes predictable discomfort, which is avoided if possible by using more of the substance. Because use is harmful and not necessary for life, the treatment goal for addiction is abstinence.

Out-of-control interactive media use can look a lot like addiction to a substance. Immersed in the interactivity, users focus on their screens, often to the exclusion of anything or anyone around them. They lose track of time. When asked to stop, they desperately want to finish up what they are doing. When asked to stop again, they can explode in anger. Separated from their screens, they can be distracted, fidgety, and anxious, calming only when they get back on screen.

Applying the language of addiction to interactive media use originated more than a quarter century ago as a fictitious diagnosis posted on an online bulletin board. Psychiatrist Ivan Goldberg, MD, parodied the complex diagnostic language of the *Diagnostic and Statistical Manual of Mental Disorders* to describe "internet addiction disorder" in the days of amber displays and dot-matrix printers.[1] To his astonishment, Goldberg was inundated by messages from many psychiatric and medical colleagues, grateful that he had taken "netaholism" seriously and asking for help. Goldberg quickly sought to clarify his satirical intentions, asserting that "to medicalize every behavior by putting it into psychiatric nomenclature is ridiculous. If you expand the concept of addiction to include everything people can overdo, then you must talk about people being addicted to books."[2]

But with so many struggling with technology and so little knowledge about what was going on, the nomenclature stuck. Kimberly Young, then a psychology doctoral student with a friend who had lost her husband to a chatroom romance, took it seriously, publishing "Internet Addiction: The Emergence of a New Clinical Disorder," in 1998.[3] Since that time, thousands of research reports and more than one hundred diagnostic terms, from *digital game addiction* to *mobile phone dependency* to *compulsive use of sexually explicit internet material* to *problematic internet use* have been proposed, the nomenclature varying with the device, platform, or application that the researcher was studying. In effect, the provocative term went viral the way other terms or trends do in the digital age: because they're catchy and sticky, not because they're grounded in rigorous science.

In 2016, half of US thirteen-to-eighteen-year-olds surveyed and 59 percent of their parents reported that they believed the teens were addicted to their devices.[4] More than three-fourths of parents and 41 percent of kids felt that the other was distracted by their devices, validated in the same survey by the 72 percent of kids and 48 percent of parents who felt that they must respond immediately to pings.[5] The GUD (Growing Up Digital) Alberta survey of 2016 asked parents and grandparents whether they felt their children and grandchildren were distracted or addicted to screens. Twenty-two percent of the parents felt that their children were addicted, but 30 percent of them felt that they themselves were addicted; 36 percent of the grandparents thought the kids were addicted.[6]

DISTRACTED OR ADDICTED?

30% of parents feel "addicted" to their own technologies, with social media as the area of greatest dependence.

22% of parents feel their children are "addicted" to technology, with the areas of greatest dependence being watching videos and video games.

36% of grandparents believe their grandchild is "addicted" to technology.

Alberta Teachers' Association, "Growing Up Digital" (infographic), *Learning Team* 21, no. 3 (Spring 2018): 2, https://legacy.teachers.ab.ca/SiteCollectionDocuments/ATA/Publications/Learning-Team/Volume%2021/Learning%20Team%2021-3.pdf.

While China and South Korea have established internet addiction disorder as a diagnosis and developed health-care infrastructures to treat it, *internet gaming disorder* is noted as needing further research in order to be considered a formal diagnosis in the fifth edition of the *Diagnostic and Statistical Manual of Mental Disorders* that Goldberg had parodied nearly two decades earlier.[7] Other arbiters of diagnostic terms are making other choices. The World Health Organization's *International Classification of Diseases, Eleventh Edition* includes a diagnosis of *gaming disorder*.[8] The clinical debate over nomenclature continues, but more to the point for parents, the debate over terms reflects a more important, fundamental difference in how the problem is understood, how young people struggling with the problem are viewed, and how we—as parents, health-care providers, and communities—respond to them. The label of addiction isn't helpful when it skews our response and fails to provide the young person with the means of righting a pattern of media use that has gone awry.

The Big Binge: Digital Appetites Out of Control

Interactive media are not only powerful tools but, unlike some substances to which one can become addicted, are a *necessary* resource. Facility with interactive media is essential for education, employment, shopping, entertainment, social life, and citizenship. During the pandemic lockdown, we were utterly dependent on interactive media for virtually (pun intended) every aspect of our lives.

Patients who come to CIMAID have lost control of their relationship with a powerful tool that is an essential part of life. The therapeutic goal for uncontrolled interactive media use is to develop or regain that control, to self-regulate their use of that necessary resource. An effective way to understand the problem and how best to respond to it, for parents and health-care providers alike, parallels not addiction but binge eating disorder. The most common eating disorder in the US, binge eating disorder is excessive, uncontrolled consumption of a necessary resource, food, even when the person is not hungry. Eating is their coping strategy for psychological distress. Binge eating is not biologically triggered by hunger nor is it stopped by satiety. There is no stopping point for binge eaters, who compulsively eat to fill a psychological need that food cannot meet. They binge secretively, withdrawing from family and friends out of shame and to protect and continue their behavior. The treatment goal is not abstinence. Eating is necessary for life. Just as binge eaters must regulate, rather than abstain from, eating, young people with problematic interactive media use must regulate and effectively use interactive media tools to function well in today's world.

Keep that parallel, and the very real distinction between disordered behavior and addiction, in mind because the words we use carry meaning and psychological impact. There is a powerful social stigma attached to addiction. It is laden with harsh judgment and "othering," distancing those who are struggling. Society perceives addicts as weak in character, helpless to resist the inexorable pull of the addiction, to be punished or pitied. For children and adolescents who are struggling, parents, teachers, clinicians, or other authority figures labeling them as addicts stigmatizes and further undermines their self-esteem, delays diagnosis, and taints recovery with punishments and shame. When addiction is invoked, not only is the young person's strength of character questioned but the label can give them permission to plead helplessness and succumb to its draw. This works against adolescents' natural developmental drive to achieve autonomy as a successful and unique individual. And it delays addressing problematic interactive media use earlier or preventing it altogether. As frustrated and angry as parents might be with their child's behaviors, most do not see their child as addicted and thus (finally) in need of treatment until they are severely impaired—and the addiction stereotype seems the only explanation. As happened with Patrick, too many patients come to CIMAID after they have precipitated or undergone a catastrophic event, dropped or failed out of school, physically threatened or attacked family members, or even attempted suicide.

Social Media: A Lifeline or Undertow?

It was her hands I noticed first. White trails of scratches were punctuated by small, dark scabs, like body modification connect-the-dots. Her fingernails were bitten ragged to the quick. Anna, sixteen, was seething as she and her parents came into CIMAID together.

"I can give you something to soothe this dry skin," I said, gently taking her hand in mine to examine it. Unexpectedly, her hand relaxed as I held it. Turning her hand over, I glimpsed many linear white scars on her forearm. She quickly pulled her hoodie sleeve down and over her hand as she withdrew it.

"That's not why we're here," her dad snapped, glaring at his daughter. "Anna is addicted to her smartphone! It is in her hand 24/7. She takes it to school, into the bathroom—she sleeps with it!"

"Everybody does!" Anna turned her back to her father and, for the first time, looked straight at me.

I looked at Anna through her shock of fading orange-on-black hair. "Tell me about your phone."

"It's where my friends are," she murmured as she looked at me quizzically, as if stating the obvious.

Anna's parents had given her the smartphone for getting all As in her last year of middle school, her father explained, adding unhappily, "And her grades have gone down ever since!"

I raised my hand so Anna was encouraged to continue.

"He moved us here where I have *no* friends," she started, before her father interrupted to report that she would come home and immediately disappear into her room, catching up and "talking" with her friends by text, images, or video chats. When her father or mother got up in the middle of the night, they would often see a faint glow under her door, so they assumed she was on the phone at all hours.

"One night Anna screamed and woke me up from a dead sleep," Dad recounted. "I ran to her room, but, as usual, her door was locked. I pounded on her door, trying to get to her. I heard her sobbing and she finally said something about a nightmare. I have to tell you, Doctor, that was the most scared I've ever been! I was locked out. I was helpless. Nightmare or not, I figured it had something to do with the phone, so I shut down her account the next day. And then she *really* blew up!"

Anna—at sixteen, already taller than her father—came home from school, got toe to toe with him in the living room, and screamed in his face, her mother said, "For Six. Straight. Minutes!" Anna's mother seethed. "I had had it with both of them! He was the one who wanted to give her that phone. I didn't. I went to the kitchen and looked up this clinic online."

Once I excused her parents from the room, I looked at Anna and, after a moment, she started to talk. Anna revealed that she had been intensely lonely after their family moved from the West Coast. She reached back out to her old friends, but only a few of them had phones. As time went on, there was less and less to talk about as they lived their separate lives. She connected to other friends online, and those friends connected her to still others.

"So how do you feel after connecting?"

Anna paused and started to say something, then stopped. After a long pause, she said, "Disappointed, I guess. Lonely."

"Always?"

"Pretty much," she shrugged.

"So why do you do it?"

"I can't *not* do it. . . . It's all I have." As Anna's trust grew over several visits, she shared that she had always had a hard time making friends. Before the move, she had a wonderful guidance counselor at her middle school who had helped her overcome her shyness and start to make close friends. "But then I was dumped into this big suburban high school knowing no one. I was frozen," she said. Feeling awkward and embarrassed and worried that she would be judged by the other students, Anna felt very alone.

And she was finding people online who felt like her: alone. When she first tentatively tried to make contact and talk about her loneliness, responses were rude: "I'm lonely, too, why don't you send me a nude?" "If you feel that bad, just off yourself!"

Anna's mood grew darker and darker. She had no one who wanted to talk to her except a group of anime fans and cosplayers who called themselves Entrance to Darkness. "They didn't particularly like each other," Anna recalled, "but at least they didn't throw me out or put me down." Those in the group challenged one another to dares, like drinking increasingly potent hot sauces and car surfing (trying to stay standing on the roof of a car doing donuts). But they seemed to have people to try those challenges with. Anna had no one.

There was someone else who, like Anna, lurked around the edges of the Entrance, and eventually they reached out to Anna. "I finally found someone I could talk to who wasn't totally mean to me. She was depressed, too, and just needed to talk." Anna and her online friend would communicate for hours, sometimes talking, sometimes just keeping a video call open as they fell asleep. Anna wanted to know her friend's name and where she lived, but the girl didn't share that. It was often late at night when Anna's friend would suggest challenges. They dripped hot candle wax on their legs and counted how many drips they could take before having to stop. They scratched their arms with needles until they drew blood, then graduated to cutting themselves with razor blades. Anna's friend said it made her feel better to cut, like she was letting the bad out.

"How did it make you feel?" I asked.

"It hurt. But I felt nothing."

On their next video call, when her friend brought out her razor blade, Anna suggested instead that they hold their breath as long as they could. Anna didn't want to admit to her friend that she found cutting scary, but she hoped the breath-holding challenge would be less so. They got on a video call to do it together, but neither could hold their breath very long. What happened next was beyond anything Anna ever imagined. "She pulled this really pretty blue scarf from her closet, tied it to her closet doorknob, and wrapped it around her neck. And then she kind of stood up and leaned away from it—so it got tighter! And she was kind of like laughing but there was no sound," Anna said. "Then it seemed like her feet slipped, and she sort of went limp. That's when I screamed and Dad came charging down the hall, and, well, you know the rest of the story."

"No. I don't." There was a long pause as Anna collected herself.

"By the time my dad went away, the video call had ended. I called and got her voicemail, which was creepy—I was listening to her voice when I thought she might be dead! I kept trying to call through the night, but it went to her voicemail every time. And I had no idea where she was or who I would call anyway."

Tweens and teens are developmentally programmed to grow into independent individuals and separate themselves from parents and family as they move toward adulthood. This is both normal and the driver of many parent-teen conflicts, large and small. As they turn their gaze outward and move away from family, adolescents seek connection with peers—others with whom they relate, share values, and try out being themselves beyond parental observation. They want to experiment with different selves, various ways to be, to push their limits outside of their parents' control and beyond their parents' and their own preconceptions. They want to be seen, to be heard, to be validated. They need to *matter*. Interactivity with friends, strangers, even NPCs (non-player characters) and AI chatbots of celebrities that respond to them allow them to feel their presence in the world. Anna couldn't have imagined that her search for friends would lead to such a moment.

Four Ways to Lose Your Way

Patrick, seeking control over his attention and anxiety, lost control of his gaming. Anna, searching for connection, got lost in social media. At CIMAID, we have seen four distinct, sometimes co-occurring manifestations of uncontrolled interactive media use: gaming, social media, pornography, and information-bingeing on text or video aggregation sites. These behaviors are occurring on a variety of devices, platforms, and applications. There is a great deal of crossover behavior—when kids have their gaming consoles confiscated by frustrated parents, they go online to information-binge on videos of others gaming or to talk about gaming on social media. What these young people have in common is their drive to interact.

Among the hundreds of children and adolescents we have seen in CIMAID, we have yet to see one who did not have an underlying psychological issue that they were avoiding by using interactive media to distract and soothe themselves. What we do see is problematic media use behaviors that are immersive due to their interactivity—distracting and soothing children and adolescents with subclinical or undertreated emotional and behavioral issues.

We have found problematic interactive media use (PIMU) to be the unifying description of what we are observing and which we characterize as a syndrome rather than a singular diagnosis.[9] In other words, PIMU is a collection of signs and symptoms of maladaptive attempts to cope with one or more underlying psychological conditions, most prominently attention deficit hyperactivity disorder (ADHD), autism spectrum disorder (ASD), anxiety, depression, and other affective and mood disorders.

When "Everybody Does It" Becomes Problematic

For most of our CIMAID patients, parents motivate the visit. Sometimes these are cases of the "worried well," where the parents are worried but the child or adolescent is well. Sometimes the young person is impaired by PIMU and their physical, mental, or social health is suffering. Either way, the young person does not believe there is a problem. Kids are frequently wary, even angry, when they first come. They feel that they are doing "what everybody else is doing" and are being brought to CIMAID to be punished and deprived of access to what makes them happy. Because parents are generally less interested in and facile with interactive media, they usually have not been engaged in their children's digital lives. Their only interactions with their kids about media are negative: "You should stop playing video games and do your homework!"

A sixteen-year-old patient once slouched into the seat in my office and, when I asked what was wrong, said, "The whole world is *should*-ing on me!" He felt judged and not good enough because all he heard was what he should and should not do. When parents or caregivers take a distant and disapproving stance toward a young person's interactive media use, the tween or teen believes that the digital environment is their private, parent-free domain, a critical part of what defines them as an individual, different from their parents. Much as the proverbial teen trifecta of sex, drugs, and rock and roll came to symbolize rebellious independence in the 1960s, games, texting, and social media are that to today's teens—something that their parents are not part of, don't understand, and don't like, which makes interactive media all the more attractive and personal to them.

ASK THE MEDIATRICIAN
Addicted to Her Phone?

*I am the mother of three daughters (fifteen, thirteen, and eleven).
Although I try to set limits, technology is ruining my family life. My oldest
daughter stares at her phone all the time. She is addicted to Instagram,
Snapchat, FaceTime, texting. When she is online, she gets anxious and
uses it more, and that makes her even more anxious. When I ask her
to stop, she rolls her eyes and ignores me. When I blocked her phone
account, she used her school computer, then borrowed a friend's phone
to stay in touch with I don't know who. Now my thirteen-year-old and
eleven-year-old want phones. I feel like I'm in a bad movie, surrounded
by teen zombies. What do you suggest?*

Parenting digital kids is challenging because we have no reference points
in our own childhoods. But you can relax. From what you have described,
your daughter is not dealing with an addiction, and she's not a zombie
who will turn your other kids into zombies. As a teenager, she is pursuing
key developmental tasks through her media use—seeking experiences,
establishing her individual identity, and connecting with peers. But perhaps the amount of time she is devoting to it, her exclusion of family,
the anxiety that builds—and the fact that she responds to the anxiety by
increasing her use—can and should be addressed.

Talk this through with your daughter directly, simply, and with compassion. First, at a time when you are not in open conflict—preferably
while driving somewhere, sealed off from the world and belted in so
you don't have to look at each other—have a conversation with her. Start
as her student. Ask her to explain to you how Instagram or Snapchat
work. Ask how she feels when she is on them. Listen to her. She may
be unhappy or uncomfortable and may actually say so as long as she
doesn't feel she's being judged or criticized by you or that she may be
punished. If the opportunity presents, tell her that you are concerned
because she seems to get anxious when she is online. Even if you can't
ask directly about her, ask for her advice on whether, when, and how her

sisters should get phones. Teens more easily see risks and problems in others than in themselves, and this may be your way to help her reflect indirectly on her own experience.

It's possible that she's feeling lots of pressure to be constantly available. Tell her that you dislike constantly being on call, so you let your boss and friends know that as of a certain time in the evening, your phone goes off. (Did you know that you can ask for overtime pay if your employer asks you to read and respond to emails after hours?) Suggest that she make herself available online only during certain hours when they do not disrupt her sleep, homework, or family time. Offer to take the blame if her friends criticize her for not being available at all hours—she can complain that Mom takes the phone away to charge it between 9:00 p.m. and 6:00 a.m., for example. This way, she can save face while reducing her anxiety and learning to manage her media use in the context of everything else she needs to do in a day.

Designed to Hook and Hold Attention

So why do so many tweens and teens spend so much time with interactive media, even if they do not have PIMU? Research shows and our clinical experience corroborates that what draws users into gaming, social media, online auctions, loot boxes, computer dating, and more is not the device, platform, or application but the variable reward systems embedded in interactive media that hook and hold our attention.[10]

What, exactly, is a variable reward system, and how does it work? Most of us know about classical conditioning: Pavlov's dogs who associated the stimulus of a bell ringing with feeding time. Once conditioned, the dogs would salivate when they heard a bell ring, whether they were fed or not. But if they were not fed, the dogs' conditioned response to the bell ringing would disappear, or extinguish, over time. To make sense out of this, experimental psychologist B. F. Skinner reversed Pavlov's experiment, rewarding mice with a food pellet each time they pushed a lever. The mice learned quickly that they would receive food when they pushed the lever, so they pushed the lever a lot—at first. But with reliable food rewards, they would stop after a while. The mice learned that they would always be rewarded with food when they pushed the lever, so they pushed it when they were hungry and stopped pushing it when they were full. Skinner experimented with varying the rewards. Sometimes the mice would get one food pellet, sometimes none, sometimes ten. With a variable reward schedule, the mice learned to push the lever more slowly, but once they learned, the mice kept pushing the lever ever more frantically—even when they were no longer hungry.[11] Varying rewards proved effective behavioral bait. They produced a high rate of the desired repetitive behaviors, and the behaviors persisted regardless of the outcome, driven by hopes that the next push of the lever would produce a big reward.

Interactive media provide extremely effective variable reward systems. In video games, variable rewards are designed into the game. For today's experimental psychologists, scholarly descendants of B. F. Skinner, game design has become one of the most highly paid career options. A player learns the central activity of an interactive game, whether it be shooting basketballs or shooting terrorists, by pursuing the activity over and over until they master it. The player receives positive reinforcement for successfully shooting a basket or a terrorist and negative reinforcement when they fail to do so. Success is rewarded with a higher, more challenging level of play with more skills or better weapons. Interactive electronic games fulfill all the criteria for an effective variable reward system: a frustrating but ultimately achievable challenge yielding immediate, valuable, but intermittent wins, fails, or near wins that are close enough to convince the player that they will win next time—and "next time" must be *now*!

When a game is played online, with other humans, variability is not only designed in but multiplied by the unpredictable variations in human behavior. In massively multiuser online role-playing games (MMORPGs) like *League of Legends*, with which millions of players around the world are engaging 24/7, the social aspect of the game can combine with the designed-in variable rewards to make the game extremely hard to leave. Not only does the thrill of success or near success motivate you but there are other players, perhaps in different time zones, who rely on you for their success. The social component, the sense that you are with comrades who understand, appreciate, and need you, is hard to resist. And they are there, playing, at all times of day or night.

Young people are uniquely susceptible to being drawn in, both by the variable rewards system and by the social connectivity of interactive media.

Still-developing impulse control is easily overpowered by the brain's social emotional limbic system. Desire overshadows logic, easily tipping the balance. This is why advertising that does not talk about the product but what using the product can make you feel or become is so effective. Social media has been called "advertising on steroids" because social connection synergizes with a variable reward system. The variable rewards of social media are created by the near infinite variability of human nature. When a user posts an image or text, there can be nearly instant response in the form of likes, LOLs, and reposts. Or nasty trolling from those who feel safe in their anonymity. Or a delayed response. Or worst of all—no response. Each of these compels further engagement. Fast, large, positive responses encourage more and similar posts. Trolling is hurtful, triggering retaliation and escalation—or silent suffering. A sluggish response builds uncertainty and insecurity, often resulting in taking down the post and posting a different, often more edgy, attention-grabbing image, video, or text. No response at all is devastating. "Does anybody see or hear me . . . ?"

For Anna, the need to feel she mattered and had a friend group, however thin the connection, led to a dark place that would hardly be considered rewarding but for the sense of acceptance and presence she found early on. For others, even when the rewards feel positive, they can become problematic.

Clickbait Hijacks Curiosity for Learning

Fifteen-year-old Isabella was "endlessly curious," by her mother's description. She was an avid and omnivorous student, eager to learn about everything that caught her interest. Isabella read very early, consuming fiction for adolescents and young adults when she was in the early grades. When she encountered upsetting and confusing adult issues like sex, she switched to nonfiction and began reading about lost tribes in the (other) Amazon, ancient history, and nuclear fusion. When she received a Chromebook for remote learning during the pandemic lockdown, she switched from books to Wikipedia, Reddit, and YouTube—but did not use her device to pay attention in class or do her homework. "What's the point? Everyone will get a Pass anyway," she said. Throughout the year of learning remotely, Isabella's parents and teachers who knew her voracious curiosity were befuddled by her lack of motivation and underachievement.

When they came to CIMAID, Isabella's parents related that it was not just her schoolwork that suffered but also her sleep, activities and hobbies she'd previously enjoyed, time with family and friends, and her mood. Isabella was a recluse with her Chromebook. Her parents had monitored Isabella's online traffic and were confident that she was not gaming, using social media, or going to concerning websites. They just saw an eclectic journey through the internet, connecting idea to idea, links in her chain of thought. Isabella revealed that she found school boring and repetitive of "stuff I already know." She was much more excited by what she learned online, starting from a news item on human-powered flight to the aerodynamics of birds' wings to how many calories a hummingbird consumes daily to the way plants are polli-nated. She thought the kids at school were "insipid" and they ostracized her as "different." Isabella saw absolutely no point in doing her schoolwork "just to satisfy grown-ups."

As with Anna and Patrick, it was the interactivity that drew Isabella in. But in her case, it was not quite the same variable rewards and their hook-and-hold effect on the brain that held her attention. Isabella loved learning. It was the actual, ever-changing rewards of exploring the near-infinite, instantly accessed fountain of human knowledge and experience that were so compelling. She was delighted by her discoveries and saw nothing in school, academic or social, that motivated her to participate there. It was not until she entered high school and teacher-parent meetings became more critical that Isabella's parents noticed that she was falling off academically.

"In middle school, her teachers just talked about how brilliant she was!" her mother explained. So they had encouraged her online exploration. But Isabella wasn't learning in an organized way, building fundamental under-standing and skills on each other. She was jumping from one interesting idea to the next, linked by gossamer-thin but spiderweb-strong threads of hot links. Isabella followed whatever grabbed her interest, covering a lot of information but in a haphazard way. Although Isabella's information bingeing appeared random, it was guided by the search engine's sophisticated digital algorithms that were recording and analyzing her choices, offering with increasing accu-racy information that the artificial intelligence of machine learning predicted would interest her. To Isabella, her online journeys felt like self-directed learn-ing. To her proud parents, her behaviors looked like research. But the time and attention she was spending on it were disrupting her academic progress and her socialization, shrinking her circle of friends, and eliminating the sports and outdoor activities that had been part of her earlier life.

In medicine, there are conditions we call "acute on chronic." These occur when an ongoing chronic medical condition both makes the patient vulnerable to and is exponentially worsened by an acute problem with the same body system, such as when a patient who has chronic asthma gets acute pneumonia. "Acute on chronic" is a good way of describing what occurred during the pandemic lockdown. Most children and teens increased their screen time on every device to which they had access—smartphones, tablets, laptops, and televisions. Split-tasking with multiple screens increased by 62 percent. And the arguments between parents and their children over screen use grew more frequent and more severe—42 percent of parents reported these arguments at least every day. Nearly half (44 percent) of the time the arguments were about *how long* children were on screens, one-third (32 percent) were about *when* they were using screens, and one in five (20 percent) were about the screen *content* children were consuming.[12] Although the COVID-19 pandemic lockdown called increased attention to PIMU behaviors, it did not cause them. It served as an accelerant of a phenomenon that had already been occurring.

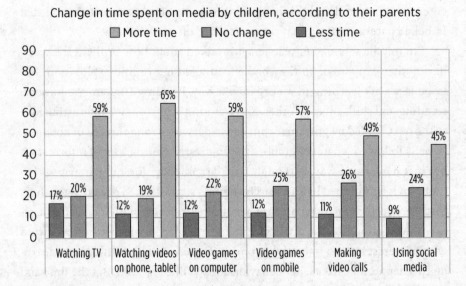

PULSE SURVEY, MARCH 2021

Change in time spent on media by children, according to their parents

Boston Children's Hospital Digital Wellness Lab

Because the brain of the child and adolescent is a work in progress—and development of the executive function of self-regulation on that same trajectory—some psychological diagnoses cannot be reliably made until adulthood. Since neurodevelopment extends well into one's twenties, evolving factors such as age, developmental stage, and living environment create a moving target for diagnosis. Some out-of-control behaviors, like temper tantrums, that are normal at one developmental stage represent problems at another. A child's developing brain and its interactions with the rapidly evolving digital environment can make it difficult to differentiate problem behaviors from adaptive "new normal" behaviors. Determining when a young person's interactive media use is problematic becomes more complex during adolescence, a time of impulsivity, experimentation, and sensation-seeking. Isabella's experience reminds us that interactive media use is not necessarily toxic. It is a tool that, used mindfully, is a healthy and necessary part of modern life. However, how it is used and how much it is used can become dysfunctional.

MEDIA Rx
But How Much Is Too Much?

Since it often seems as if every child and adolescent is staring at a smartphone, tablet, or laptop for much of their day, how does a parent recognize when their child is struggling with PIMU? Interactive media use becomes problematic when your child is impaired physically, psychologically, academically, or socially by their use of screen media. While parents are understandably annoyed by their child's screen use, nagging, reprimanding, or punishing them will only cause them to dig in and resist your efforts to change their behavior. Channel your annoyance into supportive concern by focusing on your child's well-being.

- *Academics:* Are they not doing or not turning in homework? Are their grades dropping? Do teachers report that they are using their phones or not paying attention in class? Are they reading for fun, playing sports, getting together with friends, and pursuing hobbies, or is free time always screen time?

- *Physical health:* Are they sleep-deprived due to staying up late or waking up in the middle of the night to go online? Do they have a hard time waking up in the morning? Are they sleepy during the day? Are they gaining or losing weight? Are they complaining of eye strain or pain? Neck or back pain? Headaches? Are they getting outside for the benefits of "green time"? How much of their waking time is sedentary versus active?
- *Social health:* Have they become reclusive, spending more and more time holed up with a device? Are they spending less time with family and friends? Are they missing meals? Avoiding social situations?
- *Mental health:* Are they withdrawn or irritable when not using interactive media? Do they get argumentative, even aggressive, when asked to stop using interactive media? Is there a change in their personal hygiene?

While many parents worry about how much their children use screens, the next normal (because any "new normal" will be old in a matter of weeks) for kids may appear to parents to be overuse. Most kids manage to integrate screen use into their schoolwork and social lives while maintaining their physical and mental health. Parents who see their children having trouble with academics, social situations, or physical or mental health can seek help for that problem from their teachers or school guidance counselors, pediatricians or family practitioners, or psychologists or other mental health providers. It is often these professionals who recognize the challenge presented by the young person's interactive media use and can recommend strategic steps for the child and parent.

Restoring Life Balance by Choice

In the clinic setting, recovery from PIMU begins when a child or adolescent realizes that (1) their clinician understands their attraction to and engagement with interactive media, (2) the goal is not to take interactive media away from them but to help them take control of it, and (3) parents will be asked to stop policing their child's behaviors and start supporting their successes. Once the young person trusts their clinician, they frequently become able to identify their own pain points—grades, social lives, relationships with their parents and family. When the young person realizes that they can lessen that pain by self-regulating their interactive media use, they can be guided toward balancing their lives. Most importantly, both the child and the parents need to realize that the child is in control. Recognizing and taking control of their behaviors asserts their autonomy more powerfully than defying their parents by succumbing to the siren song of interactive media clamoring for their time, attention, clicks, and dollars.

This is more easily said than done—and it is rarely done overnight. The acute-on-chronic nature of PIMU helps explain the double challenge for effective treatment. For example, youth who game uncontrollably (the acute condition) frequently have previously unknown, subclinical (no observed symptoms), undiagnosed, or undertreated chronic conditions, such as ADHD. Their impulsivity and distractibility allow them to excel at interactive electronic games, especially those like first-person shooter games that require rapid, reflexive responses to succeed. Kids with ADHD like Patrick are frequently better at such games than neurotypical children. For them, gaming is a place of mastery; its endless demands for their finely tuned hypervigilance build their confidence, a soothing contrast with the confusion and demands of the classroom, playground, or social interaction. Their gaming is not causing PIMU; it is medicating their ADHD.

Similarly, kids with anxiety—especially social anxiety, as in Anna's case—are drawn to social media as a seemingly less risky environment in which they expect to develop friendships. But the same distance that makes social media feel safe dilutes authenticity that is necessary to develop and sustain meaningful relationships. Even critical human situations, such as an online connection contemplating suicide, become performative and watched from a safe distance as high drama. And those connected with the person struggling build a sense that they are needed and thus have meaning. It is hard to have perspective on and even harder to let go of what gives you meaning.

For the perpetual learner like Isabella, the internet is a wonderland of endlessly linked information—and a minefield of clickbait. Each interesting fact, idea, and question is linked to many others. One can lose all sense of time, disappearing into an infinite rabbit warren of information, images, stories, and videos, all with associated overt and covert commercial messages. And one's movement through these mazes is automatically tracked to lead the user, in increasingly precise and powerful ways, to more of the same.

Some teens recognize PIMU in themselves and self-regulate. Others have launched pushback trends such as switching from smartphones to flip phones—even using TikTok and other platforms to encourage peers to tame tech for themselves and use the tools for good. But for many of the children and adolescents who have come to CIMAID, the underlying psychological drivers of PIMU make professional counseling and therapeutic treatment a more effective response.

Working with Clinicians to Address Your Child's PIMU

If you believe that your child is impaired by PIMU and have not been able to sustain a constructive dialogue with them about it, seek care from a professional who has experience with assessing and treating PIMU. Establish with your child or teen that you are concerned rather than angry, seeking to support your child rather than punish them. Present the clinical visit as part of your effort to help, not to deprive them of an activity important to them. They probably won't believe you, but you will be laying the groundwork for the clinician and family to take a supportive approach together.

It is important for parents to express that they, too, need help in their own and their family's media use—that they are seeking the clinician's help for themselves as well as for their child. The clinician will listen to you, demonstrate that they are not taking sides, and push back regarding parent-child conflicts that may be intruding on a child's growing autonomy and hindering recovery. Stating that this is not a situation of right versus wrong but of finding the best way to be healthy and successful, the clinician will explicitly share that it is the child who will find their way to recovery, not the clinician or the parents.

The clinician will ask for a complete physical, mental, and social health history. Has your child had problems in school or getting homework done? Does your child have difficulty sleeping and/or waking up in the morning? How does your child behave at home? How does your child eat—do they have meals with the family? Do meals happen with or without devices for your child and other family members? What are your own uses of interactive media? Does your child have a history of any medical, mental health, or educational problems? How have those been managed? Does your child take any medications? Is there any family history of educational, mental health, or substance use problems?

One-on-one with the young person, the clinician will ask what their parents got right and wrong in their story about the child's screen use, acknowledging that everyone perceives reality in different ways.

- How do they feel about their own situation and about themselves?
- If there were one thing they would change, what would that be?
- What are their pain points? Do they have physical problems like eye, neck, or back pain? Are they anxious, depressed, or moody? Do they feel lonely or wish they had more friends?
- How can the clinician help?

The clinician will try to identify and address unrecognized or undertreated conditions that might be driving PIMU behaviors. Often young people will not have shared anxiety or depression with their parents out of embarrassment or shame. Attentional problems may have gone unnoticed by the young person, who has never known anything different, or even by teachers and parents because the young person has instinctively developed work-arounds in school. The young person may have been diagnosed and treated when younger and thought to have grown out of the condition when hyperactivity or anxiety, for example, lessened. The adolescent may have physically grown so that the medication dosage that once worked is no longer enough to optimize their attention or alleviate their anxiety. In our experience, once the underlying psychological condition driving PIMU is identified and medical and psychotherapies are optimized, the problematic media use behaviors are more easily addressed.

In CIMAID, we practice media use therapy, dubbed MUT both as its acronym and because it is a mixed breed of cognitive behavioral therapy (CBT)—in which unhealthy thoughts about the self and the world are challenged with reality checks—and dialectical behavioral therapy (DBT), which works toward acceptance and change-oriented strategies, finding balance, and a middle path that is acceptable to both patients and parents. We address the young person's PIMU-related pain points with motivational enhancement therapy (MET) by helping them identify alternative coping strategies for their psychological and social distress.

Every young person struggling with PIMU is different, and their paths to recovery vary in strategy and duration. Some are able to turns things around and self-regulate quite quickly, needing only three or four visits. A majority take four to twelve months, meeting every two to four weeks. A small minority actively resist or are unable to respond to outpatient treatment and self-regulation. Inpatient psychiatric hospitalization is usually not helpful. In many cases, psychiatric hospitals offer gaming or online time as a reward for good behavior. In time, this may change—when I was a medical student, the psychiatric hospital at which I trained rewarded good behavior with cigarettes. While there are a number of residential treatment centers advertised online, most are available only to adults. A residential program called reSTART, located outside Seattle with over a decade of experience treating adults, now has a program for teens thirteen to eighteen years old.[13] Many residential treatment programs are based on, and some are combined with, programs treating addiction to alcohol or drugs. Because understanding, treatment, and even nomenclature for PIMU have not been standardized, each program has its own treatment model, and few collect rigorous outcomes data. As a result, one must rely on online reviews on sites akin to Yelp from those who have been treated there.

Some young people who are unable to achieve self-regulation of their interactive media use in an outpatient program like CIMAID have had success with outdoor behavioral health (OBH) or wilderness therapy. The core idea of OBH therapy is to help young people who are struggling with emotional, behavioral, and relational issues, such as anxiety, depression, substance use, or mood disorders, to reset. With the guidance of licensed therapists, they strive to rebuild themselves and their self-confidence in the simpler setting of the natural world. Nature is calming and centering but also implacable. The usefulness of OBH therapy for youth struggling with PIMU is that they are "off the grid" with no devices and no internet. They must deal directly with the consequences of their successes and their shortcomings, from starting a fire to interacting with others in person. Immediate positive and negative feedback in a supportive environment helps young people "find themselves." OBH therapy usually includes group living, group therapy, and mindfulness exercises as well as one-on-one counseling sessions. Some programs collect and analyze treatment outcomes, and academic centers such as the University of New Hampshire are rigorously evaluating the effectiveness of OBH therapy.[14]

While some OBH programs have helped some young people break free from PIMU, they are not a panacea, and they are not available to everyone. Because OBH therapy has not yet been standardized or formally accredited, programs are not of equal quality; nor are most covered by health insurance. The cost of OBH therapy, which usually requires two to three months, runs in the tens of thousands of dollars, which means it is functionally available only to those who can afford to pay. Some parents have dedicated their child's college fund to such treatment because they believe their child will need to control PIMU to be successful in college. Progress made by young people in such programs must be sustained and continued by thoughtful and vigilant reentry plans when the young person returns home to the environment in which they developed PIMU.

Because there is no reliable standard, there have been some OBH programs and some outpatient programs claiming to treat PIMU that have received deservedly bad press for being ineffective, even unsafe. With the increase in PIMU and parents' distress about it, there are programs that claim to cure "digital addiction" in a luxury rehab setting for large cash advances. Any program—outpatient, residential, or wilderness-based—should be thoroughly researched and vetted for the qualifications of the professionals overseeing and providing therapy, the use of evidence-based treatments, and consumer feedback from individuals and families who have used them. A key feature of legitimate and effective programs is whether they measure and report treatment outcomes. In choosing a program for one's child, it is important to do due diligence.

Insight and Action Lead to Recovery

Patrick's ten-day break from gaming in the psychiatric hospital allowed him to lower his hyperstimulation. At his first CIMAID visit, we identified his ADHD and started him on stimulant medications. He decided to play no video games at all for one month since he already had ten game-free days and then start with one non-*Fortnite* game at a time. He dove into his schoolwork. With the help of his parents, he found an organizational tutor who helped him with planning and getting his homework done. Patrick struggled in the computer lab because his friends with whom he played *Fortnite*, both at school and beyond, "kept bugging me to play." He was able to persuade his school friends to play Dungeons and Dragons in their after-school program and became their dungeon master. Patrick also joined amateur radio and robotics clubs, progressing to obtain a radio license and compete in battle robot tournaments. He never really returned to gaming, saying it was "boring," but in talking to his therapist, Patrick admitted that he was wary of how he might get "sucked back in."

Anna's panic that her "challenge partner" had died by accident or suicide resolved the morning after. Discovering that she had no cell service, Anna borrowed a phone from someone at school and reached her friend, who laughed at Anna for believing it was real. Hurt, Anna saw this as meanness and stopped communicating with the girl. Anna started to work on her anxiety with a therapist, supported by mild antianxiety medication. Once her father understood that her phone was not Anna's escape from reality but an essential part of her reality, he was able to tolerate her use of it. He also agreed not to bring *his* phone to the dinner table. Feeling that her needs were respected and that her dad was willing to adhere to the same expectations, Anna was able to coordinate her communications with online friends so that they did not interfere with homework, family meals, or sleep. She let her friends know that as of 10:00 p.m. she was offline, not because she did not care about them but because her parents "made" her. She took her phone to the kitchen for charging and did not pick it up until she left for school the next morning. Anna redirected her social efforts from online relationships to kids at her high school, but they communicated largely on their phones. Sleeping better and feeling better about herself, Anna engaged with school, made friends, joined several clubs, and tutored elementary school kids in reading. She stopped chewing her nails and scratching herself. She was recently accepted to college, where she hopes to major in psychology.

Isabella, still unwilling to "play the academic game," approached college warily. She was intrigued by the idea of learning whatever she wanted but was aware that her high school grades were wildly inconsistent. She knew she had to dig herself out of an academic hole of her own making. Isabella started paying attention in class and found that she really liked history. Coached by her therapist and a tutor, Isabella developed a schedule where she did her homework before information-bingeing. Her classmates went to SAT-prep classes and signed up with college coaches, but Isabella forgot to schedule taking the admissions exams. And then it was too late. All the testing sites near her hometown were fully booked.

Not wanting to be among her classmates during SAT weekend, she decided to visit her favorite uncle at his mountain cabin in a nearby state. Always trying to help, he checked whether there were any nearby testing sites and found a local school that still had seats available for the SAT. Persuading her to just try, even though she had not prepared, he drove Isabella to the school and dropped her off. Afterward, Isabella felt OK about the test but had no sense of how she had done. When her scores came back six weeks later, she was shocked—she'd done really well. Encouraged and energized, she started shopping for schools that she found interesting. Isabella was excited to find a small liberal arts college, where she registered for classes in botany, philosophy, anthropology, and poetry and started to explore developing her own interdisciplinary major.

MEDIA Rx
Never Too Early, Never Too Late for Prevention

When we think about preventive medicine, we usually visualize what public health calls *primary prevention*, stopping disease before it happens. In reality, much more disease is averted by *secondary prevention*, identifying a potential problem, screening for it, and treating it before it causes symptoms. *Tertiary prevention* is recognizing a disease in process and treating it effectively so that it doesn't get worse and does not spread.

Prevention of PIMU relies on modeling, mentoring, and monitoring healthy media use not only from the earliest stages of a child's media use but repeatedly through childhood and adolescence as they encounter, learn, and master different media. Share media use with your children at every stage. If they show signs of losing control or if you see behaviors or hear language that may be influenced by their interactive media use, talk about it. Children, even siblings, do not mature at the same rate, and you are the best judge, both before and after introducing a digital device or activity, of whether your child can manage it in ways that are healthy, productive, and respectful of themselves and others. It is OK to rein in their digital freedom or pause it altogether, just as you might ground them or enforce a time-out on other unhealthy or unkind behaviors.

Recognizing early signs of problematic behaviors, such as family conflict around stopping interactive media use, more secretive behavior, or irritability when offline that resolves when going back online, is critical to intervening early, definitively, and empathetically. The process of raising an adolescent is one of transferring discipline from outside in to inside out, from parents providing discipline to young people's self-discipline. Human development does not occur in a straight, ever-improving line, and it does not happen overnight. Be patient. A calm, consistent home environment for media use is a critical component in success.

Use these basic pieces of a family strategy, presented earlier and reiterated in previous chapters, as a troubleshooting guide when you feel concerned about your child or teen's media use.

YOU CAN

- *Review the shared expectations around family screen use.* Parents and siblings should have the same guidelines for fundamentals, like having no devices at the dining table or overnight in bedrooms; devices will be turned off and, if possible, physically distant when involved in family time, conversations, or doing homework. Family expectations are better than parental rules.
- *Sit down with your child and go through their typical day, from waking up to going to sleep.* Encourage them to prioritize what they want and need to do each day and create a daily schedule that ensures proper nutrition, strenuous physical activity, homework time, and adequate sleep.
- *Block out time for essential activities*, including homework, strenuous physical activity, chores, and the single most important

thing you can do, not just for your children's nutrition but for their mental health: a sit-down family meal without devices for anyone.

- *Make time in the schedule, once essential activities are done, for your child's online life.* If they game or interact with friends online, encourage your child to let their friends know when they will be online and when they will be offline so they do not feel pressure to be available 24/7. Encourage them to blame limited online time on strict parents rather than risking their friends feeling rejected.
- *Schedule a favorite activity after their online time* so the transition is more about starting, rather than stopping, something that they enjoy.
- *Turn off all screens one hour before sleeptime* to allow your child's brain to secrete melatonin, the sleep hormone. (I use *sleeptime* rather than *bedtime* because so many children and adults use screens in bed.) Adolescents, who are growing faster than at any other time since birth, need more sleep (nine to eleven hours) than they did when they were younger. Aim to establish a consistent circadian (day-night) sleeptime rhythm.
- *Call "closing time" on all screens, from TV to smartphones, and park them outside bedrooms overnight.* A common charging spot in the kitchen or other common area can reinforce that the same expectations apply to all in the family.
- *Once the schedule is decided on together with your child(ren), write it down and post it on the fridge* to avoid future disagreements on what was decided.

PIMU or the Next Normal

As unfamiliar as young people's behavior with their digital devices and applications may be to parents, it is important to be able to distinguish what is dysfunctional and what is a generational evolution of human behavior. To parent well in the digital space where children and adolescents spend so much of their time, we must understand PIMU, prevent it if possible, and recognize and intervene if a child is in trouble. Remember that our devices

258 ■ The Mediatrician's Guide

are neutral tools. It's how we use them that can help or harm us. Mindful, focused, self-regulated use of interactive screen media can support healthy child and adolescent development, but undirected and uncontrolled use is problematic and unhealthy.

As parents, teachers, clinicians, and members of society, we must be able to recognize and respond to this phenomenon in ways that are understanding and not judgmental, are comprehensive enough to include a variety of manifestations, and clearly identify the problem. Young people struggling with their interactive media use need help as early as possible. Effective recognition and treatment require an evidence-based approach by clinicians. Equally important is your own commitment to addressing the roots of your child's problematic use, to resisting marketing promises that appeal to your fears for your child, and to managing your fears of or unease in the digital environment. Take a whole-child approach as you talk with your child's physician, therapist, or guidance counselor about your child's interactive media use. Share what you have observed about your child's challenges and strengths so that your child and their care team can address the underlying conditions that drive their media use. With this understanding, your child can take meaningful steps to develop self-regulation and fully enjoy their media used effectively and wisely.

Part 3

Now What?

Chapter 12

Queen's Gambit

Claim Your Power in the Media Matrix

ontent is king. With this three-word title of a blog more than a quarter century ago, Bill Gates imagined bringing the internet to everyone, envisioning the day when online content would be something anyone anywhere could create, consume—and commercialize. He prophesized, "Anyone with a PC and a modem can publish whatever content they can create . . . allow[ing] information to be distributed worldwide at basically zero marginal cost to the publisher. Those who succeed will propel the Internet forward as a marketplace of ideas, experiences, and products—a marketplace of content."[1]

In the decades that followed content's coronation, its marketplace has exploded. The rapid development of technology has allowed almost anyone to create and consume content at any time and in any setting. Content from multibillion-dollar news, entertainment, and tech companies; to social and political movements; to pornography; to musicians; to the family, the kid, even the dog next door has flooded the digital ecosystem. We have seen the best, the worst, and the endless, time-sucking *meh* in between, remarkable only for the sheer quantity of it.

Parents and teachers have felt helpless before the attention-grabbing tsunami of media content that hooks us and the sticky techniques that hook and hold children, adolescents, and us all. Science has linked consumption of problematic content with health risk behaviors, as we have learned. But the speed with which all manner of content is churned out and the rapid evolution of the devices on which it is consumed has outpaced the best efforts of child health researchers and developmental psychologists to determine the long-term effects of exposure to media content on children and adolescents. Parents, pediatricians, teachers, and child advocates have campaigned long and hard to protect children from harmful content and have been largely frustrated because endlessly edgier content sells and legislation stalls. Children's screen time, the duration of media use, has been linked to negative physical, mental, and social health outcomes. Much of that research has been based on the assumption that media content is inherently harmful, so more time using it results in greater harm. Because media content varies so widely between the good, the bad, and the forgettable, we can no longer use screen time as the key metric of risk to children's health and development. And it is almost impossible to measure screen time in our screen-saturated world. Screen content of any type and any length is available on demand at any time of day or night on devices in nearly every room and pocket. Kids graze, moving constantly and seamlessly between the screen and the physical world. What else kids are doing (and what they are not doing) when they are using media can be as influential as the content to which they are exposed. We are now measuring *how* children and adolescents use screen media and the ways in which different uses lead to significant health and developmental outcomes. Within that nuanced understanding of screen use, science has handed parents a game-changing tool that you can leverage to your child's advantage. That tool is context—how, when, where, and with whom children use media. Therein lies your power.

If content is king, then context is queen. The ancient game of chess is built on that dual power dynamic. The king must be protected; the queen is the most powerful warrior. The context of children's media use is as critical to their well-being as the content to which they are exposed and the duration of that exposure. While available media content is difficult to control, the context of children's media use is much easier for parents to regulate because parents buy the devices; pay for apps, services, and subscriptions; introduce those devices and uses of screen media; and most importantly, set and sustain family expectations of how, when, and where media are used.

Most importantly for younger children, much of the physical environment in which children consume media is in parents' control, and parents can take the lead in creating alternative activities to screen use. This is your opportunity to bring into being the vision you have for your family life and your children's formative years. Remember the Ms—Model, Mentor, and Monitor—and start with an objective look at your own media use as part of the context you want to create for your child. When you are with your child, how do you model balanced and mindful use of your phone, texting, social media, and recreational screen time?

Your child neither knows nor cares whether you are on your device for work or for fun. You are just on your device. Asking them to stop using their devices while you are using yours is, to them, the height of hypocrisy. Shutting down your devices when you are with them means that you are present for them, enjoying undistracted family time. And it is healthier for you too. Research has shown that employees who receive and respond to after-hours emails experience increased anxiety, decreased quality of sleep, and lower relationship satisfaction because they feel they are on duty 24/7. Not just their mental health but their productivity and performance suffer.[2] (Bosses, take notice!) Both employees and employers need to be aware that in the US, the Fair Labor Standards Act (FLSA) requires employers to pay nonexempt employees for all overtime hours worked—including any after-hours emailing, texting, or talking—or face a fine.[3] EurWORK, the European Union's work rules repository, defines "a worker's right to be able to disengage from work and refrain from engaging in work-related electronic communications, such as emails or other messages, during non-work hours."[4] Since 2017, French employees have been allowed by law to switch off phones and all other devices outside of their thirty-five-hour work week.[5] According to the FLSA, US citizens are similarly protected, but most of us are not aware of this regulation and have not developed the habit of turning off our devices and focusing on our families and ourselves. This can be changed. We are all, employers and employees alike, in this together—and together we can change it. We and our families will be happier and healthier for it.

Who

Every child grows and matures differently. There is no specific age at which it is appropriate for all children to use a device or consume certain media content. Human development is not democratic. Not only is it unhealthy for all children of all ages to have access to all devices and content, but recommended ages for introducing media devices and content are just that—recommendations, not age-related rights. Know your child—some will be ready before and some after the recommended ages. Developmental readiness is a metric which applies not only to kids of various chronological ages but to neurodiverse and cognitively challenged kids as well. Seek the most developmentally optimal time to introduce each device and platform. When you believe that your child needs and is ready to responsibly use a media device, platform, or application, mentor their screen use. Your child will likely know as much, possibly more, than you about how to make that power tool work. Do not mistake technical facility for media literacy. They need you to teach them what they will use this tool for, where and when they will use it—and *explicitly* what they will *not* use it for, and where and when they will *not* use it at all. If you are uncomfortable talking to your child about pornography, sexting, cyberbullying, or any of the online realities we explored in part 2, "So What?," perhaps your child and you are not ready to initiate responsible, respectful, and healthy use of that technology that accesses them so easily.

How

How your child uses media should always be guided by the understanding that it is a power tool. This does not mean that they cannot use media for pleasure, but media should be used purposefully for learning, communicating, and, yes, entertaining—then turned off to pursue other activities when that task is complete. Limiting screen time, how long your child uses media, is not about avoiding inherently negative screen exposure but about not displacing healthier non-screen activities—including in-person time with family and friends, undistracted meals, strenuous physical activity (preferably outside), homework, and sleep. Healthy media use strategies include *not* (1) allowing screen media use to become a default behavior, (2) using screens to avoid boredom, or (3) choosing screen media when it is not the best tool for the task at hand.

Where and When

Screen use that is healthy in some contexts can be a problem if that tool is used in a place or at a time when its use detracts from the purpose of the place and time. When at school, kids' primary task is to learn from teachers, fellow students, and from screen media only when it is part of the planned curriculum. The great majority of what kids do on smartphones is a distraction from learning. Constant connectivity with parents disrupts the critical social and emotional learning of figuring out how to function as an independent individual, get along with others, and build a society of their own. Digital devices can disrupt studying if they are used for split-tasking. The psychological and nutritional benefits of a sit-down family meal are diminished when one or more have a device at the table. Phones in the bedroom harm the quality and quantity of sleep so important for children and rapidly growing adolescents.

Looking Forward

As new devices and technologies emerge, we must purposefully look for and create ways to optimize their use. In the near future, we will likely be sorting out the potential health effects of immersion in the metaverse. Currently, the metaverse and the technology that powers it remain more a novelty item than a widespread media use experience. Among other things, the VR and AR headsets are still clunky, physically and cognitively exhausting to use. What are the health effects, positive or negative, on kids?

We do not have enough experience with VR use by anybody to have valid findings on health effects. The brain's prefrontal cortex, still years or decades from being fully developed in children and adolescents, is where the dual visual inputs of VR/AR are integrated into a single three-dimensional image. Many adults are exhausted and headachy after using VR. Imagine what VR's cognitive load does to prefrontal cortexes still in construction. A child might not complain of feeling tired or headachy, but they might not have the energy or emotional tolerance to attend to the next non-screen activity or human interaction. Their brain fatigue might show up as lackluster interest, crankiness, or a short temper.

Despite these valid theoretical concerns, research has already shown beneficial effects of VR use in medical care and education. Researchers had burn patients play a VR snowball-throwing game while their wounds were being debrided, one of the most painful of all medical procedures. The VR content featured a cold arctic environment in which the patients had to concentrate to find penguins and try to hit them with snowballs. Scientists theorize that because the immersive experience flooded their audiovisual sensory systems, the patients required less pain medication for the procedure than they did without VR.[6] In education, VR has been used in storytelling through virtual experiences, from climbing Mount Everest to diving in the deepest parts of the ocean.[7] Both applications are now in use. Concerns about future risks the metaverse experience may pose for children's and teens' health and development are reasonable at this stage, while much of it remains in development. This is the time, early in the design and marketing stages, to ask the critical questions, to do rigorous research on health and developmental effects, and to offer evidence-based expectations for users.

The Digital Wellness Lab and others can work toward constantly improving digital devices, applications, and content for the future, but we must all recognize the power we have—right now—to pay attention to the contexts that we create for our own digital lives. Not only will our children be happier and healthier, but as we model and mentor, our children are learning to create healthy digital use contexts too. With awareness comes agency. I'm encouraged by what I am hearing from young people who want to find their healthy life balance.

Tipping the Scales

Jeff sat down gingerly on the front edge of the armless chair in the examination room, avoiding the backrest. Jeff and his family had recently moved from another state. This was our first visit. He had come in to get help managing his acne, but I was more immediately struck by how overweight he was. At fourteen Jeff weighed one hundred and ninety-seven pounds, sixty pounds over a healthy weight for his age and height. He said that his acne had gone from bad to worse in the past six months. "It's all over my chest and back." After several years and many heavily advertised acne remedies, Jeff's mom thought it was time to see a doctor. Looking over records from his childhood pediatrician, I saw that he had no chronic medical conditions and was on no medications. He had grown from a healthy, sturdy toddler to a husky boy. As a preteen, when his friends had gotten involved in sports and scouts, Jeff had opted out. He was a big fan of Japanese anime, and he spent hours watching online.

"I'm learning Japanese!" he told me proudly.

"What else do you do for fun?" I asked as I took his blood pressure, elevated at 150/85.

"I play games with my anime characters."

"Who do you play with?"

"Online friends. That's how I'm learning Japanese. They're in Japan. Oh, can you write me a note to get out of gym class? My hips and knees hurt when I run."

"When do you watch anime?"

"Whenever I can. Mostly at night after my homework is done."

"And when do you game?"

"Before my family wakes up. Japan time is, like, exactly opposite of ours, so they get home from school around four o'clock." Jeff was waking up at 4:00 a.m. to game after staying up until midnight or later watching anime. Because his schedule was so different, he no longer ate meals with his family, preferring to take plates of food and snacks to eat in his room while watching anime.

"What do you want to do about your weight?"

"Nothing to do. I've tried everything. Nothing works."

Although Jeff was overweight compared to healthy standards, he was closer to the average when compared to his peers. Obesity among children has doubled and for adolescents has more than tripled in the last several decades.[8] Pre-pandemic obesity prevalence was nearly one child in five (19.7 percent) on average.[9] The proportion increased steadily with children's ages:

- 12.7 percent among two-to-five-year-olds,[10]
- 20.7 percent among six-to-eleven-year-olds,[11] and
- 22.2 percent among twelve-to-nineteen-year-olds.[12]

Like Jeff, many of the 14.7 million obese children and adolescents had obesity-related conditions, including elevated blood pressure, high cholesterol, type 2 diabetes, joint pain, and breathing problems, such as asthma and sleep apnea.

The strong link between increased television viewing and risk of obesity was one of the main drivers of the 1999 American Academy of Pediatrics recommendations for screen time limits. A longitudinal study of the rapid increase of childhood obesity in the 1980s found a strong relationship between average daily TV viewing and risk of being overweight among ten-to-fifteen-year-olds, with as much as 60 percent of the new-onset overweight attributable to excess television viewing.[13] Obesity is now the leading preventable cause of death in the United States with 47 percent more life-years lost than those attributed to tobacco use. Obesity and associated cardiometabolic risk factors such as elevated blood pressure and cholesterol levels in adulthood have been associated with greater screen time in childhood.[14] Community-based screen time reduction programs have resulted in reduced weight gain in children, demonstrating a cause-and-effect relationship.[15]

The initial and logical response to these findings was to conclude that being overweight was the result of sedentary screen time displacing strenuous physical activity. Contrary to first impressions, however, the relationship between television viewing and obesity may not be driven solely by sedentary behavior. Interventions that reduced screen time resulted in participants being less overweight, but there was no significant increase in strenuous physical activity—instead of watching television, children would read or play quietly, remaining relatively sedentary.[16]

More than 90 percent of studies seeking the mechanism of increased risk of obesity have shown that increased screen time was associated with less sleep.[17] Sleep deprivation has been shown to contribute to weight gain by altering sensitivity to appetite-regulating hormones, thus increasing hunger and decreasing feelings of satiety. Inadequate sleep results in increased snacking, especially at nighttime, on comfort foods that tend to provide more calories and less nutrition.[18] Children and adolescents who watch videos, game, text, or use social media at night, disrupting their quality and quantity of sleep, are more likely to be overweight.[19]

Public health research has associated obesity and being overweight in children with exposure to food advertising on television. Limitations on advertising to children that had been in place since 1946 were deregulated by Ronald Reagan in the 1980s, allowing commercials for energy-dense/nutrient-poor foods high in fat, salt, and sugar (aka junk food) to proliferate on children's television programming after 1983.[20] A review of research on the effects of food and beverage television advertising, "advergaming" (integrating products into interactive online games), and social media targeting children has shown a significant effect on children's food choices, food intake, and nagging behaviors on parents' food purchasing.[21] Cognitively unable to discern the persuasive intent of food advertising, particularly in advergames or social media that seem to be entertainment or messages from friends, children have been found to increase automatic eating when ads are embedded in animated entertainment.[22] Even a single thirty-second ad influences brand preference.[23] In a randomized controlled trial, the gold standard of research, children preferred the taste of branded fast food in side-by-side taste tests.[24]

Concern for the demonstrated correlation between television viewing and obesity motivated the AAP recommendation for a two-hour time limit for using all screens. But are all screens equal? Specifically, are the obesity-related effects of using all screens similar? A study conducted by Digital Wellness Lab team members (before the Lab formally existed) sought to answer that question. We used Measuring Youth Media Exposure (MYME), an innovative, multimodal research method that quantifies and records how children use television, computers, video games, and smartphones, to compare screen use of thirteen-to-fifteen-year-olds with measurements of body mass index (BMI).[25] No significant association was found between overall screen time and BMI. Only greater durations of paying primary attention to television were significantly associated with increased BMI. What is different about how we use television that it alone drives the relationship between screen time and risk of obesity?

Contextual Clues to Behavioral Cues

When we looked at the contexts in which each of these screens were used, there was one glaring difference. Uniquely, television viewing left the users' hands free. Computers, video games, and smartphones kept the media user's hands busy. And what did the television viewers do with their hands? They fed themselves. Not with nutritious, balanced meals, but with heavily advertised snack foods high in fat, salt, and sugar, stimulating their taste buds with the intensity that their eyes and ears were being stimulated. And because they wanted to limit interruptions of their viewing, they would grab the whole bag of chips or tub of ice cream from the kitchen and eat until it was all gone, distracted by the screen from their body's hunger and satiety cues. This study demonstrated that the context in which the screen was used, eating while watching, was a powerful, perhaps the most powerful, factor influencing young people's risk of obesity.

I didn't scold Jeff about his food choices, lack of exercise, or even his screen use. Instead, we talked about lifestyle factors that were changeable. He was surprised that I didn't mention dieting or exercising at that first visit but suggested that he could try tweaking just one habit—his media use—and see what happened. When he thought about it, he realized that most days he spent about seven hours watching anime videos and another two hours gaming with his friends in Japan and had not eaten a meal with his family in the three months since they moved. I suggested that just for one month, he cut his screen time in half, stop snacking while watching, get eight hours of sleep, and have one sit-down meal with his family each day. He agreed, reasoning that it still left him with four and a half hours to do as he pleased. Considering that he often just watched anime to fill the time, we listed other activities he wanted to try instead. He was quick to buy in: "I could learn to draw anime myself!"

When Jeff returned four weeks later, he had lost eleven pounds and normalized his blood pressure without any restrictions on his diet or increased exercise. At first, cutting back on screen time was harder than he had anticipated, so he took his flatscreen out of his bedroom and started doing his homework on the dining room table. He pulled out his phone to show me a drawing he made of his favorite anime character—using the computer and some of his screen time. He went outside to do yard work with his dad, which, he was surprised to realize, made him feel better. While he was outside, he met his neighbor who went to the same high school. He was invited to shoot hoops together. "I wasn't very good," he admitted, "but at least he said we should do it again."

MEDIA Rx
Choose a Mindful Media Diet That Promotes a Healthy Balance of Screen Time, Meal Time, and Movement

Any time we bring awareness and appreciation to something routine, it becomes more enjoyable. If we take a little time and attention to notice our habits around eating, screen time, and movement, we can heighten the pleasures of all three—and reap the health benefits.

YOU CAN

- *Promote mindful food consumption and mindful media consumption.* Eat when you eat and watch when you watch.
- *Eat at least one sit-down, screen-free meal together each day as a family*, and talk to each other about your day. No screens should be present, visible, or audible during meals.
- *Remember to choose developmentally optimal content lengths consistent with your child's attention span at each age*, and turn it off when the program is done.
- *Help your child recognize and feel empowered to call out, question, or avoid media content that promotes stereotypes about weight and attractiveness.* They may sometimes choose the clichéd programming, but a candid conversation about toxic messaging can help them avoid objectifying themselves and questioning their self-worth.
- *Avoid watching commercials whenever possible.* Use ad-free video streaming services, watch recorded videos, or fast-forward through commercials. When commercials are unavoidable, try improvisational "ad-busting" by making fun of ads, challenging their truth, and questioning their motives.
- *Shop and cook together with your child from an early age* so that they learn not only that eating is sustenance but shared sensory experience and bonding with loved ones.
- *Make fruits and vegetables plentiful and always available in the home.* Limit the availability of high-fat, salty, and sugary snacks.
- *Make time for physical activity each day.* Encourage children and teens to play outside, join a sports team, or use a local community center. Play together and do chores together as a family. Make it fun!

The screen time limits recommended by the AAP were proposed when broadcast television was the only screen used by most children. The physical contexts in which children consumed media were limited by the fact that televisions were static pieces of furniture. When the AAP recommended that televisions be only in public family spaces, many parents, to their credit, removed televisions from children's bedrooms, amid loud protests. Broadcast television had fixed schedules, so parents could determine which shows of what lengths their children would view. Regulated by the FCC, broadcasters limited certain types of content to be broadcast at child-viewing times. Child-friendly programming of shorter lengths was limited to daytime and early evening, while more adult-oriented and longer content was shown during later hours. Under those conditions, screen time limits were a rough but quantifiable attempt to restrict the amount and quality of media content children consumed.

Despite the best of intentions, screen time limits didn't work. If the family's after-school limit was one hour, kids would rush home and turn on the television to watch or play video games. At the end of the prescribed hour, what would happen? Absolutely nothing. Then after an hour and twenty minutes, Mom or Dad came to remind the child that they went over time and there would always be whining, negotiating, and anger. "Can I finish my program? Can't I level up in my game?" The problem with screen time limits, even when screen time was measurable, is that they made screen time the forbidden fruit. Like chocolate cake, anything that needs to be restricted is something that kids will desire and do anything they can to get more of. So there was conflict every time the limit was reached or exceeded. Screen time limits were not evidence-based, created conflict, and ultimately were rendered obsolete by the evolution of mobile devices and screen content on demand.

Just because screen time limits are obsolete doesn't mean we shouldn't limit screen time. We were going at it all wrong. We approached screens as something that was OK in small doses but harmful at more than two hours a day. Kids (and many parents) didn't buy that after one hundred and twenty minutes, screens transformed from tolerable to toxic. Scare tactics do not work in health education, as we learned from trying to combat smoking by dissecting black lungs in science class. What matters is not that screen time is inherently toxic but that it is *displacing* healthier activities—like sleep, getting outdoors, exercising, reading, doing homework, hanging out with friends and family, daydreaming, and imagining the new. Screens, now ubiquitous, offer a path of least resistance to kill time. Time is all we get in life, so why would we want to kill it? And screens don't really kill time; they dissolve it.

Once kids are on screens, they lose track of time and place, making it hard for them to extract themselves from what is a weak substitute for a healthy, diversified lifestyle.

When Jeff started having dinner with his family, he stuck to his commitment to leave his phone and tablet outside the dining room. But he immediately noticed that his father was silently eating with one hand while scrolling through emails with his opposite thumb. Jeff's mother would laugh from time to time with the television show still running in the kitchen. No one spoke. Jeff felt lonely. He started to talk about what had happened at school that day, but neither parent responded—or even seemed to hear him. He stood and picked up his plate, ready to walk with it to his bedroom, but after a minute, Jeff put his plate down, walked into the kitchen, and turned off the television.

"Why'd you do that?" his mother asked.

"I stabbed my algebra teacher with a pencil today."

"*What?* Honey, did you hear that?" Jeff's mom asked his dad.

"Uh-huh."

"Put your phone down. We should talk. Your son is in trouble!"

The rising anxiety in Mom's voice caused Dad to lower his phone. "What?"

"Tell him, Jeff. Tell him what you did!"

"I didn't do anything. I just wanted to stab her with a pencil because she made fun of one of my answers on a quiz. I just wanted to talk about my day. How were yours?"

That was the beginning of his family's transition to a sit-down meal every day, a meal without devices or distractions. And they started to talk to each other, both about what had happened that day at school or work and to plan family vacations. After a while, Jeff's mom invited him into the kitchen, and he discovered that he loved to cook. He even invented a Doritos omelet and served it to mixed reviews one Sunday morning. His interest in cooking took Jeff to the supermarket with his mother so he could choose his own ingredients for the meal he was preparing. As the weather warmed, Jeff more frequently played basketball with his neighbor, first HORSE, then HIPPOPOTAMUS, then one-on-one. Over the next few months, Jeff became more aware of and regulated his diet and exercise. He continued to lose weight, though much more slowly than he had at first. Most importantly, he began to feel better, both physically and about himself.

A World of Worry: Loneliness, Anxiety, Depression

Avoiding social situations for fear of public embarrassment or humiliation is the textbook description of social anxiety disorder. And for some young people, that's the description of adolescence. Social media and texting provide youth with tentative connections. The psychosocial context in which they use social media—what they communicate, how they communicate it, and what they expect from it—varies from person to person and even within an individual at different points in time. For many, social media can serve as a fertile, safer-feeling space for expressing interest in another. Private enough to avoid feeling awkward, yet public enough that plausible deniability and emotional escape remains possible, electronic contact proves to be a healthy transition zone from stranger to friend for many young people. But for some, the anxiety of progressing from the comfort of social media to in-person contact can be overwhelming.

Social media feels safe because it connects but does not demand connectedness. It is easy to reach out and show interest in someone, but it is equally easy to abuse or (worse) ignore someone reaching out. Social interest is gauged by number and speed of responses. Unfortunately, this quantifies human feelings, which, at their truest, generate a quality, not a score. As adolescents mature socially and emotionally, many move beyond advertising themselves to increasing openness and honesty as they seek deeper, more genuine relationships. Maturing relationships move closer emotionally and physically, and as they do, many young people decrease or abandon social media use in favor of being together in person.

It is too easy for digital devices and platforms to become walls rather than bridges between us. Encourage young people to open themselves and move closer to each other by upgrading their connections with each other.

- Instead of tweeting, text.
- Instead of texting, call or, better yet, video call.
- Instead of calling, meet in person.

Of course, this applies to people one knows well—not those met online or not known beyond the persona they present in social media. (See the important cautionary note in the box below.) One must be cautious about strangers meeting and grooming kids online, exploiting kids' loneliness in order to hurt them, but these are relatively rare events. Amplified by news media, these stories worry parents. But the kids are even more worried about being embarrassed in front of peers. It is much more common to see a line of teens sitting side by side at recess or a social event, all on their phones, texting rather than turning their heads to look at and talk to each other. Anxiety about being exposed can wall us off from each other.

It is too easy for socially anxious youth to stay in the transition space of social media, establishing but not evolving relationships. Seeking connection but feeling vulnerable, some expect more from social media than it can give. Anxiety brings them to social media because it feels safer but keeps them from opening themselves to an authentic connection. When young people get stuck, their feelings of inadequacy are reinforced, leading to depression. When young people push through their fear of embarrassment and get together in person, they can realize that they are not the only ones figuring out how to connect. Making themselves open and vulnerable allows their empathy, humility, and humor to blossom. Being authentic allows deep, meaningful trust and intimacy to develop. You can say (and show) a lot with a smartphone, but you can't learn to kiss with it.

Important note: This advice to upgrade connections applies only with friends one knows IRL. Children and adolescents must be extremely cautious with strangers met online who seek to connect in person. Even if they submit a photo, you cannot trust that they are who they say they are. Sexual predators will misrepresent themselves as a peer to build trust and groom young people, exploiting kids' loneliness. It is important that youth always use critical thinking when online to protect themselves from harm. As a rule, it is best to keep contacts made online strictly online.

Upward Comparisons a Downer

Rigorous scientific research has shown that adolescents who are anxious get more anxious and those who are depressed get more depressed when they use social media.[26] Because of their anxiety and depression, they engage in upward social comparison, looking at the glowing posts of others showing the best of themselves and their lives. Comparing their own anxiety- and depression-filtered realities against idealized images posted by others, they feel worse.

A patient of mine who was active on social media, but struggling with anxiety and depression, had developed problem drinking during her first semester at the University of Southern California. Seeking help, she was introduced to the work of a student across the country from her and shared her introduction with me at her annual physical. Larissa May, a student at prestigious Vanderbilt University and a fashion influencer with hundreds of thousands of followers on social media, had found herself feeling anxious, depressed, and terribly alone. Seeking to understand why she felt so bad, she had a flash insight that she was comparing the whole of her lived reality to social media posts that showed only part of others' stories—just the good part. Realizing that she, too, was showing only her best but yearning to be seen, she founded #HalfTheStory, a storytelling platform where users can be just the way they are. There she courageously told her whole story and urged others to do so. May started a youth movement in which she has activated thousands of adolescents and young adults to reclaim their mental health not by shutting down social media but by using it to be truthful about their whole selves and empathetic to the truths of others. #HalfTheStory was the first youth-led organization to spearhead the digital wellness conversation with policymakers and big tech, building a collective of youth around the globe to fight for their future.[27]

While there is much public debate over whether social media and smartphones cause adolescent anxiety and depression, this speculation is based on a measured rise of adolescent anxiety and depression paralleling the increase in adolescent smartphone ownership and social media use. Research tells a different story. Even those who propose that social media and smartphones may cause anxiety and depression acknowledge that those who use little or no social media as well as those who use social media a lot have poorer mental health outcomes than those who use social media moderately.[28] Our research at the Digital Wellness Lab has shown that

- 55 percent of adolescents and 45 percent of parents observed social media use to be more beneficial than detrimental to adolescent mental health, particularly during the isolation of COVID-19 lockdowns.[29]

- The majority of adolescents felt that their use of social media made them feel socially connected (79 percent) and emotionally supported by their peers (69 percent) and made friend relationships better (50 percent).[30]

However, 46 percent felt worse about their bodies.[31] What I have observed in more than thirty years of caring for adolescents is that for many, feeling anxious, exhilarated, frustrated, scared, happy, confused, contented, insecure, and tragically sad, often in rapid succession, is part of adolescent social emotional development. Social media and its 24/7 availability via smartphones are not the cause of adolescent anxiety and depression but serve as accelerants of social emotional stimuli and amplifiers of psychological response.

It is not how much but how young people use screens, and particularly social media, that influences their emotional well-being. The context for using social media—the mood they are in at the moment, those they are with, what image they want to project, what they want to show and avoid showing—is more telling than what is on the screen. Their context for using screens incorporates two worlds: their inner world, which is accessible to parents only as much as their teens' insight and confidence allow them to articulate, and their outward-facing world, where you can encourage enjoyment of non-screen activities, support get-togethers with friends, and guide them toward a rich diversity of experience.

A Room with a View: The Right People at the Right Time

Adolescents use social media more than any other age group because it is a safer-feeling environment to engage with key developmental tasks, particularly identity formation and connecting with peers. Adolescence is a time of exploration and, for better or worse, experimentation. Many use social media actively, reaching out to form relationships and affinity groups over everything from shared fandom to issues of social justice. Particularly for young people who feel they do not fit in where they live because of their race, politics, religion, gender, or sexuality, social media can allow them to find the community they do not have in their physical world. Marginalized, ostracized, sometimes bullied in their communities and even in their homes, these youth find their way on social media.[32]

Julian was referred to me by the doctor who served an exclusive, all-male New England boarding school. After several months of Julian's first year there, he had stopped doing homework, he was falling asleep in class, and his grades had plummeted. When his housemaster discovered that Julian was gaming on his laptop instead of doing homework and his roommate complained that his gaming often continued after lights out, Julian's laptop was confiscated. All of his homework was converted to paper. Julian started doing his homework and going to bed on time, but after a few days, he began falling asleep in class again. The doctor found him to be healthy, with no organic reason to be as drowsy as he was. One morning, several weeks later, Julian was found sound asleep in the window seat of his dorm's common room, his head on another student's laptop. He had resumed his all-night sessions online by "borrowing" other students' devices while they slept. Unsure of whether to punish or obtain clinical help for him, the school sent Julian to CIMAID.

Surprisingly perhaps, Julian welcomed the medical attention. He described how lonely he felt far from his home in Texas, how he had found friends online first through gaming, then continued their interactions on a social media platform where they could interact and play with each other as self-created avatars. This was the first visit of what became a clinical relationship that lasted several years. Over time, reassured of confidentiality, Julian revealed that he had felt uncomfortable in his male body since first grade but had not revealed it to his family or friends because he did not know how they might respond. Now far from home, Julian shared a new chosen name—Julie—and *she/her/hers* pronouns. Gaming was a way to distract herself from her interior struggle; social media provided an opportunity to interact with others through her female avatar.

Online, Julie had found a group of friends that, like her, had gender dysphoria and were experimenting with being their true selves, identifying as female.

"They understand. And they have helped me feel OK about myself for the first time," Julie said. "Now they are helping me figure out what to do." Compared to their heterosexual and cisgender peers, LGBTQ+ youth are at higher risk for depression, self-harm, and suicidal ideation and completion.[33] LGBTQ+ youth actively use social media as a place where they can figure out who they are, how they fit into the human constellation, and who can and will support their mental health in difficult times.[34] After completing her CIMAID treatment program, Julie, supported by the online friend group, went on to seek gender-affirming care—but not before weathering hateful and threatening online attacks on the social media platform to which she and her online friends had retreated for safety. Now a college student and more assertive than when younger, Julie reluctantly bid farewell to the online community that had been so supportive though a crucial time, advising those friends to move to kinder spaces.

As in Julie's case, social media algorithms designed to target markets for advertisers can bring together people with shared interests, activities, and life-styles. The digital ecosystem has created universally accessible but previously unavailable spaces where those who feel marginalized in their physical worlds can find a community of peers who affirm, support, and share life with them. Unfortunately, for those who fear and hate anyone other than those with whom they identify, social media can create concentrations of those they seek to victimize. Julie found acceptance and ultimately a sturdy sense of self on social media but also encountered discrimination, hatred, and threats. How Julie used social media at first was liberating, healthy self-actualization. But when less healthy human behavior changed the digital environment, Julie was aware and strong enough to pivot away. It was *how* Julie used, then chose *not to use*, social media that helped her through a difficult time in her life. Connection in that context meant everything.

Socialize Your Child to Social Media

Because of the unique self-consciousness, curiosity, emotional lability, and incomplete impulse control in the adolescent stage of neurodevelopment, it is important to create context and mentor your adolescent as they begin to use interactive media. Stay in touch with them and keep the door open for nonjudgmental communication as they navigate the digital ecosystem. They will run across images and information that intrigue, confuse, upset, and scare them. They need you to parent and be there for them. How they use social media is critical to their health outcomes. Although you aren't part of their conversation on social media, you create the context of conversation between you two, one in which you are reliably approachable, reasonable, and supportive in the way you engage. It is in that context that your child becomes confident they can count on you.

ASK THE MEDIATRICIAN
How Can I Change the Social Media Conversation?

For my teen and her friends, social media is the sea they swim in, even when it seems they're drowning in the drama. How can I change the conversation when I'm not in it?

You're clearly a seasoned forecaster when it comes to reading the cues from your daughter and her friends. Even when adolescents know that using social media makes them feel bad, they are loath to let go. Although this seems counterintuitive to adults, the worse teens feel, the harder they cling to their smartphones. While many of us use our phone more than we need to due to FOMO (fear of missing out), adolescents and pre-adolescents struggle with the even more potent FOBLO (fear of being left out).[35] While their emotions rise and fall with the amount and rapidity of likes they receive, being ignored or ghosted is even worse. They fear that if they are offline, they will cease to exist, at least in the digital environment. Because of FOMO/FOBLO, 29 percent of teens reported sleeping with their smartphone in their bed, and 36 percent of them admitted to waking up to respond to messages.[36] The resulting sleep deficit contributes to daytime sleepiness and anxiety,[37] and sleep disruptions can prevent brain housekeeping and the consolidation of learning that occurs in deep rapid eye movement (REM) sleep.[38] Adolescents who were more invested in and used social media more overall and at night experienced poorer sleep quality, lower self-esteem, and higher levels of anxiety and depression.[39]

Research has found different wellness outcomes from using social media in different ways. Passive social media use, such as browsing others' posts, has been found to trigger upward self-comparison, poorer body image, and life dissatisfaction, while active social media use, like reaching out to others and creating something new, elicits positive feedback and social connectedness.[40] However, communications theories challenge the passive/active use dichotomy, arguing that all media use, receptive as well as interactive, is active in nature.[41]

There are so many media messages available to us that we actively choose which we pay attention to based on how we feel at the time. The way that the messages we choose affect us depends on the psychological, social, and situational context in which we receive them—and those contexts, as well as personalities, differ from person to person. Studies testing passive/active media use theories in real time found that passive use resulted in negative well-being for 10 percent of adolescents; the remaining 90 percent felt a positive or no effect.[42] A follow-up study found that for 11 percent of adolescents, both active and passive use led to negative effects and for 12 percent both active and passive use led to positive effects on affective wellness.[43]

The effects that social media use has on adolescent well-being vary from individual to individual and context to context. The idea that we can recognize the effect of our own inner context on how we feel and respond on social media, that we can assert control over the context in which we engage with others, is something your daughter may find useful.

In the meantime, you know your child or adolescent better than anyone. Recognizing how, in the context of media use, they are likely to respond to different stimuli, you are the best companion for them as they explore digital environments and explain them to you. In the best mentorship tradition, you will be both teaching and learning from them.

As obvious as stormy waters may be from the beach, you're right to recognize when it's not helpful to dive in. But when you make quieter waters a constant in your own space, your daughter will come to experience the alternative herself and know she can always find you there, a calm port in the social storm.

Research on the effects of media use on child and adolescent health continues to deliver nuanced insights on the effects of both media content used and the contexts in which they are used. In an age when screens are ubiquitous, time spent on screens is not about what children are doing. It is about what they are *not* doing—sleeping, exercising, studying, socializing, imagining . . . just being.

In a struggle to meet preconceived screen time limits, we fail and we feel guilty. But we can change the equation. We can control the contexts we create in which we and our children use media, the screen habits we model for them, the screen skills we mentor, and the memories we make with them when we are off screens.

Chapter 13

The Art of Living

Curiosity and Creativity as Context for Childhood

Childhood is an adventure. As children grow up, they encounter novel situations, people, events, environments, problems to be solved, and stories to tell. Experience by experience, they build their knowledge of the world, learn about others, find their identities, express themselves, and figure out how to be productive and happy. With the advent of the digital age, the reach of children and adolescents to the larger world expanded exponentially. With the introduction of smartphones, children's and adolescents' ability to direct and control their reach increased dramatically—and so did the proportion of their waking hours spent on screens.

The sheer volume of unsolicited information pouring at kids presents new educational challenges. In addition to learning how to drill down and focus research on subjects of interest, children and adolescents have to filter out what is distracting from what is essential. Broad surface knowledge instantly available on any subject blunts curiosity and disincentivizes digging deeper. Facts, misinformation, even disinformation are presented as equivalents, requiring extensive source-checking and general distrust. Algorithms designed to profile consumers and drive personalized commercial messages have created echo chambers where users receive information and ideas that they already agree with and like.

Ironically, as our connectivity has increased, our connectedness with each other and the world has diminished. Instead of bringing us closer, in many ways screens have distanced us. Interactive media are constantly available, uncritical, and easier than other humans. Any experience can be accessed virtually. We have lost touch with the world and with each other—and we didn't miss or even notice it. Leaving the hospital after one long, exhausting day, stepping onto the city sidewalk, I turned west toward the parking lot and was greeted by a glorious gold-purple-orange-pink sunset. I was instantly uplifted, energized by this unexpected gift. Smiling spontaneously, I looked around at the hundreds of others on the sidewalk. Every one of them was staring at their phones held close. They did not see the sunset.

Marvin had struggled in middle school, both academically and behaviorally. He had been suspended twice, once for getting into a teacher's face and physically threatening her and once for suspicion of supplying cannabis edibles to a classmate who was caught with them. He had entered high school with a dark reputation. Teachers were alerted, and the students who came from his middle school warned other students. Marvin began his freshman year badly. He tried out for the basketball team but got into a fistfight with another student and was asked to leave. Avoided by other students for years, Marvin sought out comfort online, gaming deep into the night and struggling to wake up in the morning. He would make it to school late, missing his first-period English class and sometimes his second-period civics class. History kept repeating itself. Teachers and students alike were wary of Marvin and weary of his behaviors. In the second quarter, he was moved down a level in English, so his schedule shifted and he was forced to take an art class to keep his credits up. Marvin walked into his first art class and took a seat alone at the paint-spattered worktable farthest away from the other students. Mr. Perez, all muscle and as wide as he was tall, walked into the room carrying a huge block of damp clay. He made a beeline for Marvin and slammed the clay down on the table, hard. "Beat the crap out of that . . . please." Marvin looked up at Mr. Perez with a mixture of confusion and annoyance. "Do it! I will tell you when you and the clay are ready." Not knowing what else to do, Marvin began to punch and knead the clay. Mr. Perez turned to the class and said, "Welcome to 3D Art. We will begin by making vessels." He engaged the class with a discussion about what vessels were, how they were used historically, and why they were considered art. Marvin kept kneading.

Screens all around us, and particularly those in our pockets, have made looking at those screens reflexive. Whenever we have even a brief moment, our FOMO and kids' FOBLO compel us to pull the screens out. The screens suck us in with their variable rewards, we lose track of time, and we use them for longer than that moment. Once young people are engaged in gaming, social media, even doomscrolling, it is hard for them to disengage. And when it is a parent who is asking them to rejoin life—to come to dinner, do homework, go to bed, or just have some family time—annoyance, anger, even aggression can be triggered. If we are to effectively guide children and adolescents through the diverse menu of experiences that will help them learn, grow, and become resilient, it is essential to make those experiences fun, social, and available to compete with the 24/7 siren song of screen media. Remember, the goal is not to restrict or ban screens but to use them mindfully. Part of mindful use of these power tools is to turn them on to do what they do well—and to turn them off when they are not the best tool for the task or when there is no task at all. Screens too easily become a default behavior, the path of least resistance, displacing experiential learning, recreational play in the physical environment, even daydreaming. (Daydreaming? What use is that?!)

Mr. Perez assigned a "snapsketch" of the vessels the students imagined making, handing out large sheets of paper and pencils. He put down the paper and pencils in front of Marvin and pointed at his hunk of clay. "You're done. Grab that and follow me." Relieved he wouldn't have to draw, Marvin followed Mr. Perez into a back room. In the middle sat a small table with a round plate on a vertical shaft. "Slam that down right in the middle." Mr. Perez sat, threw a switch, and the plate began to turn. Dipping his hands in a water bowl, Mr. Perez silently, almost hypnotically, drew the formless mass of clay up into a tall vase. Marvin was mesmerized. "Can I do that?" were the first words he spoke. Mr. Perez stopped the potter's wheel. "You must!" Mr. Perez said, smashing his fist down and reducing the vase into a blob of clay. Marvin was stunned. "Why did you do that?" Mr. Perez stood up and indicated that Marvin should sit. "Because you are going to make something that is better."

As we recovered from the Great Recession of 2008, IBM interviewed more than fifteen hundred corporate CEOs from thirty-three industries and sixty countries to determine what qualities were most important for leadership.[1] Contradicting expectations that they would point to disciplined management, a majority of the CEOs cited creativity as the most important leadership criterion. But what is creativity? How do we measure it? And is it different from intelligence?

Most succinctly, creativity is alternating divergent thinking—generating new ideas—and convergent thinking—combining those ideas to imagine the new. Intelligence, as measured by intelligence quotient (IQ) tests, is reasoning, using one's fund of knowledge to solve problems. Since intelligence was first measured in the early 1900s, the average IQ of children and adolescents has risen by about three points every decade, a phenomenon called the Flynn effect.[2] This steady increase in intelligence is thought to be the result of richer information environments and increased focus on complex, abstract thinking in education, along with improved nutrition and more genetic mixing due to greater mobility.[3]

Creativity has been measured since the 1960s with the Torrance Tests of Creative Thinking (TTCT).[4] Education scholar Kyung Hee Kim found that the average of children's creative thinking scores rises steadily through the preschool years to peak at third grade, level off through sixth grade, then steadily decrease, believed to be the result of increased conformity of thinking as schooling increasingly focuses on logic, reasoning, and getting to the Right Answer. Population creativity scores rose in parallel with IQ scores until 1990. While IQ scores have continued to rise, TTCT scores have decreased significantly since 1990, with the most serious declines for kindergarten through third grade—formerly the developmental stage with the greatest increase in creative thinking.[5] When education researcher Jonathan Plucker compared children's IQ and creative thinking scores with their adult accomplishments, he found that adult innovative success was correlated with creative thinking three times more strongly than with IQ scores.[6]

Mr. Perez went back to the main art classroom, and Marvin wet his hands and went to work on his clay. Imitating Mr. Perez, he would start to draw the clay upward and it would spin off and splat on the floor. Marvin picked it up and started again and again and again. The bell rang and the other students left the classroom, but Marvin kept at it, totally focused.

Mr. Perez came in and watched Marvin for a moment. "Do you have another class now?"

"Lunch," Marvin replied without looking up. "Can I stay?"

"Of course."

Resilience Is a Creative Act

Creativity, from music-making to building forts to dress-up role-playing, is natural to children but frequently undervalued and forgotten as they grow older and advance in school. In school and in our communities, we treat art as an academic elective or a luxury available only to those who can afford cello lessons or children's theater troupes. And art is not the only avenue for creativity. Every discipline, every environment, every relationship offers the opportunity to be creative. Creativity is a human essential. It can be practiced in every community, every school, and every home. But one has to put down one's phone, turn off the television, and exercise creativity, wrestle with it like clay on a wheel, and make it one's own.

Creative expression of our shared humanity is the most important vessel of history and culture. We remember Leonardo da Vinci's work but not the merchants who funded it. We hum a Mozart tune but cannot name the emperor for whom he composed it. Creativity stimulates our brain in ways that no other activity does. When music starts playing, toddlers start swaying. By middle school, most kids stand self-consciously against the walls at dances. When one asks a kindergarten class who is an artist, everyone raises their hand. By the time they are in fourth grade, just a few raise their hand, because art has been downplayed in school and the children believe that only a select few are good enough to have been praised. The sounds, shapes, and movements that come naturally to young children have been evaluated by adults and found wanting if they are not a Picasso or a Yo-Yo Ma. The true value of art to children, and to all of us, is the making of it, not the judging of it.

Children are natural, instinctual artists, imagining and creating all the time, whether they are building sandcastles, singing to themselves, or acting out swordfights with sticks. Humans have been creating since our earliest ancestors molded clay and painted on cave walls. Philosophers and anthropologists have proposed that the drive to create art, to shape our understanding of the human condition, is encoded in our DNA. It has been essential to our ability to make sense out of and adapt to our world, passing these traits down to future generations.

Just as creativity can be taught *out* of children, it can be taught *into* them, developed and nurtured at home and in school, not just in art class. Instead of teaching to the test and focusing on the Right Answer (which AI will now generate faster and more accurately), education that encourages curiosity, celebrates uniqueness, and provides stability to take risks and fail produces creative, confident, and resilient adults. *Celebrating* rather than *discouraging* the endless curiosity of the preschooler who asks "Why?" a hundred times a day is an investment in their future. Helpful as it may seem to satisfy the question, responding with the Right Answer is not as good for the child as "Let's figure it out!" Modeling and encouraging problem-solving rather than googling triggers their left brain to gather facts and their right brain to scan for remembered experiences. Defocused attention—mind wandering or daydreaming—produces partially formed ideas. Then focused attention pulls together these alternative perspectives, unseen patterns, and complex abstractions into—aha!—the new. Divergent/convergent thinking can turn the toddler's "Why?" into the adolescent's "Why not?" While there are clearly some people who are naturally more inclined to think divergently, neuropsychologist Rex Jung has found that the ability to switch between divergent and convergent thinking, aka creativity, can be developed and nurtured through practice.[7]

Giving children the tools and intention of problem-solving serves to do more than nurture creativity; it builds grit and resilience. We live in anxious times. Anxiety and depression are on the rise, most acutely among children and adolescents. Anxiety is a stress response paralyzed by a feeling of helplessness; depression is grief potentiated by hopelessness. In an environment that is challenging, constantly changing, and sometimes confusing, problem-solving skills provide adaptability—flexibility, optimism, and confidence that with passion, perseverance, and humor one can survive and thrive. Confronted with overwhelming problems, we will be tempted to suppress our creativity and fall back on rigid, predetermined rules. Finding the Right Answer may calm chaos in the short run but does not develop or model for our children the creative resilience to manage the unexpected. Creativity is not a luxury reserved for those who can afford it. Creativity is an essential brain function that keeps us engaged, open, positive, and motivated. If we don't play, experiment, disrupt, imagine, our ability to innovate is limited and our social and emotional well-being is at risk.

Mark Runco, a professor of cognitive psychology, asks his college students to list all the obstacles that might prevent them from graduating. Then he asks them to pick just one and think up as many solutions as possible. Students who exercised divergent-convergent thinking and did best at both identifying and creatively solving problems had better interpersonal relationships. Those who were able to list problems quickly but their creative inflexibility stymied them on solutions had higher rates of despair and suicidal ideation, even when controlling for anxiety and depression. He also found that those who did better in both problem-finding and problem-solving had better relationships with others, because they were able to identify and creatively solve problems that arose.[8]

Marvin not only stayed through lunch, trying again and again to make the vessel, but asked to come back after school and keep trying. Mr. Perez would clean the studio and prepare for the next day and Marvin would sit at the wheel. Sometimes they would talk; mostly they worked silently. Sometimes Marvin asked for help and Mr. Perez explained how Marvin might do it. Mr. Perez never again demonstrated what to do: "It is not about what your eyes see, it is what your fingers feel." Marvin's mind wandered and his fingers learned.

The Brain Craves IRL Freedom and Fun

Since the 1990s, the science of neuroaesthetics has brought together neurology, cognitive science, psychology, public health, engineering, design, education, humanities, and the arts to study how creativity nurtures brain development and improves learning, memory, speech, mental health, and quality of life. We are drawn to aesthetic experiences because they make us feel good. They feel good because they link our senses with our emotions and our thoughts in ways that connect us with the world and with each other. Each of us connects our sensations, feelings, and thoughts in unique ways that define our individuality and our selfhood. We each experience the same painting, book, or piece of music differently, but we do it together. As we sit in the dark theater watching a movie, the aesthetic experience is both intensely personal and universal, connecting us with each other.

Creating art, whether it be performing a sock puppet play or humming a tune, engages, builds, and nurtures the brain in complex ways through sensory experience. We may see, hear, smell, touch, and taste what we create. A meal, a song, a dance, a poem, a painting enters us through our senses, stirs our emotions, and is interpreted cognitively, stimulating and linking our brains' sensory, limbic, and higher cortical functions in ways that are our very own. Artmaking has been used to heal and to teach from the shamans of our neolithic ancestors to our preschool teachers of today. Art doesn't have to be made "well" (an arbitrarily subjective concept anyway); it just has to be made.

Art is fun and interesting enough to compete with screens and it is available to all regardless of their financial resources—but it requires a little more effort from both the parent and the child. It is that effort, hands-on or engagement with materials and direct involvement of inner resources, that helps children grow healthy, smart, and social. We can harness the power of neuroaesthetics by redirecting a child's attention from a screen to the physical world. It is the process, not the product, that helps them grow healthier, smarter, and kinder.

Marvin kept coming back to Mr. Perez's studio, not just for advanced art classes, but in his free time, especially when stressed academically, challenged socially, or when he just needed to think. It was not just the artmaking but Mr. Perez's unspoken unconditional acceptance and confidence in Marvin that drew him back. Marvin felt psychologically safe, and his self-confidence grew. Sometimes Marvin would do just what Mr. Perez did when they first met: draw up a tall cylinder and squish it back down over and over again. His mind would wander, and he would solve problems. He thought about his biology class and about his relationship with his father. He thought about his crush and how he might start to talk to her. He thought about songs he loved that were stuck in his head as earworms. Marvin was in good company. Great thinkers through time have found favorite activities that allow the mind to wander, refreshing the brain and stimulating their thinking. While they wrestled with problems to solve, Albert Einstein played his violin and Fred Rogers swam laps.[9]

In 1997, neuroscientists were using functional MRI to image real-time neural activity to map the brain regions involved in various cognitive and physical tasks. They discovered that between tasks, when the research subject was lying in the MRI tube waiting for instructions, much larger and more diverse regions of the brain became active. The scientists had discovered a neural network that they misnamed the *default mode network* because it was found when the subject was not doing anything. But when asked what they were doing, research subjects revealed that their minds were wandering. When studying which regions of the brain registered color, for example, a subject may have been shown the color red. Awaiting the next task, they recalled that the red tomatoes in their garden needed to be picked and were probably overripe so they would make tomato sauce with them using Grandma's recipe but Grandma died last year and they miss her terribly but they met a second cousin for the first time at her funeral. When we day-dream, we move from sensation to associations to memories to feelings to ideas, much the way a butterfly moves from flower to flower. Neuroscientists are now focusing on the so-called default mode network as the divergent thinking source of creativity.[10] Others are examining its role in our sense of self, that unique amalgam of experiences, sensations, relationships, dreams, memories, joys and sorrows, hopes and hurts that is duplicated in no one else.

While it is important to avoid letting screen media displace creativity, digital devices and applications are not the enemy of creativity. As powerful tools of information and imagery, screen media can be harnessed to create the new. The cover of this book is created from many selfies and photos of lives lived that have been brought together into the image of a child, a visual metaphor of what we are talking about in this book, that we are all amalgams of many experiences. The digital ecosystem is rich with opportunities to experience art and artists at work from Carnegie Hall to street musicians, the Museum of Modern Art to murals in neighborhoods around the world. YouTube videos feature musicians, dancers, visual artists, and sculptors who welcome us into their work. That work can occur anywhere, with anything. Witness British artist Andy Goldsworthy, who works with nature and time as both his materials and his collaborators in land art.[11] Create experiential activities for your child and have them create experiences for you to move through and beyond the screen to your child's unique imagination.

Play Isn't Frivolous—It's Joyful Brain-Building

Dylan, whom I treated as a preschooler for injuries sustained in an imaginary shoot-out, is currently in college studying social robotics. Throughout his childhood and adolescence, he and his sister had tea parties with imaginary friends; got into cosplay, where they took on different characters (sometimes switching genders); played Dungeons and Dragons; chased Pokémon charac-ters around their neighborhood; and built a fort to welcome Klingons when they arrived. Dylan even learned some Klingon so they could talk, but his sister refused. These fantasized alternate realities, which psychologists call *paracosms*, helped them to manage strong feelings, to learn that reality is what they pay attention to, and to ideate their future. Many famous artists, from Hieronymus Bosch to Salvador Dalí, and writers, from the Brontë sisters to C. S. Lewis, developed paracosms. More surprisingly perhaps, a Michigan State University study found that many MacArthur Foundation "genius grant" winners created paracosms as children.[12]

"Play is the work of childhood." Although frequently credited to Maria Montessori, whose educational method harnessed children's natural way of learning, or Jean Piaget, the father of developmental psychology, it was first articulated nearly a century earlier by Friedrich Froebel (1782–1852), the founder of kindergarten. These visionary pioneers of early childhood understood that child's play is not frivolous but a biological imperative to figure out how the world and those they share it with work.

It is through play that children experiment with and master the world and themselves. A Digital Wellness Lab pulse survey, as well as empirical observations from CIMAID, revealed that the social aspects of interactive digital play with friends were more, and often more important, than the game itself. The children and adolescents talked about social gaming as hanging out with their friends rather than a competition to win.[13]

Like creativity, free, unstructured play is too often devalued by parents in favor of activities with a purpose—learning a skill, improving at a sport, practicing on an instrument, excelling academically. Sociologists have observed that children are seen by some as "human becomings" rather than "human beings."[14] What they mean by that is that many adults see children as adults-in-the-making. Adult-organized play may meet specific learning goals, but it assumes that the child is incompetent and directs their play toward building competence. It can be reasonably concluded that video games, being designed by adults who set clear rules and goals, are adult-directed play. And adult-directed play is not play at all according to Dr. Peter Gray, a child psychologist and educator at Boston College. Gray sees child-directed play as neither a distraction nor a needed break from education. It *is* education of the most important and essential kind. He sees the current mental health and relational struggles of youth as the outcome of the decline and disappearance of free, child-directed play.[15]

Children live in the here and now, a place where child-directed, spontaneous, free play can break out. Adult-directed play focuses on what it *does* for children. Free play belongs to children—what it *means* is what is important to them. Children like to move. They learn to be adventurous and master their fears by taking risks. They master fine motor skills by building a tower with blocks and gross motor skills by kicking it down. They develop their own play narrative and work together to make it happen. They learn to negotiate and get along with those with whom they play. While it may appear to be directionless to adult eyes, child-directed free play contributes to outcomes that most parents seek for their child: healthy growth and development, learning, creativity, and physical, mental, and social wellness.[16]

How does free play do this? By being:

- Intrinsically motivated, happening for its own sake rather than goal oriented.
- Spontaneous and voluntary, initiated and self-directed by the children playing, who have the freedom to choose and the freedom to quit.
- Diverse, incorporating the ideas and imaginations of the different ages, abilities, and cultures of the children involved.
- Social, unfolding in a social emotional context which requires players to meet the needs and desires of others as well as themselves to sustain play.
- Imaginative, freeing children from their immediate environments and circumstances through creative transformations of materials and make-believe improvisation to develop and be enveloped in a world of their own making.
- Stimulating, often emotionally or physically risky and absorbing, allowing them to achieve a flow state.
- Open-ended and self-governed by children negotiating and building an internal structure that has clear guidelines that are adaptable as the play evolves.
- Emotionally resonant, intense, often joyful but often laden with a wide variety of feelings that resonate with their inner lives and help them make sense of their world in a fictional setting.

As with creating art, it is not the immediate outcome of free play but the process that produces both immediate and long-term benefits. The evidence for such benefits is compelling enough that Michael Yogman, MD, professor of pediatrics at Harvard Medical School, wrote a recommendation that pediatricians write prescriptions for play, later endorsed by the American Academy of Pediatrics.[17] Yogman saw children's well visits to their pediatrician as an opportunity to prescribe outdoor play—for children *and* parents—as a way to "emphasize the strengths of parents to share joyful discovery through play with their children . . . Play is brain building," concluding that playful learning enhances children's literacy, numeracy, executive function, creativity, problem-solving, and social emotional skills of cooperation and collaboration. Importantly, it buffers adversity and stress.[18]

While adult-directed play can help children develop skills and teamwork, it does so in an outside-in framework. Working together in free play demands that children develop that discipline from the inside out and work together with others, unconstrained by adult rules. Video games are the easier alternative to which many children default—directed play with adult-determined rules and objectives that do not demand the kind of skills that are learned, practiced, and challenged in free play. However, video games are not the only option for play in the digital space. The Digital Futures Commission, a UK nonprofit "dedicated to placing children's interests at the center of the design of the digital world,"[19] followed its in-depth look at the qualities of free play that promote healthy development with *Playful by Design*, a study of how children, adolescents, and families played online and how those experiences met, modified, or did not meet criteria for developmentally optimal free play.[20] The children studied felt that the digital games they played were social, diverse, stimulating, immersive, and imaginative. They felt that the experiences were reasonably open-ended and gave a sense of achievement and emotional resonance. However, they were not as enthused about the opportunities for risk-taking or the safety of the digital products they used. Few of them felt digital products offered voluntary play. Most interesting, both in the Digital Futures Commission study and the observations of the Digital Wellness Lab and CIMAID, were the creative ways that young people developed their own free play with digital devices, applications, and games. These ranged from drawing and storytelling with distant relatives on video conferencing apps to playing hide-and-seek for hidden devices to playing a shooter game and refusing to shoot, hiding from predators with your friends for as long as possible. It is encouraging to realize that on the cusp of the immersive 3D metaverse, young people can bring their creativity, imagination, and risk-taking even to products that were designed with different outcomes in mind.

Bring Back Boredom

Perhaps the most difficult challenge to overcome in finding healthier alternatives to screens is our cultural aversion to boredom. All of us, children and adults alike, have too easily evaded boredom by having screens available to us during virtually all of our waking hours. Kids get on the school bus and stare silently at their phones. Adults do the same when they step on an elevator. Locked in our downward gaze, we no longer look at the world around us or talk to each other. It is easier and less challenging to absorb the continuous feed of stimulus available on our phones.

In 1905, dubbed by twentieth-century scholars as his "miraculous year," Albert Einstein wrote four scientific papers on which theoretical physics is built, ending up with his famous equation, $E=mc^2$, which gave rise to the atomic age. At that time, Einstein was not working in a laboratory or teaching at a university. He was working as a low-level patent clerk in Switzerland.[21] The boring predictability of his job allowed Einstein's imagination to run free, to travel through space and time. Boredom is the crucible of imagination, creativity, and innovation, not just because it provides a space in which to imagine but because it is an uncomfortable vacuum, nudging us to fill it with new ideas, images, and sounds. All of us, children and adults alike, too often forfeit the opportunity to think the new when we default to whatever game, meme, text, or advertisement happens to be on our phones. Corporations spend billions to grab our attention and we give it away for free. We owe it to our children and to the future they will imagine to bring back boredom.

Cultivate Green Time

"Look deep, deep into nature, and then you will understand everything better," wrote Albert Einstein, reflecting on the nature of the universe in a personal correspondence.[22] One can imagine him walking to his job at the patent office beside the River Aare, watching the swirls and eddies of the water and reflecting on the nature of the universe. He found that his most productive work was done on long walks in nature.[23] For many of us, our focus on screens has distanced us from the natural world. Kids play *Fortnite*;

they don't climb trees. Kids text each other instead of hanging out in the park. Many go to academic or computer camps in the summer set in school buildings, not in the woods. We have lost touch with nature—and we have suffered. Disconnected from the natural world of which we are a part, we have become disconnected from each other and from ourselves. All of us, kids and adults alike, need to "touch grass."

Most of us suffer from nature-deficit disorder, a condition coined by author Richard Louv in his book *Last Child in the Woods*.[24] Our default setting on life has become screen-facing, and our physical, emotional, and mental health have suffered. Children do not depend on or even fully use their senses; Chinese researchers have linked computer use to an increase in near-sightedness, adaptive evolution driven by our near-constant use of screens.[25] Increases in ADHD have been associated with screen use, but spending time in nature has been shown to improve attention.[26] Time in nature has been prescribed by pediatricians to intervene on and prevent obesity and related illnesses like type 2 diabetes.[27] An Australian survey of preschool children ages two to five showed that increased time playing outdoors compared to screen time was associated with improved social skills, such as joining play in open, direct ways and calm, easygoing cooperation.[28] A meta-analysis of 186 research studies from around the world found screen time to be associated with poorer psychological outcomes of anxiety, depression, and academic performance and "green time" in nature to be protective.[29] These outcomes were most pronounced in early and late adolescence and among youth of lower economic resources who were living in urban settings. A recent study found that even a brief intervention of a ten-day nature experience showed a significant improvement in stress levels, happiness, and life satisfaction, with greatest change found among those with the highest levels of screen time.[30] Research continues to show that even modest steps to spend more time out-doors, like walking the family dog, can make a difference in your child's media use and its impact on their health and well-being.[31]

The challenge we face is that in the space of a single generation, children's culture has shifted from children actively playing outdoors until the dinner bell rang into staying "safe" indoors, dependent on virtual experiences to be brought to them. Mobile media offered the chance of disconnecting from the television or computer and becoming more active, but for many children it has served to continue screen use outdoors and to add more screens to be used simultaneously indoors. This cultural shift has transformed childhood from an active, exploratory time of growth and development in which outdoors and nature featured prominently to a more sequestered, sedentary, isolated passage to young adulthood.

The trade-off in child and adolescent health has been costly. Obesity, diabetes, attention problems, anxiety, depression, substance use, aggression, and a profound sense of disconnection from the larger world—all of these have become urgent public health issues. No longer worrisome statistical projections on the horizon, these are problems plaguing children right now. Green time has proven to have a healing effect on all of them.

MEDIA Rx
The Green Hour: Make the Most of Green Time and Screen Time

You can use media to get kids moving, exploring, and interacting with the outdoor world around them. Research on creative play and health by the Centers for Disease Control and Prevention and the American Academy of Pediatrics shows the best way to connect young people to a lifelong concern for nature, wildlife, and the outdoors is through regular positive experiences. In *Friending Fresh Air: Connecting Kids to Nature in the Digital Age*, the National Wildlife Federation promotes the goal of an hour a day outside—a "green hour"—and offers tips on how to use technology to help your child connect with nature.[32]

YOU CAN

- *Inspire and plan your nature-based experiences* by exploring online links to outdoor adventures.
- *Keep a record of your experiences* by taking photos and making videos.
- *Create a nature journal* that catalogs outdoor adventures and discoveries with your kids and the effect it has on their (and your) mood.
- *Share photos, video clips, and a travelogue-style letter* about the adventure with family or friends who live at a distance.

From grit to grandeur, the sensory experience of nature stimulates healthy responses in the brain and body. Spending time outdoors gives all children a visceral sense of connection to the natural world and their place in it. They can watch clouds morph into thunderheads and the struggle of a fly caught in a spider web. They can watch but cannot control the beauty and tragedy of life unfolding. They learn how their own choices and actions affect the natural world. In subsequent books, Louv explored what children's lives might be like if they were as immersed in nature as they are in technology and proposed five hundred ways that children and families might connect with nature in their daily lives.[33]

The benefits of nature are increasingly important as an antidote to the stressful, high-pressured lives of children and the adults who care for them. For many children, being immersed in nature has a calming and focusing effect. "Forest bathing"—spending time in the woods for its therapeutic benefits—and other immersion experiences in natural settings have become popular in many cultures to relieve stress, support self-regulation, focus attention, calm the mind and body, and restore energy. Nature helps children, adolescents, and us all feel less stressed and interact in positive ways. As a research study at the University of Rochester revealed, being in or even just looking at nature makes human beings more human. It makes us healthier, happier, calmer, and kinder.[34]

Active play and physical movement support healthy brain development. Time outdoors spent in parks and open space gives kids a chance to play and problem-solve, to co-create make-believe scenarios. All of this lays the foundation for learning in any environment. Studies have shown that connecting children to nature helps them academically—children in schools with environmental education programs score higher on standardized tests in math, reading, writing, and listening.[35] Exposure to environment-based education significantly increases student performance on tests of their critical thinking skills.[36] There are a growing number of outdoor, nature-based preschools and fewer but also increasing K–12 schools around the US and the world.[37]

Key benefits of nature and outdoor play include:

- Natural sensory stimulation, including visual, sound, touch, smell, and spatial senses.
- Spending time outside raises levels of vitamin D, helping protect children from future bone problems, heart disease, diabetes, and other health issues.
- Play protects children's emotional development, whereas loss of free time in combination with a hurried lifestyle can be a source of stress and anxiety and may contribute to depression. Children who spend much of their time indoors watching television or playing video games can become isolated and withdrawn, even those who are connecting online. Screen-free time with other children builds essential social skills for two-way conversation, collaboration, negotiation, reading social cues, socialization, and other life skills.
- A child who connects with nature is more likely to grow up to be an adult who cares about the environment and practices good stewardship of natural resources. That's an investment in long-term health—for your child, for all of us, and for the earth.
- For parents, spending time with your child outdoors offers unique opportunities to share experiences and make memories, exploring, being playful and creative in nature.

Nature has been used as therapy with children who have a range of challenges or special needs and as occupational therapy with neurodiverse children, building their confidence and physical strength.[38] When young people struggling with PIMU are unable to achieve self-regulation of their interactive media use in the outpatient setting of CIMAID, our most successful option for a higher level of care is wilderness or OBH therapy. Nature lowers the need for constant hyperstimulation but demands one's attention and taking responsibility for oneself and others. If a young person wants to stay dry, they have to work with others to set up a tent. If they want to eat, they must learn to make a fire and to cook. Addressing problem behaviors by building personal and social responsibility, OBH therapy programs include one-on-one and group therapy sessions, hiking and other strenuous physical exercise, psychologically challenging adventure experiences like rock climbing, and mindfulness training through yoga and meditation.

Media can be an ally when we use it to support introducing children to nature, sparking their curiosity and desire to explore further. Screens can be a special window into the wonders of nature, from the hidden world of microbes to our planet's diverse and extreme habitats to the farthest reaches of the cosmos. There's nothing inherently wrong with wow-worthy online videos from mountaintops to deep ocean trenches, beaches to backwoods. But the brain and body are not fooled. Nature itself—the real thing—offers experiences and sensations that can't be replicated on or replaced by any screen.

ASK THE MEDIATRICIAN
Ruminating over Recess: Playground or Screen Play?

My third grader prefers to spend recess in the school's media center on computers instead of outdoors on the playground. I'm glad she can sharpen her tech skills, and the kids have indoor gym class three times a week, but I'm concerned—is she missing something important?

You have reason for concern about your daughter missing out on outdoor recess. In addition to being a great way to get exercise, outdoor play has many cognitive, social, emotional, and physical benefits for children.

Outdoor recess offers a break from the normal pressures of the school day and provides an opportunity to experience nature, not just physical activity. Nature has rhythms and rules of its own that neither software nor the fanciest gym can duplicate. Watching a robin feed its young or ants carrying food back to their nest can be a wonderful way to learn about nature's rhythms and can calm and center your child.

Unlike solo play in the media center, outdoor recess is communal. It's great for social emotional development, a key task of elementary education. Having a safe, supervised time for free play allows kids to play games, create imaginary worlds, and develop a social structure where they learn to confront challenges and resolve conflicts. While computer games and videos can introduce a range of content from reading to science, the direct experience of the outdoors and the complexity of nature and face-to-face interaction with peers are uniquely valuable.

- Talk with your daughter about her recess choices. Why does she prefer to skip outdoor recess? If she's avoiding the social scene, she may need some coaching in how to step outside her comfort zone, be creative in finding things to do with others, and join her peers on the playground.
- If she feels ostracized or bullied, communicate your concern with your daughter's teachers so that they can address the situation. They can help your daughter to choose outdoor recess, help her habituate to the playground dynamic, and let you know how she is doing.
- Explain to your daughter the benefits of being outdoors that the media center can't provide. Share some of your favorite childhood experiences of playing outside with friends, but don't romanticize it—stories of your own recess challenges and how you managed them can be equally motivating.
- Encourage your daughter to balance her playtime and suggest trying to go outside for recess at least twice a week to start. Once she chooses to go outside, talk to her regularly about her experiences in a way that lets her reflect on the good and access your help addressing the more difficult. Compliment her on her successes and encourage her to increase the frequency of her outdoor play as the school year progresses.

Nature can help guide us to meet the challenges of living and raising children well in the physical-digital environment. Psychologist Catherine Steiner-Adair likens the family to an ecosystem: diverse, hardy, fragile, and resilient. "Each of us wants our family to grow and thrive, to endure in the best sense of that word," she wrote in *The Big Disconnect: Protecting Childhood and Family Relationships in the Digital Age*. "The garden teaches us to persevere and remain hopeful, knowing full well we can't control the weather." But we can cultivate what she called a "sustainable family" by providing day to day, moment to moment, "the most loving, supportive, and uniquely human context for healthy growth and development." She observed, "The threat to sustainable families is in not adapting, not opening the circle for new people and new ideas, generative connections and new technology."[39] Our media use and the context we create for it can strengthen family connectedness or dilute it. That's up to us.

As you think about both content and context for media use, remember that you have more power to effect change than you may realize. Art, music, dance, and other creative pursuits or pastimes are sadly undervalued in the context of our children's lives at school and are often an option but not a priority after school, where homework gets top billing. Creativity, play, and getting out in nature—think of those elements as the context you want to create for your child, and be creative yourself about using media as a resource without relying on it.

As consumers we can purposefully invest our resources in those devices, games, apps, and subscriptions that offer content that we want our children to learn. With a fresh focus on context, remember that it is the media content and the context in which we use it that make the experience, and any health effects, positive or negative. As we have seen time and again with existing technologies, any safety setting designed by tech companies can be hacked around by users who do not want to be restricted. Kids are especially adept at this and eager to share their work-arounds with their peers.

Interactive media use needs to be limited not because its content is universally toxic but because of what children and adolescents are *not* doing during the long, open-ended hours they are immersed on screens, having lost track of time. Remember, content may be king, but context is queen, the most powerful and flexible piece on our chess board. The context of children's interactive media use—the developmental stage of the child, how that child is using interactive media, where and when they are using it—are all controllable. When and where children are using interactive media can be contained by when and where we capture their infectious curiosity and natural creativity with non-screen adventures from basketball to baking, martial arts to dance, parkour to orienteering. Free play with others, reading, and downtime to get bored and fill with their imagination are the most important and the most difficult to arrange for the same reason—they are self-structured. As with using media as a family, pursuing alternative activities together serves both to model and to bond around healthy behaviors. What is most protective for youth, and for us all, is engaging media with our children, mastering these tools, and creating the contexts in which we and our children are empowered to shape our digital environment to be healthier, safer, and more inclusive and empathetic. This calls us to be mindful in our screen use, be balanced in our screen and non-screen activities, and above all, be present with and for our children.

Chapter 14

Yes, You Can!

Finding the Healthy, Happy Medium

I t's too much! I just don't think I can deal with it. Her younger sister doesn't worry me at all. She couldn't care less about boys." Nicki's mom burst into tears as Nicki had stepped away to the bathroom to collect a urine sample before meeting with me for her checkup. "They asked her to pee in a cup. Do they think she might be pregnant?"

I reassured her that it was routine to ask for a urine sample and that we would not do a pregnancy test unless it seemed warranted. Nicki's mother leaned in. "Can you at least test for drugs? I just have no idea what she is doing when she goes out."

When I'd first met Nicki, now seventeen, her mom was worried about her getting in trouble with strangers online. Now Nicki was going out into the real world to meet friends rather than going online. The worry had not abated, only changed focus. When I asked how Nicki was doing, her mom softened.

"She's gotten all of her college applications in. Her grades got better after she started doing her homework in the dining room—thanks for that idea—so she is pretty hopeful and looking forward to college. Probably because she'll finally get away from me and her dad!" she said with a rueful smile.

As you've seen in the stories of children, teens, and their parents throughout this book, and possibly experienced yourself, parenting is a constant work in progress, now more than ever. We must remember that with each child, we are raising, teaching, and enjoying a unique human being. Each is moving through the arc of human development in different ways and at different rates. The psychosocial environment of our children's formative years continues to evolve as the boundaries between the physical and the digital become increasingly unclear. This will be more unclear as the projected immersive

3D virtual/augmented reality environment becomes more established. As we have seen, the digital environment can affect children's and adolescents' development in positive and negative ways as young people are continuously growing themselves, bringing themselves into focus, and interacting with the physical-digital environment and each other to create and shape their future.

Children's behaviors, the ways that they and everyone around them live their lives, are constantly adapting to new tools and processes available to them. Today smartphones, smartwatches, and smart houses are nearly ubiquitous, but soon they will be replaced by the tools of virtual and augmented reality. Many of the tasks we now do, from driving cars to writing college essays, may be supported or done by AI. We are engaged, as parents, individuals, and citizens of the world, in an ongoing process with three moving elements, as I mentioned at the outset of this book—the developing human, the physical-digital environment affecting and reflecting that development, and the transformation of all of our behaviors as we learn to control and avoid being controlled by these powerful digital tools.

Surprising even to me, I began work on this book in the years before social media and smartphones transformed our lives. I have been learning about and advising, in the clinic, in talks, and in writing, how to parent in a screen-filled world since the time when televisions were the screens about which parents, teachers, and pediatricians worried. I did not know then how the screen world would change (and neither, frankly, did the futurists). Now, again without knowing exactly what the future holds, I am optimistic about and for children, adolescents, and their parents.

Parenting and life itself are a journey without a known destination. I have learned a lot in my journey as a parent, as a pediatrician, as a filmmaker, and as a researcher of child health in an increasingly screen-saturated and screen-dependent world. All of that exploring, from the quaint days of the black-and-white television on which I secretly watched Abbott and Costello movies instead of going to church, until today, when I can explore real and fictional 3D worlds through a VR headset, has led me to where this journey started. Which is not an allegiance to a "back to basics" core set of principles defining the parent-child relationship but to a deep understanding of how fundamental aspects of time-tested parenting strategies can be applied in fresh ways to evolve with the physical-digital environment and our children's experiences and aspirations.

What I don't know is what the future of screen media holds, which is why I have explored with you the foundational concepts of how we humans of all ages respond to screens and to each other. You can apply these fundamental principles to interactive media yet to be invented. If I were to talk about specific devices, applications, or platforms, that information would be obsolete in a few years, if not months.

What I do know is that most parents care deeply about and want to do the best by their children. You have good parenting instincts and skills, but many of you are not confident and hesitate to use them in a world so different from the one in which you grew up. You are confused and concerned by what you see, worried about your children's future, and unsure of how to proceed. And you may feel guilty that you haven't parented them as well as you could. Let go of the guilt. Apply that energy to learning to live, love, and raise children in the world we have, for better or for worse. All that you need is to learn, in part from your children, the physical-digital ecosystem in which your children live, moving seamlessly between what we used to call *real* and *virtual*—then translate your good instincts and skills into that environment. This is not a far-fetched notion. You do some version of it every single day as you navigate this media-infused world yourself.

This book has explored the digital ecosystem, its promise and its perils, and acknowledged that the exploration is never done. You have the tools to navigate the digital world, and to *listen* to your children when they talk (or text) and to *talk (or text)* so they will listen. Part 1 first examined the "What?" of normal human development and an even-handed look at the positive and negative *effects* that screen use can have on that development and a child's health. In part 2, "So What?," we explored the consequences of potential *risks to children's physical, mental, and social health* posed by media content to which they are exposed. And in part 3, "Now What?," we've focused on the *context* in which media are used and *actions that you can take* to optimize your children's media use by shaping the contexts in which they use them. As you continue the adventurous journey of parenting, you can dive back into those chapters as your child moves through developmental stages or as you confront health concerns.

What follows is "Ages and Stages: A Digital Wellness Primer," which lists developmental stages from infancy to young adulthood and the ways that screen use can influence the developing human at each stage. But as the digital ecosystem evolves and research continues to generate new evidence-based findings, some of those principles and strategies will evolve with it. For the most up-to-date information on how your child's age and stage can benefit from and avoid risk in the digital ecosystem, please visit the online Family Digital Wellness Guide at https://digitalwellnesslab.org/parents/family-digital-wellness-guide. But you now have what you need to parent effectively in the environment we are in and in what it will evolve into. Keep in mind the original 3Ms—plus two.

YOU CAN

- **Model** the screen use and the interpersonal behaviors you want to see in your children.
- **Mentor** your children's screen use as you introduce each power tool when they need that tool and can, in your judgment, handle it responsibly and with respect for themselves and others.
- **Monitor** your children's screen use, especially at the beginning, and be prepared to increase or reduce their autonomy in the digital ecosystem as they demonstrate their abilities and digital citizenship.
- **Make memories** by spending non-screen time together—they, and you, will not remember video games played or movies watched as powerfully as family meals, dance parties, playing basketball, or taking a walk—and those with whom you did them.
- **Master** the digital ecosystem with your children by combining all five Ms, knowing when to put your device down and be present for your children, modeling healthy behaviors for them, mentoring and learning from their exploration of the physical-digital world, enjoying media with and parenting them in the digital space as you do in physical space, and knowing when to enrich their lives and experience by turning screens off and making memories.

As exciting and concerning as the ongoing digital revolution can be, and as frustrating as our children's behaviors can be, we must always remember why we wanted to bring these new humans into the world. Let's remember to enjoy them, to laugh at their behaviors and our mistakes, and keep moving forward. Early on, the geniuses who created the digital revolution were focused on launching the killer app. Now that we are in the midst of that ongoing evolution, we, as parents and as fellow humans, should focus on developing what I call our "killer BEs." They are:

- *Be mindful.* Use our powerful digital tools for what they do well and turn them off when they are not the best tool for the activity.
- *Be balanced.* Use intention to integrate screen use and non-screen activities.
- *Be bored.* Shake off the tendency to default to a screen and use the discomfort of nothing to do and the available space in your attentive mind to imagine the new.
- *Be present.* Consciously put down your devices so their near-infinite connectivity with strangers does not undermine our deep and sustaining connectedness with those we love.

The joy of raising healthy, smart, kind kids in our screen-saturated world lies in being present. Their childhood is fleeting. Supporting them in experiencing all they can during this precious time helps them be healthy in body and mind. Their fearless curiosity and willingness to take risks will build their intelligence. But being healthy and smart are no longer enough in today's media-infused physical-digital environment. Kindness is as essential for a child to thrive. How our children respect and treat themselves, and how they respect and treat others, defines the world as they experience it and as they create it for others. Our schemas—our expectations and assumptions about how the world works, and our place and our behaviors in it—are created by the media storylines and stereotypes we consume and those we create. Sadly, our most primitive survival instincts can easily be triggered in the digital environment. The voices of bigotry and contempt for others have been amplified by algorithms engineered to grab the most attention, which makes the world less safe for us all. "Othering" people who appear different or with whom we disagree can too easily become a viral call to fear and hate. But by recognizing that we are all in this together, that it is not us versus them but *us with us*, we can make the physical-digital ecosystem safer and demand the same from tech, entertainment, and policymakers.

You and your family can make this happen by flexing your clout as media consumers. While there is much talk about multibillion-dollar media and tech companies controlling our choices, let's remember where their billions of dollars came from: our pockets.

We have all spent our dollars on devices, games, apps, and streaming subscriptions that were the most attractive to us at the time. However, knowing what we know now and remembering that all media are educational, we can purposefully direct our dollars toward those devices, games, apps, and subscriptions that deliver media content that we want our children to learn in contexts where healthier activities are not displaced.

While much concern has been voiced and much legislation has been proposed to protect children from media, the tech and entertainment industries invest largely successfully in protecting their products from being restricted by law. And they have used those freedoms to produce and promote what the market shows we most desire.

But if we, as parents, teachers, and others who care for children, are educated and empowered—as you are now—and as consumers we make choices that are consistent with our intentions, market forces will change the content offered. If we no longer pay for content that is hindering children's optimal development, placing them at risk, or harming their health, then producing and distributing that content will be unprofitable. If we invest in our children's learning and well-being by modeling, mentoring, and monitoring the consumption of healthy media in healthy ways, even the megacorporations will follow the money. In their quest to reclaim and retain customers, they will redirect some of the millions they spend on countering adverse publicity, lobbying policymakers, and legal defense toward rigorous scientific research on improving a second bottom line: the physical, mental, and social well-being of their users. That bottom line will allow them to maintain and grow their consumers rather than drive them away. They will be able to do well while doing good.

It won't be a quick or easy process, but if we act as informed, determined, and consistent consumers who care about children and the future that they will create and live in, we will succeed in changing the products brought to market. This has already been a journey and will continue to be one. Rest assured, you are not alone. We are in this together, all of us. Set aside your fears for courage, your confusion for confidence, and your guilt for compassion and a sense of humor. You are and you have what you need to be the best parent for your child. You can do it. Yes, you can!

Part 4

Ages and Stages:
A Digital Wellness Primer

Digital wellness, in mind, body, and relationships, is best achieved by taking a balanced approach, enjoying the positive affordances of our powerful screen tools and avoiding or intervening early on negative influences. Digital wellness is not an end state but an ongoing process of intentional engagement with our physical-digital environment. Seeking digital wellness is, and always will be, a work in progress, both because the digital ecosystem is always evolving and because we will always be less than perfect.

In raising and caring for children today, we are dealing with three moving targets:

- Human development from infancy through childhood and adolescence into adulthood
- Our rapidly evolving digital environment that is both affecting and reflecting human development
- The transformation of our behavior since we have integrated digital devices and applications into our lives

While we understand the biological progression of child development, we know that every child is unique and travels their own developmental path. This primer summarizes human development in broad stages, but few children will fit neatly into a single stage. One or more aspects of your child's development may be ahead or behind age estimates here, so read back or ahead of their age to find the most recognizable issues and helpful suggestions. For example, body image issues most commonly arise in teens, so that is where this primer discusses them, but they may first occur in tweens or school-age children. Similarly, while cyberbullying is more prevalent in tweens, it may occur for the first time in the teen or young-adult years. Seek out your concerns wherever they appear and read ahead to be prepared. If you are entering at the tween or teen age, it would be helpful to read earlier stages for healthy media habits that ideally start as early as possible but can be established at any age.

For basic fundamentals, this primer plus the experience and attention that you bring to parenting are a good foundation. For constantly updated information on the current state of the physical-digital environment and strategies to optimize child health and development in it, and for full references to sources (also in the chapter notes), please seek out the Family Digital Wellness Guide online at https://digitalwellnesslab.org/parents/family-digital-wellness-guide.

The Five Key Questions of Media Literacy

Media literacy is the foundation and the goal not only for our children but for us as parents. With that in mind, use these key questions to keep your own media literacy sharp—and growing. Remember that advertisers, marketers, and influencers are targeting *you* as well as your children. When your children are able to have these conversations, use these questions as prompts. But in the meantime, notice when messages in your environment are designed to persuade you of something—perhaps about products, but also about parenting itself. Notice how you respond to those messages—first immediately, then after you have thought about them for a while. Practice deconstructing those messages by asking yourself the five key questions of media literacy you'll also help your child learn to ask. Then keep the questions in mind as you move through all of your child's ages and stages:

- Who created this message, and what did they want it to do?
- What techniques are used to attract your attention?
- What lifestyles, values, and points of view are represented?
- How might different people interpret this message differently?
- What is omitted from this message?

A final and important caveat: These recommendations are to actively parent your growing child in the digital space, practicing the full five Ms

—modeling, mentoring, monitoring, making memories with your child, and mastering screen media. Digital parenting is hands-on and more involved than most of us, including myself, have been doing. Unfortunately, we have defaulted some of our parenting to the electronic babysitter and only now are realizing how we could have done it better. Please do not let these recommendations make you feel guilty for the past, but also do not let them feel like too much to do now. We are all in this ongoing work in progress together. Let us solve the future together and remember to enjoy our children and our moments with them to the fullest.

Digital Wellness—Birth to Kindergarten

Science Says . . .

Infants (birth through eighteen months) experience **rapid brain development, exploration, and learning as they begin engaging with their family and immediate environment.** Babies begin to **smile and imitate their caregivers' expressions**. Physically, they advance rapidly from lifting their head to rolling over and sitting up, and around eight to twelve months, to crawling, exploring their expanding world.

By one year, babies can **understand language** and may begin to babble, imitate spoken language, or even say their **first words**. While their words may be hard to understand at first, babies are **learning to communicate** and practicing the give-and-take of conversation. Infants soak up the richness and warmth of their physical world. Screens are cool, distant, and in comparison, poor imitations of life. While an infant's attention will be drawn to a screen's novel images and sounds due to the orienting response, it is unclear whether they are able to decode them into something meaningful. Recognizing the sound and image of a known loved one may be the earliest that infants connect what they see on screen with their physical world, but their attention is limited by their still-developing brain.

The Mediatrician Recommends . . .

☐ When you are with your child at home, on the playground, or pushing their stroller, *be with them. Put your phone away when they are awake*. There will be plenty of time to catch up when they nap. Don't miss out on this very special but fleeting time when you fill their world and they fill yours. Look at them, read their facial expressions, let them read yours, and be present.

☐ *Preferably use non-screen media* with your infant. Read books, listen, and dance to your favorite music (OK, you dance and hold your infant, but they will be dancing soon enough). You will find that they will always equate that music with joy, connection, and well-being.

☐ Always *introduce new media with your infant on your lap* or next to you so you can sense their responses and so they associate warmth, safety, and your presence with screen use.

☐ Ideally, your infant's first screen experience will be *three-to-five-minute video chats* with family and friends whom they have already met in person.

☐ *Interact on screen with respect and empathy* for others. Even babies who aren't yet talking can understand and learn from the words you're using and your tone of voice.

☐ *Avoid exposing your infant to screens used by others.* Even programming as seemingly harmless as a sporting event is, at best, distracting for both the infant and those to whom the infant is looking for connection. More commonly, loud emotional responses by viewers can be confusing and upsetting to the infant, who, unable to understand the abrupt shift, experiences it as a disconnect with those around them.

☐ *Make memories* of these very special times with them so that you and your child have them to remember when you frustrate each other in the future. Solo screen time spent mindlessly engaged in TV shows and video games quickly fades from mind, but we all remember playing catch or cooking or walks in the woods together. Shared activities—even screen-based word games or others—make memories stick.

Science Says . . .

Toddlers (eighteen months to three years) begin to venture beyond the cocoon of their nuclear family to meet peers in daycare or playgrounds. They start with **parallel play** alongside other children, then **engage in mutual play**. Their **emotions can swing wildly** as their exploration of the world becomes **increasingly independent** and cognitively challenging.

Infants and toddlers are acutely attuned to people and the physical world; they **learn by interacting** with others and their environment.

The Mediatrician Recommends . . .

☐ Continue to *prioritize books, music, and non-screen play.*

☐ When they seem ready, *start watching child-centered, interactive educational programming* with your child on your lap or in physical contact next to you.

☐ *Talk and ask questions about what your child is seeing and hearing.* Point things out, ask questions, and model prosocial reactions.

☐ *Be aware of media portrayals of gender and race.* Children notice differences as young as three months old and internalize these messages by preschool.

☐ *Model and teach critical viewing* the moment they start viewing.

☐ *When their attention wanes, change to a fun non-screen activity.* Consider this simple formula for estimating your child's attention span: 2–3 × age in years = minutes of attention span.

☐ *Establish mealtimes as screen-free* for everyone. When parents use devices during meals, families lose out on important bonding time and children's behaviors and eating practices suffer. During meals, turn off all screens and leave tablets and smartphones outside the room.

☐ *Resist the powerful temptation to use screen media as the electronic babysitter.* It will establish expectations in your child that will be hard to break later.

☐ *Support self-regulation development.* Avoid handing over a smartphone or giving screen access to calm your child's tantrums—you will be rewarding that tantrum and ensuring that it will happen again.

☐ Remember that *interacting with humans and the physical world* is richer than any screen at this age.

Science Says . . .

Preschoolers (ages three to five) are becoming ever **more independent**, forming their own opinions, developing friendships, and exploring the world **beyond their nuclear family.** They like to know **what to expect and why.** They are **developing routines, learning rules**, and displaying **complex emotional reactions to situations.** Preschoolers are **self-oriented** and can engage in **extensive make-believe** play, including imaginary friends and multiple self-identities (even within short periods of time!). Preschoolers are learning to **navigate relationships, regulate their emotions,** and **test limits.** They are **rapidly developing language skills and social skills**, with storytelling becoming increasingly important. Preschoolers continue to **learn best from interactions with others, free play, and self-directed curiosity.** It is best to limit their screen time, preferably to less than two hours total (including video chatting) per day, with an adult caregiver present, on prosocial media that encourage interaction, such as answering questions.

The Mediatrician Recommends . . .

- ☐ *Develop social, emotional, and cognitive skills.* Your time with your child is best spent interacting directly with one another without the distraction of screens and other devices.
- ☐ *Limit your own screen use* when with your child. When on a screen, you are not present with your child. Behavioral health outcomes are poorer for children whose parents are on their devices during meals or interactions.
- ☐ *Do not let your child's screen use displace* more productive, developmentally optimal experiences like *free play, artmaking, strenuous physical exercise* (outdoors if possible), and *interacting with friends.*
- ☐ *Treat screen media as a tool* to be used purposefully, not as a special treat given for being good or denied for being bad.
- ☐ *Avoid using screens to comfort or to regulate your child's emotions.* Support your child's developing emotion self-regulation skills by practicing co-regulation and self-regulation that involve personal interaction with you or others or with hands-on play that does not involve screens or media.
- ☐ *Change from screen to a non-screen activity when attention wanes* (2–3 × age in years = minutes of attention). Be alert for even brief lapses in their gaze to avoid attention regrabs.
- ☐ While getting together in person is always better, *use video chat to spend time limited to your child's attention span* with loved ones who are far away. Encourage them to talk directly to your toddler, sing songs, play games, or repeat actions to imitate (such as hand clapping).

Preschoolers can show artwork, demonstrate new skills ("Look what I can do!"), or tell stories.

☐ *Seek out interactivity in receptive screen media,* such as programs in which characters ask questions of viewers. Model responding to the screen for the child when they start watching such shows.

☐ *Select TV shows, movies, and books that show a variety of human differences*—including gender, race, ethnicity, and ability. Ask questions and make observations that notice and *celebrate differences* as enriching.

☐ Preschoolers can hold a conversation and talk with you about what they're seeing. *Ask questions* about what they think the characters are feeling or how they might react if they were in the story.

☐ *Limit screen time to no more than two hours total per day*, in short, fully attentive sessions.

☐ *Turn off all screens at least one hour before naps or bedtime* so their brains can better secrete melatonin and they can get naturally drowsy and sleep better.

Digital Wellness—School Age

Science Says . . .

Grade-schoolers (ages six to nine) predominantly watch television (more than 90 percent watch regularly), and more than two-thirds of parents report that their children use interactive media such as tablets, smartphones, gaming consoles, and computers.[1] Parents and caregivers report struggling with decisions about oversight, enforcement, and balance of their children's media habits at this age.

Grade-schoolers become physically **stronger and more coordinated**, more **independent**, and much more **aware of themselves and their bodies**. Going to school presents their first extended opportunity to function as **individuals among peers**, rather than a member of a family. This **social emotional learning** is even more important than academics during the early school years, and the independence necessary for this learning can be **disrupted by phone use in school**.

School-age children begin to **form more complex relationships** with peers. They may test boundaries, break rules, and try on new identities as they **seek acceptance by others**. Peers become increasingly important as they form friendships and alliances.

Physically, grade-schoolers undergo rapid periods of change. There is typically wide variation in height and weight between children of the same age. They need at least one hour of physical activity daily[2] and the development of **healthy eating and exercise** habits is particularly important.

Grade-school children begin to develop longer attention spans, with the **ability to focus on a single task** for up to an hour by age nine. They begin to **make more complex decisions,** reflecting, problem-solving, and contributing meaningfully to their family and peer groups. Children at this age begin to develop self-regulation and self-awareness, understanding themselves in relation to others and managing their emotions.

Grade-school children can begin to **use screen media more purposefully**. Engaged co-viewing and **gaming** with parents and peers can offer opportunities for relationship-building and learning. At this age, children can develop meaningful relationships through video games and other interactive forms of online play. Developmentally optimal screen content can support improved academic performance, enriched knowledge, and increased literacy.

The Mediatrician Recommends . . .

☐ *Develop schedules* in anticipation of the first day of real school. Now that a school schedule will anchor their day, it is a good time to capitalize on your child's excitement to be growing up and work with them to establish daily schedules for weekdays and weekend days. If your child feels heard and develops the schedules with you, they have ownership in those schedules and are more likely to adhere to them. This is just like seat belts are always on before the car starts once they graduate from a car seat—a given that is part of the process of growing up.

☐ *Create family expectations, not rules.* Rules from parent to child are made to be broken. Expectations created and adhered to together are more effective. Authoritative (not authoritarian) parenting, in an atmosphere of mutual respect, is superior to authoritarian parenting, both because it is working together flexibly to optimize family life and because it works better. It feels far worse to have your parent disappointed in you for failing to meet expectations than angry at you for breaking a rule.

☐ *Avoid screen time limits* that cause conflicts and parental guilt and never really work. Sit down with your child and approach their twenty-four-hour day as an empty glass that you fill together with their necessary and desired activities.

☐ *Work backward from wake-up:* Start from the time they must wake up in time to eat breakfast, brush their teeth, and get to school and work backward to a bedtime that gives them at least eight hours of sleep and a no-screens time one hour earlier so they can better produce melatonin and slow down toward sleep.

☐ *Work forward from school return:* Because the times that children return home from school and family schedules vary widely, the time between school return and no-screens time needs to be customized to your reality. Whatever time they get home from school, they should eat a snack immediately to bump up their blood glucose, get some strenuous physical activity if they haven't gotten it at school or after school, then assess their homework situation.

☐ *A sit-down family meal* each day is the most important tradition you can establish for balanced nutrition and for everyone's mental health. It is important to have time together as a family to decompress, reconnect, and enjoy each other. It is essential that you do this with . . .

☐ *No devices at or visible from the dinner table*—children *and* adults. The shared meal experience, so nourishing for mind, body, and spirit, is easily lost in distracted attention to devices.

☐ *Model healthy media behavior* for your children: *be* the change you want to *see*. Even before they use or get devices of their own, remember that they are watching and learning from you. Model prosocial behavior for them through your own interactive and social media use. Follow positive accounts, share videos and posts that demonstrate the best parts of human interaction, and avoid making posts that attack others.

☐ *Put down your devices (preferably in another room) when with your child*, especially during mealtimes, before bed, and while engaged in conversations. Intentionally avoid device use during family time, such as when you're watching a movie together, playing a board game, or attending your child's sporting event.

☐ *Develop media literacy together.* Until they are about seven or eight, children are unable to understand persuasive intent and are thus more vulnerable to advertising. As they get older, children begin to develop a deeper understanding of advertising, influencers, and disinformation and what the producers of these campaigns are trying to get them to do or think. Co-engagement with media alongside your child offers an opportunity to build their critical thinking about what they are seeing. When you see an advertisement or persuasive message, ask your child:

- what they think is attractive (or not) about it,
- who they think created the message,
- what the message is trying to get them to think, believe, or do,
- whether or not they agree with that message.

☐ *Mentor their media use,* introducing each device, application, or platform sitting side by side with them. Remember that the smartphones we have in our pockets are power tools more than one million (that's 1,000,000) times more powerful than the computer that landed people on the moon. Teach them to master interactive media the way you will teach them to master another powerful, freeing tool: an automobile (white-knuckled, beside them in the front seat).

☐ *Tablets are frequently the best first device* because of the easy touch screen interface. Introduce them with respect for both the power of the device and application *and* for your child. Make it clear that how they handle a tablet will demonstrate to you when they are ready for more mobile devices like a smartphone. (See **Tweens** for the smartphone discussion.)

☐ *Explicitly talk about:*

- when your child is and is not to use media power tools,
- how they are to use them with respect for themselves and others,
- where it is OK and not OK to go online, and
- with whom they are and are not able to interact online, and
- decide with them what the consequences should be if/when they don't meet the expectations you make together. If you are not ready to talk to your child about pornography, for example, consider whether you are ready to give them a device where they can (and will) come upon pornography.

☐ *Game with your child.* Video games offer a bonding and shared coping opportunity for families of grade-school children. Children love to be experts and to share their expertise with others, particularly when they can teach their parents something. Ask your child what they are playing, what they like about it, and if you can play with them. You can ask that they teach you how to play and then ask questions along the way ("What should I do next?" "Which button do I push to make my next move?"). If they are playing social games, such as *Roblox*, *Fortnite*, or *Minecraft*, you can ask them to introduce you to their friends and to tell you more about them and how they met.

☐ *Consider violent-action screen games carefully.* Research on the effects of playing violent games is mixed but does indicate at least short-term negative effects on aggression, empathy, and schoolwork. But research also indicates that open-world action games can have positive effects on one's attention and ability to learn. I recommend that parents avoid violent games with their younger children. If you decide to allow grade-schoolers or tweens to play action games, then you should play with your child at the beginning, observe how your child behaves when playing, and after the game, talk about what is happening on the screen and how they feel about it.

☐ *Establish effective study habits early.* Homework presents a great opportunity to build focused academic work patterns and self-regulation, even in the earliest years of schooling. Create a quiet, comfortable space with good lighting and no distractions for your child to do schoolwork. Support your child's effective study habits by setting expectations for use of screens during homework and study time—place phones and tablets in another room, turn off televisions, and singletask with laptops if required for schoolwork.

☐ *Guide your child toward developmentally optimal content from reliable educational sources and monitor sites intermittently* as they and your child change. If your child has moved on developmentally, find new optimal sites as they age up.

☐ *Manage access to devices and content* as your grade-schooler uses them independently. Just because their brains can manage the device, their prefrontal cortex, which controls executive functions like impulse control, future thinking, and self-monitoring, is still about two decades from full development.

☐ *Balance the digital and the physical.* Healthy children require physical activity, creativity, and in-person interactions with peers and family members. Excessive screen media exposure has been correlated with obesity and long-term negative health outcomes. Encourage and model healthy screen media use that is purposeful and balanced with a rich diversity of in-person human relationships, outdoor play, sports, art, and reading.

Digital Wellness—Tweens (Ages Ten to Twelve)

Science Says . . .

As their brains have matured, tweens are able to tackle higher-level schoolwork. In the United States, many tweens transition from elementary to middle school, where academic demands increase—but they pale compared to the heat of social dynamics as they turn toward peers for acceptance and approval. Middle school brings **new expectations** from teachers, **new independence**, and **focus on privacy** for tweens—which translates into **new distance from parents**. **More capable of logical and abstract thought**, tweens plunge into practical tasks, problem-solving, and negotiating the intricacies of social structures and the drama of friendships.

Being perceived as popular and cool takes on great importance. Puberty has begun for some, but not for others. With the increased hormones of early adolescence, some tweens experience notable physical changes with increased variability in height, body odor, and secondary sexual development among kids of the same age. As social relationships continue to increase in importance, tweens are **excruciatingly self-conscious** and seek to be attractive to others. As part of normative development, tweens may be sorting out their sexuality and relationships, with non-romantic friendships often dominating. Many tweens are **aspirational**, trying to dress, speak, and act like admired adolescents or idolized celebrities. They want smartphones, both to see what is cool and to be cool. However, the combination of their **exploration, confusion, and competition** with mobile devices can result in their private struggles, crushes, and cruelties becoming very public.

While **testing the limits** of their independence, tweens need boundaries and the safety of their relationships with parents and other caregivers. At this age, children can begin to **use media more independently** but **still need the mentorship and oversight** of adults.

The Mediatrician Recommends . . .

☐ *Create a shared media use agreement.* Tweens appreciate boundaries and fairness; they crave guided independence. Sitting down with your child to craft a media use agreement that addresses how everyone in the household uses television, tablets, computers, smartphones, game consoles, and other devices can set expectations and opportunities for using media independently and together. It's important that tweens have input on the agreement and that everyone signs on.

☐ *Be transparent and collaborative.* It is important for the whole family to have a healthy, balanced engagement with the digital ecosystem because tweens are highly aware of adult media use patterns that seem hypocritical, such as a parent who does not allow their child to play video games but spends hours on their smartphone or social media.

☐ *Approach your decision thoughtfully about a smartphone for your child*, just as you will when your child wants to get their driver's license. Tweens want smartphones and ask for them again and again, personifying the "nag factor" that marketers seek as wireless companies reach deeper and deeper into childhood. Many parents have come to believe that their capability to reach their kids 24/7 is an important part of parenting, but having a smartphone at school distracts from learning and undermines valuable social emotional learning to be independent.

☐ *Consider what tools they need to meet their needs and compare those needs to what a smartphone offers.* Think about your child's activities and tasks. They have school and homework. They have household chores. They may have outside activities like organized sports. Of all smartphone functions, the only ones that are needed by tweens are talking and texting to communicate with friends and family or to arrange transportation. A flip phone will meet those needs. Everything else on a smartphone is a potential distraction. France has banned phones in school since 2018, and while enforcement has had mixed results, students without phones have been able to focus on lessons and each other.

☐ *Treat a smartphone like you would treat a power tool.* It is a tool that can provide possibilities and freedom but, used thoughtlessly, can hinder or harm the user and others. It should be provided when the child *needs* and *can use* that tool responsibly and with respect for themselves and others. When your child of any age asks for a smartphone, ask them why they want it. If their answer is "Because everyone else has one," they are not understanding it as a power tool or planning to use it that way.

☐ Many parents want their children to fit in with their peers and will get them a smartphone believing that will help. Observe tweens with smartphones and you will see that they focus on their phones, not on each other—even when they are side by side. *Smartphones distract not only from academics but also from the all-important social emotional learning that occurs in school.* Smartphones do not help tweens fit in. They separate them from their peers.

☐ *Smartphones provide strangers access to your child*, not only by the corporations whose apps are installed but by many individuals and organizations they and you do not even know. COPPA prohibits collection of personal information of anyone under the age of thirteen, but children using smartphones remain vulnerable. The available evidence indicates that best practices are to avoid getting a smartphone for a tween, meeting their needs with a flip phone (some adolescents, frustrated with their distraction, are trading their smartphones in for flip phones).

☐ *Review and update their established daily schedule and media use plan at least annually* as their school demands and interests evolve. Continuing to get a good night's sleep becomes even more important as tweens approach puberty. Homework becomes more demanding and time-consuming as academic demands ramp up toward high school. Help your tween turn off screens an hour before sleep and leave all devices outside the bedroom overnight. Get them an alarm clock so that when they obtain a smartphone, it does not become their device to wake up. As your tween's independence increases and their reasoning matures, they will have opinions about what media devices and applications they want to use. They are more likely to adhere to family expectations when they have had input on those expectations.

☐ *Discuss with your child devices and applications they want to use.* Ask what content they want to use, whether you may view them together, what your concerns might be, and why you have those concerns. You can still make the decision that is in your child's best interests, even if it's not in line with their desires, but it's important for them to feel heard and to understand why you have made the decision.

☐ *Discuss openly what your tween may see online.* Many parents find it harder to have the "internet talk" than the sex talk. As uncomfortable as the sex talk is, most parents feel they know more about sex than their children. They cannot say the same about the internet. Many children first encounter pornography online while they are still in elementary school. For most tweens, pornography is unnerving and confusing during a developmental stage where they are starting their sexual awareness. As they approach puberty, children naturally become more interested in exploring their own sexuality and use the internet to search for sexual images and information in order to deepen their own understanding of sex and sexuality. Though it's likely to make parents and kids uncomfortable, it's important to begin having conversations about the objectification of women and inaccuracy of sexual behavior portrayed in pornography.

☐ *Have open access to your child's online presence and activity from the beginning.* When you mentor your child with a new device or platform, decide their usernames and passwords together. They will most likely object to you having access to their accounts, but explain that it is a condition of them having those accounts. Talk frankly with them; tell them that you love, respect, and are confident in them but that their brain is still developing and they need your support and guidance to stay healthy and safe. You won't need to check in on them constantly, but your child will learn and practice self-regulation more quickly if you can.

☐ *Establish expectations around use of social media.* Although it is a COPPA violation for children under thirteen to be on social media, research indicates that at least a third of pre-adolescent children are on sites such as TikTok, Instagram, Snapchat, and Facebook. Your tween will likely want to join them but to do so, they, with or without your knowledge, will need to lie about their age. While it would be best for them to wait until they are thirteen or older to add the distraction of social media, it is most important for you to be fully aware of their social media presence and behaviors whenever they start. If they get on social media without your knowledge (and many will), you will not be available to them when they encounter difficulties.

☐ *Tweens will want VR and AR.* While the promised metaverse is yet to arrive and the sales of still-primitive VR/AR headsets have been sluggish, this technology is highly desired by tweens who, along with teens, will be early adopters. Resolving 3D imagery takes a lot of the brain's executive function horsepower. Even adults with mature prefrontal cortexes struggle with 3D, often coming out of movies exhausted and headachy. Once the novelty of VR/AR wears off, many young people abandon them for more manageable screens.

☐ *Be present and active in the digital life of your tween* about pornography, misinformation, disinformation, hate sites that channel racism, misogyny, xenophobia, homophobia, transphobia, and all manner of "otherphobia." Since their brain executive functions are still developing, tweens can be particularly vulnerable to curated, altered, and outright fake images and videos online. Teach them to be skeptical of what they hear, read, and see and to verify everything.

☐ *Decide together and set up online accounts with your child.* Most apps, streaming services, and games require that users have accounts with specific permissions and preferences. Rather than setting up these accounts for your child, or allowing them to do it independently, I recommend setting them up together so you can discuss and make decisions together about preferences, permissions, and limits.

☐ *Teach tweens the "Grandma Rule."* When they begin to create, post, and communicate online, they must be aware that their online behaviors can always be seen by others. Since most kids love, respect, and want to be respected by their grandmother, with whom they have a special, nonjudgmental relationship, teach them "Don't post anything online that you don't want Grandma to see."

☐ *Explicitly address cyberbullying.* With greater focus on peer relationships comes potential for bullying, ostracism, shunning, or other exclusionary behaviors. Your tween may be a victim, bully, bystander, or any combination at different times, since power differentials are less clear in the digital than in the physical world. Kids who are bullied online are at greater risk than their peers for depression and anxiety. They may obsessively watch their device, hide it when a parent walks by, withdraw from friends and family, and/or become upset after being online or when asked to get offline. Talk with your child on a regular basis about what they are seeing and hearing both online and in person. Ask them non-shaming questions such as "I heard from a friend that there is a lot of cyberbullying at his child's school. Does that happen at your school?" Report bullying when you hear about it. If your child was doing the bullying, even in retaliation, talk to them about it. Ask what was happening for them at this time, how it felt, how they think it felt for the victim, and what they think they could do to make the situation better for the victim.

☐ *Build healthy decision-making skills both on- and offline.* When they are online, children of any age will find themselves making choices quickly and often on their own. You can help them to make healthy choices by asking them to consider potential positive benefits and negative consequences of each choice. Describe your own risk-benefit analysis of different situations, from the mundane decisions like what to wear to an event to heavy choices like how to talk to or about others. Let them make safe mistakes in places like social gaming where they can make—and rebound from—poor choices with lower risk of serious consequences. Ask your child what went wrong and what they might do differently next time.

Digital Wellness—Teens and Young Adults

Science Says . . .

Adolescence (ages thirteen to eighteen) is an active period of change finalizing the shift from childhood to adulthood. Teens are **maturing physically, sexually, and cognitively** while they also develop **more complex and nuanced relationships** with peers and seek even greater independence from parents and primary caregivers.

Friends become the predominant connection during adolescence, offering a safe space and emotional independence from parents and other caregivers.

Teens form more mature friendships and romantic relationships and they begin to feel a **greater need to establish their own sexual identity**. Social connectedness is integral to teens' long-term wellness outcomes.

Though their brains haven't yet achieved the maturity levels of adulthood, teens' brains become more capable of future thinking and logical problem-solving. They are developing more complex understandings of human relationships, emotional nuance, and their own morals and values systems.

As they strike off more independently into the online world, teens need opportunities to **take risks with safety nets** and to use their caregivers for support and guidance.

Nearly 100 percent of teens report having access to a smartphone or home computer, and nearly half of teens report that they are online "almost constantly." Sixty percent of teens report using computers to do their homework every day.[3] Moving seamlessly between the digital and physical, teens and young adults are **engaged in a constant, frequently simultaneous interaction** with what they experience as a single environment.

As young adults (ages nineteen to twenty-five) exit their teen years, they begin to take on identities and activities **driven by their own interests**, instead of those determined by parental authority figures. They **may move away** from their family home, often to apartments or college settings, as they **shift into adult roles**, pursuing careers, hobbies, and more mature platonic and romantic relationships.

Young adults' relationships with their parents become more equal and the influence of same-age peers begins to wane as they begin to feel more comfortable in their own identities and interests. As they enter new environments and relationships, they begin building new habits, routines, and support systems and take on key functions of daily life, such as health insurance, financial management, and their own physical safety. Eighty-four percent of young adults report using social media regularly. Despite their full independence, young adults **still need the support and guidance of their families to navigate new pressures and decisions** of adulthood.

The Mediatrician Recommends . . .

☐ *Talk to teens early and often about screens and interactive media* that are important parts of their social lives, education, and entertainment choices. These can be light, matter-of-fact conversations about what they are doing and what choices they are making online. Unlike earlier stages where parents have provided structure and discipline as guardrails, these conversations are to learn what your teen is experiencing, advise them on life lessons while learning new digital developments from them, and build skills for lifelong digital wellness by transferring screen discipline from outside in to inside out. Empower your child to maximize the potential benefits of their interactive media and technology use while minimizing the potential harms.

☐ *Review and revise your family media use agreement* to address everyone's evolving use of digital devices and applications and to set mutual expectations. Research indicates that simpler is better and that keeping written details of the agreement available for frequent review can support stronger adherence. As your child grows increasingly independent, you can help them to maintain a healthier, more balanced engagement with the digital world.

☐ *Support and respect your teen's media boundaries and intervene only when necessary to help them stay safe and healthy online.* Content shared through social media has the potential to reach a large audience, regardless of privacy settings. Talk with your teen about the permanency of the internet and how, once something is shared, they lose control of that message or image. Sit down with your teen to walk through the privacy settings on each of their accounts, and friend them on their social media accounts. Ask before you post about your teen online; no matter how proud you are of them, they have a right to control how their image and information are shared online, even by their parents.

☐ *AI, particularly generative AI chatbots, has changed education.* While there is legitimate concern about the effects of AI on learning, it parallels the fears that arose when calculators entered the math classroom. AI is a powerful tool that can scan trillions of resources online and generate a reasonably reliable evidence base. It *can* generate papers and pass professional board exams, but it makes mistakes, sometimes huge mistakes. Generative AI operates on probability, not reasoning. Because of this, AI can put together sentences that are convincing but not true. Students will learn to check the sources of AI's evidence base, develop original ideas, and support them with reasoning of their own.

If they do not, they may very well graduate with a solid B average having learned little—or face severe consequences if and when their cheating is discovered!

☐ *Introduce social media thoughtfully, one platform at a time.* Social media offers opportunities for connection across geographic, cultural, and social divides. However, it can be filled with misinformation, hate, bullying, hypersexualization, and other potentially harmful influences. Parents may introduce and support their teen's social media access when they feel their child can manage that environment. Social media platforms should be introduced by the parent, side by side with the teen, with close monitoring. Do your homework together to understand the goals and parameters of each platform and make clear goals and red flags with the child. Explore each site together, discussing how social media should and should not be used. Once your teen is using it on their own, remain available for questions, concerns, and nonjudgmental help when your teen needs it.

☐ *Be intentional about providing a smartphone.* On average, parents now provide these powerful computers to their child around age ten, often to ensure their child has the ability to easily communicate with the parents and stay safe when away from home. A smartphone offers children nearly unrestricted access to everyone and everything online, however, and should be treated as the powerful tool that it is. When you and your child are ready to get their first smartphone, sit down and ask your child what they want to do with the phone. Have a frank conversation about how, when, and where the phone can (and cannot) be used and what the consequences should be when expectations aren't met. Maintain access to your child's phone and apps. Continue to set the expectation that you will randomly check in on their accounts and review their usage.

☐ *Resist the urge to check in with your child when they're at school.* School is your child's opportunity to establish their independence. You also want to model responsible use, and calling your child outside of emergencies will demonstrate an acceptance of phone use during school hours.

☐ *Help your teen get the sleep they need.* Teens and young adults need eight to ten hours of sleep each night to maintain their health and well-being. Screen media use in adolescence is associated with taking longer to fall asleep, getting less sleep, and experiencing more sleep disruptions. Continue to support your teen in setting a regular and consistent bedtime and provide a space away from their bedroom where they can charge all devices overnight. Provide your teen with an alarm clock so they don't have a need to keep their phone in their room.

☐ *Help teens learn to love their bodies.* When you see photos of celebrities and others online, ask your teen how realistic the images seem. Ask whether they know anyone who looks like that, what it might take to look like that, and whether they believe the person looks like their photo in real life. Discuss your child's ideas about beauty and ideal bodies and how they developed these concepts.

☐ *Talk about the dangers of cell phones in the car.* Many youths begin driving independently by their late teens, around the same age that they gain independent use of their cell phones. Distracted driving is extremely dangerous, claiming thousands of lives annually. You can instill safe habits that will carry them through life while your child is learning to drive.

  ○ Model safe behavior. Never text while driving or look at your phone while the car is in motion. When you need to change the playlist, send a text, or make a call, pull over in a safe place and put the car in Park before doing so.

  ○ Require that phones be turned off and set out of reach when your child is driving.

  ○ If your child needs their phone to play music, help them set up a playlist, set it to play, and place it outside of their reach before they start the car.

  ○ Set expectations and clear consequences for risky behavior behind the wheel. Loss of car and/or phone would give your teen a chance to reflect and recover these privileges.

☐ *Maintain situational awareness.* Many adolescents sport headphones on their ears or around their necks when they are out in the world. Help yours establish and maintain situational awareness when out in public, riding a bike, or driving a car by removing their headphones or earbuds. If they cannot hear what is around them, they cannot anticipate danger to themselves or others. Headphones make them a target

for theft or assault because they advertise that the wearer has money
and is tuned out.

☐ *Openly discuss sexting with your teen.* The transmission and receipt of
sexually explicit images and content has been correlated with riskier
sexual behaviors. Sexting is illegal for children under the age of eighteen in many states; sending sexually explicit photos of minors may be
considered sexual exploitation or child pornography. Choose a time
when you and your child are calm and can focus on the conversation.
Sexting is not uncommon among even young teens; keep in mind that
this behavior may seem commonplace and safe to your child. Provide
young people with access without shame to accurate information about
sexuality and sexual behavior, and help them to understand the importance of a caring relationship to healthy, fulfilling sexual activity.

☐ *Protect your child from sextortion* by having frank discussions about
sex as a normal human activity and not a source of shame. Catfishing
has led to financial scams and, in several cases, death by suicide of the
ashamed adolescent.

☐ *Talk with your young adult about online dating.* Dating apps have transformed romance and sex. Nearly half of young adults—and well over
half of adults who identify as LGBTQ+—report having used online
dating sites or apps. While online dating is prevalent and largely safe,
a notable percentage of users report experiencing problematic behavior, such as harassment or threats of physical harm. Meeting potential
romantic or sexual partners like buying online has, for some, made
romantic relationships superficial and sex transactional. Talk with your
child about who they are meeting online, how they are confirming that
each person is who they say they are, and how they are staying safe
when meeting in person.

☐ *Help your teen learn from their mistakes.* When your child has made
a harmful decision, such as trying a potentially dangerous viral challenge or sharing a hurtful image on social media that they regret, ask
them calmly why they made the choice they made, what they were
hoping to achieve, and what they might do differently next time. If
their behavior violated your family's media use agreement, talk with
your teen about the consequences you had agreed upon and implement
those consequences.

☐ *Continue to help your teen advance their media literacy.* Advertising, product placement, and influencer marketing can greatly affect teens' attitudes and behaviors regarding their health and well-being. As teens and young adults develop their own sets of beliefs and values, these influences can be particularly important. Ask your child to show you some of the influencers they follow on social media. Ask them what they like about each and what they think that person or company is trying to get them to think or do. Talk about news items with your teen and ask them what they think about them. Might there be other perspectives on an event? What might the news reporter be wanting them to think, and why? What does your teen believe about the event?

☐ *Support your teen's development of digital management skills.* As they begin to navigate the digital ecosystem more independently, your teen will be making important decisions every day. When your teen is encountering a problem or decision, online or offline, resist the urge to step in and solve it for them. Instead, ask probing questions to help them to arrive at a solution on their own. What are the potential positive and negative consequences for each possible decision? Share your own decision-making processes. If you have a social media account, show your child your posts. Tell them why you posted and whether you received the responses for which you were hoping. Empowering them to address problems and make decisions on their own will support your teen's long-term positive life outcomes.

Acknowledgments

This book is a child raised by a global village that I wish to thank. Since I began working on it in 2007, it is now an adolescent, and as with all adolescents, I must let it go into the world.

In all truth, it would never have been born without the gracious, patient, and kind midwifery of Teresa Barker. Although we have yet to meet IRL, Teresa has made this book happen. Over countless video meetings, she has motivated me to get my research, reflections, and recommendations down on the page. She has patiently tolerated my missing deadline after deadline when my other jobs of parent, clinician, researcher, teacher, and public health policy advocate have intervened. When I have felt overwhelmed, she has encouraged me to keep writing. When I have tried to coast, she has firmly gotten me back on track. And when I have despaired that the digital ecosystem was changing so fast that anything I wrote would be partly obsolete by the time it is published, she has insisted that I keep going because devices, applications, and platforms will change but we humans will still need to live well and raise kids well in the future physical-digital environment. She reminded me many times that the fundamentals of our relationships with screens, whether they be televisions or smartphones, if managed mindfully, will help us all be healthier, smarter, and kinder to each other. Teresa, thank you isn't enough.

As you have likely noticed, there are hundreds of references to the research on which this book and my clinical practice are based. Kaitlin Allair Tiches has been nothing short of remarkable. She has tracked down vaguely remembered research in close to twenty different disciplines, found new research, and corrected my memory many times. All in a matter of minutes and way too frequently at off hours. AI has nothing on her!

Over the years, many hands have helped to shape this clay vessel. I am deeply in debt to Dr. Philip McRae of the Alberta Teachers' Association, with whom I have designed and conducted research, taught many educators, offered guidance to the front lines of education and childcare through the difficulties of the pandemic, and devised productive applications of the earliest iterations of generative AI. Julie Polvinen operationalized giving sick kids a voice by handing them camcorders and saying, "Teach us!" Kristelle Lavallee Collins worked with me to write more than four hundred responses to parents, teachers, and clinicians who sought to Ask the Mediatrician online and recorded with me a full season of *Ask the Mediatrician* podcasts. Lauren Rubenzahl sat across my kitchen table for months helping me shape the very first version of what was to become *The Mediatrician's Guide*. Amanda Bauch expertly shepherded me toward my first journey in book publishing. Meaghan Porter has had the patience and will to oversee and nurture the adventure of working with me—without her focused attention and generous encouragement, *The Mediatrician's Guide* would still be a pipe dream. Thank you to publisher Matt Baugher for coming to my presentation to parenting influencers and responding as a parent. Additional thanks to book designer Kait Lamphere, copyeditor Dawn Hollomon, senior director of marketing Sicily Axton and marketing manager Hannah Harless, and the full HarperCollins team. Thanks to proofreaders Amy Kerr, Kelsey Michener, Merry MacIvor, Janna Walkup, Phil Newman, and Andrew Buss for their meticulous attention to detail in polishing the text and notes. Thanks as well to our literary agents, Katherine Flynn and Madeleine Morel.

I am grateful to the many smart and compassionate clinicians from whom I have had the honor and privilege to learn not just the science of pediatric medicine but the art and humanity of it. T. Berry Brazelton, MD, helped me discover the magic of the newborn; Lewis First, MD, the fun of doctoring the tween; and Bob Masland, MD, the tentative, then brilliant joy of an adolescent discovering that someone really cares and really listens to them. In particular, I want to honor the courage and the faith in me shown by my mentor in adolescent medicine, S. Jean Emans, MD. She listened to every unconventional idea I proposed: "I want to give video camcorders to kids and have them show and tell us about the illness experience from the inside out!" "I want to try to publish medical research with embedded video data." "I want to develop a method for measuring kids' active use and ambient exposure to screen media and use it to follow the health and development of hundreds of them in places around the world for ten years." She listened, asked a few pointed questions, and let me try again and again and again if it wasn't funded or didn't quite work the first, second, or third time.

I feel fortunate to have trained, worked, and taught at the finest pediatric hospital in the world, Boston Children's Hospital. Its greatness lies not in its cutting-edge technology and phenomenal facilities but in the people it attracts. I have learned so much from the nurses, social workers, psychologists, nutritionists, child life specialists, and, yes, the clowns and the dogs who care for our young patients.

I am humbled by the courage, the hope, and the joy of the young people for whom it has been my honor to care. I can only mention a few exemplars; I hope that they can represent all (and you know who you are) for whom I have cared and from whom I have learned so much: Mel, who started angry at the world and everyone in it, but has now become a powerful voice of advocacy; Esther, whose smile lit up the world and whose hugs were healing; Nathan, who said, "I want to be a doctor just like you"; and Nick, who, when I felt defeated that his life could not be saved, comforted me by saying, "You can't always cure but you can always heal."

I must acknowledge all that I learned from my parents' models of service to others and the value of getting as much education as one can get. I might never have become the Mediatrician if not for my experiences as a filmmaker. Of special note must be Francis Coppola, who told me at breakfast in 1979 that future technology would enable an eight-year-old girl from Ohio to be the Mozart of cinema. I met Francis on a location shoot with my mentor in filmmaking, Akira Kurosawa. While my nearly two years as his assistant director on *Kagemusha* were hard—sometimes painfully hard—work, I learned from him and from his films that a true hero is not perfect but is always becoming, constantly striving to better themselves, and the villain believes that they are complete.

I am grateful to those in technology, entertainment, and health care who have had the foresight and courage to drop their defenses and work with me to realize the audaciously contrarian initiative of the Digital Wellness Lab at Boston Children's Hospital. Antigone, Bill, Carolyn, Jordan, three Michaels, Peter, Steve, Tami—you know who you are, and I hope that you have felt the depth of my gratitude and camaraderie. After decades of polarization, we have come together to bring our respective skill sets to bear on building a better digital environment for us all and for future generations to be healthier, smarter, and kinder to each other. The Digital Wellness Lab was built on the tireless investigation of David Bickham, PhD, and his research teams and would never have realized the fullness of its implementation without the expert management of Cori Stott, EdM, MBA. Others in our village providing valued insight and unflagging support include Rebecca Barker, Steve Weiner, Aaron and Lauren Weiner and their digital natives, Rachel and Kristen Rau and their digital natives, Dolly Joern, Leslie Rowan, Sue Shellenbarger, and Margaret Browning.

Finally, and most importantly, I cannot adequately express my gratitude to Lydia, my partner in life, in pediatric medicine, in child health research, and most importantly, in raising two exceptional young men, Jason and Ian, who tolerated years of my excessive screen time working on this book. Not without objection, however, because as healthy, smart, and not-always-kind kids, they have been known to call me a "screenager" and challenged my apparent hypocrisy as the Mediatrician. Criticism acknowledged and accepted. I am present with you now.

On behalf of the children and families who will benefit, I honor and thank you all.

Michael Rich, MD, MPH

Notes

Introduction

1. Hilda K. Kabali et al., "Exposure and Use of Mobile Media Devices by Young Children," *Pediatrics* 136, no. 6 (2015): 1044–50, https://doi:10.1542/peds.2015-2151.

2. Victoria Rideout et al., *Common Sense Census: Media Use by Tweens and Teens, 2021* (San Francisco: Common Sense Media, 2022); https://www.common sensemedia.org/sites/default/files/research/report/8-18-census-integrated -report-final-web_0.pdf; Victoria Rideout et al., *Common Sense Census: Media Use by Kids Age Zero to Eight, 2020* (San Francisco: Common Sense Media, 2020), 2020_zero_to_eight_census_final_web.pdf.

3. Melina R. Uncapher et al., "Media Multitasking and Cognitive, Psychological, Neural, and Learning Differences," *Pediatrics* 140, Supplement 2 (2017): S62–S66, https://doi:10.1542/peds.2016-1758D.

4. Emily A. Vogels, Risa Gelles-Watnick, and Navid Massarat, "Teens, Social Media and Technology 2022," Pew Research Center, August 10, 2022, https://www.pewresearch.org/internet/2022/08/10/teens-social-media-and -technology-2022/.

5. Jason M. Nagata et al., "Screen Time Use Among US Adolescents During the COVID-19 Pandemic: Findings From the Adolescent Brain Cognitive Development (ABCD) Study," *JAMA Pediatrics* 176, no. 1 (2022): 94–96, https://doi:10.1001/jamapediatrics.2021.4334.

6. ParentsTogether Foundation, "Survey Shows Parents Alarmed as Kids' Screen Time Skyrockets During COVID-19 Crisis," ParentsTogether Foundation, April 23, 2020, https://parents-together.org/survey-shows-parents-alarmed-as -kids-screen-time-skyrockets-during-covid-19-crisis/.

7. ParentsTogether Foundation, "Survey Shows Parents Alarmed."

8. Sarah Shevenock, "YouTube, Netflix and Gaming: A Look at What Kids Are Doing with Their Increased Screen Time," Morning Consult, August 20, 2020, https://morningconsult.com/2020/08/20/youtube-netflix-and-gaming-a-look -at-what-kids-are-doing-with-their-increased-screen-time/.

9. Committee on Public Education, "Children, Adolescents, and Television," *Pediatrics* 107, no. 2 (2001): 423–6, https://doi:10.1542/peds.107.2.423.

10. Victoria Rideout et al., *Common Sense Census: Media Use by Tweens and Teens, 2021* (San Francisco: Common Sense Media, 2022), https://www.common sensemedia.org/sites/default/files/research/report/8-18-census-integrated -report-final-web_0.pdf.

11. David S. Bickham, Summer Moukalled, and Michael Rich, "Young People's Media Use and Remote Schooling Experiences During the COVID-19 Pandemic" (paper presented at the Technology, Mind and Society, 2021, Conference Proceedings).

12. Matthew D. Lieberman, *Social: Why Our Brains Are Wired to Connect*, 1st ed. (New York: Crown Publishers, 2013); Robert Boyd and Peter J. Richerson, "Culture and the Evolution of Human Cooperation," *Philos Trans R Soc Lond B Biol Sci* 364, no. 1533, November 12, 2009: 3281–8, https://doi:10.1098/rstb.2009 .0134; Esther Herrmann et al., "Humans Have Evolved Specialized Skills of Social Cognition: The Cultural Intelligence Hypothesis," *Science* 317, no. 5843 (2007): 1360–66, https://doi:doi:10.1126/science.1146282.

Chapter 1: Raising Children Well in a World of Screens

1. E. B. White, "Removals," in *One Man's Meat*, 13th ed. (Thomaston, ME: Tilbury House, 2003).

2. Emily A. Vogels, Risa Gelles-Watnick, and Navid Massarat, "Teens, Social Media, and Technology 2022," Pew Research Center, August 10, 2022, https://www .pewresearch.org/internet/2022/08/10/teens-social-media-and-technology-2022/.

3. Michael B. Robb. *The New Normal: Parents, Teens, Screens, and Sleep in the United States* (San Francisco: Common Sense Media, 2019), 2019-new-normal-parents -teens-screens-and-sleep-united-states-report.pdf.

4. Victoria Rideout et al., *Common Sense Census: Media Use by Tweens and Teens, 2021* (San Francisco: Common Sense Media, 2022), https://www.common sensemedia.org/sites/default/files/research/report/8-18-census-integrated -report-final-web_0.pdf.

5. *Star Wars Episode IV: A New Hope*, directed by George Lucas (1977; Century City, CA: Twentieth Century Fox, 1982), DVD.

6. Bruce E. Wexler, *Brain and Culture: Neurobiology, Ideology, and Social Change* (Cambridge, MA: MIT Press, 2006), 101.

7. Wexler, *Brain and Culture*, 102.

8. Jack Flynn, "20 Vital Smartphone Usage Statistics [2023]: Facts, Data, and Trends on Mobile Use in the U.S.," Zippia.com., April 3, 2023, https://www .zippia.com/advice/smartphone-usage-statistics/.

9. Jewish Broadcasting Service, "'Tech Shabbat: The Power of Unplugging One Day a Week'—A Conversation with Tiffany Shlain," YouTube video, August 20, 2021, 49:36, https://youtu.be/mZqJjpoLIBQ?si=qn3cQst4265_rLTx.

10. Jenny S. Radesky et al., "Patterns of Mobile Device Use by Caregivers and Children During Meals in Fast Food Restaurants," *Pediatrics* 133, no. 4 (April 2014): e843–9, https://doi.org/10.1542/peds.2013-3703.

11. Jeff Grabmeier, "Warning to Adults: Children Notice Everything," *Ohio State News*, August 5, 2019, https://news.osu.edu/warning-to-adults-children-notice-everything/.

12. David S. Bickham, Summer Moukalled, and Michael Rich, "Young People's Media Use and Remote Schooling Experiences During the COVID-19 Pandemic" (paper presented at the Technology, Mind and Society, 2021, Conference Proceedings).

13. Melina R. Uncapher and Anthony D. Wagner, "Minds and Brains of Media Multitaskers: Current Findings and Future Directions," *Proceedings of the National Academy of Sciences* 115, no. 40 (2018): 9889–96, https://www.pnas.org/doi/10.1073/pnas.1611612115.

14. Melina R. Uncapher et al., "Media Multitasking and Cognitive, Psychological, Neural, and Learning Differences," *Pediatrics* 140, Supplement 2 (2017): S62–S66, https://doi:10.1542/peds.2016-1758D; Uncapher and Wagner, "Minds and Brains of Media Multitaskers"; Susanne E. Baumgartner et al., "The Relationship Between Media Multitasking and Executive Function in Early Adolescents," *The Journal of Early Adolescence* 34, no. 8 (2014): 1120–44, https://doi:10.1177/0272431614523133.

15. Wikipedia, s.v. "Cinnamon Challenge," last modified October 2, 2023, https://en.wikipedia.org/wiki/Cinnamon_challenge.

16. Amelia Grant-Alfieri, Judy Schaechter, and Steven E. Lipshultz, "Ingesting and Aspirating Dry Cinnamon by Children and Adolescents: The 'Cinnamon Challenge,'" *Pediatrics* 131, no. 5 (2013): 833–35, https://doi.org/10.1542/peds.2012-3418.

17. Nancy Keates, "Just a Spoonful of Cinnamon Makes the Internet Rounds: 'Challenge' to Swallow Spice Finds Takers, Millions of Viewers; Warning Parents," *The Wall Street Journal*, March 19, 2012, https://www.wsj.com/articles/SB10001424052702304537904577279663808279888.

Chapter 2: What Is Digital Wellness?

1. Boston Children's Digital Wellness Lab, "Welcome to the Digital Wellness Lab," https://digitalwellnesslab.org/about/.

2. *Babies*, directed by Thomas Balmès (2010; Focus Features), DVD.

3. Council on Communications and Media et al., "Media and Young Minds," *Pediatrics* 138, no. 5 (November 2016), https://doi.org/10.1542/peds.2016-2591.

4. Monique K. LeBourgeois et al., "Digital Media and Sleep in Childhood and Adolescence," *Pediatrics* 140, Supplement 2 (2017): S92–S96, https://doi.org/10.1542/peds.2016-1758J.

5. Giuseppe Curcio, Michele Ferrara, and Luigi De Gennaro, "Sleep Loss, Learning Capacity, and Academic Performance," *Sleep Medicine Reviews* 10, no. 5 (October 2006): 323–37, https://doi.org/10.1016/j.smrv.2005.11.001.

6. Candice A. Alfano and Amanda L. Gamble, "The Role of Sleep in Childhood

Psychiatric Disorders," *Child and Youth Care Forum* 38, no. 6 (2009): 327–40, https://doi.org/10.1007/s10566-009-9081-y.

7. Sujay Kansagra, "Sleep Disorders in Adolescents," *Pediatrics* 145, Supplement 2 (2020): S204–S09, https://doi.org/10.1542/peds.2019-2056I.

8. Kansagra, "Sleep Disorders."

9. Beatriz Gómez-González et al., "Role of Sleep in the Regulation of the Immune System and the Pituitary Hormones," *Annals of the New York Academy of Sciences* 1261, no. 1 (July 2012): 97–106, https://doi.org/10.1111/j.1749-6632.2012.06616.x.

10. Simin Cao and Hui Li, "A Scoping Review of Digital Well-Being in Early Childhood: Definitions, Measurements, Contributors, and Interventions," *International Journal of Environmental Research and Public Health* 20, no. 4 (2023): 3510, https://doi.org/10.3390/ijerph20043510.

11. Kelly Johnston, "Engagement and Immersion in Digital Play: Supporting Young Children's Digital Well-Being," *International Journal of Environmental Research and Public Health* 18, no. 19 (2021): 10179, https://doi.org/10.3390/ijerph 181910179.

12. Johnston, "Engagement and Immersion in Digital Play"; Helen Beetham, "Building Digital Capabilities Framework: The Six Elements Defined" (Bristol, UK: JISC, 2015), accessed October 24, 2023, https://repository.jisc.ac.uk/8846/1 /2022_Jisc_BDC_Individual_Framework.pdf.

13. Johnston, "Engagement and Immersion in Digital Play."

14. Zhen Xing Ong et al., "Measuring Online Well-Being: A Scoping Review of Subjective Well-Being Measures," *Frontiers in Psychology* 12 (March 11, 2021): 616637, https://doi.org/10.3389/fpsyg.2021.616637.

15. Bjorn Nansen et al., "Children and Digital Well-Being in Australia: Online Regulation, Conduct, and Competence," *Journal of Children and Media* 6, no. 2 (2012): 237–54, https://doi.org/10.1080/17482798.2011.619548.

16. Audrey Yue et al., "Developing an Indicator Framework for Digital Well-Being: Perspectives from Digital Citizenship," accessed October 24, 2023, https://ctic.nus.edu.sg/resources/CTIC-WP-01(2021).pdf.

17. "Infant Vision: Birth to 24 Months of Age," American Optometric Association, n.d., https://www.aoa.org/healthy-eyes/eye-health-for-life/infant-vision?sso=y; Janette Atkinson, Oliver Braddick, and Fleur Braddick, "Acuity and Contrast Sensitivity of Infant Vision," *Nature* 247, no. 5440 (February 1974): 403–4, https:// doi.org/10.1038/247403a0; Angela M. Brown et al., "The Contrast Sensitivity of the Newborn Human Infant," *Investigative Ophthalmology and Visual Science* 56, no. 1 (2015): 625–32, https://doi.org/10.1167/iovs.14-14757; Susan M. Ludington-Hoe, "What Can Newborns Really See?," *American Journal of Nursing* 83, no. 9 (1983): 1286–89, https://doi.org/10.1097/00000446-198383090-00015.

18. Kerstin Uvnäs Moberg and Danielle K. Prime, "Oxytocin Effects in Mothers and Infants During Breastfeeding," *Infant* 9, no. 6 (2013): 201–6, https://www .infantjournal.co.uk/pdf/inf_054_ers.pdf.

19. Naomi Scatliffe et al., "Oxytocin and Early Parent-Infant Interactions: A Systematic Review," *International Journal of Nursing Sciences* 6, no. 4 (2019): 445–53, https://doi.org/10.1016/j.ijnss.2019.09.009.

20. Jeannette T. Crenshaw, "Healthy Birth Practice #6: Keep Mother and Baby Together—It's Best for Mother, Baby, and Breastfeeding," *The Journal of Perinatal Education* 23, no. 4: 211–17, https://doi.org/10.1891/1058-1243.23.4.211.

21. Ruth Feldman, "Parent-Infant Synchrony and the Construction of Shared Timing; Physiological Precursors, Developmental Outcomes, and Risk Conditions," *Journal of Child Psychology and Psychiatry* 48, no. 3–4 (2007): 329–54, https://doi.org/https://doi.org/10.1111/j.1469-7610.2006.01701.x.

22. Feldman, "Parent-Infant Synchrony."

23. Charles A. Nelson, Nathan A. Fox, and Charles H. Zeanah, "The History of Child Institutionalization in Romania," chap. 3 in *Romania's Abandoned Children: Deprivation, Brain Development, and the Struggle for Recovery* (Cambridge, MA: Harvard University Press, 2014), 39–69.

24. Kirsten Weir, "The Lasting Impact of Neglect: Psychologists Are Studying How Early Deprivation Harms Children—and How Best to Help Those Who Have Suffered from Neglect," *Monitor on Psychology* 48, no. 6 (June 2014): 36, https://www.apa.org/monitor/2014/06/neglect.

25. Charles A. Nelson et al., "Cognitive Recovery in Socially Deprived Young Children: The Bucharest Early Intervention Project," *Science* 318, no. 5858 (December 2007): 1937–40, https://doi.org/10.1126/science.1143921; Charles A. Nelson, Nathan A. Fox, and Charles H. Zeanah, "Socioemotional Development," chap. 10 in *Romania's Abandoned Children: Deprivation, Brain Development, and the Struggle for Recovery* (Cambridge, MA: Harvard University Press, 2014), 227–65.

26. Weir, "The Lasting Impact of Neglect"; Kathryn L. Hildyard and David A. Wolfe, "Child Neglect: Developmental Issues and Outcomes," *Child Abuse and Neglect* 26, no. 6 (June 2002): 679–95, https://doi.org/10.1016/S0145-2134(02)00341-1.

27. American Academy of Pediatrics, "Cell Phones Take Parents' Attention Away from Kids on Playgrounds," *EurekAlert!*, April 25, 2015, https://www.eurekalert.org/news-releases/815247; Craig W. O'Brien, "Injuries and investigated deaths associated with playground equipment, 2001–2008," *US Consumer Product Safety Commission* (2009), https://www.cpsc.gov/s3fs-public/pdfs/playground.pdf.

28. Jenny S. Radesky et al., "Maternal Mobile Device Use During a Structured Parent-Child Interaction Task," *Academic Pediatrics* 15, no. 2 (March–April 2015): 238–44, https://doi.org/10.1016/j.acap.2014.10.001; "Patterns of Mobile Device Use by Caregivers and Children During Meals in Fast Food Restaurants," *Pediatrics* 133, no. 4 (April 2014): e843–9, https://doi.org/10.1542/peds.2013-3703.

29. Jessa Reed, Kathy Hirsh-Pasek, and Roberta Michnick Golinkoff, "Learning

on Hold: Cell Phones Sidetrack Parent-Child Interactions," *Developmental Psychology* 53, no. 8 (2017): 1428–36, https://doi.org/10.1037/dev0000292.

30. *Diane Sawyer Reporting*, "Screentime," aired May 3, 2019, on ABC.

31. Edward Tronick, "Still Face Experiment Dr. Edward Tronick," March 25, 2016, YouTube video, 2:49, https://www.youtube.com/watch?v=YTTSXc6sARg.

32. William Beardslee, *When a Parent Is Depressed: How to Protect Your Children from Effects of Depression in the Family* (Boston: Little Brown and Company, 2003).

33. Marshall McLuhan, *Understanding Media: The Extensions of Man* (Cambridge, MA: MIT Press, 1964).

Chapter 3: Hungry Brains

1. Aida Gómez-Robles et al., "Relaxed Genetic Control of Cortical Organization in Human Brains Compared with Chimpanzees," *Proceedings of the National Academy of Sciences USA* 112, no. 48 (2015): 14799–804, https://doi.org/10.1073/pnas.1512646112; Chet C. Sherwood and Aida Gómez-Robles, "Brain Plasticity and Human Evolution," *Annual Review of Anthropology* 46, no. 1 (2017): 399–419, https://doi.org/10.1146/annurev-anthro-102215-100009.

2. Frederico A. C. Azevedo et al., "Equal Numbers of Neuronal and Nonneuronal Cells Make the Human Brain an Isometrically Scaled-Up Primate Brain," *Journal of Comparative Neurology* 513, 5 (2009): 532–41, https://doi.org/10.1002/cne.21974; Shawn F. Sorrells et al., "Human Hippocampal Neurogenesis Drops Sharply in Children to Undetectable Levels in Adults," *Nature* 555, no. 7696 (March 2018): 377–81, https://doi.org/10.1038/nature25975.

3. Suzana Herculano-Houzel et al., "The Elephant Brain in Numbers," *Frontiers in Neuroanatomy* 8 (June 2014), https://doi.org/10.3389/fnana.2014.00046; Heidi S. Mortensen et al., "Quantitative Relationships in Delphinid Neocortex," *Frontiers in Neuroanatomy* 8 (November 2014), https://doi.org/10.3389/fnana.2014.00132.

4. Rebecca C. Knickmeyer et al., "A Structural MRI Study of Human Brain Development from Birth to 2 Years," *The Journal of Neuroscience: The Official Journal of the Society for Neuroscience* 28, no. 47 (2008): 12176–82, https://doi.org/10.1523/JNEUROSCI.3479-08.2008; Junko Matsuzawa et al., "Age-Related Volumetric Changes of Brain Gray and White Matter in Healthy Infants and Children," *Cerebral Cortex* 11, no. 4 (2001): 335–42, https://doi.org/10.1093/cercor/11.4.335.

5. JP Bourgeois, "Synaptogenesis, Heterochrony and Epigenesis in the Mammalian Neocortex," *Acta Paediatrica* 86, no. S422 (1997): 27–33, https://doi.org/10.1111/j.1651-2227.1997.tb18340.x; Center on the Developing Child at Harvard University, *From Best Practices to Breakthrough Impacts: A Science-Based Approach to Building a More Promising Future for Young Children and Families* (2016), https://harvardcenter.wpenginepowered.com/wp-content/uploads/2016/05/From_Best_Practices_to_Breakthrough_Impacts-4.pdf; Peter R. Huttenlocher and

Arun S. Dabholkar, "Regional Differences in Synaptogenesis in Human Cerebral Cortex," *The Journal of Comparative Neurology* 387, no. 2 (1997): 167–78, https://doi .org/10.1002/(SICI)1096-9861(19971020)387:2<167::AID-CNE1>3.0.CO;2-Z.

6. Huttenlocher and Dabholkar, "Regional Differences"; Deborah Phillips et al., *From Neurons to Neighborhoods: The Science of Early Childhood Development* (Washington, DC: National Academy Press, 2000).

7. Phillips et al., *From Neurons to Neighborhoods*.

8. Phillips et al., *From Neurons to Neighborhoods*.

9. American Academy of Pediatrics, "Newborn Reflexes," Healthychildren.org, updated March 8, 2022, https://www.healthychildren.org/English/ages-stages /baby/Pages/newborn-reflexes.aspx.

10. Ross A. Thompson, "Early Attachment and Later Development: Reframing the Questions," in *Handbook of Attachment: Theory, Research, and Clinical Applications*, 3rd ed., edited by Jude Cassidy and Phillip R. Shaver (New York: The Guilford Press, 2016), 330–48; Nancy S. Weinfield et al., "Individual Differences in Infant-Caregiver Attachment: Conceptual and Empirical Aspects of Security," in *Handbook of Attachment*, 2nd ed. (2008), 78–101.

11. Megan E. Harrison et al., "Systematic Review of the Effects of Family Meal Frequency on Psychosocial Outcomes in Youth," *Canadian Family Physician* 61, no. 2 (February 2015): e96–106, https://www.ncbi.nlm.nih.gov/pmc/articles /PMC4325878/pdf/0610e96.pdf.

12. Roma Jusiene et al., "Screen Use During Meals among Young Children: Exploration of Associated Variables," *Medicina* 55, no. 10 (October 2019): 688, https://doi.org/10.3390/medicina55100688; Jenny S. Radesky et al., "Patterns of Mobile Device Use by Caregivers and Children During Meals in Fast Food Restaurants," *Pediatrics* 133, no. 4 (April 2014): e843–9, https://doi.org/10.1542 /peds.2013-3703.

13. Daniel A. Abrams et al., "Neural Circuits Underlying Mother's Voice Perception Predict Social Communication Abilities in Children," *Proceedings of the National Academy of Sciences USA* 113, no. 22 (May 2016): 6295–300, https:// doi.org/10.1073/pnas.1602948113; Anthony J. DeCasper and William P. Fifer, "Of Human Bonding: Newborns Prefer Their Mothers' Voices," *Science* 208, no. 4448 (1980): 1174–76, https://doi.org/10.1126/science.7375928; Donna L. Mumme, Anne Fernald, and Carla Herrera, "Infants' Responses to Facial and Vocal Emotional Signals in a Social Referencing Paradigm," *Child Development* 67, no. 6 (1996): 3219–37, https://doi.org/10.1111/j.1467-8624.1996.tb01910 .x; Alexandra R. Webb et al., "Mother's Voice and Heartbeat Sounds Elicit Auditory Plasticity in the Human Brain before Full Gestation," *Proceedings of the National Academy of Sciences USA* 112, no. 10 (March 2015): 3152–7, https:// doi.org/10.1073/pnas.1414924112.

14. J. Christopher Edgar et al., "The Maturation of Auditory Responses in Infants and Young Children: A Cross-Sectional Study from 6 to 59 Months," *Frontiers*

in Neuroanatomy 9, no. 131 (October 2015), https://doi.org/10.3389/fnana
.2015.00131; Sarah Lippé, Natasa Kovacevic, and Anthony Randal McIntosh,
"Differential Maturation of Brain Signal Complexity in the Human Auditory
and Visual System," *Frontiers in Human Neuroscience* 3, no. 48 (November 2009),
https://doi.org/10.3389/neuro.09.048.2009.

15. Center on the Developing Child at Harvard University, *From Best Practices to Breakthrough Impacts*; Lisa S. Scott and Natalie H. Brito, "Supporting Healthy Brain and Behavioral Development During Infancy," *Policy Insights from the Behavioral and Brain Sciences* 9, no. 1 (2022): 129–36, https://doi.org/10.1177 /23727322211068172.

16. Sérgio Gomes da Silva and Ricardo Mario Arida, "Physical Activity and Brain Development," *Expert Review of Neurotherapeutics* 15, no. 9 (2015): 1041–51, https://doi.org/10.1586/14737175.2015.1077115.

17. Michael Yogman et al., "The Power of Play: A Pediatric Role in Enhancing Development in Young Children," *Pediatrics* 142, no. 3 (2018): e20182058, https://doi.org/10.1542/peds.2018-2058.

18. Melissa Fay Greene, "30 Years Ago, Romania Deprived Thousands of Babies of Human Contact," *The Atlantic* (July/August, 2020), https://www.theatlantic .com/magazine/archive/2020/07/can-an-unloved-child-learn-to-love/612253/; Charles H. Zeanah et al., "Attachment in Institutionalized and Community Children in Romania," *Child Development* 76, no. 5 (2005): 1015–28, https://doi .org/10.1111/j.1467-8624.2005.00894.x.

19. Charles A. Nelson, Nathan A. Fox, and Charles H. Zeanah, "Socioemotional Development," chap. 10 in *Romania's Abandoned Children: Deprivation, Brain Development, and the Struggle for Recovery* (Cambridge, MA: Harvard University Press, 2014), 227–65.

20. Greene, "30 Years Ago, Romania Deprived Thousands of Babies of Human Contact."

21. Charles A. Nelson, Nathan A. Fox, and Charles H. Zeanah, "Early Institutionalization and Brain Development," chap. 8 in *Romania's Abandoned Children: Deprivation, Brain Development, and the Struggle for Recovery* (Cambridge, MA: Harvard University Press, 2014), 182–210.

22. Taryn W. Morrissey, "Multiple Child-Care Arrangements and Young Children's Behavioral Outcomes," *Child Development* 80, no. 1 (2009): 59–76, https://doi.org/10.1111/j.1467-8624.2008.01246.x.

23. Center on the Developing Child at Harvard University, *From Best Practices to Breakthrough Impacts*.

24. Deborah Phillips et al., *From Neurons to Neighborhoods: The Science of Early Childhood Development* (Washington, DC: National Academy Press, 2000).

25. Ruth Graham, "The Rise and Fall of Baby Einstein," *Slate*, December 19, 2017, https://slate.com/technology/2017/12/the-rise-and-fall-of-baby-einstein.html.

26. Victoria J. Rideout, Elizabeth A. Vandewater, and Ellen A. Wartella, *Zero to*

Six: Electronic Media in the Lives of Infants, Toddlers, and Preschoolers, The Henry J. Kaiser Family Foundation (2003), 10.

27. American Academy of Pediatrics Committee on Public Education, "Media Education," *Pediatrics* 104, no. 2, pt 1 (1999): 341–43, https://doi.org/10.1542/peds.104.2.341.

28. Daniel R. Anderson and Katherine Hanson, "What Researchers Have Learned About Toddlers and Television," *Zero to Three* 33, no. 4 (March 2013): 4–10; Council on Communications and Media, "Media Use by Children Younger Than 2 Years," *Pediatrics* 128, no. 5 (November 2011): 1040–5, https://doi.org/10.1542/peds.2011-1753; Council on Communications and Media, "Media and Young Minds," *Pediatrics* 138, no. 5 (November 2016): e20162591, https://doi.org/10.1542/peds.2016-2591.

29. "Fairplay Baby Einstein Product Detail," Fairplay, https://fairplayforkids.org/wp-content/uploads/archive/Attachment%203%20-%20BE%20words,%20da%20vinci,%20numbers.pdf, 3.

30. Frederick J. Zimmerman, Dimitri A. Christakis, and Andrew N. Meltzoff, "Associations Between Media Viewing and Language Development in Children Under Age 2 Years," *The Journal of Pediatrics* 151, no. 4 (2007): 364–68, https://doi.org/10.1016/j.jpeds.2007.04.071.

31. Michael B. Robb, Rebekah A. Richert, and Ellen A. Wartella, "Just a Talking Book? Word Learning from Watching Baby Videos," *British Journal of Developmental Psychology* 27, no. 1 (2009): 27–45, https://doi.org/10.1348/026151008X320156.

32. Graham, "The Rise and Fall of Baby Einstein"; Tamar Lewin, "No Einstein in Your Crib? Get a Refund," *New York Times,* October 23, 2009, https://www.nytimes.com/2009/10/24/education/24baby.html.

33. Columbia University Irving Medical Center, "The Orienting Reflex: The Foundation of Relational Health," https://nurturescienceprogram.org/the-orienting-reflex-the-foundation-of-relational-health/; Ivan Sechenov, *Reflexes of the Brain,* translated by S. Belsky (Cambridge, MA: MIT Press, 1965).

34. Nelson Cowan, *Attention and Memory: An Integrated Framework,* Oxford Psychology Series, No. 26 (New York: Oxford University Press, 1995).

35. Leslie B. Cohen, Eric R. Gelber, and Marilee A. Lazar, "Infant Habituation and Generalization to Differing Degrees of Stimulus Novelty," *Journal of Experimental Child Psychology* 11, no. 3 (1971): 379–89, https://doi.org/10.1016/0022-0965(71)90043-9.

36. Marie Evans Schmidt et al., "The Effects of Background Television on the Toy Play Behavior of Very Young Children," *Child Development* 79, no. 4 (2008): 1137–51, https://doi.org/10.1111/j.1467-8624.2008.01180.x.

37. Samuel Ball and Gerry Ann Bogatz, *The First Year of Sesame Street: An Evaluation* (Princeton, NJ: Educational Testing Service, 1970); Joan Ganz Cooney, *The Potential Uses of Television in Preschool Education: A Report to the Carnegie*

Corporation of New York (New York: Carnegie Corporation, 1966); Shalom M. Fisch and Rosemarie T. Truglio, eds., *G Is for Growing: Thirty Years of Research on Children and Sesame Street* (New York: Routledge Communication, 2000); "The Joan Ganz Cooney Center," Sesame Workshop, https://www.sesameworkshop.org/what-we-do/research-and-innovation/joan-ganz-cooney-center.

38. Georgette L. Troseth and Judy S. DeLoache, "The Medium Can Obscure the Message: Young Children's Understanding of Video," *Child Development* 69, no. 4 (1998): 950–65, https://doi.org/10.1111/j.1467-8624.1998.tb06153.x.

39. Dimitri A. Christakis et al., "Audible Television and Decreased Adult Words, Infant Vocalizations, and Conversational Turns: A Population-Based Study," *Archives of Pediatrics and Adolescent Medicine* 163, no. 6 (2009): 554–58, https://doi.org/10.1001/archpediatrics.2009.61.

40. Dimitri A. Christakis et al., "Early Television Exposure and Subsequent Attentional Problems in Children," *Pediatrics* 113, no. 4 (2004): 708–13, https://doi.org/10.1542/peds.113.4.708; Sheri Madigan et al., "Associations Between Screen Use and Child Language Skills: A Systematic Review and Meta-Analysis," *JAMA Pediatrics* 174, no. 7 (July 2020): 665–75, https://doi.org/10.1001/jamapediatrics.2020.0327; Frederick Zimmerman, Dimitri A. Christakis, and Andrew N. Meltzoff, "Associations Between Media Viewing and Language Development in Children under Age 2 Years," *The Journal of Pediatrics* 151, no. 4 (2007): 364–68, https://doi.org/10.1016/j.jpeds.2007.04.071.

41. Daniela Avelar et al., "Children and Parents' Physiological Arousal and Emotions During Shared and Independent E-Book Reading: A Preliminary Study," *International Journal of Child-Computer Interaction* 33, Issue C (2022), https://doi.org/10.1016/j.ijcci.2022.100507; Ofra Korat, Adina Shamir, and Shani Heibal, "Expanding the Boundaries of Shared Book Reading: E-books and Printed Books in Parent-Child Reading as Support for Children's Language," *First Language* 33, no. 5 (2013): 504–23, https://doi.org/10.1177/0142723713503148; Reading Rockets, Colorin Colorado, and LD OnLine, "How to Read an E-Book with Your Child," Ed Tech and Digital Media (2013), https://www.readingrockets.org/topics/ed-tech-and-digital-media/articles/how-read-e-book-your-child.

42. Naomi Scatliffe et al., "Oxytocin and Early Parent-Infant Interactions: A Systematic Review," *International Journal of Nursing Sciences* 6, no. 4 (2019): 445–53, https://doi.org/10.1016/j.ijnss.2019.09.009.

43. Lauren J. Myers et al., "Baby Facetime: Can Toddlers Learn from Online Video Chat?" *Developmental Science* 20, no. 4 (2017): e12430, https://doi.org/10.1111/desc.12430.

44. Joan L. Luby et al., "Maternal Support in Early Childhood Predicts Larger Hippocampal Volumes at School Age," *Proceedings of the National Academy of Sciences USA* 109, no. 8 (2012): 2854–59, https://doi.org/10.1073/pnas.1118003109.

45. Patricia K. Kuhl et al., "Infants' Brain Responses to Speech Suggest Analysis by Synthesis," *Proceedings of the National Academy of Sciences USA* 111, no. 31

(July 2014): 11238–45, https://doi.org/10.1073/pnas.1410963111; David J. Lewkowicz and Amy M. Hansen-Tift, "Infants Deploy Selective Attention to the Mouth of a Talking Face When Learning Speech," *Proceedings of the National Academy of Sciences* 109, no. 5 (2012): 1431–36, https://doi.org/10.1073/pnas.1114783109.

46. Carlo Maria Di Liegro et al., "Physical Activity and Brain Health," *Genes* 10, no. 9 (2019): 720, https://www.mdpi.com/2073-4425/10/9/720.

47. Suzanne E. Mol et al., "Added Value of Dialogic Parent-Child Book Readings: A Meta-Analysis," *Early Education and Development* 19, no. 1 (2008): 7–26, https://doi.org/10.1080/10409280701838603; Rosa Catharina Teepe, I. Molenaar, and L. Verhoeven, "Technology-Enhanced Storytelling Stimulating Parent-Child Interaction and Preschool Children's Vocabulary Knowledge," *Journal of Computer Assisted Learning* 33, no. 2 (2016): 123–36, https://doi.org/https://doi.org/10.1111/jcal.12169.

48. Melissa L. Danielson et al., "Prevalence of Parent-Reported ADHD Diagnosis and Associated Treatment Among U.S. Children and Adolescents, 2016," *Journal of Clinical Child and Adolescent Psychology* 47, no. 2 (March–April 2018): 199–212, https://doi.org/10.1080/15374416.2017.1417860.

49. Daniel J. Levitin, "Too Much Information, Too Many Decisions: The Inside History of Cognitive Overload," in *The Organized Mind: Thinking Straight in the Age of Information Overload* (New York: Penguin Group, 2014).

50. Annie Swanepoel et al., "How Evolutionary Thinking Can Help Us to Understand ADHD," *BJPsych Advances* 23, no. 6 (2018): 410–18, https://doi.org/10.1192/apt.bp.116.016659; David J. Pettitt et al., "Abnormal Glucose Tolerance During Pregnancy in Pima Indian Women: Long-Term Effects on Offspring," *Diabetes* 40, Supplement 2 (December 1991): 126–30, https://doi.org/10.2337/diab.40.2.s126.

51. Ine Beyens, Patti M. Valkenburg, and Jessica Taylor Piotrowski, "Screen Media Use and ADHD-Related Behaviors: Four Decades of Research," *Proceedings of the National Academy of Sciences USA* 115, no. 40 (October 2018): 9875–81, https://doi.org/10.1073/pnas.1611611114.

52. Beyens, Valkenburg, and Piotrowski, "Screen Media Use and ADHD-Related Behaviors."

53. Dimitri A. Christakis et al., "Early Television Exposure and Subsequent Attentional Problems in Children," *Pediatrics* 113, no. 4 (2004): 708–13, https://doi.org/10.1542/peds.113.4.708.

54. Kevin P. Madore and Anthony D. Wagner, "Multicosts of Multitasking," *Cerebrum* (2019), https://www.ncbi.nlm.nih.gov/pmc/articles/PMC7075496/pdf/cer-04-19.pdf.

55. Adrian F. Ward et al., "Brain Drain: The Mere Presence of One's Own Smartphone Reduces Available Cognitive Capacity," *Journal of the Association for Consumer Research* 2, no. 2 (2017): 140–54, https://doi.org/10.1086/691462.

56. Chaelin K. Ra et al., "Association of Digital Media Use with Subsequent Symptoms of Attention-Deficit/Hyperactivity Disorder Among Adolescents," *JAMA* 320, no. 3 (Jul 2018): 255–63, https://doi.org/10.1001/jama.2018.8931.

57. Madore and Wagner, "Multicosts of Multitasking."

Chapter 4: Lonely Hearts

1. Amy Randall Parish, "Female Relationships in Bonobos (*Pan paniscus*)," *Hu Nat* 7, no. 1 (1996): 61–96, https://doi.org/10.1007/BF02733490.

2. Brian Hare and Vanessa Woods, *Survival of the Friendliest: Understanding Our Origins and Rediscovering Our Common Humanity* (New York: Random House, 2020).

3. Emily A. Vogels, Risa Gelles-Watnick, and Navid Massarat, "Teens, Social Media, and Technology 2022," *Pew Research Center*, August 10, 2022, https://www.pewresearch.org/internet/2022/08/10/teens-social-media-and-technology-2022/.

4. Vogels, Gelles-Watnick, and Massarat, "Teens, Social Media, and Technology 2022."

5. Amazing Videos, "Funny Infant Kid Crying for Mobile—Best funny baby video compilation of 2015," YouTube video, June 10, 2015, 1:34, https://www.youtube.com/watch?v=c_XyWbxGNFQ.

6. Columbia University Irving Medical Center, "The Orienting Reflex: The Foundation of Relational Health," https://nurturescienceprogram.org/the-orienting-reflex-the-foundation-of-relational-health/.

7. Judy S. DeLoache et al., "Do Babies Learn from Baby Media?" *Psychological Science* 21, no. 11 (2010): 1570–74, https://doi.org/10.1177/0956797610384145; Council on Communications and Media, "Media and Young Minds," *Pediatrics* 138, no. 5 (November 2016), https://doi.org/10.1542/peds.2016-2591; Rebekah A. Richert et al., "Word Learning from Baby Videos," *Archives of Pediatrics and Adolescent Medicine* 164, no. 5 (2010): 432–37, https://doi.org/10.1001/archpediatrics.2010.24.

8. Webkinz, Ganz, https://www.webkinz.com/.

9. Michael Thompson, Catherine O'Neill-Grace, and Lawrence J. Cohen, *Best Friends, Worst Enemies: Understanding the Social Lives of Children* (New York: Ballantine Books, 2002).

10. Michael Thompson, interviewed by Teresa Barker and Michael Rich, June 3, 2023.

11. Susanne A. Denham, *Emotional Development in Young Children* (New York: Guilford Press, 1998).

12. Kate Cowan et al., "Children's Digital Play During the COVID-19 Pandemic: Insights from the Play Observatory," *Journal of E-Learning and Knowledge Society* 17, no. 3 (2021): 8–17, https://doi.org/10.20368/1971-8829/1135590; Jessica Navarro, "Fortnite: A Context for Child Development in the U.S. During

COVID-19 (and Beyond)," *Journal of Children and Media* 15, no. 1 (2020): 13–16, https://doi.org/10.1080/17482798.2020.1858435; Victoria J. Rideout and Michael B. Robb, *The Role of Media During the Pandemic: Connection, Creativity, and Learning for Tweens and Teens* (San Francisco: Common Sense Media, 2021), 8-18-role-of-media-research-report-final-web.pdf.

13. Cowan et al., "Children's Digital Play"; Navarro, "Fortnite"; Rideout and Robb, *The Role of Media During the Pandemic.*

14. Cowan et al., "Children's Digital Play"; Navarro, "Fortnite"; Rideout and Robb, *The Role of Media During the Pandemic.*

15. Cowan et al., "Children's Digital Play"; Navarro, "Fortnite"; Rideout and Robb, *The Role of Media During the Pandemic.*

16. Paul Hodkinson, "Bedrooms and Beyond: Youth, Identity, and Privacy on Social Network Sites," *New Media and Society* 19, no. 2 (2017): 272–88, https://doi.org/10.1177/1461444815605454; Patti M. Valkenburg, Alexander P. Schouten, and Jochen Peter, "Adolescents' Identity Experiments on the Internet," *New Media and Society* 7, no. 3 (2005): 383–402, https://doi.org/10.1177/1461444805052282; Joanna C. Yau and Stephanie M. Reich, "Buddies, Friends, and Followers: The Evolution of Online Friendships," in *Online Peer Engagement in Adolescence: Positive and Negative Aspects of Online Social Interaction*, edited by Nejra Van Zalk and Claire P. Monks (New York: Routledge, 2020).

17. Helen Morgan et al., "The Role of the Avatar in Gaming for Trans and Gender Diverse Young People," *International Journal of Environmental Research and Public Health* 17, no. 22 (2020): 8617, https://doi.org/10.3390/ijerph17228617.

18. David Bickham, Summer Moukalled, and Michael Rich, "Young People's Media Use and Remote Schooling Experiences During the COVID-19 Pandemic" (paper presented at the Technology, Mind and Society, 2021, Conference Proceedings).

19. LinkedIn Talent Solutions, *2019 Global Talent Trends: The Four Trends Transforming Your Workplace*, 2019, https://business.linkedin.com/talent-solutions/global-talent-trends?trk=bl-po.

20. Michelle L. Kusel, "The Influence of Social Networking on Socially Responsible Leadership" (PhD diss., Loyola University, 2019).

21. Children's Online Privacy Protection Act of 1998, 15 U.S.C. §§ 6501–6506, 2000.

22. Colleen McClain, "How Parents' Views of Their Kids' Screen Time, Social Media Use Changed During COVID-19," Pew Research Center, April 28, 2022, https://www.pewresearch.org/fact-tank/2022/04/28/how-parents-views-of-their-kids-screen-time-social-media-use-changed-during-covid-19/; Victoria J. Rideout et al., *Common Sense Census: Media Use by Tweens and Teens, 2021* (San Francisco: Common Sense Media, 2022); Shalynn Weeden, Bethany Cooke, and Michael McVey, "Underage Children and Social Networking," *Journal of Research on Technology in Education* 45, no. 3 (2013): 249–62, https://doi.org/10.1080/15391523.2013.10782605.

23. Adam E. Barry et al., "Alcohol Marketing on Twitter and Instagram: Evidence of Directly Advertising to Youth/Adolescents," *Alcohol and Alcoholism* 51, no. 4 (2016): 487–92, https://doi.org/10.1093/alcalc/agv128; Megan A. Moreno and Jennifer M. Whitehill, "Influence of Social Media on Alcohol Use in Adolescents and Young Adults," *Alcohol Research* 36, no. 1 (2014): 91–100, https://arcr.niaaa.nih.gov/media/128/download?inline; Jacqueline Nesi et al., "Friends' Alcohol-Related Social Networking Site Activity Predicts Escalations in Adolescent Drinking: Mediation by Peer Norms," *Journal of Adolescent Health* 60, no. 6 (2017): 641–47, https://doi.org/10.1016/j.jadohealth.2017.01.009.

24. Rideout et al., *Common Sense Census: Media Use by Tweens and Teens, 2021*.

25. Anna Fleck, "What Do You Want to Be When You Grow Up?" *Statista*, November 22, 2022, https://www.statista.com/chart/28802/childhood -aspirations-in-china-us-uk/.

26. David Bickham, Summer Moukalled, and Michael Rich, "Young People's Media Use and Remote Schooling Experiences During the COVID-19 Pandemic" (paper presented at the Technology, Mind and Society, 2021, Conference Proceedings).

27. Marcus Carter et al., "Situating the Appeal of *Fortnite* Within Children's Changing Play Cultures," *Games and Culture* 15, no. 4 (2020): 453–71, https:// doi.org/10.1177/1555412020913771; Alexa Hiebert and Kathy Kortes-Miller, "Finding Home in Online Community: Exploring TikTok as a Support for Gender and Sexual Minority Youth Throughout COVID-19," *Journal of LGBT Youth 20*, no. 4 (2021): 800–17, https://doi.org/10.1080/19361653.2021.2009953; Jessica Navarro, "Fortnite: A Context for Child Development in the U.S. During Covid-19 (and Beyond)," *Journal of Children and Media* 15, no. 1 (2020): 13–16, https://doi.org/10.1080/17482798.2020.1858435.

28. American Psychological Association, "Health Advisory on Social Media Use in Adolescence," May 2023, https://www.apa.org/topics/social-media-internet /health-advisory-adolescent-social-media-use.

29. APA, "Health Advisory."

30. Jean M. Twenge et al., "Increases in Depressive Symptoms, Suicide-Related Outcomes, and Suicide Rates Among U.S. Adolescents after 2010 and Links to Increased New Media Screen Time," *Clinical Psychological Science* 6, no. 1 (2018): 3–17, https://doi.org/10.1177/2167702617723376.

31. Jean M. Twenge and W. Keith Campbell, "Associations Between Screen Time and Lower Psychological Well-Being Among Children and Adolescents: Evidence from a Population-Based Study," *Preventative Medicine Reports* 12 (December 2018): 271–83, https://doi.org/10.1016/j.pmedr.2018.10.003.

32. Jasmine N. Khouja et al., "Is Screen Time Associated with Anxiety or Depression in Young People? Results from a UK Birth Cohort," *BMC Public Health* 19, no. 1 (January 2019): 82, https://doi.org/10.1186/s12889-018-6321-9.

33. Linda Charmaraman et al., "Associations of Early Social Media Initiation on Digital Behaviors and the Moderating Role of Limiting Use," *Computers*

in Human Behavior 127 (2022): 107053, https://doi.org/10.1016/j.chb.2021
.107053; Karin M. Fikkers, Jessica Taylor Piotrowski, and Patti M. Valkenburg,
"A Matter of Style? Exploring the Effects of Parental Mediation Styles on Early
Adolescents' Media Violence Exposure and Aggression," *Computers in Human
Behavior* 70 (2017): 407–15, https://doi.org/10.1016/j.chb.2017.01.029.

34. Jean M. Twenge and Thomas E. Joiner, "U.S. Census Bureau–Assessed
Prevalence of Anxiety and Depressive Symptoms in 2019 and During the 2020
COVID-19 Pandemic," *Depression and Anxiety* 37, no. 10 (2020): 954–56, https://
doi.org/https://doi.org/10.1002/da.23077; Kathleen B. Watson et al., "Chronic
Conditions Among Adults Aged 18–34 Years—United States, 2019," *Morbidity
and Mortality Weekly Report 2022* 71, no. 30 (2022): 964–70, http://dx.doi.org/10
.15585/mmwr.mm7130a3.

35. Bernice A. Pescosolido et al., "Trends in Public Stigma of Mental Illness in the
US, 1996–2018," *JAMA Network Open* 4, no. 12 (2021): e2140202, https://doi.org
/10.1001/jamanetworkopen.2021.40202; A. H. Weinberger et al., "Trends in
Depression Prevalence in the USA from 2005 to 2015: Widening Disparities in
Vulnerable Groups," *Psychological Medicine* 48, no. 8 (2018): 1308–15, https://doi
.org/10.1017/S0033291717002781.

36. Office of the U.S. Surgeon General, *Protecting Youth Mental Health: The U.S.
Surgeon General's Advisory,* 2021, https://www.hhs.gov/sites/default/files
/surgeon-general-youth-mental-health-advisory.pdf.

37. Centers for Disease Control and Prevention, *Youth Risk Behavior Surveillance
Data Summary & Trends Report: 2009–19,* 2020, https://www.cdc.gov
/healthyyouth/data/yrbs/pdf/YRBSDataSummaryTrendsReport2019-508.pdf.

38. Sally C. Curtin, "State Suicide Rates Among Adolescents and Young Adults
Aged 10–24: United States 2000–2018," *National Vital Statistics Reports* 69, no. 11
(2020), https://stacks.cdc.gov/view/cdc/93667.

39. Sally C. Curtin et al., "Provisional Numbers and Rates of Suicide by Month
and Demographic Characteristics: United States, 2020," *NVSS: Vital Statistics
Rapid Release* 70, no. 16 (2021), https://stacks.cdc.gov/view/cdc/110369.

40. Evan Tarver, "3 Social Media Networks Before Facebook," Investopedia,
September 13, 2022, https://www.investopedia.com/articles/markets
/081315/3-social-media-networks-facebook.asp#:~:text=In%202003%2C%20
Friendster%20was%20a,Internet%20company%20at%20the%20time.

41. United States Census Bureau, "Age and Sex," *American Community Survey,
ACS 1-Year Estimates Subject Tables, Table S0101,* 2022, https://data.census.gov
/table?q=United+States+age&g=010XX00US.

42. Stacy Jo Dixon, "Number of Social Media Users in the United States from
2019–2028," Statista, November 6, 2023, https://www.statista.com/statistics
/278409/number-of-social-network-users-in-the-united-states/.

43. Office of the U.S. Surgeon General, *Our Epidemic of Loneliness and Isolation:
The U.S. Surgeon General's Advisory on the Healing Effects of Social Connection and*

Community, 2023, https://www.hhs.gov/sites/default/files/surgeon-general
-social-connection-advisory.pdf.

44. Viji Diane Kannan and Peter J. Veazie, "US Trends in Social Isolation, Social Engagement, and Companionship: Nationally and by Age, Sex, Race/Ethnicity, Family Income, and Work Hours, 2003–2020," SSM - Population Health 21 (2023): 101331, https://doi.org/10.1016/j.ssmph.2022.101331.

45. Farhana Mann et al., "Loneliness and the Onset of New Mental Health Problems in the General Population," *Social Psychiatry and Psychiatric Epidemiology* 57, no. 11 (2022): 2161–78, https://doi.org/10.1007/s00127-022-02261-7.

46. Office of the U.S. Surgeon General, *Social Media and Youth Mental Health: The U.S. Surgeon General's Advisory*, 2023, https://www.hhs.gov/sites/default/files/sg-youth-mental-health-social-media-advisory.pdf.

47. Mann et al., "Loneliness and the Onset of New Mental Health Problems."

48. Emily A. Vogels, Risa Gelles-Watnick, and Navid Massarat, "Teens, Social Media, and Technology 2022," Pew Research Center, August 10, 2022, https://www.pewresearch.org/internet/2022/08/10/teens-social-media-and-technology-2022/.

49. American Psychological Association, "Health Advisory on Social Media Use in Adolescence," May 2023, https://www.apa.org/topics/social-media-internet/health-advisory-adolescent-social-media-use; Yalda T. Uhls, Nicole B. Ellison, and Kaveri Subrahmanyam, "Benefits and Costs of Social Media in Adolescence," *Pediatrics* 140, Supplement 2 (2017): S67–S70, https://doi.org/10.1542/peds.2016-1758.

50. Vogels, Gelles-Watnick, and Massarat, "Teens, Social Media, and Technology 2022"; Eline Frison and Steven Eggermont, "The Impact of Daily Stress on Adolescents' Depressed Mood: The Role of Social Support Seeking Through Facebook," *Computers in Human Behavior* 44 (2015): 315–25, https://doi.org/10.1016/j.chb.2014.11.070.

51. Kira E. Riehm et al., "Associations Between Time Spent Using Social Media and Internalizing and Externalizing Problems Among US Youth," *JAMA Psychiatry* 76, no. 12 (2019): 1266, https://doi.org/10.1001/jamapsychiatry.2019.2325.

52. Melissa G. Hunt et al., "No More FOMO: Limiting Social Media Decreases Loneliness and Depression," *Journal of Social and Clinical Psychology* 37, no. 10 (2018): 751–68, https://doi.org/10.1521/jscp.2018.37.10.751.

53. Victoria Rideout and Michael B. Robb, *Social Media, Social Life: Teens Reveal Their Experiences* (San Francisco: Common Sense Media, 2018), 2018-social-media-social-life-executive-summary-web.pdf.

54. Olivia Carville, "TikTok's Viral Challenges Keep Luring Young Kids to Their Deaths," *Bloomberg*, November 29, 2022, https://www.bloomberg.com/news/features/2022-11-30/is-tiktok-responsible-if-kids-die-doing-dangerous-viral-challenges.

55. Clare Dyer, "Social Media Content Contributed to Teenager's Death 'in More than a Minimal Way,' Says Coroner," *BMJ* 379 (2022): o2374, https://doi.org/10.1136/bmj.o2374.

56. Jacqueline Nesi and Mitchell J. Prinstein, "Using Social Media for Social Comparison and Feedback-Seeking: Gender and Popularity Moderate Associations with Depressive Symptoms," *Journal of Abnormal Child Psychology* 43, no. 8 (2015), 1427–38, https://doi.org/10.1007/s10802-015-0020-0; Annalise G. Mabe, K. Jean Forney, and Pamela K. Keel, "Do You 'Like' My Photo? Facebook Use Maintains Eating Disorder Risk," *International Journal of Eating Disorders* 47, no. 5 (2014): 516–23, https://doi.org/10.1002/eat.22254.

57. David Bickham et al., *Adolescent Media Use: Attitudes, Effects, and Online Experiences* (Boston, MA: Boston Children's Hospital Digital Wellness Lab, 2022), https://digitalwellnesslab.org/wp-content/uploads/Pulse-Survey_Adolescent-Attitudes-Effects-and-Experiences.pdf.

58. Michelle P. Hamm et al., "Prevalence and Effect of Cyberbullying on Children and Young People: A Scoping Review of Social Media Studies," *JAMA Pediatrics* 169, no. 8 (2015): 770–77, https://doi.org/10.1001/jamapediatrics.2015.0944; Mohammed Alhajji, Sarah Bass, and Ting Dai, "Cyberbullying, Mental Health, and Violence in Adolescents and Associations with Sex and Race: Data from the 2015 Youth Risk Behavior Survey," *Global Pediatric Health* 6 (2019), https://doi.org/10.1177/2333794X19868887.

59. Rea Alonzo et al., "Interplay Between Social Media Use, Sleep Quality, and Mental Health in Youth: A Systematic Review," *Sleep Medicine Reviews* 56 (2021): 101414, https://doi.org/10.1016/j.smrv.2020.101414; Michael Rich, Michael Tsappis, and Jill R. Kavanaugh, "Problematic Interactive Media Use Among Children and Adolescents: Addiction, Compulsion, or Syndrome?," in *Internet Addiction in Children and Adolescents: Risk Factors, Assessment, and Treatment*, ed. Kimberly S. Young and Cristiano Nabuco De Abreu (New York: Springer Publishing Company, 2017), 3–28.

60. "The Inspired Internet Pledge," Boston Children's Hospital Digital Wellness Lab, https://inspiredinternet.org/.

61. Monica Anderson et al., "Connection, Creativity and Drama: Teen Life on Social Media in 2022," Pew Research Center, November 16, 2022, https://www.pewresearch.org/internet/2022/11/16/connection-creativity-and-drama-teen-life-on-social-media-in-2022/.

62. Jessica Gall Myrick, "Emotion Regulation, Procrastination, and Watching Cat Videos Online: Who Watches Internet Cats, Why, and to What Effect?," *Computers in Human Behavior* 52 (2015): 168–76, https://doi.org/10.1016/j.chb.2015.06.001.

63. Jessica Taylor Piotrowski and Patti M. Valkenburg, "Finding Orchids in a Field of Dandelions: Understanding Children's Differential Susceptibility to Media Effects," *American Behavioral Scientist* 59, no. 14 (2015): 1776–89, https://doi.org/10.1177/0002764215596552.

64. Jay N. Giedd et al., "Brain Development During Childhood and Adolescence: A Longitudinal MRI Study," *Nature Neuroscience* 2, no. 10 (1999): 861–63, https://doi.org/10.1038/13158.
65. Susan A. Carlson et al., "Influence of Limit-Setting and Participation in Physical Activity on Youth Screen Time," *Pediatrics* 126, no. 1 (July 2010): e89–96, https://doi.org/10.1542/peds.2009-3374.
66. Vivek H. Murthy, MD, *Together: The Healing Power of Human Connection in a Sometimes Lonely World* (New York: Harper, 2023), 113.
67. Jamie Nesbitt Golden, "South Side Storytelling Workshop Teaches Young Adults to Use Their Phones to Change the World," Block Club Chicago, July 6, 2023, https://blockclubchicago.org/2023/07/06/south-side-storytelling -workshop-teaches-young-adults-to-use-their-phones-to-change-the-world/.
68. Boston Children's Hospital Digital Wellness Lab, https://inspiredinternet pledge.org.

Chapter 5: What's Love Got to Do with IT?

1. Zhiying Yue, "Sexual Media and Behaviors," in *Encyclopedia of Child and Adolescent Health (First Edition)*, edited by Bonnie Halpern-Felsher (Oxford: Academic Press, 2023), 239–47.
2. Alexandra C. Kirsch and Sarah K. Murnen, "'Hot' Girls and 'Cool Dudes': Examining the Prevalence of the Heterosexual Script in American Children's Television Media," *Psychology of Popular Media Culture* 4, no. 1 (2015): 18–30, https://doi.org/10.1037/ppm0000017.
3. Sarah M. Coyne et al., "Contributions of Mainstream Sexual Media Exposure to Sexual Attitudes, Perceived Peer Norms, and Sexual Behavior: A Meta-Analysis," *Journal of Adolescent Health* 64, no. 4 (2019): 430–36, https://doi.org/10 .1016/j.jadohealth.2018.11.016.
4. Coyne et al., "Contributions of Mainstream Sexual Media Exposure to Sexual Attitudes."
5. Coyne et al., "Contributions of Mainstream Sexual Media Exposure to Sexual Attitudes."
6. US Department of Health and Human Services, "Increase the Proportion of Adolescents Who Get Formal Sex Education before Age 18 Years—Fp-08," https://health.gov/healthypeople/objectives-and-data/browse-objectives /family-planning/increase-proportion-adolescents-who-get-formal-sex -education-age-18-years-fp-08.
7. Guttmacher Institute, "Sex and HIV Education," last updated September 2023, https://www.guttmacher.org/state-policy/explore/sex-and-hiv-education; Laura D. Lindberg and Leslie M. Kantor, "Adolescents' Receipt of Sex Education in a Nationally Representative Sample, 2011–2019," *Journal of Adolescent Health* 70, no. 2 (2022): 290–97, https://doi.org/10.1016/j.jadohealth.2021.08.027; US Department of Health and Human Services, and Centers for Disease Control

and Prevention, *Results from the School Health Policies and Practices Study* (Washington, DC: CDC, 2017), https://www.cdc.gov/healthyyouth/data/shpps /pdf/shpps-results_2016.pdf.

8. Guttmacher Institute, "US Adolescents' Receipt of Formal Sex Education," February 2022, https://www.guttmacher.org/fact-sheet/adolescents-teens -receipt-sex-education-united-states.

9. Paola Miano and Chiara Urone, "What the Hell Are You Doing? A PRISMA Systematic Review of Psychosocial Precursors of Slut-Shaming in Adolescents and Young Adults," *Psychology and Sexuality* (2023): 1–17, https://doi.org/10.1080 /19419899.2023.2213736.

10. Walpurga Antl-Weiser, "The Anthropomorphic Figurines from Willendorf," *Wissenschaftliche Mitteilungen Niederösterreichisches Landesmuseum* 19 (2008): 19–30, https://www.zobodat.at/pdf/WM_19_0019-0030.pdf.

11. Teresa Nelson, "Minnesota Prosecutor Charges Sexting Teenage Girl with Child Pornography," *American Civil Liberties Union*, January 5, 2018, https:// www.aclu.org/news/juvenile-justice/minnesota-prosecutor-charges-sexting -teenage-girl-child-pornography.

12. Jessica Ringrose et al., *A Qualitative Study of Children, Young People, and "Sexting": A Report Prepared for the NSPCC*, National Society for the Prevention of Cruelty to Children (London: NSPCC, 2012), https://eprints.lse.ac.uk/44216 /1/_Libfile_repository_Content_Livingstone%2C%20S_A%20qualitative %20study%20of%20children%2C%20young%20people%20and%20%27 sexting%27%20%28LSE%20RO%29.pdf.

13. Rachel Simmons, "The 'Slut List' as Badge of Honor: Breaking News?" *HuffPost*, November 28, 2009, https://www.huffpost.com/entry/the-slut-list-as -badge-of_b_302435.

14. Susanna Paasonen, "Pornification and the Mainstreaming of Sex," *Oxford Research Encyclopedia of Criminology and Criminal Justice* (Oxford: Oxford University Press, 2016), https://doi.org/10.1093/acrefore/9780190264079.013.159.

15. Michael B. Robb and Supreet Mann, *Teens and Pornography* (San Francisco: Common Sense Media, 2023), https://www.commonsensemedia.org/sites /default/files/research/report/2022-teens-and-pornography-final-web.pdf.

16. Robb and Mann, *Teens and Pornography*, 6.

17. Beata Bothe et al., "Problematic and Non-Problematic Pornography Use Among LGBTQ Adolescents: A Systematic Literature Review," *Current Addiction Reports* 6, no. 4 (2019): 478–94, https://doi.org/10.1007/s40429-019-00289-5.

18. Daniel Delmonaco and Oliver L. Haimson, "'Nothing That I Was Specifically Looking For': LGBTQ+ Youth and Intentional Sexual Health Information Seeking," *Journal of LGBT Youth* 20, no. 4 (2022): 818–35, https://doi.org/10.1080 /19361653.2022.2077883.

19. Centers for Disease Control and Prevention, *Youth Risk Behavior Survey Data Summary and Trends Report: 2011–2021* (Washington, DC: CDC, 2023), 11,

https://www.cdc.gov/healthyyouth/data/yrbs/pdf/YRBS_Data-Summary
-Trends_Report2023_508.pdf.

20. Victoria J. Rideout et al., *Common Sense Census: Media Use by Tweens and Teens, 2021* (San Francisco: Common Sense Media, 2022), 22, https://www .commonsensemedia.org/sites/default/files/research/report/8-18-census -integrated-report-final-web_0.pdf; "Teens and Mobile Phones," Pew Research Center, April 20, 2010, https://www.pewresearch.org/internet/2010/04/20 /teens-and-mobile-phones-3.

21. Niki Fritz et al., "A Descriptive Analysis of the Types, Targets, and Relative Frequency of Aggression in Mainstream Pornography," *Archives of Sexual Behavior* 49, no. 8 (2020): 3041–53, https://doi.org/10.1007/s10508-020-01773-0.

22. "The 2022 Year in Review," PornHub, December 8, 2022, https://www .pornhub.com/insights/2022-year-in-review; "New BBFC Research Reveals Children Are More Exposed to Sites Specialising in Non-Photographic Pornography, Compared to Adults," British Board of Film Classification, https://www.bbfc.co.uk/about-us/news/new-bbfc-research-reveals-children -are-more-exposed-to-sites-specialising-in-non-photographic-pornography -compared-to-adults.

23. Brenda K. Wiederhold, "How COVID Has Changed Online Dating—and What Lies Ahead," *Cyberpsychology, Behavior, and Social Networking* 24, no. 7 (2021): 435–36, https://doi.org/10.1089/cyber.2021.29219.editorial.

24. Andrej Hadji-Vasilev, "25 Online Dating Statistics and Trends in 2023," *Cloudwards*, March 16, 2023, https://www.cloudwards.net/online-dating -statistics.

25. Artur Acelino Francisco L. N. Queiroz et al., "Vulnerability to HIV Among Older Men Who Have Sex with Men Users of Dating Apps in Brazil," *The Brazilian Journal of Infectious Diseases* 23, no. 5 (2019): 298–306, https://doi .org/10.1016/j.bjid.2019.07.005; Ashlee N. Sawyer, Erin R. Smith, and Eric G. Benotsch, "Dating Application Use and Sexual Risk Behavior Among Young Adults," *Sexuality Research and Social Policy* 15, no. 2 (2018): 183–91, https://doi .org/10.1007/s13178-017-0297-6.

26. Monica Anderson, Emily A. Vogels, and Erica Turner, "The Virtues and Downsides of Online Dating," Pew Research Center, February 6, 2020, https://www.pewresearch.org/internet/2020/02/06/the-virtues-and -downsides-of-online-dating; Kristin Veel and Nanna Bonde Thylstrup, "Geolocating the Stranger: The Mapping of Uncertainty as a Configuration of Matching and Warranting Techniques in Dating Apps," *Journal of Aesthetics and Culture* 10, no. 3 (2018): 43–52, https://doi.org/10.1080/20004214.2017.1422924.

27. Perry Stein, "FBI Warns of Explosion of 'Sextortion' Cases Targeting Boys, Teens," *The Washington Post*, December 19, 2022, https://www.washingtonpost .com/national-security/2022/12/19/sextortion-children-fbi-online.

28. Stein, "FBI Warns."

29. Stein, "FBI Warns."
30. Ginger Allen, "I-Team: New Data Shows More Young People Are Getting Catfished," CBS Texas, December 16, 2022, https://www.cbsnews.com/texas/news/younger-people-getting-catfished.
31. Allen, "I-Team."
32. Amanda Watts, Tina Burnside, and Zoe Sottile, "Virginia Man Accused of 'Catfishing' Teen Before Killing Her Family, Police Say," CNN, November 28, 2022, https://www.cnn.com/2022/11/28/us/austin-edwards-riverside-catfishing-murders/index.html.
33. Robin Abcarian, "Opinion: 'Catfishing' Murder Serves a Reminder That Kids Are Easy Prey," *Virginian Pilot*, December 9, 2022, https://www.pilotonline.com/2022/12/09/opinion-catfishing-murder-serves-a-reminder-that-kids-are-easy-prey.
34. Pranshu Verma, "AI Fake Nudes Are Booming. It's Ruining Real Teens' Lives," *Washington Post*, November 5, 2023, https://www.washingtonpost.com/technology/2023/11/05/ai-deepfake-porn-teens-women-impact/.
35. *The Breakfast Club*, directed by John Hughes (Universal City, CA: Universal Pictures, 1985), film.

Chapter 6: The Teachable Moment

1. E. B. White, "Removals," in *One Man's Meat*, 13th ed. (Thomaston, ME: Tilbury House, 2003).
2. Winthrop Jordan, *The Americans* (Boston: McDougal Littell, 1996), 798.
3. "Number of Telephones in Use and Households with Radio and Television Sets in the United States from 1876 to 1986," *Statista*, graph, 2023, retrieved from https://www-statista-com.ezp-prod1.hul.harvard.edu/statistics/1247483/us-number-telephones-radio-tv-historical.
4. Newton N. Minow, *Television and the Public Interest*, speech, May 9, 1961, https://www.americanrhetoric.com/speeches/newtonminow.htm.
5. Fred Rogers, "Senate Statement on PBS Funding [Video recording and transcript on the page]," American Rhetoric, https://www.americanrhetoric.com/speeches/fredrogerssenatetestimonypbs.htm.
6. Rogers, "Senate Statement on PBS Funding."
7. Rogers, "Senate Statement on PBS Funding."
8. Fred Rogers, "Fred Rogers: Look for the Helpers," YouTube video, April 15, 2013, 0:57, https://www.youtube.com/watch?v=-LGHtc_D328.
9. Sesame Street, "Sesame Street: Show Open Season 1," YouTube video, April 10, 2009, 0:53, https://www.youtube.com/watch?v=jfQSp92L88I.
10. Michael Davis, *Street Gang: The Complete History of Sesame Street* (New York: Viking Books, 2009), 8.
11. Gerald S. Lesser, *Children and Television: Lessons from Sesame Street,* first ed. (New York: Random House, 1974).

12. Shalom M. Fisch and Rosemarie T. Truglio, eds., *G Is for Growing: Thirty Years of Research on Children and Sesame Street* (New York: Routledge Communication, 2000).

13. Fisch and Truglio, eds., *G Is for Growing*.

14. Maura Hohman, "This 'Mister Rogers' Moment Broke Race Barriers. It's Just as Powerful Today," *Today*, June 8, 2020, https://www.today.com/popculture /how-mister-rogers-pool-moment-broke-race-barriers-t183635.

15. Dartmouth Office of Communications, "Revisiting Fred Rogers' 2002 Commencement Address," March 27, 2018, https://home.dartmouth.edu/news /2018/03/revisiting-fred-rogers-2002-commencement-address.

16. Alexandra C. Kirsch and Sarah K. Murnen, "'Hot' Girls and 'Cool Dudes': Examining the Prevalence of the Heterosexual Script in American Children's Television Media," *Psychology of Popular Media Culture* 4, no. 1 (2015): 18–30, https://doi.org/10.1037/ppm0000017.

17. Shalom M. Fisch, *Children's Learning from Educational Television: Sesame Street and Beyond* (London: Routledge Communication, 2014).

18. Aletha C. Huston et al., "Sesame Street Viewers as Adolescents: The Recontact Study," in *G Is for Growing: Thirty Years of Research on Children and Sesame Street*, edited by Shalom M. Fisch and Rosemarie T. Truglio (New York: Routledge Communication, 2000), 131–43.

19. Dale Kunkel and Julie Canepa, "Broadcasters' License Renewal Claims Regarding Children's Educational Programming," *Journal of Broadcasting and Electronic Media* 38, no. 4 (1994): 397–416, https://doi.org/10.1080/08838159409364275.

20. "ParentFurther.com Barney vs Power Rangers," YouTube video, October 19, 2011, 7:26, https://www.youtube.com/watch?v=LXbS4Uaaiww.

21. Caroline O'Sullivan, "Professional Wrestling: Can Watching It Bring Out Aggressive and Violent Behaviors in Children?" ERIC (1999), https://files.eric .ed.gov/fulltext/ED431526.pdf.

22. Jim Waxmonsky and Eugene V. Beresin, "Taking Professional Wrestling to the Mat: A Look at the Appeal and Potential Effects of Professional Wrestling on Children," *Academic Psychiatry* 25 (2001): 125–31, https://link.springer.com /article/10.1176/appi.ap.25.2.125.

23. Robert H. Durant et al., "Viewing Professional Wrestling on Television and Engaging in Violent and Other Health Risk Behaviors," *Southern Medical Journal* 101, no. 2 (2008): 129–37, https://doi.org/10.1097/SMJ.0b013e31815d247d.

24. Silvia Galdi and Francesca Guizzo, "Media-Induced Sexual Harassment: The Routes from Sexually Objectifying Media to Sexual Harassment," *Sex Roles* 84, no. 11 (2021): 645–69, https://doi.org/10.1007/s11199-020-01196-0.

25. Victoria J. Rideout, Ulla G. Foehr, and Donald F. Roberts, *Generation M2: Media in the Lives of 8- to 18-Year-Olds*, The Henry J. Kaiser Foundation (2010), https:// www.kff.org/wp-content/uploads/2013/04/8010.pdf.

26. Jenny S. Radesky et al., "Patterns of Mobile Device Use by Caregivers and

Children During Meals in Fast Food Restaurants," *Pediatrics* 133, no. 4 (Apr 2014): e843–9, https://doi.org/10.1542/peds.2013-3703.

27. Jenny S. Radesky et al., "Longitudinal Associations Between Use of Mobile Devices for Calming and Emotional Reactivity and Executive Functioning in Children Aged 3 to 5 Years," *JAMA Pediatrics* 177, no. 1 (2022): 62–70, https://doi .org/10.1001/jamapediatrics.2022.4793.

28. Kaitlyn E. May and Anastasia D. Elder, "Efficient, Helpful, or Distracting? A Literature Review of Media Multitasking in Relation to Academic Performance," *International Journal of Educational Technology in Higher Education* 15, no. 13 (2018), https://doi.org/10.1186/s41239-018-0096-z.

29. Victoria J. Rideout and Michael B. Robb, *The Common Sense Census: Media Use by Tweens and Teens, 2019* (San Francisco: Common Sense Media, 2019), https:// www.commonsensemedia.org/sites/default/files/research/report/2019 -census-8-to-18-full-report-updated.pdf.

30. Helena Lewis-Smith et al., "A Short-Form Drama Series Created for the Digital Media Environment: A Randomised Controlled Trial Exploring Effects on Girls' Body Satisfaction, Acceptance of Appearance Diversity, and Appearance-Related Internalised Racism," *Body Image* 47 (2023), https://doi.org/10.1016/j .bodyim.2023.08.002.

31. Paloma Escamilla-Fajardo, Mario Alguacil, and Samuel López-Carril, "Incorporating TikTok in Higher Education: Pedagogical Perspectives from a Corporal Expression Sport Sciences Course," *Journal of Hospitality, Leisure, Sport and Tourism Education* 28 (2021): 100302, https://doi.org/10.1016/j.jhlste.2021.100302.

32. Sarah Jerasa and Trevor Boffone, "BookTok 101: TikTok, Digital Literacies, and Out-of-School Reading Practices," *Journal of Adolescent and Adult Literacy* 65, no. 3 (2021): 219–26, https://doi.org/10.1002/jaal.1199.

33. Yu-Ju Lan, Yao-Tin Sung, and Kuo-En Chang, "A Mobile-Device-Supported Peer-Assisted Learning System for Collaborative Early EFL Reading," *Language Learning and Technology* 11, no. 3 (2007): 130–51, https://www .lltjournal.org/item/10125-44121/; Jeremy Roschelle et al., "Scaffolding Group Explanation and Feedback with Handheld Technology: Impact on Students' Mathematics Learning," *Educational Technology Research and Development* 58, no. 4 (2010): 399–419, https://doi.org/10.1007/s11423-009-9142-9; Gustavo Zurita and Miguel Nussbaum, "Computer Supported Collaborative Learning Using Wirelessly Interconnected Handheld Computers," *Computers and Education* 42, no. 3 (2004): 289–314, https://doi.org/10.1016/j.compedu.2003.08.005.

34. Peggy A. Ertmer, Anne Ottenbreit-Leftwich, and Cindy S. York, "Exemplary Technology-Using Teachers: Perceptions of Factors Influencing Success," *Journal of Computing in Teacher Education* 23, no. 2 (2006): 55–61, https://files.eric .ed.gov/fulltext/EJ876918.pdf; Marie-Anne Mundy, Lori Kupczynski, and Rick Kee, "Teacher's Perceptions of Technology Use in the Schools," *SAGE Open* 2, no. 1 (2012), https://journals.sagepub.com/doi/full/10.1177/2158244012440813;

Janell D. Wilson, Charles C. Notar, and Barbara Yunker, "Elementary In-Service Teacher's Use of Computers in the Elementary Classroom," *Journal of Instructional Psychology* 30, no. 4 (2003): 256–64, link.gale.com/apps/doc/A112686159/EAIM?u=anon~26bf0a16&sid=sitemap&xid=901ae932.

35. Shayl F. Griffith et al., "Apps as Learning Tools: A Systematic Review," *Pediatrics* 145, no. 1 (2020), https://doi.org/10.1542/peds.2019-1579.

36. "New Approach Needed to Deliver on Technology's Potential in Schools," OECD web archive, September 15, 2015, https://web-archive.oecd.org/2015-09-16/371671-new-approach-needed-to-deliver-on-technologys-potential-in-schools.htm.

37. Alexis R. Lauricella and Missi Jacobson, "iPads in First Grade Classrooms: Teachers' Intentions and the Realities of Use," *Computers and Education Open* 3 (2022): 100077, https://doi.org/10.1016/j.caeo.2022.100077.

38. Samantha Murphy Kelly, "ChatGPT Passes Exams from Law and Business Schools," CNN Business, January 26, 2023, https://www.cnn.com/2023/01/26/tech/chatgpt-passes-exams/index.html.

39. Phil McRae, "Myth: Blended Learning Is the Next Ed-Tech Revolution—Hype, Harm, and Hope," *Alberta Teachers' Association Magazine* 95, no. 4 (2015): 11–17.

40. Victoria J. Rideout and Michael B. Robb, *The Common Sense Census: Media Use by Kids Age Zero to Eight, 2020* (San Francisco: Common Sense Media, 2020), https://www.commonsensemedia.org/sites/default/files/research/report/2020_zero_to_eight_census_final_web.pdf; *Common Sense Census: Media Use by Tweens and Teens, 2021* (San Francisco: Common Sense Media, 2022), https://www.commonsensemedia.org/sites/default/files/research/report/8-18-census-integrated-report-final-web_0.pdf.

41. Connections Academy, "New Parent Survey Reveals Why K-12 Students Attend Online Schools Full Time," June 24, 2014, https://www.multivu.com/players/English/7067853-connections-academy-parent-survey-why-k-12-students-attend-online-schools-full-time/.

42. David Bickham, Summer Moukalled, and Michael Rich, "Young People's Media Use and Remote Schooling Experiences During the COVID-19 Pandemic" (paper presented at the Technology, Mind and Society, 2021, Conference Proceedings); Rideout et al., *Common Sense Census: Media Use by Tweens and Teens.*

43. Vikki Katz and Victoria Rideout, *Learning at Home While Under-Connected: Lower-Income Families During the COVID-19 Pandemic* (New America Foundation, 2021), https://www.newamerica.org/education-policy/reports/learning-at-home-while-underconnected; Katherine Schaeffer, "What We Know About Online Learning and the Homework Gap Amid the Pandemic," Pew Research Center, October 1, 2021, https://www.pewresearch.org/fact-tank/2021/10/01/what-we-know-about-online-learning-and-the-homework-gap-amid-the-pandemic.

44. Suevon Lee, "On Eve of Boston Public Schools' First Day, One Last Push to Get Students to Come to School," WBUR, September 7, 2022, https://www

.wbur.org/news/2022/09/07/boston-back-to-school-absenteeism; Bianca Vázquez Toness, "One in Five Boston Public School Children May Be Virtual Dropouts," *Boston Globe*, May 23, 2020, https://www.bostonglobe.com/2020 /05/23/metro/more-than-one-five-boston-public-school-children-may-be -virtual-dropouts.

45. Marshall McLuhan, *Understanding Media: The Extensions of Man* (Cambridge, MA: MIT Press, 1964).
46. Albert Bandura, *Social Learning Theory* (Englewood Cliffs: Prentice Hall, 1977).
47. McLuhan, *Understanding Media*.
48. George Santayana, *The Life of Reason: Or, The Phases of Human Progress* (New York: Charles Scribner's Sons, 1906), 284.
49. Kimberly M. Thompson and Fumie Yokota, "Violence, Sex, and Profanity in Films: Correlation of Movie Ratings with Content," *Medscape General Medicine* 6, no. 3 (2004): 3, https://www.ncbi.nlm.nih.gov/pmc/articles/PMC1435631/.

Chapter 7: Insidious Influencers, Consuming Passions

1. Kristen Elmore, Tracy M. Scull, and Janis B. Kupersmidt, "Media as a 'Super Peer': How Adolescents Interpret Media Messages Predicts their Perception of Alcohol and Tobacco Use Norms," *Journal of Youth and Adolescence* 46, no. 2 (2017): 376–87, https://doi.org/10.1007/s10964-016-0609-9.
2. Eric Stice and Heather E. Shaw, "Adverse Effects of the Media Portrayed Thin-Ideal on Women and Linkages to Bulimic Symptomatology," *Journal of Social and Clinical Psychology* 13, no. 3 (1994): 288–308, https://doi.org/10.1521 /jscp.1994.13.3.288.
3. Jean Kilbourne, *Can't Buy My Love: How Advertising Changes the Way We Think and Feel* (New York: Simon and Schuster, 1999), 90.
4. Kilbourne, *Can't Buy My Love*, 90–91.
5. Rachael Berman, "Depictions, Perceptions, and Harm: An Interview with Media Critic Jean Kilbourne," *TheHumanist.com*, August 3, 2017, https:// thehumanist.com/features/interviews/depictions-perceptions-harm-interview -media-critic-jean-kilbourne.
6. Jean Piaget and Barbel Inhelder, *The Psychology of the Child* (New York: Basic Books, 1969).
7. Piaget and Inhelder, *The Psychology of the Child*.
8. Dafna Lemish, "Viewers in Diapers: The Early Development of Television Viewing," in *Natural Audiences: Qualitative Research of Media Uses and Effects*, edited by T. R. Lindlof (Norwood, NJ: Ablex Publishing Corp, 1987), 33–57; Patti M. Valkenburg and Joanne Cantor, "The Development of a Child into a Consumer," *Journal of Applied Developmental Psychology* 22, no. 1 (2001): 61–72, https://doi.org/10.1016/S0193-3973(00)00066-6.
9. Valkenburg and Cantor, "The Development of a Child."
10. Piaget and Inhelder, *The Psychology of the Child*.

11. Dan S. Acuff, *What Kids Buy and Why: The Psychology of Marketing to Kids*, edited by Robert H. Reiher (New York: Free Press, 1997); Heather L. Kirkorian, Ellen A. Wartella, and Daniel R. Anderson, "Media and Young Children's Learning," *The Future of Children* 18, no. 1 (2008): 39–61, https://doi.org/10.1353/foc.0 .0002; Dafna Lemish, *Children and Television: A Global Perspective* (Malden, MA: Blackwell Publishing, 2007).

12. Holly K. M. Henry and Dina L. G. Borzekowski, "The Nag Factor: A Mixed-Methodology Study in the US of Young Children's Requests for Advertised Products," *Journal of Children and Media* 5, no. 3 (2011): 298–317, https://doi.org /10.1080/17482798.2011.584380.

13. Jean Kilbourne, *Can't Buy My Love: How Advertising Changes the Way We Think and Feel* (New York: Simon and Schuster, 2000), 27.

14. Piaget and Inhelder, *The Psychology of the Child*.

15. Brian Wilcox et al., *Report of the APA Task Force on Advertising and Children: Psychological Issues in the Increasing Commercialization of Childhood* (Washington, DC: APA, 2004), https://www.apa.org/pi/families/resources/advertising -children.pdf.

16. MediaSmarts website, Canada's Centre for Digital Media Literacy, https:// mediasmarts.ca.

17. Media Power Youth website, https://mediapoweryouth.org.

18. E. B. White, "Removals," in *One Man's Meat*, 13th ed. (Thomaston, ME: Tilbury House, 2003).

19. Marshall McLuhan, *Understanding Media: The Extensions of Man* (Cambridge, MA: MIT Press, 1964), 25.

20. Matteo Cinelli et al., "The Echo Chamber Effect on Social Media," *Proceedings of the National Academy of Sciences* 118, no. 9 (2021): e2023301118, https://doi.org /10.1073/pnas.2023301118.

21. Piaget and Inhelder, *The Psychology of the Child*.

22. Sandra L. Calvert, "Children as Consumers: Advertising and Marketing," *The Future of Children* 18, no. 1 (2008): 205–34, https://doi.org/10.1353/foc.0.0001.

23. Trudy Hui Hui Chua and Leanne Chang, "Follow Me and Like My Beautiful Selfies: Singapore Teenage Girls' Engagement in Self-Presentation and Peer Comparison on Social Media," *Computers in Human Behavior* 55 (2016): 190–97, https://doi.org/10.1016/j.chb.2015.09.011; Giovanna Mascheroni, Jane Vincent, and Estefanía Jimenez, "'Girls Are Addicted to Likes So They Post Semi-Naked Selfies': Peer Mediation, Normativity, and the Construction of Identity Online," *Cyberpsychology: Journal of Psychosocial Research on Cyberspace* 9, no. 1 (2015): 5, https://doi.org/10.5817/CP2015-1-5.

Chapter 8: A More Perfect Me

1. Eric Stice and H. E. Shaw, "Adverse Effects of the Media Portrayed Thin-Ideal on Women and Linkages to Bulimic Symptomatology," *Journal of Social and*

Clinical Psychology 13, no. 3 (1994): 288–308, https://doi.org/10.1521/jscp.1994.13 .3.288.

2. Sydney M. Hartman-Munick et al., "Association of the Covid-19 Pandemic with Adolescent and Young Adult Eating Disorder Care Volume," *JAMA Pediatrics* 176, no. 12 (2022): 1225–32, https://doi.org/10.1001/jamapediatrics .2022.4346; Anna C. Schlissel et al., "Anorexia Nervosa and the Covid-19 Pandemic Among Young People: A Scoping Review," *Journal of Eating Disorders* 11, no. 1 (2023): 122, https://doi.org/10.1186/s40337-023-00843-7.

3. Jacinthe Dion et al., "Correlates of Body Dissatisfaction in Children," *The Journal of Pediatrics* 171 (2016): 202–07, https://doi.org/10.1016/j.jpeds.2015.12.045.

4. Sharon Hayes and Stacey Tantleff-Dunn, "Am I Too Fat to Be a Princess? Examining the Effects of Popular Children's Media on Young Girls' Body Image," *British Journal of Developmental Psychology* 28, no. 2 (2010): 413–26, http:// dx.doi.org/10.1348/026151009X424240; Professional Association for Childcare and Early Years, "Children as Young as 3 Unhappy with Their Bodies," August 31, 2016, https://www.pacey.org.uk/news-and-views/news/archive /2016-news/august-2016/children-as-young-as-3-unhappy-with-their-bodies.

5. Stephanie R. Damiano et al., "Dietary Restraint of 5-Year-Old Girls: Associations with Internalization of the Thin Ideal and Maternal, Media, and Peer Influences," *International Journal of Eating Disorders* 48, no. 8 (2015): 1166–69, https://doi.org/10.1002/eat.22432.

6. Amy I. Nathanson and Renée A. Botta, "Shaping the Effects of Television on Adolescents' Body Image Disturbance: The Role of Parental Mediation," *Communication Research* 30, no. 3 (2003): 304–31, https://doi.org/10.1177 /0093650203030003003.

7. Duane Hargreaves and Marika Tiggemann, "Longer-Term Implications of Responsiveness to 'Thin-Ideal' Television: Support for a Cumulative Hypothesis of Body Image Disturbance?" *European Eating Disorders Review* 11, no. 6 (2003): 465–77, https://doi.org/10.1002/erv.509; Rachel F. Rodgers and Tiffany Melioli, "The Relationship Between Body Image Concerns, Eating Disorders, and Internet Use, Part I: A Review of Empirical Support," *Adolescent Research Review* 1, no. 2 (2016): 95–119, https://doi.org/10.1007/s40894-015 -0016-6; Eric Stice et al., "Relation of Media Exposure to Eating Disorder Symptomatology: An Examination of Mediating Mechanisms," *Journal of Abnormal Psychology* 103, no. 4 (1994): 836–40, https://doi.org/10.1037/0021 -843X.103.4.836.

8. Natalie Angier, "Drugs, Sports, Body Image, and G.I. Joe," *New York Times*, December 22, 1998, https://www.nytimes.com/1998/12/22/science/drugs -sports-body-image-and-gi-joe.html.

9. Harrison G. Pope, Katharine A. Phillips, and Roberto Olivardia, *The Adonis Complex: How to Identify, Treat, and Prevent Body Obsession in Men and Boys* (New York: Free Press, 2002).

10. Jason M. Nagata et al., "Muscle-Building Behaviors from Adolescence to Emerging Adulthood: A Prospective Cohort Study," *Preventive Medicine Reports* 27 (2022): 101778, https://doi.org/10.1016/j.pmedr.2022.101778.

11. Allison Lin et al., "Dry Scooping and Other Dangerous Pre-Workout Consumption Methods: A Quantitative Analysis," *Pediatrics* 149, no. 1, Meeting Abstracts, (February 2022): 204, https://publications.aap.org/pediatrics/article/149/1%20Meeting%20Abstracts%20February%202022/204/185966/Dry-Scooping-and-Other-Dangerous-Pre-workout.

12. Lin et al., "Dry Scooping."

13. Kyle T. Ganson et al., "Prevalence and Correlates of Dry Scooping: Results from the Canadian Study of Adolescent Health Behaviors," *Eating Behaviors* 48 (2023): 101705, https://doi.org/10.1016/j.eatbeh.2023.101705.

14. Dale Duncan, "Dry Scooping: A Risky Dietary Practice Common Among Adolescents and Young Adults," *Neuroscience News*, February 10, 2023, https://neurosciencenews.com/dry-scooping-health-22482/#:~:text=Analyzing%20data%20from%20over%202%2C700,times%20over%20that%20time%20period.

15. The Dove Self-Esteem Project, *Girls and Beauty Confidence: The Global Report*, 2017, https://assets.unilever.com/files/92ui5egz/production/43439da93d53ada63d6e2bac732657040a27e770.pdf/dove-girls-beauty-confidence-report-infographic.pdf.

16. The Dove Self-Esteem Project, *Girls and Beauty Confidence*.

17. S. Leung et al., *Youth Survey Report 2022*, Mission Australia (Sydney, NSW: Mission Australia, 2022), http://hdl.voced.edu.au/10707/651728.

18. Reuters Staff, "Apple Sells 1 Million New iPhones," *Reuters*, July 14, 2008, https://www.reuters.com/article/business-apple-iphone-dc-idITN1445985820080714.

19. Debbie Ging and Sarah Garvey, "'Written in These Scars Are the Stories I Can't Explain': A Content Analysis of Pro-Ana and Thinspiration Image Sharing on Instagram," *New Media and Society* 20, no. 3 (2018): 1181–200, https://doi.org/10.1177/1461444816687288.

20. Carolyn Costin, "Thin Commandments," Eatingdisorders.com, https://eatingdisorders.com/specific/thin-commandments.

21. Ging and Garvey, "'Written in These Scars.'"

22. Ging and Garvey, "'Written in These Scars.'"

23. Atte Oksanen et al., "Pro-Anorexia and Anti-Pro-Anorexia Videos on YouTube: Sentiment Analysis of User Responses," *Journal of Medical Internet Research* 17, no. 11 (2015): e256, https://doi.org/10.2196/jmir.5007.

24. Georgia Wells, Jeff Horwitz, and Deepa Seetharaman, "Facebook Knows Instagram Is Toxic for Teen Girls, Company Documents Show," *The Wall Street Journal*, September 14, 2021, https://www.wsj.com/articles/facebook-knows-instagram-is-toxic-for-teen-girls-company-documents-show-11631620739?mod=hp_lead_pos7&mod=article_inline.

25. *60 Minutes*, "Whistleblower: Facebook Research Showed Instagram Is Worse

for Teenagers Than Other Social Media," YouTube video, October 3, 2021, 3:50, https://www.youtube.com/watch?v=oT2sMDCW_2k.

26. Bobby Allyn, "Here Are 4 Key Points from the Facebook Whistleblower's Testimony on Capitol Hill," NPR, October 5, 2021, https://www.npr.org/2021 /10/05/1043377310/facebook-whistleblower-frances-haugen-congress.

27. Alyssa N. Saiphoo and Zahra Vahedi, "A Meta-Analytic Review of the Relationship Between Social Media Use and Body Image Disturbance," *Computers in Human Behavior* 101 (2019): 259–75, https://doi.org/10.1016/j.chb .2019.07.028.

28. Saiphoo and Vahedi, "A Meta-Analytic Review."

29. Jasmine Fardouly et al., "Social Comparisons on Social Media: The Impact of Facebook on Young Women's Body Image Concerns and Mood," *Body Image* 13 (2015): 38–45, https://doi.org/10.1016/j.bodyim.2014.12.002; Annalise G. Mabe, K. Jean Forney, and Pamela K. Keel, "Do You 'Like' My Photo? Facebook Use Maintains Eating Disorder Risk," *International Journal of Eating Disorders* 47, no. 5 (2014): 516–23, https://doi.org/10.1002/eat.22254.

30. Saiphoo and Vahedi, "A Meta-Analytic Review."

31. Siân A. McLean, Susan J. Paxton, and Eleanor H. Wertheim, "Does Media Literacy Mitigate Risk for Reduced Body Satisfaction Following Exposure to Thin-Ideal Media?" *Journal of Youth and Adolescence* 45, no. 8 (2016): 1678–95, https://doi.org/10.1007/s10964-016-0440-3; "The Role of Media Literacy in Body Dissatisfaction and Disordered Eating: A Systematic Review," *Body Image* 19 (2016): 9–23, https://doi.org/10.1016/j.bodyim.2016.08.002; Susan J. Paxton, Siân A. McLean, and Rachel F. Rodgers, "'My Critical Filter Buffers Your App Filter': Social Media Literacy as a Protective Factor for Body Image," *Body Image* 40 (2022): 158–64, https://doi.org/10.1016/j.bodyim.2021 .12.009.

32. Marisa Minadeo and Lizzy Pope, "Weight-Normative Messaging Predominates on TikTok—a Qualitative Content Analysis," *PLOS ONE* 17, no. 11 (2022): e0267997, https://doi.org/10.1371/journal.pone.0267997; Emily A. Vogels, Risa Gelles-Watnick, and Navid Massarat, "Teens, Social Media, and Technology 2022," Pew Research Center, August 10, 2022, https://www .pewresearch.org/internet/2022/08/10/teens-social-media-and-technology -2022.

33. Minadeo and Pope, "Weight-Normative Messaging"; Tracy L. Tylka et al., "The Weight-Inclusive Versus Weight-Normative Approach to Health: Evaluating the Evidence for Prioritizing Well-Being over Weight Loss," *Journal of Obesity* 2014 (2014): 983495, https://doi.org/10.1155/2014/983495.

34. Center for Countering Digital Hate, *AI and Eating Disorders: How Generative AI Is Enabling Users to Generate Harmful Eating Disorder Content*, August 2023, https://counterhate.com/wp-content/uploads/2023/08/230705-AI-and-Eating -Disorders-REPORT.pdf.

Chapter 9: Wirelessly Wired

1. "Smoking and Tobacco Use: Diseases and Death," Centers for Disease Control and Prevention, last reviewed July 29, 2022, https://www.cdc.gov/tobacco /data_statistics/fact_sheets/fast_facts/diseases-and-death.html.

2. "Youth and Tobacco Use," Centers for Disease Control and Prevention, last reviewed November 10, 2022, https://www.cdc.gov/tobacco/data_statistics /fact_sheets/youth_data/tobacco_use/index.htm.

3. Martha N. Gardner and Allan M. Brandt, "'The Doctors' Choice Is America's Choice': The Physician in US Cigarette Advertisements, 1930–1953," *American Journal of Public Health* 96, no. 2 (2006): 222–32, https://doi.org/10.2105/ajph .2005.066654.

4. "Tobacco Use Among Children and Teens," American Lung Association, last updated May 31, 2023, https://www.lung.org/quit-smoking/smoking-facts /tobacco-use-among-children.

5. Matthew C. Farrelly et al., "The Influence of the National Truth® Campaign on Smoking Initiation," *American Journal of Preventive Medicine* 36, no. 5 (2009): 379–84, https://doi.org/10.1016/j.amepre.2009.01.019; David R. Holtgrave et al., "Cost–Utility Analysis of the National Truth® Campaign to Prevent Youth Smoking," *American Journal of Preventive Medicine* 36, no. 5 (2009): 385–88, https://doi.org/10.1016/j.amepre.2009.01.020.

6. "Tobacco Industry Marketing," Centers for Disease Control and Prevention, last reviewed May 14, 2021, https://www.cdc.gov/tobacco/data_statistics/fact _sheets/tobacco_industry/marketing/index.htm.

7. "Youth and Tobacco Use," CDC.

8. Leo Burnett, advertisement, "Now More to Like Than Ever: Marked Improvement in Marlboro Filter Does Not Disturb Famous Marlboro Flavor," August 19, 1958, https://www.industrydocuments.ucsf.edu/tobacco/docs/#id =xkhn0117.

9. Unknown, "Come to Marlboro Country," 1981, https://www.industry documents.ucsf.edu/tobacco/docs/#id=ngbk0022.

10. Dale Carnegie, *How to Win Friends and Influence People* (New York: Pocket Books, 1982), 14, retrieved from https://archive.org/details /howtowinfriendsi00carn/page/14/mode/2up?q="pride+and+vanity".

11. Eunice Park-Lee et al., "Tobacco Product Use Among Middle and High School Students—United States, 2022," *Morbidity and Mortality Weekly Report* 71, no. 45 (2022): 1429–35, http://dx.doi.org/10.15585/mmwr.mm7145a1.

12. Maria Cooper et al., "Notes from the Field: E-Cigarette Use among Middle and High School Students—United States, 2022," *Morbidity and Mortality Weekly Report* 71, no. 40 (2022): 1283–85, http://dx.doi.org/10.15585/mmwr .mm7140a3.

13. National Center for Chronic Disease Prevention and Health Promotion (US) Office on Smoking and Health, *Preventing Tobacco Use Among Youth and Young*

Adults: A Report of the Surgeon General (CDC, 2012), https://www.ncbi.nlm.nih
.gov/books/NBK99237/.

14. Annemarie Charlesworth and Stanton A. Glantz, "Smoking in the Movies
Increases Adolescent Smoking: A Review," *Pediatrics* 116, no. 6 (2005): 1516–28,
https://doi.org/10.1542/peds.2005-0141.

15. Michael A. Tynan et al., "Tobacco Use in Top-Grossing Movies—United States,
2010–2018," *Morbidity and Mortality Weekly Rep* 68, no. 43 (2019): 974–78, http://
dx.doi.org/10.15585/mmwr.mm6843a4.

16. Smoke Free Media, https://smokefreemedia.ucsf.edu.

17. Nada Adibah et al., *Smoking in Movies: 2020* (NORC at the University of
Chicago, 2021), https://truthinitiative.org/sites/default/files/media/files/2022
/01/NORC%20report_v6.pdf.

18. Digital Wellness Lab at Boston Children's Hospital, "Alcohol, Tobacco, and
Drugs," https://digitalwellnesslab.org/parents/alcohol-tobacco-and-drugs.

19. Lindsay M. Squeglia, Joanna Jacobus, and Susan F. Tapert, "The Influence
of Substance Use on Adolescent Brain Development," *Clinical EEG and
Neuroscience* 40, no. 1 (2009): 31–38, https://doi.org/10.1177/155005940904
000110.

20. National Highway Traffic Safety Administration, "Drunk Driving," https://
www.nhtsa.gov/risky-driving/drunk-driving#age-5056.

21. National Institute on Alcohol Abuse and Alcoholism, "Get the Facts About
Underage Drinking," updated July 2023, https://www.niaaa.nih.gov
/publications/brochures-and-fact-sheets/underage-drinking.

22. Raimee H. Eck et al., "Company-Specific Revenues from Underage Drinking,"
Journal of Studies on Alcohol and Drugs 82, no. 3 (2021): 368–76, https://doi.org/10
.15288/jsad.2021.82.368.

23. Kimberly M. Thompson and Fumie Yokota, "Depiction of Alcohol, Tobacco,
and Other Substances in G-Rated Animated Feature Films," *Pediatrics* 107,
no. 6 (2001): 1369–74, https://doi.org/10.1542/peds.107.6.1369.

24. Thompson and Yokota, "Depiction of Alcohol."

25. Cristel Antonia Russell et al., "Television's Cultivation of American Adolescents'
Beliefs About Alcohol and the Moderating Role of Trait Reactance," *Journal of
Children and Media* 8, no. 1 (2014): 5–22, https://doi.org/10.1080/17482798.2014
.863475.

26. Janis B. Kupersmidt, Tracy M. Scull, and Erica Weintraub Austin, "Media
Literacy Education for Elementary School Substance Use Prevention: Study of
Media Detective," *Pediatrics* 126, no. 3 (2010): 525–31, https://doi.org/10.1542
/peds.2010-0068.

27. Christine A. Edwards et al., "Out of the Smokescreen: Does an Anti-Smoking
Advertisement Affect Young Women's Perception of Smoking in Movies and
Their Intention to Smoke?" *Tobacco Control* 13, no. 3 (2004): 277, https://doi.org
/10.1136/tc.2003.005280; Cornelia Pechmann and Chuan-Fong Shih, "Smoking

Scenes in Movies and Antismoking Advertisements Before Movies: Effects on Youth," *Journal of Marketing* 63, no. 3 (1999): 1–13, https://doi.org/10.1177/002224299906300301.

28. Eunice Park-Lee et al., "Tobacco Product Use Among Middle and High School Students—United States, 2022," *Morbidity and Mortality Weekly Report* 71, no. 45 (2022): 1429–35, http://dx.doi.org/10.15585/mmwr.mm7145a1.

29. Victor C. Strasburger and The Council on Communications and Media, "Children, Adolescents, Substance Abuse, and the Media," *Pediatrics* 126, no. 4 (2010): 791–99, https://doi.org/10.1542/peds.2010-1635.

30. Jie Guo et al., "Developmental Relationships Between Adolescent Substance Use and Risky Sexual Behavior in Young Adulthood," *Journal of Adolescent Health* 31, no. 4 (2002): 354–62, https://doi.org/10.1016/S1054-139X(02)00402-0.

31. Sandra C. Jones, "Alcohol-Branded Merchandise Ownership and Drinking," *Pediatrics* 137, no. 5 (2016): e20153970, https://doi.org/10.1542/peds.2015-3970.

Chapter 10: Lessons in Fear and Loathing

1. Christina Pazzanese, "U.S. Hurtles Toward New Record for Mass Shootings," *Harvard Gazette*, October 31, 2023, https://news.harvard.edu/gazette/story/2023/10/u-s-hurtles-toward-new-record-for-mass-shootings-says-atf-director/; BBC News, "How Many US Mass Shootings Have There Been in 2023?," October 26, 2023, https://www.bbc.com/news/world-us-canada-41488081.

2. Jason E. Goldstick, Rebecca M. Cunningham, and Patrick M. Carter, "Current Causes of Death in Children and Adolescents in the United States," *New England Journal of Medicine* 386, no. 20 (2022): 1955–56, https://doi.org/10.1056/NEJMc2201761.

3. Melonie Heron, "Deaths: Leading Causes for 2019," *National Vital Statistics Reports* 70, no. 9 (July 2021): 1–114, https://dx.doi.org/10.15620/cdc:107021.

4. Albert Bandura, Dorothea Ross, and Sheila A. Ross, "Imitation of Film-Mediated Aggressive Models," *Journal of Abnormal and Social Psychology* 66, no. 1 (1963): 3–11, https://doi.org/10.1037/h0048687.

5. Albert Bandura, *Social Learning Theory* (Englewood Cliffs, NJ: Prentice Hall, 1977).

6. Jennifer E. Lansford, "Aggression: Revisiting Bandura's Bobo Doll Studies," in *Developmental Psychology: Revisiting the Classic Studies*, edited by Alan Slater and Paul C. Quinn (London: SAGE, 2012), 176–90.

7. Leonard D. Eron, "Relationship of TV Viewing Habits and Aggressive Behavior in Children," *Journal of Abnormal and Social Psychology* 67, no. 2 (1963): 193–96, https://doi.org/10.1037/h0043794.

8. Monroe M. Lefkowitz et al., *Growing Up to Be Violent: A Longitudinal Study of the Development of Aggression* (New York: Pergamon Press, 1977).

9. Lefkowitz et al., *Growing Up to Be Violent*.

10. L. Rowell Huesmann et al., "Stability of Aggression over Time and

Generations," *Developmental Psychology* 20, no. 6 (1984): 1120–34, https://doi.org /10.1037/0012-1649.20.6.1120.

11. Brad J. Bushman and L. Rowell Huesmann, "Effects of Televised Violence on Aggression," in *Handbook of Children and the Media*, edited by Dorthy Singer and Jerome Singer (Thousand Oaks, CA: Sage Publications, 2001), 234.

12. Craig A. Anderson and Brad J. Bushman, "Human Aggression," *Annual Review of Psychology* 53, no. 1 (2002): 27–51, https://doi.org/10.1146/annurev.psych.53 .100901.135231; "Media Violence and the General Aggression Model," *Journal of Social Issues* 74, no. 2 (2018): 386–413, https://doi.org/10.1111/josi.12275.

13. Sumiko Iwao, Ithiel de Sola Pool, and Shigeru Hagiwara, "Japanese and US Media: Some Cross-Cultural Insights into TV Violence," *Journal of Communication* 31, no. 2 (1981): 28–36, https://doi.org/10.1111/j.1460-2466.1981.tb01225.x.

14. Nicole Martins and Karyn Riddle, "Reassessing the Risks: An Updated Content Analysis of Violence on U.S. Children's Primetime Television," *Journal of Children and Media* 16, no. 3 (2022): 368–86, https://doi.org/10.1080/17482798 .2021.1985548.

15. Alessandro Gabbiadini et al., "Acting Like a Tough Guy: Violent-Sexist Video Games, Identification with Game Characters, Masculine Beliefs, and Empathy for Female Violence Victims," *PLOS ONE* 11, no. 4 (2016): e0152121, https://doi .org/10.1371/journal.pone.0152121; Silvia Galdi and Francesca Guizzo, "Media-Induced Sexual Harassment: The Routes from Sexually Objectifying Media to Sexual Harassment," *Sex Roles* 84, no. 11 (2021): 645–69, https://doi.org/10 .1007/s11199-020-01196-0; Steven J. Kirsh, "Cartoon Violence and Aggression in Youth," *Aggression and Violent Behavior* 11, no. 6 (2006): 547–57, https://doi.org /10.1016/j.avb.2005.10.002.

16. Peter Fischer et al., "The Effects of Risk-Glorifying Media Exposure on Risk-Positive Cognitions, Emotions, and Behaviors: A Meta-Analytic Review," *Psychological Bulletin* 137, no. 3 (2011): 367–90, https://doi.org/10.1037 /a0022267; Joan Tucker, Jeremy Miles, and Elizabeth D'Amico, "Cross-Lagged Associations Between Substance Use-Related Media Exposure and Alcohol Use During Middle School," *Journal of Adolescent Health* 53, no. 4 (2013): 460–64, https://doi.org/10.1016/j.jadohealth.2013.05.005.

17. Galdi and Guizzo, "Media-Induced Sexual Harassment: The Routes from Sexually Objectifying Media to Sexual Harassment"; Kirsh, "Cartoon Violence and Aggression in Youth"; Nicole Martins and Karyn Riddle, "Reassessing the Risks: An Updated Content Analysis of Violence on U.S. Children's Primetime Television," *Journal of Children and Media* 16, no. 3 (2022): 368–86, https://doi .org/10.1080/17482798.2021.1985548.

18. Yael Shany and Yaacov B. Yablon, "The Contribution of Face-to-Face and Embedded Mediation to Early Childhood Aggression After Watching Violent Media Content," *Psychology of Violence* 11, no. 6 (2021), 519–28, https://doi.org /10.1037/vio0000385; Jennifer Ruh Linder and Nicole E. Werner, "Relationally

Aggressive Media Exposure and Children's Normative Beliefs: Does Parental Mediation Matter?" *Family Relations* 61, no. 3 (July 2012): 488–500, https://doi .org/10.1111/j.1741-3729.2012.00707.x.

19. Justin H. Chang and Brad J. Bushman, "Effect of Exposure to Gun Violence in Video Games on Children's Dangerous Behavior with Real Guns: A Randomized Clinical Trial," *JAMA Network Open* 2, no. 5 (2019): e194319, https://doi.org/10.1001/jamanetworkopen.2019.4319; Kelly P. Dillon and Brad J. Bushman, "Effects of Exposure to Gun Violence in Movies on Children's Interest in Real Guns," *JAMA Pediatrics* 171, no. 11 (2017): 1057–62, https://doi .org/10.1001/jamapediatrics.2017.2229.

20. Patrick E. Jamieson and Daniel Romer, "The Association Between the Rise of Gun Violence in Popular US Primetime Television Dramas and Homicides Attributable to Firearms, 2000–2018," *PLOS ONE* 16, no. 3 (2021): e0247780, https://doi.org/10.1371/journal.pone.0247780.

21. Steven Stack, "Contributing Factors to Suicide: Political, Social, Cultural, and Economic," *Preventive Medicine* 152 (2021): 106498, https://doi.org/10.1016/j .ypmed.2021.106498.

22. John Gramlich, "What the Data Says About Gun Deaths in the U.S.," Pew Research Center, updated April 26, 2023, https://pewrsr.ch/448q4hU.

23. Corinne David-Ferdon et al., "Vital Signs: Prevalence of Multiple Forms of Violence and Increased Health Risk Behaviors and Conditions among Youths—United States, 2019," *Morbidity and Mortality Weekly Report* 70, no. 5 (2021): 167–73, https://doi.org/10.15585/mmwr.mm7005a4; Forrest Stuart, "Code of the Tweet: Urban Gang Violence in the Social Media Age," *Social Problems* 67, no. 2 (2020): 191–207, https://doi.org/10.1093/socpro/spz010.

24. Jih-Hsuan Lin, "Do Video Games Exert Stronger Effects on Aggression Than Film? The Role of Media Interactivity and Identification on the Association of Violent Content and Aggressive Outcomes," *Computers in Human Behavior* 29, no. 3 (2013): 535–43, https://doi.org/10.1016/j.chb.2012.11.001.

25. Douglas A. Gentile, Christopher L. Groves, and Ronald J. Gentile, "The General Learning Model: Unveiling the Teaching Potential of Video Games," in *Learning by Playing: Video Gaming in Education*, edited by Fran C. Blumberg, 121–42 (Oxford: Oxford University Press, 2014), 134.

26. Daphne Bavelier and C. Shawn Green, "The Cognitive Neuroscience of Video Games," in *Digital Media: Transformations in Human Communication*, edited by Paul Messaris and Lee Humphreys (New York: Peter Lang Publishing, 2007), 211–24.

27. James C. Rosser et al., "The Impact of Video Games on Training Surgeons in the 21st Century," *Arch Surg* 142, no. 2 (February 2007): 181–6, https://doi.org /10.1001/archsurg.142.2.181.

28. James Alex Bonus, Alanna Peebles, and Karyn Riddle, "The Influence of Violent Video Game Enjoyment on Hostile Attributions," *Computers in Human*

Behavior 52 (2015): 472–83, https://doi.org/10.1016/j.chb.2015.05.044; Youssef Hasan, Laurent Begue, Michael Scharkow, and Brad J. Bushman, "The More You Play, the More Aggressive You Become: A Long-Term Experimental Study of Cumulative Violent Video Game Effects on Hostile Expectations and Aggressive Behavior," *Journal of Experimental Social Psychology* 49, no. 2 (2013): 224–27, https://doi.org/10.1016/j.jesp.2012.10.016.

29. Jordan Sirani, "The 10 Best-Selling Video Games of All Time," IGN, updated October 16, 2023, https://www.ign.com/articles/best-selling-video-games-of -all-time-grand-theft-auto-minecraft-tetris.

30. Craig A. Anderson and Karen E. Dill, "Video Games and Aggressive Thoughts, Feelings, and Behavior in the Laboratory and in Life," *Journal of Personality and Social Psychology* 78, no. 4 (2000): 772–90, https://www.apa.org /pubs/journals/releases/psp784772.pdf; Douglas A. Gentile, Sarah Coyne, and David A. Walsh, "Media Violence, Physical Aggression, and Relational Aggression in School Age Children: A Short-Term Longitudinal Study," *Aggressive Behavior* 37, no. 2 (2011): 193–206, https://doi.org/10.1002/ab.20380.

31. Zhaojun Teng et al., "Violent Video Game Exposure and (Cyber)Bullying Perpetration Among Chinese Youth: The Moderating Role of Trait Aggression and Moral Identity," *Computers in Human Behavior* 104 (2020): 106193, https:// doi.org/10.1016/j.chb.2019.106193.

32. Leonard Berkowitz, "Some Effects of Thoughts on Anti- and Prosocial Influences of Media Events: A Cognitive-Neoassociation Analysis," *Psychological Bulletin* 95, no. 3 (May 1984): 410–27, https://doi.org/10.1037/0033 -2909.95.3.410.

33. Nelly Alia-Klein et al., "Reactions to Media Violence: It's in the Brain of the Beholder," *PLOS ONE* 9, no. 9 (2014): e107260, https://doi.org/10.1371/journal .pone.0107260.

34. Ian Hawkins et al., "Extensions of the Proteus Effect on Intergroup Aggression in the Real World," *Psychology of Popular Media* 10, no. 4 (2021): 478–87, https:// doi.org/10.1037/ppm0000307.

35. Johanna Burkhardt and Wolfgang Lenhard, "A Meta-Analysis on the Longitudinal, Age-Dependent Effects of Violent Video Games on Aggression," *Media Psychology* 25, no. 3 (2022): 499–512, https://doi.org/10.1080/15213269 .2021.1980729.

36. Anna T. Prescott, James D. Sargent, and Jay G. Hull, "Metaanalysis of the Relationship Between Violent Video Game Play and Physical Aggression over Time," *Proceedings of the National Academy of Sciences* 115, no. 40 (2018): 9882–88, https://doi.org/10.1073/pnas.1611617114.

37. Anat Shoshani, and Maya Krauskopf, "The Fortnite Social Paradox: The Effects of Violent-Cooperative Multi-Player Video Games on Children's Basic Psychological Needs and Prosocial Behavior," *Computers in Human Behavior* 116 (2021): 106641, https://doi.org/10.1016/j.chb.2020.106641.

38. Zhaojun Teng et al., "Violent Video Game Exposure and (Cyber)Bullying Perpetration Among Chinese Youth: The Moderating Role of Trait Aggression and Moral Identity," *Computers in Human Behavior* 104 (2020): 106193, https://doi.org/10.1016/j.chb.2019.106193.

39. Dave Grossman and Gloria DeGaetano, *Stop Teaching Our Kids to Kill: A Call to Action Against TV, Movie, and Video Game Violence*, revised and updated edition (New York: Harmony Books, 2014).

40. S. L. A. Marshall, *Men Against Fire: The Problem of Battle Command* (Norman, OK: University of Oklahoma Press, 1947).

41. Brad J. Bushman, "'Boom, Headshot!': Violent First-Person Shooter (FPS) Video Games That Reward Headshots Train Individuals to Aim for the Head When Shooting a Realistic Firearm," *Aggressive Behavior* 45, no. 1 (2019): 33–41, https://doi.org/10.1002/ab.21794.

42. Grossman and DeGaetano, *Stop Teaching Our Kids to Kill*.

43. Joe Nocera, "Unlearning Gun Violence," *New York Times*, November 11, 2013, https://www.nytimes.com/2013/11/12/opinion/nocera-unlearning-gun-violence.html.

44. Brad J. Bushman et al., "Gun Violence Trends in Movies," *Pediatrics* 132, no. 6 (2013): 1014–18, https://doi.org/10.1542/peds.2013-1600.

45. Resolve S.168, 188th (2013–2014), The 193rd General Court of the Commonwealth of Massachusetts (2013), https://malegislature.gov/Bills/188/Senate/S168.

46. Nicholas L. Carnagey and Craig A. Anderson, "The Effects of Reward and Punishment in Violent Video Games on Aggressive Affect, Cognition, and Behavior," *Psychological Science* 16, no. 11 (2005): 882–89, https://doi.org/10.1111/j.1467-9280.2005.01632.x.

47. Andrew Webster, "'Grand Theft Auto V' Sets Record by Earning $1 Billion in Just Three Days," *The Verge*, September 20, 2013, https://www.theverge.com/2013/9/20/4752458/grand-theft-auto-v-earns-one-billion-in-three-days.

48. University of California Santa Barbara, *National Television Violence Study*, edited by M. Seawell (Thousand Oaks, CA: Sage, 1997); *National Television Violence Study Volume 2*, edited by M. Seawell (Thousand Oaks, CA: Sage, 1998); *National Television Violence Study Volume 3* (Thousand Oaks, CA: Sage, 1998).

49. Jean Piaget, *The Construction of Reality in the Child* (New York: Basic Books, 1954).

50. Victor C. Strasburger, Amy B. Jordan, and Ed Donnerstein, "Health Effects of Media on Children and Adolescents," *Pediatrics* 125, no. 4 (2010): 756–67, https://doi.org/10.1542/peds.2009-2563; Lauren Hale et al., "Youth Screen Media Habits and Sleep: Sleep-Friendly Screen Behavior Recommendations for Clinicians, Educators, and Parents," *Child and Adolescent Psychiatric Clinics of North America* 27, no. 2 (April 2018): 229–45, https://doi.org/10.1016/j.chc.2017.11.014.

51. Fumie Yokota and Kimberly M. Thompson, "Violence in G-Rated Animated Films," *JAMA: The Journal of the American Medical Association* 283, no. 20 (2000): 2716–20, https://doi.org/10.1001/jama.283.20.2716.

52. Kimberly M. Thompson and Kevin Haninger, "Violence in E-Rated Video Games," *JAMA* 286, no. 5 (2001): 591–98, https://doi.org/10.1001/jama.286.5.591.

53. Chris Kohler, "July 29, 1994: Videogame Makers Propose Ratings Board to Congress," *Wired*, July 29, 2009, https://www.wired.com/2009/07/dayintech-0729.

54. Kimberly M. Thompson and Fumie Yokota, "Violence, Sex, and Profanity in Films: Correlation of Movie Ratings with Content," *Medscape General Medicine* 6, no. 3 (2004): 3, http://www.medscape.com/viewarticle/480900.

55. Robin M. Kowalski and Susan P. Limber, "Psychological, Physical, and Academic Correlates of Cyberbullying and Traditional Bullying," *Journal of Adolescent Health* 53, no. 1, Supplement (2013): S13–S20, https://doi.org/10.1016/j.jadohealth.2012.09.018; Michele L. Ybarra, Marie Diener-West, and Philip J. Leaf, "Examining the Overlap in Internet Harassment and School Bullying: Implications for School Intervention," *Journal of Adolescent Health* 41, no. 6, Supplement (2007): S42–S50, https://doi.org/10.1016/j.jadohealth.2007.09.004.

56. Sameer Hinduja and Justin W. Patchin, *Bullying Beyond the Schoolyard: Preventing and Responding to Cyberbullying*, 3rd ed. (Thousand Oaks, CA: Corwin Press, 2009).

57. Michael Rothfeld and Christina Caron, "After Teen's Suicide, a New Jersey Community Grapples with Bullying," *New York Times*, February 13, 2023, https://www.nytimes.com/2023/02/13/nyregion/nj-teen-suicide-bullying-school.html.

58. Shari Kessel Schneider et al., "Cyberbullying, School Bullying, and Psychological Distress: A Regional Census of High School Students," *American Journal of Public Health* 102, no. 1 (2012): 171–77, https://doi.org/10.2105/ajph.2011.300308.

59. Emily A. Vogels, "Teens and Cyberbullying 2022," Pew Research Center, December 15, 2022, https://www.pewresearch.org/internet/2022/12/15/teens-and-cyberbullying-2022/.

60. Monica Anderson, "A Majority of Teens Have Experienced Some Form of Cyberbullying," Pew Research Center, September 27, 2018, https://www.pewresearch.org/internet/2018/09/27/a-majority-of-teens-have-experienced-some-form-of-cyberbullying/.

61. U.S. Department of Education, *Student Reports of Bullying: Results from the 2017 School Crime Supplement to the National Crime Victimization Survey* (NCES, 2019), https://nces.ed.gov/pubs2019/2019054.pdf.

62. Dieter Wolke, Kirsty Lee, and Alexa Guy, "Cyberbullying: A Storm in a Teacup?" *European Child and Adolescent Psychiatry* 26, no. 8 (2017): 899–908, https://doi.org/10.1007/s00787-017-0954-6.

63. Sally Ho, "Cyberbullying on the Rise with Girls 3 Times More Likely to Be Harassed," *PBS News Hour,* July 26, 2019, https://www.pbs.org/newshour/nation/cyberbullying-on-the-rise-with-girls-3-times-more-likely-to-be-harassed.

64. Vogels, "Teens and Cyberbullying 2022."

65. Vogels, "Teens and Cyberbullying 2022."

66. Valerie A. Earnshaw et al., "Bullying Among Lesbian, Gay, Bisexual, and Transgender Youth," *Pediatric Clinics of North America* 63, no. 6 (2016): 999–1010, https://doi.org/10.1016/j.pcl.2016.07.004.

67. Sameer Hinduja and Justin W. Patchin, "Bullying, Cyberbullying, and Suicide," *Archives of Suicide Research* 14, no. 3, (2010): 206–21, https://doi.org/10.1080/13811118.2010.494133.

68. "Effects of Bullying," US Department of Health and Human Services, StopBullying.gov, last reviewed May 21, 2021, https://www.stopbullying.gov/bullying/effects.

69. Shay Arnon et al., "Association of Cyberbullying Experiences and Perpetration with Suicidality in Early Adolescence," *JAMA Network Open* 5, no. 6 (2022): e2218746-e46, https://doi.org/10.1001/jamanetworkopen.2022.18746; Charisse L. Nixon, "Current Perspectives: The Impact of Cyberbullying on Adolescent Health," *Adolescent Health, Medicine and Therapeutics* 5 (2014): 143–58, https://doi.org/10.2147/AHMT.S36456; Justin W. Patchin and Sameer Hinduja, "Cyberbullying and Self-Esteem," *Journal of School Health* 80, no. 12 (2010): 614–21, https://doi.org/10.1111/j.1746-1561.2010.00548.x; Shari Kessel Schneider et al., "Cyberbullying, School Bullying, and Psychological Distress: A Regional Census of High School Students," *American Journal of Public Health* 102, no. 1 (2012): 171–77, https://doi.org/10.2105/ajph.2011.300308.

70. Arnon et al., "Association of Cyberbullying Experiences."

71. Arianna Prothero, "How Educators and Teens Disagree on What's Harming Students' Mental Health, in Charts," *EducationWeek,* October 24, 2023, https://www.edweek.org/leadership/how-educators-and-teens-disagree-on-whats-harming-students-mental-health-in-charts/2023/10.

72. Nixon, "Current Perspectives."

73. Traci L. Wike and Mark W. Fraser, "School Shootings: Making Sense of the Senseless," *Aggression and Violent Behavior* 14, no. 3 (2009): 162–69, https://doi.org/10.1016/j.avb.2009.01.005.

74. William E. Copeland et al., "Adult Psychiatric Outcomes of Bullying and Being Bullied by Peers in Childhood and Adolescence," *JAMA Psychiatry* 70, no. 4 (2013): 419–26, https://doi.org/10.1001/jamapsychiatry.2013.504; Elizabeth Englander et al., "Defining Cyberbullying," *Pediatrics* 140, Supplement 2 (2017): S148–S51, https://doi.org/10.1542/peds.2016-1758U.

75. Sharon Padgett and Charles E. Notar, "Bystanders Are the Key to Stopping Bullying," *Universal Journal of Educational Research* 1, no. 2 (2013): 33–41, https://files.eric.ed.gov/fulltext/EJ1053992.pdf.

76. Caitlin Elsaesser et al., "Parenting in a Digital Age: A Review of Parents' Role in Preventing Adolescent Cyberbullying," *Aggression and Violent Behavior* 35 (2017): 62–72, https://doi.org/10.1016/j.avb.2017.06.004.

Chapter 11: Virtually Hooked

1. David Wallis, "Just Click No," *New Yorker*, January 5, 1997, https://www .newyorker.com/magazine/1997/01/13/just-click-no.
2. Wallis, "Just Click No."
3. Kimberly S. Young, "Internet Addiction: The Emergence of a New Clinical Disorder," *Cyberpsychology and Behavior* 1, no. 3 (1998): 237–44, https://doi.org /10.1089/cpb.1998.1.237.
4. Laurel J. Felt and Michael B. Robb, *Technology Addiction: Concern, Controversy, and Finding Balance* (San Francisco: Common Sense Media, 2016), https:// www.commonsensemedia.org/sites/default/files/research/report/2016_csm _technology_addiction_executive_summary.pdf.
5. Felt and Robb, *Technology Addiction*.
6. Philip McRae, "Growing Up Digital Alberta: Parent and Grandparent Perspectives on Digital Technology, Health, and Learning" (Alberta, Canada: Alberta Teachers' Association, 2018), https://legacy.teachers.ab.ca /SiteCollectionDocuments/ATA/About/Education%20Research/Promise% 20and%20Peril/COOR-101-10-1%20GUD%20Phase%202%20-%20 Infographic %202018%20(web).pdf.
7. American Psychiatric Association, *Diagnostic and Statistical Manual of Mental Disorders: DSM-5*, 5th ed. (Washington, DC: APA, 2013).
8. World Health Organization, *International Classification of Diseases*, Eleventh Revision (ICD-11) (2023), https://icd.who.int/browse11.
9. Michael Rich, Michael Tsappis, and Jill R. Kavanaugh, "Problematic Interactive Media Use Among Children and Adolescents: Addiction, Compulsion, or Syndrome?," in *Internet Addiction in Children and Adolescents: Risk Factors, Assessment, and Treatment*, ed. Kimberly S. Young and Cristiano Nabuco De Abreu (New York: Springer Publishing Company, 2017), 3–28.
10. Robert C. Lorenz et al., "Video Game Training and the Reward System," *Frontiers in Human Neuroscience* 9 (2015), https://doi.org/10.3389/fnhum.2015.00040.
11. Charles B. Ferster and B. F. Skinner, *Schedules of Reinforcement* (New York: Appleton-Century-Crofts, 1957).
12. David Bickham, Summer Moukalled, and Michael Rich, "Young People's Media Use and Remote Schooling Experiences During the COVID-19 Pandemic" (paper presented at the Technology, Mind and Society, 2021, Conference Proceedings).
13. reStart Life, "Too Much Screen Time?: Reconnect with Your Inner Greatness," https://www.restartlife.com/program/services-for-teens/.
14. Website for Outdoor Behavioral Healthcare Center, University of New

Hampshire in the College of Health and Human Services, https://www
.obhcenter.org/.

Chapter 12: Queen's Gambit

1. Heath Evans, "'Content Is King'—Essay by Bill Gates 1996," January 27, 2019,
   https://medium.com/@HeathEvans/content-is-king-essay-by-bill-gates-1996
   -df74552f80d9.
2. William Becker et al., "Killing Me Softly: Organizational E-Mail Monitoring
   Expectations' Impact on Employee and Significant Other Well-Being,"
   Journal of Management 47, no. 4 (2019): 1024–52, https://doi.org/10.1177
   /0149206319890655.
3. "Employment Law Guide," US Department of Labor, December 2019, https://
   webapps.dol.gov/elaws/elg/minwage.htm.
4. "Right to Disconnect," Eurofund, December 1, 2021, https://www.eurofound
   .europa.eu/observatories/eurwork/industrial-relations-dictionary/right-to
   -disconnect.
5. David Z. Morris, "New French Law Bars Work Email After Hours," *Fortune*,
   January 1, 2017, https://fortune.com/2017/01/01/french-right-to-disconnect
   -law.
6. Hunter G. Hoffman et al., "Virtual Reality Pain Control During Burn Wound
   Debridement in the Hydrotank," *The Clinical Journal of Pain* 24, no. 4 (2008):
   299–304, https://doi.org/10.1097/AJP.0b013e318164d2cc; Theresa McSherry et al.,
   "Randomized, Crossover Study of Immersive Virtual Reality to Decrease
   Opioid Use During Painful Wound Care Procedures in Adults," *Journal of
   Burn Care and Research* 39, no. 2 (2018): 278–85, https://doi.org/10.1097/BCR
   .0000000000000589.
7. Website for the Everest Virtual Reality Experience, 2019, https://www.everest
   virtualreality.com/; website for *Titanic VR*, 2018, http://www.titanicvr.io.
8. Craig M. Hales et al., "Prevalence of Obesity Among Adults and Youth: United
   States, 2015–2016," *NCHS Data Brief*, no. 288 (Oct 2017): 1–8, https://stacks.cdc
   .gov/view/cdc/49223.
9. Brian Stierman et al., *National Health and Nutrition Examination Survey 2017–
   March 2020 Prepandemic Data Files Development of Files and Prevalence Estimates
   for Selected Health Outcomes*, in *National Center for Health Statistics Reports*, no. 158
   (2021): 1–21, https://stacks.cdc.gov/view/cdc/106273.
10. Stierman et al., *National Health and Nutrition Examination Survey.*
11. Stierman et al., *National Health and Nutrition Examination Survey.*
12. Stierman et al., *National Health and Nutrition Examination Survey.*
13. Steven L. Gortmaker et al., "Television Viewing as a Cause of Increasing
    Obesity Among Children in the United States, 1986–1990," *Archives of Pediatrics
    and Adolescent Medicine* 150, no. 4 (Apr 1996): 356–62, https://doi.org/10.1001
    /archpedi.1996.02170290022003.

14. Cleveland Clinic, "Cleveland Clinic Study Finds Obesity as Top Cause of Preventable Life-Years Lost," *EurekAlert!*, April 22, 2017, https://www .eurekalert.org/news-releases/738629; Russell M. Viner and Tim J. Cole, "Television Viewing in Early Childhood Predicts Adult Body Mass Index," *The Journal of Pediatrics* 147, no. 4 (October 2005): 429–35, https://doi.org/10.1016/j .jpeds.2005.05.005.

15. Leonard H. Epstein et al., "A Randomized Trial of the Effects of Reducing Television Viewing and Computer Use on Body Mass Index in Young Children," *Archives of Pediatrics & Adolescent Medicine* 162, no. 3 (2008): 239–45, https://doi.org/10.1001/archpediatrics.2007.45.

16. Leigh Ramsey Buchanan et al., "Reducing Recreational Sedentary Screen Time: A Community Guide Systematic Review," *American Journal of Preventive Medicine* 50, no. 3 (March 2016): 402–15, https://doi.org/10.1016/j.amepre .2015.09.030; Epstein et al., "A Randomized Trial of the Effects of Reducing Television Viewing."

17. Lauren Hale and Stanford Guan, "Screen Time and Sleep Among School-Aged Children and Adolescents: A Systematic Literature Review," *Sleep Medicine Reviews* 21 (2015): 50–58, https://doi.org/10.1016/j.smrv.2014.07.007.

18. Alison L. Miller, Julie C. Lumeng, and Monique K. LeBourgeois, "Sleep Patterns and Obesity in Childhood," *Current Opinion in Endocrinology, Diabetes and Obesity* 22, no. 1 (2015): 41–47, https://doi.org/10.1097/MED .0000000000000125.

19. Campbell Foubister et al., "Time Spent on Social Media Use and BMI Z-Score: A Cross-Sectional Explanatory Pathway Analysis of 10798 14-Year-Old Boys and Girls," *Pediatric Obesity* 18, no. 5 (March 2023): e13017, https://doi.org/10 .1111/ijpo.13017.

20. Margaret Gamble and Nancy Cotugna, "A Quarter Century of TV Food Advertising Targeted at Children," *American Journal of Health Behavior* 23, no. 4 (1999): 261–267, https://doi.org/10.5993/AJHB.23.4.3; Irvin Molotsky, "Reagan Vetoes Bill Putting Limits on TV Programming for Children," *New York Times*, November 7, 1988, https://www.nytimes.com/1988/11/07/us/reagan-vetoes -bill-putting-limits-on-tv-programming-for-children.html.

21. Catherine M. Mc Carthy, Ralph de Vries, and Joreintje D. Mackenbach, "The Influence of Unhealthy Food and Beverage Marketing Through Social Media and Advergaming on Diet-Related Outcomes in Children—A Systematic Review," *Obesity Reviews* 23, no. 6 (2022): e13441, https://doi.org/10.1111/obr .13441.

22. Jennifer L. Harris, John A. Bargh, and Kelly D. Brownell, "Priming Effects of Television Food Advertising on Eating Behavior," *Health Psychology* 28, no. 4 (2009): 404–13, https://doi.org/10.1037/a0014399.

23. Dina L. G. Borzekowski and Thomas N. Robinson, "The 30-Second Effect: An Experiment Revealing the Impact of Television Commercials on Food

Preferences of Preschoolers," *Journal of the American Dietetic Association* 101, no. 1 (2001): 42–46, https://doi.org/10.1016/S0002-8223(01)00012-8.

24. Thomas N. Robinson et al., "Effects of Fast Food Branding on Young Children's Taste Preferences," *Archives of Pediatrics and Adolescent Medicine* 161, no. 8 (2007): 792–97, https://doi.org/10.1001/archpedi.161.8.792.

25. David S. Bickham et al., "Characteristics of Screen Media Use Associated with Higher BMI in Young Adolescents," *Pediatrics* 131, no. 5 (2013): 935–41, https://doi.org/10.1542/peds.2012-1197.

26. Elroy Boers et al., "Association of Screen Time and Depression in Adolescence," *JAMA Pediatrics* 173, no. 9 (2019): 853–59, https://doi.org/10.1001/jamapediatrics.2019.1759.

27. Website for #Halfthestory, https://www.halfthestoryproject.com.

28. Jean M. Twenge, "More Time on Technology, Less Happiness? Associations Between Digital-Media Use and Psychological Well-Being," *Current Directions in Psychological Science* 28, no. 4 (2019): 372–79, https://doi.org/10.1177/0963721419838244.

29. David S. Bickham et al., *Adolescent Media Use: Attitudes, Effects, and Online Experiences,* Boston Children's Hospital Digital Wellness Lab (Boston, MA: 2022), https://digitalwellnesslab.org/wp-content/uploads/Pulse-Survey_Adolescent-Attitudes-Effects-and-Experiences.pdf.

30. Bickham et al., *Adolescent Media Use.*

31. Bickham et al., *Adolescent Media Use.*

32. Jessica N. Fish et al., "'I'm Kinda Stuck at Home with Unsupportive Parents Right Now': LGBTQ Youths' Experiences with COVID-19 and the Importance of Online Support," *Journal of Adolescent Health* 67, no. 3 (2020): 450–52, https://doi.org/10.1016/j.jadohealth.2020.06.002.

33. Ester di Giacomo et al., "Estimating the Risk of Attempted Suicide Among Sexual Minority Youths: A Systematic Review and Meta-Analysis," *JAMA Pediatrics* 172, no. 12 (2018): 1145–52, https://doi.org/10.1001/jamapediatrics.2018.2731; Madeleine Irish et al., "Depression and Self-Harm from Adolescence to Young Adulthood in Sexual Minorities Compared with Heterosexuals in the UK: A Population-Based Cohort Study," *The Lancet Child and Adolescent Health* 3, no. 2 (2019): 91–98, https://doi.org/10.1016/S2352-4642(18)30343-2; Geoffrey L. Ream, "What's Unique About Lesbian, Gay, Bisexual, and Transgender (LGBT) Youth and Young Adult Suicides? Findings from the National Violent Death Reporting System," *Journal of Adolescent Health* 64, no. 5 (2019): 602–7, https://doi.org/10.1016/j.jadohealth.2018.10.303.

34. Matthew N. Berger et al., "Social Media's Role in Support Networks Among LGBTQ Adolescents: A Qualitative Study," *Sexual Health* 18, no. 5 (2021): 421–31, https://doi.org/10.1071/SH21110; Matthew N. Berger et al., "Social Media Use and Health and Well-Being of Lesbian, Gay, Bisexual, Transgender,

and Queer Youth: Systematic Review," *Journal of Medical Internet Research* 24, no. 9 (2022): e38449, https://doi.org/10.2196/38449.

35. Ine Beyens, Eline Frison, and Steven Eggermont, "'I Don't Want to Miss a Thing': Adolescents' Fear of Missing Out and Its Relationship to Adolescents' Social Needs, Facebook Use, and Facebook Related Stress," *Computers in Human Behavior* 64 (2016): 1–8, https://doi.org/10.1016/j.chb.2016.05.083; Linda Charmaraman et al., "Associations of Early Social Media Initiation on Digital Behaviors and the Moderating Role of Limiting Use," *Computers in Human Behavior* 127 (2022): 107053, https://doi.org/10.1016/j.chb.2021.107053; Holly Scott, Stephany M. Biello, and Heather Cleland Woods, "Identifying Drivers for Bedtime Social Media Use Despite Sleep Costs: The Adolescent Perspective," *Sleep Health* 5, no. 6 (2019): 539–45, https://doi.org/10.1016/j.sleh.2019.07.006.

36. Michael B. Robb, *The New Normal: Parents, Teens, Screens, and Sleep in the United States* (San Francisco: Common Sense Media, 2019), https://www.common sensemedia.org/sites/default/files/research/report/2019-new-normal-parents -teens-screens-and-sleep-united-states-report.pdf.

37. H. R. Colton and B. M. Altevoght, eds., "Sleep Disorders and Sleep Deprivation: An Unmet Public Health Problem," Institute of Medicine (US) Committee on Sleep Medicine and Research (Washington, DC: National Academies Press, 2006), https://www.ncbi.nlm.nih.gov/books/NBK19961/.

38. Jose L. Cantero et al., "Sleep-Dependent Theta Oscillations in the Human Hippocampus and Neocortex," *The Journal of Neuroscience* 23, no. 34 (2003): 10897–903, https://doi.org/10.1523/jneurosci.23-34-10897.2003; Gahan Fallone, Judith A. Owens, and Jennifer Deane, "Sleepiness in Children and Adolescents: Clinical Implications," *Sleep Medicine Reviews* 6, no. 4 (2002): 287–306, https://doi.org/10.1053/smrv.2001.0192.

39. Heather Cleland Woods and Holly Scott, "#Sleepyteens: Social Media Use in Adolescence Is Associated with Poor Sleep Quality, Anxiety, Depression, and Low Self-Esteem," *Journal of Adolescence* 51 (2016): 41–49, https://doi.org/10.1016 /j.adolescence.2016.05.008.

40. Philippe Verduyn et al., "Passive Facebook Usage Undermines Affective Well-Being: Experimental and Longitudinal Evidence," *Journal of Experimental Psychology: General* 144, no. 2 (April 2015): 480–8, https://doi.org/10.1037 /xge0000057; "Do Social Network Sites Enhance or Undermine Subjective Well-Being? A Critical Review," *Social Issues and Policy Review* 11, no. 1 (2017): 274–302, https://doi.org/10.1111/sipr.12033; "Social Comparison on Social Networking Sites," *Current Opinion in Psychology* 36 (2020): 32–37, https:// doi.org/10.1016/j.copsyc.2020.04.002; Philippe Verduyn et al., "Do Social Networking Sites Influence Well-Being?: The Extended Active-Passive Model," *Current Directions in Psychological Science: A Journal of the American Psychological Society* 31, no.1 (2022): 62–68, https://doi.org/10.1177/09637214211053637.

41. Patti M. Valkenburg et al., "Social Media Browsing and Adolescent Well-Being:

Challenging the 'Passive Social Media Use Hypothesis,'" *Journal of Computer-Mediated Communication* 27, no. 1 (2022): zmab015, https://doi.org/10.1093/jcmc/zmab015.

42. Ine Beyens et al., "The Effect of Social Media on Well-Being Differs from Adolescent to Adolescent," *Scientific Reports* 10, no. 1 (2020): 10763, https://doi.org/10.1038/s41598-020-67727-7.

43. Ine Beyens et al., "Social Media Use and Adolescents' Well-Being: Developing a Typology of Person-Specific Effect Patterns," *Communication Research* (2021), https://doi.org/10.1177/00936502211038196.

Chapter 13: The Art of Living

1. Austin Carr, "The Most Important Leadership Quality for CEOs? Creativity," *Fast Company*, May 18, 2010, https://www.fastcompany.com/1648943/most-important-leadership-quality-ceos-creativity.

2. Lisa H. Trahan et al., "The Flynn Effect: A Meta-Analysis," *Psychological Bulletin* 140, no. 5 (2014): 1332–60, https://doi.org/10.1037/a0037173.

3. Michael E. Martinez, "How Experience Cultivates Intelligence," in *Future Bright: A Transforming Vision of Human Intelligence* (New York: Oxford University Press, 2013), 155–94, https://doi.org/10.1093/acprof:osobl/9780199781843.003.0006.

4. Paul E. Torrance, "Torrance Tests of Creative Thinking," *Educational and Psychological Measurement* (1966), https://psycnet.apa.org/doiLanding?doi=10.1037%2Ft05532-000.

5. Kyung Hee Kim, "The Creativity Crisis: The Decrease in Creative Thinking Scores on the Torrance Tests of Creative Thinking," *Creativity Research Journal* 23, no. 4 (2011): 285–95, https://doi.org/10.1080/10400419.2011.627805.

6. Jonathan A. Plucker, "Is the Proof in the Pudding? Reanalyses of Torrance's (1958 to Present) Longitudinal Data," *Creativity Research Journal* 12 (2): 103–14, https://doi.org/10.1207/s15326934crj1202_3.

7. Rex Jung et al., "The Structure of Creative Cognition in the Human Brain," *Frontiers in Human Neuroscience* 7, art. 330 (2013), https://doi.org/10.3389/fnhum.2013.00330.

8. David K. Carson and Mark A. Runco, "Creative Problem Solving and Problem Finding in Young Adults: Interconnections with Stress, Hassles, and Coping Abilities," *The Journal of Creative Behavior* 33, no. 3 (1999): 167–88, https://doi.org/10.1002/j.2162-6057.1999.tb01195.x.

9. Walter Isaacson, *Einstein: His Life and Universe* (New York: Simon and Schuster, 2007); Maxwell King, *The Good Neighbor: The Life and Work of Fred Rogers* (New York: Abrams Press, 2018).

10. Simone Kuhn et al., "The Importance of the Default Mode Network in Creativity—a Structural MRI Study," *The Journal of Creative Behavior* 48, no. 2 (2014): 152–63, https://doi.org/10.1002/jocb.45; Ben Shofty et al., "The Default

Network Is Causally Linked to Creative Thinking," *Molecular Psychiatry* 27, no. 3 (2022): 1848–54, https://doi.org/10.1038/s41380-021-01403-8.

11. Andy Goldsworthy, "Andy Goldsworthy Natural Sculptures with Ice, Stone and More | Rivers and Tides | Documentary Central," YouTube video, September 11, 2022, 1:34:04, https://www.youtube.com/watch?v=AT7VBmd4J6w.

12. Michele Root-Bernstein and Robert Root-Bernstein, "Imaginary Worldplay in Childhood and Maturity and Its Impact on Adult Creativity," *Creativity Research Journal* 18, no. 4 (2006): 405–25, https://doi.org/10.1207 /s15326934crj1804_1.

13. David S. Bickham et al., *Adolescent Media Use: Attitudes, Effects, and Online Experiences,* Boston Children's Hospital Digital Wellness Lab (Boston, MA: 2022), https://digitalwellnesslab.org/wp-content/uploads/Pulse-Survey _Adolescent-Attitudes-Effects-and-Experiences.pdf.

14. Emma Uprichard, "Children as 'Being and Becomings': Children, Childhood, and Temporality," *Children and Society* 22, no. 4 (2008): 303–13, https://doi.org /10.1111/j.1099-0860.2007.00110.x.

15. Peter Gray, "The Decline of Play and the Rise of Psychopathology in Children and Adolescents," *American Journal of Play* 3, no. 4 (2011): 443–63, https://files .eric.ed.gov/fulltext/EJ985541.pdf.

16. Kate Cowan, *A Panorama of Play—A Literature Review,* Digital Futures Commission (London: 5Rights Foundation, 2020), https:// digitalfuturescommission.org.uk/wp-content/uploads/2022/02/A-Panorama -of-Play-A-Literature-Review.pdf.

17. Michael Yogman et al., "The Power of Play: A Pediatric Role in Enhancing Development in Young Children," *Pediatrics* 142, no. 3 (2018): e20182058, https://doi.org/10.1542/peds.2018-2058.

18. Michael Yogman, personal communication with the author, September 14, 2023.

19. Digital Futures Commission website, 5Rights Foundation, https://digital futurescommission.org.uk/.

20. Sonia Livingstone and Kruakae Pothong, *Playful by Design: A Vision of Free Play in a Digital World,* Digital Futures Commission (London: 5Rights Foundation, 2021), https://digitalfuturescommission.org.uk/wp-content/uploads/2021/11 /A-Vision-of-Free-Play-in-a-Digital-World.pdf.

21. Maria Violaris, "Einstein at the Patent Office," *The Oxford Scientist,* February 7, 2020, https://oxsci.org/einstein-at-the-patent-office.

22. Albert Einstein, personal communication to his stepdaughter Margot Einstein, after his sister Maja's death, 1951; quoted by Hanna Loewy in A&E Television *Einstein Biography,* VPI International, 1991.

23. Walter Isaacson, *Einstein: His Life and Universe* (New York: Simon and Schuster, 2007).

24. Richard Louv, *Last Child in the Woods: Saving Our Children from Nature-Deficit Disorder* (Chapel Hill, NC: Algonquin Books, 2008).

25. Jiaxing Wang et al., "Progression of Myopia in School-Aged Children After COVID-19 Home Confinement," *JAMA Ophthalmology* 139, no. 3 (2021): 293–300, https://doi.org/10.1001/jamaophthalmol.2020.6239.

26. Sanne W. C. Nikkelen et al., "Media Use and ADHD-Related Behaviors in Children and Adolescents: A Meta-Analysis," *Developmental Psychology* 50, no. 9 (2014): 2228–41, https://doi.org/10.1037/a0037318; Kirsten Weir, "Nurtured by Nature," *Monitor on Psychology* 51, no. 3 (2020): 50, https://www.apa.org/monitor/2020/04/nurtured-nature.

27. Leyla E. McCurdy et al., "Using Nature and Outdoor Activity to Improve Children's Health," *Current Problems in Pediatric and Adolescent Health Care* 40, no. 5 (2010): 102–17, https://doi.org/10.1016/j.cppeds.2010.02.003.

28. Trina Hinkley et al., "Cross Sectional Associations of Screen Time and Outdoor Play with Social Skills in Preschool Children," *PLOS One* 13, no. 4 (2018): e0193700, https://doi.org/10.1371/journal.pone.0193700.

29. Tassia K. Oswald et al., "Psychological Impacts of 'Screen Time' and 'Green Time' for Children and Adolescents: A Systematic Scoping Review," *PLOS ONE* 15, no. 9 (2020): e0237725, https://doi.org/10.1371/journal.pone.0237725.

30. Michael Mutz, Johannes Müller, and Arne Göring, "Outdoor Adventures and Adolescents' Mental Health: Daily Screen Time as a Moderator of Changes," *Journal of Adventure Education and Outdoor Learning* 19, no. 1 (2019): 56–66, https://doi.org/10.1080/14729679.2018.1507830.

31. Hayley Christian et al., "Dog Walking Is Associated with More Outdoor Play and Independent Mobility for Children," *Preventive Medicine* 67 (2014): 259–63, https://doi.org/10.1016/j.ypmed.2014.08.002.

32. *Friending Fresh Air: Connecting Kids to Nature in the Digital Age*, National Wildlife Federation (Reston, VA: National Wildlife Federation, 2013), https://www.nwf.org/~/media/PDFs/Be%20Out%20There/BOTTechReport85x11FINAL.ashx.

33. Richard Louv, *The Nature Principle: Reconnecting with Life in a Virtual Age* (Chapel Hill, NC: Algonquin Books, 2012); *Vitamin N: The Essential Guide to a Nature-Rich Life* (Chapel Hill, NC: Algonquin Books, 2016).

34. Netta Weinstein, Andrew K. Przybylski, and Richard M. Ryan, "Can Nature Make Us More Caring? Effects of Immersion in Nature on Intrinsic Aspirations and Generosity," *Personality and Social Psychology Bulletin* 35, no. 10 (2009): 1315–29, https://doi.org/10.1177/0146167209341649.

35. Oksana Bartosh et al., "Improving Test Scores Through Environmental Education: Is It Possible?," *Applied Environmental Education and Communication* 5, no. 3 (2006): 161–69, https://doi.org/10.1080/15330150600912937.

36. Julie (Athman) Ernst and Martha Monroe, "The Effects of Environment-Based Education on Students' Critical Thinking Skills and Disposition Toward Critical Thinking," *Environmental Education Research* 10, no. 4 (2004): 507–22, https://doi.org/10.1080/1350462042000291038.

37. Kate Bianchi, "The Ultimate List of Forest Schools, Outdoor-Based and

Nature-Inspired Schools of the USA," *The Forest Homeschool*, January 8, 2021, https://naturallykatey.wordpress.com/2021/01/08/list-of-forest-schools-outdoor-based-nature-inspired-schools-in-the-us.

38. Amber Amaya, "Neurodiversity in Nature: Occupational Therapy in the Outdoors Helps Children Find Confidence," *Children and Nature Network*, March 2023, https://www.childrenandnature.org/resources/neurodiversity-in-nature-occupational-therapy-in-the-outdoors-helps-children-find-confidence.

39. Catherine Steiner-Adair and Teresa Barker, *The Big Disconnect: Protecting Childhood and Family Relationships in the Digital Age*, 1st ed. (New York: Harper, 2013), 260–64.

Part 4: Ages and Stages: A Digital Wellness Primer

1. Brooke Auxier et al., "1. Children's Engagement with Digital Devices, Screen Time," from the *Parenting Children in the Age of Screens* report, Pew Research Center, July 28, 2020, https://www.pewresearch.org/internet/2020/07/28/childrens-engagement-with-digital-devices-screen-time/.

2. "School-Age Children Development," Mount Sinai Today Blog, 2023, https://www.mountsinai.org/health-library/special-topic/school-age-children-development.

3. Emily A. Vogels, Risa Gelles-Watnick, and Navid Massarat, "Teens, Social Media, and Technology 2022," Pew Research Center, August 10, 2022, https://www.pewresearch.org/internet/2022/08/10/teens-social-media-and-technology-2022/.

Index

About the Authors

Michael Rich, MD, MPH, is an associate professor of pediatrics at Harvard Medical School and practices adolescent medicine at Boston Children's Hospital. Pediatrician, child health researcher, father, and filmmaker, Dr. Rich is the founder and director of the Digital Wellness Lab and the first evidence-based medical program addressing physical, mental, and social health issues associated with digital technology use, the Clinic for Interactive Media and Internet Disorders (CIMAID). As the Mediatrician, Dr. Rich offers research-based, actionable, and practical answers to parents', educators', and clinicians' questions about children's and adolescents' media use and the positive and negative implications for their health and development.

Teresa Barker, a nonfiction book cowriter specializing in parenting, family, health, and memoir subjects, lives in Chicago.